A TEXT BOOK OF

CLOUD COMPUTING

(ELECTIVE – III)

FOR

SEMESTER – II

FINAL YEAR (B.E.) DEGREE COURSE IN COMPUTER ENGINEERING

As Per the New Revised Syllabus of Savitribai Phule Pune University, Pune.

(2012 Pattern)

NITIN N. SAKHARE
M.E. (Computer Networks)
Assistant Professor
Comp. Engg. Deptt.
Vishwakarma Institute of
Information Technology (VIIT),
Kondhwa, Pune.

SHITAL A. SALVE
M.E. (Computer)
Assistant Professor,
Comp. Engg. Deptt.
Modern Education Society
College of Engineering,
Shivajinagar, Pune.

NIRALI
PRAKASHAN
ADVANCEMENT OF KNOWLEDGE

N 3738

CLOUD COMPUTING (BE COMP. SEM. II)   ISBN 978-93-5164-897-0

Second Edition   :   January 2017

©   :   Authors

Published By :   (Polyplate)

NIRALI PRAKASHAN

Abhyudaya Pragati, 1312, Shivaji Nagar,
Off J.M. Road, PUNE – 411005
Tel - (020) 25512336/37/39, Fax - (020) 25511379
Email : niralipune@pragationline.com

☞ **DISTRIBUTION BRANCHES**

PUNE

Nirali Prakashan   :   119, Budhwar Peth, Jogeshwari Mandir Lane, Pune 411002, Maharashtra
Tel : (020) 2445 2044, 66022708, Fax : (020) 2445 1538
Email : bookorder@pragationline.com, niralilocal@pragationline.com

Nirali Prakashan   :   S. No. 28/27, Dhyari, Near Pari Company, Pune 411041
Tel : (020) 24690204 Fax : (020) 24690316
Email : dhyari@pragationline.com, bookorder@pragationline.com

MUMBAI

Nirali Prakashan   :   385, S.V.P. Road, Rasdhara Co-op. Hsg. Society Ltd.,
Girgaum, Mumbai 400004, Maharashtra
Tel : (022) 2385 6339 / 2386 9976, Fax : (022) 2386 9976
Email : niralimumbai@pragationline.com

☞ **DISTRIBUTION BRANCHES**

JALGAON

Nirali Prakashan   :   34, V. V. Golani Market, Navi Peth, Jalgaon 425001,
Maharashtra, Tel : (0257) 222 0395, Mob : 94234 91860

KOLHAPUR

Nirali Prakashan   :   New Mahadvar Road, Kedar Plaza, 1st Floor Opp. IDBI Bank
Kolhapur 416 012, Maharashtra. Mob : 9850046155

NAGPUR

Pratibha Book Distributors :   Above Maratha Mandir, Shop No. 3, First Floor,
Rani Jhanshi Square, Sitabuldi, Nagpur 440012, Maharashtra
Tel : (0712) 254 7129

DELHI

Nirali Prakashan   :   4593/21, Basement, Aggarwal Lane 15, Ansari Road, Daryaganj
Near Times of India Building, New Delhi 110002
Mob : 08505972553

BENGALURU

Pragati Book House   :   House No. 1, Sanjeevappa Lane, Avenue Road Cross,
Opp. Rice Church, Bengaluru – 560002.
Tel : (080) 64513344, 64513355,Mob : 9880582331, 9845021552
Email:bharatsavla@yahoo.com

CHENNAI

Pragati Books   :   9/1, Montieth Road, Behind Taas Mahal, Egmore,
Chennai 600008 Tamil Nadu, Tel : (044) 6518 3535,
Mob : 94440 01782 / 98450 21552 / 98805 82331,
Email : bharatsavla@yahoo.com

niralipune@pragationline.com | www.pragationline.com

Also find us on f www.facebook.com/niralibooks

PREFACE TO THE SECOND EDITION

We are glad and excited to announce that the First Edition of this book received an overwhelming response from the engineering student community, compelling us to release its **Second Edition** within a very short period of time.

This thoroughly revised **Second Edition** has been **updated** with **additional matter**, many solved problems, including **all University Examination Papers** and Numerous Exercises for practice.

Special care has been taken to maintain high degree of accuracy in the theory and numericals throughout the book.

We take this opportunity to express our sincere thanks to Dineshbhai Furia of Nirali Prakashan, a reputed pioneer in the publication field. Our special thanks to Jignesh Furia and Mrs. Nirali Verma for their effective cooperation and great care in bringing out this revised edition. We also appreciate the efforts of M. P. Munde and the entire staff of Engineering Books Deptt. of Nirali Prakashan namely Mrs. Deepali Lachake (Co-ordinator) and Mrs. Shilpa Kale for bringing this book to the students in a timely manner.

We sincerely hope that this "**Second Edition**" will also be warmly received by all concerned as in the past.

Valuable suggestions from our esteemed readers to improve the book are most welcome and highly appreciated.

Pune   **–Authors**

PREFACE TO THE FIRST EDITION

It gives us great pleasure to bring out the book on **"Cloud Computing"**. This book is strictly written as per the New Revised Syllabus of Savitribai Phule Pune University, Pune (2012 Pattern) for the students of final year degree course in Computer Engineering.

The book is as per New Revised Examination Scheme which has been implemented from this academic year. According to this, In-Semester Examination carries 30 Marks over first three units and End-Semester Examination carries 70 Marks over entire syllabus of which the first three units will carry 20 Marks and units 4, 5 and 6 will carry 50 Marks.

We have given **Sample Question Papers of In-Semester University Examination (30 Marks) and End-Semester University Examination (70 Marks) in this book for the practice.**

This book has been written to satisfy the needs of undergraduate syllabus of the Computer Engineering Course in most of the Universities. We are quite sure that this book will serve its purpose very well for Computer and IT Engineering Students.

The subject matter is presented in simple form so as to enable the students to understand the subject easily. Sufficient care is taken to present the subject matter in the point wise form in most of the units. The book consists of six units, which cover the entire syllabus.

We are gratefully acknowledge co-operation from **Shri. Dineshbhai Furia, Shri. Jignesh Furia, Mrs. Nirali Verma, Shri. M.P. Munde** and **Mrs. Deepali Lachake** (Co-ordinator) of **Nirali Prakashan.**

Also, it is important to mention invaluable moral support of our beloved family members, who consistently encouraged us for better work.

Despite the best efforts taken by authors, it is possible that some unintentional errors might have taken place. Authors would gratefully acknowledge if any of these is pointed out.

Suggestions and comments for further improvement of this book will be gratefully received and acknowledged from the students, teachers and others. Feel free to write.

Pune   **Authors**

SYLLABUS

Unit I : Introduction   **6 Hrs**

Introduction, Roots of Cloud Computing: From mainframe to Cloud, Benefits of Cloud Computing SOA, Web services, Web 2.0, Mashups, Grid computing, Utility computing, Hardware virtualization, Essentials of Cloud characteristics, Challenges, Cloud economics, Role of Networks in Cloud Computing: Cloud types and service models, Cloud computing platforms : Openstack, Opennimbus, Eucalyptus Primary Cloud Service models, Cloud Services brokerage, Primary cloud deployment models, cloud computing reference model, The greenfield and brownfield deployment options

Unit II : Virtualization   **8 Hrs.**

Introduction, Characteristics of Virutalized environments, Taxonomy of Virtualization techniques, Pros and Cons of Virtualization, Technology examples: Xen, KVM, Vmware, Microsoft Hyper-V

Unit III : Storage in Cloud   **8 Hrs.**

Storage system architecture, Big data, Virtualize data centre(VDC) architecture, VDC Environment, server, storage, networking, desktop and application virtualization techniques and benefits, Virtual Machine Components and Process of converting physical to VMs, Block and file level storage virtualization, Virtual Provisioning, and automated storage tiering, VLAN, VSAN and benefits, Network traffic management techniques in VDC, Cloud file systems: GFS and HDFS, BigTable, HBase and Dynamo. Features and comparisons among GFS,HDFS.

Unit IV : Cloud computing platforms   **6 Hrs.**

Infrastructure as Service, best-of breed cloud infrastructure components, cloud ready converged infrastructure, Virtual machine provisioning and migration services, Anatomy of Cloud infrastructure, Distributed management of virtual infrastructure, scheduling techniques, SLA Commitment

Unit V : Cloud monitoring and management   **8 Hrs.**

Introduction and architecture for federated cloud computing, Performance prediction for HPC on Cloud. SLA management: Types of SLA, Life cycle of SLA, Traditional approaches of SLA. service catalog, service ordering process, management and functional interfaces of services , cloud portal and its functions, cloud interface standards along with SOAP and REST, system integration and work-ow modeling, cloud service life-cycle phases: service planning, service creation, service operation, and service termination Control layer, its functions and benefits, element and unified manager, software defined approach and techniques for managing IT resources

Unit VI : Security in Cloud Computing   **6 Hrs.**

Introduction, Global Risk and Compliance aspects in cloud environments and key security terminologies, Technologies for Data security, Data security risk, Cloud computing and identity, Digital identity and access management, Content level security, Security-As-A-Cloud Service

CONTENTS

INTRODUCTION TO CLOUD COMPUTING

1.1 INTRODUCTION TO CLOUD COMPUTING

1.1.1 What is Cloud Computing?

- Cloud computing is nothing but a specific style of computing where everything from computing power to infrastructure, business applications are provided "as a service". It's a computing service rather than a product.

- In cloud, shared resources, software's and information is provided as a metered service over the network. When the end user accesses some service is cloud, he is not aware of where that service is coming from or what is platform being used or where it is being stored.

- Cloud computing is not a new technology, it's just a way of using old services effectively. Now lets have look on history of cloud computing.

In 1960's '**John McCarthy**' stated that

"*Computation may someday be organized as a **Public Utility***".

This is the actual concept we use in cloud computing today.

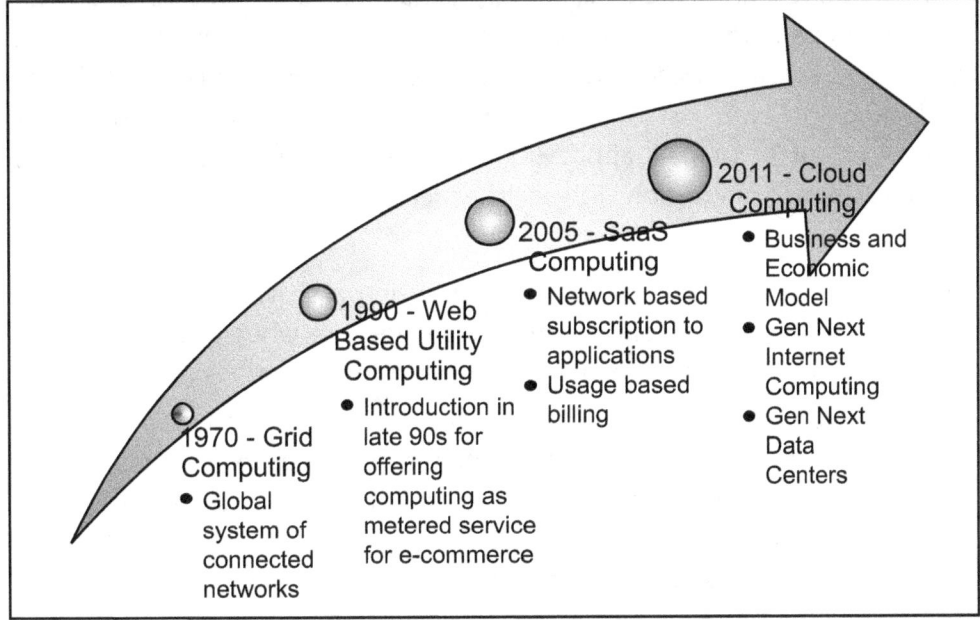

Fig. 1.1 : Evolution of Cloud Computing

In 1990's Telecommunication companies commercialized large networks by offering **VPN (Virtualized Private Network)** service for communications using the advancement of the internet calling them '**Telecom Cloud**'.

From there we got the term "**Cloud**".

1.1.2 Definition

According to NIST's Definition of Cloud Computing

Cloud computing is a model for enabling convenient, on-demand network access to a shared pool of configurable computing recourses (e.g. networks, servers, storage , applications and services) that can be rapidly provisioned and released with minimal management effort or service provider interaction.

1.1.3 Characteristics

- On-Demand Self Services
- Multi Tenancy
- Broad network access
- Resource pooling
- Rapid elasticity
- Measured service

On Demand Self-Services

In cloud computing, resources are available on demand, means if you require a service like data storage, it can be made available in couple of minutes just by approaching the vendor like Amazon Web Services), Microsoft, Google, IBM and Salesforce.com.. Or if you need a survey conducting tool, you just have to approach SaaS (Software as a service) provider. Computer services such as email, applications, network or server service can be provided without requiring human interaction with each service provider.

Multi Tenancy

- Multi-tenant literally means multiple users using a shared pool of resources. Multi Tenacity refers to a principle in software architecture where a single instance of the software runs on a server, serving multiple client organizations (tenants).

A tenant is a group of users who share broad network access a common access with specific privileges to the software instance. With a multitenant architecture, a software application is designed to virtually partition its data and configuration, and each client organization works with a customized virtual application instance. With a multitenant architecture, a software application is designed to provide every tenant a dedicated share of the instance including its data, configuration, user management, tenant individual functionality and non-functional properties.

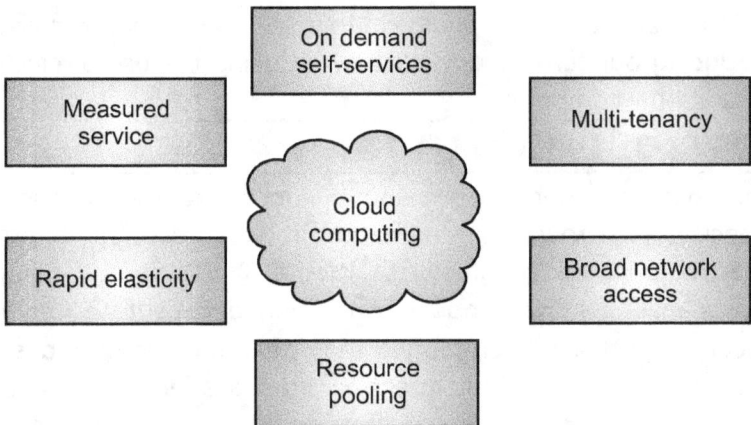

Fig. 1.2 : Essential characteristics of cloud computing

Broad Network Access

Cloud Capabilities are available over the network and accessed through standard mechanisms that promote use by heterogeneous thin or thick client platforms such as mobile phones, laptops and PDAs.

Broad network access includes private clouds that operate within a company's firewall, public clouds, or a hybrid deployment.

Resource Pooling

Service multiple customers from the same physical resources, by securely separating the resources on logical level. The provider's computing resources are pooled to serve multiple consumers using a multi-tenant model, with different physical and virtual resources dynamically assigned and reassigned according to consumer demand. There is a sense of location independence in that the customer generally has no control or knowledge over the exact location of the provided resources but may be able to specify location at a higher level of abstraction (e.g., country, state or datacenter). Examples of resources include storage, processing, memory and network bandwidth.

Rapid Elasticity

Capabilities can be elastically provisioned and released, in some cases automatically, to scale rapidly outward and inward as needed. For the user, the capabilities available for provisioning often appear to be unlimited and can be appropriated in any quantity at any time. Resources are provisioned and released on-demand and/or automated based on triggers or parameters. This will make sure your application will have exactly the capacity it needs at any point of time

Measured Service

Resource usage are monitored, measured, and reported (billed) transparently based on utilization. In short, pay for use. Cloud systems automatically control and optimize resource use by leveraging a metering capability at some level of abstraction appropriate to the type of service (e.g., storage, processing, bandwidth and active user accounts). Resource usage can be monitored, controlled and reported, providing transparency for the provider and consumer.

As we have seen in the above paragraph, in cloud computing, resources are used efficiently, we are actually reducing our carbon foot print by reducing the use of electricity, which was being wasted in traditional computing.

1.2 ROOTS OF CLOUD COMPUTING

We can track the roots of clouds computing by observing the advancement of several technologies, especially in hardware (virtualization, multi-core chips), Internet technologies (Web services, service-oriented architectures, Web 2.0), distributed computing (clusters, grids), and systems management (autonomic computing, data center automation).

Some of these technologies have been tagged as hype in their early stages of development; however, they later received significant attention from academia and were sanctioned by major industry players. Consequently, a specification and standardization process followed, leading to maturity and wide adoption. The emergence of cloud computing itself is closely linked to the maturity of such technologies. We present a closer look at the technologies that form the base of cloud computing, with the aim of providing a clearer picture of the cloud ecosystem as a whole.

From Mainframe to Cloud

We are currently experiencing a switch in the IT world, from in-house generated computing power into utility-supplied computing resources delivered over the Internet as Web services. This trend is similar to what occurred about a century ago when factories, which used to generate their own electric power, realized that it is was cheaper just plugging their machines into the newly formed electric power grid. Computing delivered as a utility can be defined as "on demand delivery of infrastructure, applications, and business processes in a security-rich, shared, scalable, and based computer environment over the Internet for a fee"

This model brings benefits to both consumers and providers of IT services. Consumers can attain reduction on IT-related costs by choosing to obtain cheaper services from external providers as opposed to heavily investing on IT infrastructure and personnel hiring. The "on-demand" component of this model allows consumers to adapt their IT usage to rapidly increasing or unpredictable computing needs. Providers of IT services achieve better operational costs; hardware and software infrastructures are built to provide multiple solutions and serve many users, thus increasing efficiency and ultimately leading to faster Return On Investment (ROI) as well as lower Total Cost of Ownership (TCO)

Benefits of Cloud Computing

- **Reduced Cost** : Cloud technology is paid incrementally, saving organizations money.
- **Increased Storage** : Organizations can store more data than on private computer systems.
- **Highly Automated** : No longer do IT personnel need to worry about keeping software up to date.
- **Flexibility** : Cloud computing offers much more flexibility than past computing methods.
- **More Mobility** : Employees can access information wherever they are, rather than having to remain at their desks.

- **Allows IT to Shift Focus** : No longer having to worry about constant server updates and other computing issues, government organizations will be free to concentrate on innovation.
- **Scalability** : You can scale your businesses storage needs seamlessly rather than having to go out and purchase expensive programs or hardware. A not-for-profit ran a cookbook project and was able to pay for all the cloud apps they needed to create, implement and market their project on a month to month basis. They didn't have to purchase a piece of hardware, buy software licenses or worry about overloading their servers.
- **Automatic Updates** : There is no need for IT to worry about paying for your future updates in terms of software and hardware.
- **Remote Access** : Employees, partners and clients can access, and update information wherever they are, rather than having to run back the office.
- **Disaster Relief** : With your company's data safely stored on secure data centers instead of your server room (previously known as your storage closet), losing power due to hurricanes, earthquakes or a construction worker cutting the power lines, you are back at work as long as you have an internet connection.
- **Ease of Implementation** : Your IT team may not like this, but implementing cloud services is as easy as, well, setting up a LinkedIn page.
- **Skilled Vendors** : Who would you rather manage and protect your data? A company such as InfoStreet (with over 16 years' experience serving enterprise clients), IBM or Amazon or your IT staff.
- **Response Time** : Cloud computing accomplishes a better response time in most cases than your standard server and hardware.
- **Even Playing Field for Small Firms** : This allows small companies to compete more effectively with some of the larger businesses, balancing the playing field. Your small business can utilize the same tools that Fortune 100 companies use and can do this because with cloud computing, your business will only pay for what you need.

Business Benefits of Cloud Computing

Almost Zero Upfront Infrastructure Investment : If you have to build a large scale system, it may cost a fortune to invest in real estate, physical security, hardware (racks, servers, routers, backup power supplies), hardware management (power management, cooling), and operations personnel. Because of the high upfront costs, the project would typically require several rounds of management approvals before the project could even get started. Now, with utility-style cloud computing, there is no fixed cost or startup cost.

Just-in-Time Infrastructure : In the past, if your applications became popular and your systems or your infrastructure did not scale, you became a victim of your own success. Conversely, if you invested heavily and did not get popular, you became a victim of your failure. By deploying applications in-the-cloud with just-in-time self-provisioning, you do not have to worry about pre-procuring capacity for large-scale systems. This increases agility, lowers risk, and lowers operational cost because you scale only as you grow and only pay for what you use.

More Efficient Resource Utilization.

System administrators usually worry about procuring hardware (when they run out of capacity) and higher infrastructure utilization (when they have excess and idle capacity). With the cloud, they can manage resources more effectively and efficiently by having the applications request and relinquish resources on-demand.

Usage-Based Costing.

With utility-style pricing, you are billed only for the infrastructure that has been used. You are not paying for allocated infrastructure but instead for unused infrastructure. This adds a new dimension to cost savings. You can see immediate cost savings (sometimes as early as your next month's bill) when you deploy an optimization patch to update your cloud application. For example, if a caching layer can reduce your data requests by 70%, the savings begin to accrue immediately and you see the reward right in the next bill. Moreover, if you are building platforms on the top of the cloud, you can pass on the same flexible, variable usage-based cost structure to your own customers.

Reduced Time to Market.

Parallelization is one of the great ways to speed up processing. If one compute-intensive or data-intensive job that can be run in parallel takes 500 hours to process on one machine, with cloud architectures, it would be possible to spawn and launch 500 instances and process the same job in 1 hour. Having available an elastic infrastructure provides the application with the ability to exploit parallelization in a cost-effective manner reducing time to market.

Technical Benefits of Cloud Computing

Some of the technical benefits of cloud computing includes :

Automation : "Scriptable Infrastructure" : You can create repeatable build and deployment systems by leveraging programmable (API-driven) infrastructure.

Auto Scaling : You can scale your applications up and down to match your unexpected demand without any human intervention. Auto-scaling encourages automation and drives more efficiency.

Proactive Scaling : Scale your application up and down to meet your anticipated demand with proper planning understanding of your traffic patterns so that you keep your costs low while scaling.

More Efficient Development Life Cycle : Production systems may be easily cloned for use as development and test environments. Staging environments may be easily promoted to production.

Improved Testability : Never run out of hardware for testing. Inject and automate testing at every stage during the development process. You can spawn up an "instant test lab" with preconfigured environments only for the duration of testing phase.

Disaster Recovery and Business Continuity : The cloud provides a lower cost option for maintaining a fleet of DR servers and data storage. With the cloud, you can take advantage of geo-distribution and replicate the environment in other location within minutes.

"Overflow" the Traffic to the Cloud : With a few clicks and effective load balancing tactics, you can create a complete overflow-proof application by routing excess traffic to the cloud

SOA, Web Services, Web 2.0, and Mashups

The emergence of Web Services (WS) open standards has significantly contributed to advances in the domain of software integration. Web services can glue together applications running on different messaging product platforms, enabling information from one application to be made available to others, and enabling internal applications to be made available over the Internet. Over the years a rich WS software stack has been specified and standardized, resulting in a multitude of technologies to describe, compose, and orchestrate services, package and transport messages between services, publish and discover services, represent Quality of Service (QoS) parameters, and ensure security in service access.

WS standards have been created on top of existing ubiquitous technologies such as HTTP and XML, thus providing a common mechanism for delivering services, making them ideal for implementing a Service-Oriented Architecture (SOA). The purpose of a SOA is to address requirements of loosely coupled, standards-based, and protocol-independent distributed computing. In a SOA, software resources are packaged as "services," which are well-defined, self-contained modules that provide standard business functionality and are independent of the state or context of other services. Services are described in a standard definition language and have a published interface.

The maturity of WS has enabled the creation of powerful services that can be accessed on-demand, in a uniform way. While some WS are published with the intent of serving end-user applications, their true power resides in its interface being accessible by other services. An enterprise application that follows the SOA paradigm is a collection of services that together perform complex business logic. This concept of gluing services initially focused on the enterprise Web, but gained space in the consumer realm as well, especially with the advent of Web 2.0. In the consumer Web, information and services may be programmatically aggregated, acting as building blocks of complex compositions, called service mashups. Many service providers, such as Amazon, del.icio.us, Facebook, and Google, make their service APIs publicly accessible using standard protocols such as SOAP and REST. Consequently, one can put an idea of a fully functional Web application into practice just by gluing pieces with few lines of code. In the Software as a Service (SaaS) domain, cloud applications can be built as compositions of other services from the same or different providers. Services such user authentication, e-mail, payroll management, and calendars are examples of building blocks that can be reused and combined in a business solution in case a single, ready-made system does not provide all those features. Many building blocks and solutions are now available in public marketplaces. For example, programmable web1 is a public repository of service APIs and mashups currently listing thousands of APIs and mashups. Popular APIs such as Google Maps, Flickr, YouTube, Amazon eCommerce, and Twitter, when combined, produce a variety of interesting solutions, from finding video game retailers to weather maps. Similarly, Salesforce.com's offers AppExchange, which enables the sharing of solutions developed by third-party developers on top of Salesforce.com components.

Grid Computing

Grid computing enables aggregation of distributed resources and transparently access to them. Most production grids such as TeraGrid and EGEE seek to share compute and storage resources distributed across different administrative domains, with their main focus being speeding up a broad range of scientific applications, such as climate modeling, drug design, and protein analysis. A form of distributed and parallel computing, whereby a 'super and virtual computer' is composed of a cluster of networked, loosely coupled computers acting in concern to perform very large tasks.

A key aspect of the grid vision realization has been building standard Web services-based protocols that allow distributed resources to be "discovered, accessed, allocated, monitored, accounted for, and billed for, etc., and in general managed as a single virtual system." The Open Grid Services Architecture (OGSA) addresses this need for standardization by defining a set of core capabilities and behaviors that address key concerns in grid systems.

Utility Computing

The "packaging of computing resources, such as computation and storage, as a metered service similar to a traditional public utility, such as electricity. With increasing popularity and usage, large grid installations have faced new problems, such as excessive spikes in demand for resources coupled with strategic and adversarial behavior by users. Initially, grid resource management techniques did not ensure fair and equitable access to resources in many systems. Traditional metrics (throughput, waiting time, and slowdown) failed to capture the more subtle requirements of users. There were no real incentives for users to be flexible about resource requirements or job deadlines, nor provisions to accommodate users with urgent work. In utility computing environments, users assign a "utility" value to their jobs, where utility is a fixed or time-varying valuation that captures various QoS constraints (deadline, importance, satisfaction). The valuation is the amount they are willing to pay a service provider to satisfy their demands. The service providers then attempt to maximize their own utility, where said utility may directly correlate with their profit. Providers can choose to prioritize high yield (i.e., profit per unit of resource) user jobs, leading to a scenario where shared systems are viewed as a marketplace, where users compete for resources based on the perceived utility or value of their jobs. Further information and comparison of these utility computing environments are available in an extensive survey of these platforms.

1.3 CLOUD PROVIDER

A service provider that offers customers storage or software services available via a private (private cloud) or public network (cloud). Cloud provider is a company which hosts the servers on its premises and make the services available on-demand. Some examples of cloud providers are Google, Amazon, Rackspace, Microsoft etc.

Hardware Virtualization

Cloud computing services are usually backed by large-scale data centers composed of thousands of computers. Such data centers are built to serve many users and host many disparate applications. For this purpose, hardware virtualization can be considered as a perfect fit to overcome most operational issues of data center building and maintenance.

The idea of virtualizing a computer system's resources, including processors, memory, and I/O devices, has been well established for decades, aiming at improving sharing and utilization of computer systems. Hardware virtualization allows running multiple operating systems and software stacks on a single physical platform. As depicted in Fig. 1.3, a software layer, the Virtual Machine Monitor (VMM), also called a hypervisor, mediates access to the physical hardware presenting to each guest operating system a Virtual Machine (VM), which is a set of virtual platform interfaces. The advent of several innovative technologies multi-core chips, paravirtualization, hardware-assisted virtualization, and live migration of VMs-has contributed to an increasing adoption of virtualization on server systems. Traditionally, perceived benefits were improvements on sharing and utilization, better manageability, and higher reliability. More recently, with the adoption of virtualization on a broad range of server and client systems, researchers and practitioners have been emphasizing three basic capabilities regarding management of workload in a virtualized system, namely isolation, consolidation, and migration. Workload isolation is achieved since all program instructions are fully confined inside a VM, which leads to improvements in security. Better reliability is also achieved because software failures inside one VM do not affect others. Moreover, better performance control is attained since execution of one VM should not affect the performance of another VM. The consolidation of several individual and heterogeneous workloads onto a single physical platform leads to better system utilization. This practice is also employed for overcoming potential software and hardware incompatibilities in case of upgrades, given that it is possible to run legacy and new operation systems concurrently.

Workload migration, also referred to as application mobility, targets at facilitating hardware maintenance, load balancing, and disaster recovery. It is done by encapsulating a guest OS state within a VM and allowing it to be suspended, fully serialized, migrated to a different platform, and resumed immediately or preserved to be restored at a later date. A VM's state includes a full disk or partition image, configuration files, and an image of its RAM.

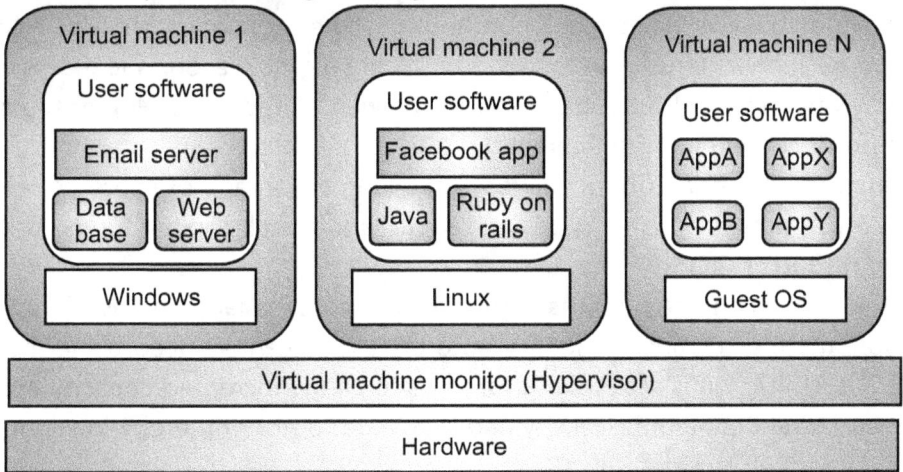

Fig. 1.3 : A hardware virtualized server hosting three virtual machines, each one running distinct operating system and user level software stack.

Challenges in the Cloud

While the cloud service offerings present a simplistic view of IT in case of IaaS or a simplistic view of programming in case PaaS or a simplistic view of resources usage in case of SaaS, the underlying systems level support challenges are huge and highly complex. These stem from the need to offer a uniformly consistent and robustly simplistic view of computing while the underlying systems are highly failure-prone, heterogeneous, resource hogging, and exhibiting serious security shortcomings. Invariably either in the IaaS or PaaS or SaaS cloud services, one is proffered features that smack of full network reliability; or having "instant" or "zero" network latency; or perhaps supporting "infinite" bandwidth; and so on. But then robust distributed systems are built while keeping mind that are these fallacies that must be studiously avoided at design time as well as during implementations and deployments. Cloud computing has the ironical role of projecting this idealized view of its services while ensuring that the underlying systems are managed realistically. In fact the challenges in implementing cloud computing services are plenty :

1.4 CLOUD ECONOMIC AND BENEFITS

1.4.1 Economic Context

- Like energy, computing has become an essential component of any economy. Historically, the size of an economy was directly related to the energy it consumed.
- Likewise, a person's professional growth, the growth of an organization, or the growth of a country as a whole can directly be related to the computing power they use.
- Rising energy costs, combined with a growing global awareness of the potential impact of climate change due to carbon emissions puts a renewed focus on energy usage and its associated carbon footprint.
- The challenge today is to increase computing power consumption with lower energy consumption. Every enterprise in the world is facing a global economic recession that has profoundly affected all developed countries as well as those developing countries that produce products sold in those markets.
- Uncertain times also bring opportunities, but taking advantage of strategic opportunities typically must now be done quickly without additional capital funds or additional corporate resources.
- For Information Technology (IT) managers, energy cost management is not a small issue. In addition, the maintenance of legacy enterprise data centers absorb the majority of IT budgets and IT managers are looking for ways to create increased capacity and flexibility within their current computing facility and hardware footprint thereby lowering costs and increasing their Return On Assets (ROA).
- Because capacity planning for traditional enterprise data centers must accommodate the company's peak load periods, there is typically very low server utilization during non-

peak periods which, depending on the industry, may be most of the year. The last few years have seen a trend in data center management towards server virtualization which allows faster deployment of specialized server configurations and towards higher server density without increasing the size of the data center or its staff overhead or even higher energy consumption.

- However, these alternatives still require significant investments and long-term technology commitments and there has been increasing attention paid to alternatives that provide the pay-as-you-go options, unlimited scalability, quick deployment, and the minimal maintenance requirements. Cloud computing is a computing paradigm that promises to meet all these requirements.

1.4.2 Economic Benefits

- Occasionally used to refer to the economics of cloud computing, the term "Cloudonomics" was coined by Joe Weinman.
- He examined the strategic advantages provided by public utility cloud services over private clouds and traditional data centers.
- He posits that public utility clouds are fundamentally different than traditional data center environments and private clouds.
- For individual enterprises, cloud services provide benefits that broadly fall into the categories of lowering overall costs for equivalent services (you pay only for what you use), increased strategic flexibility to meet market opportunities without having to forecast and maintain on-site capacity, and access to the advantages of cloud provider's massive capacity : instant scalability, parallel processing capability which reduces task processing time and response latency, system redundancy which improves reliability, and better capability to repel botnet attacks.
- Further, public cloud vendors can achieve unparalleled efficiencies compared to data centers and private clouds because they are able to scale their capacity to address the aggregated demand of many enterprises, each having different peak demand periods.
- This allows for much higher server utilization rates, lower unit costs, and easier capacity planning netting a much higher return on assets than is possible for individual enterprises.
- Finally, because the location of the public cloud vendor's facilities are not tied to the parochial interests of the individual clients, they are able to locate, scale, and manage their operations to take optimum advantage of reduced energy costs, skilled labor pools, bandwidth, or inexpensive real estate.
- These are not the only benefits that have been identified. Matzke suggests that the levels of required skills or specialized expertise along with the required economies of scale drive the optimum choice for resourcing IT initiatives.

- For him, the availability of scalable skills combined with other economies of scale are among the compelling benefits of cloud computing. This is especially true for enterprises that are located in labor markets that have very few or only very expensive IT staff resources available with the requisite skills.

1.4.3 Economic Costs

- The costs associated with cloud computing facing early adopters include the potential costs of service disruptions; data security concerns; potential regulatory compliance issues arising out of sensitive data being transferred, processed or stored beyond defined borders.
- Limitations in the variety and capabilities of the development and deployment platforms currently available; difficulties in moving proprietary data and software from one cloud services provider to another; integration of cloud services with legacy systems.
- Cost and availability of programming skills needed to modify legacy application to function in the cloud environment; legacy software CPU-based licensing costs increasing when moved to a cloud platform, etc.

1.4.4 Company Size and the Economic Costs and Benefits of Cloud Computing

- The economic costs or benefits of implementing cloud services vary depending upon the size of the enterprise and its existing IT resources/overheads including legacy data center infrastructure, computer hardware, legacy software, maturity of internal processes, IT staffing and technical skill base.
- These determine the strategic costs and benefits that accrue to individuals and corporations depending upon their relative size.
- In the past, large corporations have had an advantage over small corporations in their access to capital and their ability to leverage their existing human, software, and hardware resources to support new marketing and strategic initiatives.
- However, since the advent of cloud computing, the barriers to entry for a particular market or market segment for a startup company have been dramatically reduced and cloud computing may have tipped the balance of strategic advantage away from the large established corporations towards much more nimble small or startup companies.
- A small, dedicated, and talented team of individuals can now pool their individual talents to address a perceived market need without an immediate need for a venture capital funds to provide the necessary IT infrastructure.
- There are a number of cloud providers who provide software development environments that include the requisite software development tools, code repositories, test environments, and access to a highly scalable production environment on pay-as-you-go basis.
- Also contributing to this trend is the open-source movement. While licensing issues, support, and feature considerations may dissuade larger enterprises from using open

source software in the development and deployment of their proprietary products, the availability of open source software in nearly every software category has been a boon to SMEs, the self-employed, and start-ups.

- As these small companies grow into midsize and large companies they face changing cost equations that modify the relative costs and benefits of cloud computing.

- For instance, at certain data traffic volumes the marginal costs of operating on a cloud provider's infrastructure may become more expensive than providing the necessary IT infrastructure in-house.

- At that point, there may be advantages of a mixed-use strategy in which some of the applications and services are brought in-house and others continue to be hosted in the cloud. The following tables will identify the differences that SMEs and large enterprises face in both the benefits and costs of cloud services.

1.4.5 The Economics of Green Clouds

- The development of green data centers and green clouds is shaped by two important factors. The first is a global awareness of the devastating potential of climate change due to human activity primarily through carbon emissions.

- The second is the rising costs of energy. These two factors have focused IT infrastructure planning and decision-making on energy cost reduction, dynamic resource allocation strategies and have moved green issues from the category of nice-to-do to strategically important for all midsize and large corporations.

- Public cloud providers locate their data centers where bandwidth, cheap energy, abundant water for cooling, and proximity to markets are optimal.

- Google and other cloud providers have focused on creative approaches to efficient resource usage including not only electricity usage but also water recycling and equipment recycling upon disposal.

- Through purchasing servers and other equipment designed to minimize energy usage and in the modular design and management of their data centers, these cloud providers minimize the non-computing energy overhead and maximize their utilization rates through the dynamic allocation of computing resources.

- This combination of lower energy overhead amortized over a much higher server utilization rate allows cloud suppliers to provide computing services far more efficiently with a much smaller energy and carbon footprint.

- Because of the scale of operations of large cloud providers, they are able to achieve efficiency rates and server utilization rates that are unachievable in even large corporate data center operations.

- Thus, cloud computing holds the promise of not only providing attractive cost savings at the enterprise level but also may contribute to the larger societal objectives of energy efficiency and environmental protection and sustainable development.

1.5 CLOUD SERVICE MODELS

In cloud, everything from storage to computation is provided as a service. Depending in the nature of service, it is divided into following services :

- Software as a service (SaaS)
- Platform as a Service (PaaS)
- Infrastructure as a Service (IaaS)

1.5.1 Software as a Service (SaaS)

Software as service is cloud deployment model in which a software is built centrally by provider and is given for use to the end users on-demand via a thin client like web browser. Here instead of buying a software, user pays per use.

- SaaS is model of software deployment where an application is hosted as service provided to customers across internet.
- Where Applications (word processor, CRM etc) or Application Services (mail, schedule, calendar) execute in the **cloud** using the interconnectivity of the internet to propagate data. SaaS has become a common delivery model for most business applications, including accounting, collaboration, Customer Relationship Management (CRM), Enterprise Resource Planning (ERP), invoicing, Human Resource Management (HRM), Content Management (CM) and service desk management. SaaS has been incorporated into the strategy of all leading enterprise software companies.

Benefits of SaaS

- **Faster Time to Market of Business Apps**

  Means the time, application is ready for use, can be made available to end user. Suppose, a SaaS provider develops an application, he does not have to market it, no need to the licensing, what all he has to do is just make that available on centralized server.

- **Any Time any Where Access**

  Means if I purchase a software service, I can use it anywhere and on any device as I don't have to actually install it on my PC, I just have to access the service through a web browser. So a software service purchased can be accessible on my desktop, laptop or any other media device.

- **Elimination of Licensing Risk**

  As we have all seen, piracy is a big issue at the moment in software industry, but if make all software's as service, piracy can be controlled on larger extent. Also, to the licensing of software is a big overhead, which can be avoided by the use of SaaS.

- **Elimination of Version Compatibility**

  Here, we are maintaining the software centrally. So any changes or updates to the software can be made available to all users in just one commit to the central server. So, compatibility and version controlling is a very easy task for the software provider.

- **Reduced Hardware Foot Print**

  As we can access any software services on just a click of a web browser, there is no need to buy the expensive hardware to install the software. Any commodity hardware can be used to access the services.

- **Lower Operating and Maintenance Cost**

  Software is service is developed and maintained on centralized server, so there is an efficient use of space and energy, which ultimately results in low cost of operating. Also, if there is any need of upgradation, can be achieved through minimum resources, which reduces the maintenance cost when compared to traditional computing

- **Consumption Based Expenditure**

  As it's a pay per use model, we can access the services only when required and pay for only that usage, which makes it cost and energy effective.

Challenges of SaaS

- **Extension of the On-premises Security Model to the SaaS Provider (data privacy and ownership)**

  Here, from computation to storage, we don't have direct control on data. So, our data will always be with SaaS provider and we have to be dependent on its availability.

- **Governance and Billing Management**

  Pay per use model has to be customized depending on the end user's preference. Some common pay per use models are as follows

- Per user per month
- Per transaction
- Per GB of storage per month

Sometimes its difficult to keep governance on such usage, for that there is need of good metering devices.

- **Synchronization of Client and Vendor Migration**

  Sometimes if there is a need to change the software service provider, migration from one such provider to other is a difficult thing as every software provider uses its own way of storage and computation. So migration of already existing data from one provider is not possible as of now, as there is no standardization followed in SaaS industry.

- **Need of Good Connectivity**

  As all service are available on clouds, and nothing is present on local machine, we have to be dependant on internet connectivity. Performance of that service is greatly affectedby speed and availability of the network. But we live in the edge of 3G and 4G network services, so connectivity is not a big issue at the moment.

1.5.2 Platform as a Service (PaaS)

Platform as a service is a cloud model, in which a computation platform is provided as a service to end user. PaaS is mainly used by developers to deploy their code on public cloud. Once the code is deployed, from computation to storage everything happens in cloud, at provider's end. PaaS offerings facilitate the deployment of applications without the cost and complexity of buying and managing the underlying hardware and software and provisioning hosting capabilities, providing all of the facilities required to support the complete life cycle of building and delivering web applications and services entirely available from the Internet.

In PaaS,

- Applications are built on the 'Cloud platform, using variety of technologies. Like Java, Python, .NET, Ruby etc.
- PaaS offers development environments that can be used to develop 'cloud-ready' applications.
- Has got inherent dynamic scaling capabilities
- Development environment + runtime = Provides everything a developer needs to build an application
- Developer only needs to deploy his code on platform and rest will be taken care by PaaS provider.

Benefits of PaaS

- **Enables Developer to Focus on the Application Code and the Business Logic**

  In PaaS, we only have to deploy the code, irrespective of what is the run time platform, its capacity, database storage. So it makes developer to focus on code building rather than wasting time in buying the server space, buying the hardware, buying the database etc.

- **Natural fit for Development, Testing and Production Environments**

  In development environment, it is expected to make the environments available quick and ready to use, so PaaS becomes a natural fit for development. Also, if someone wants to try some web application's success, then he can first try launching that application on PaaS and if successful, can be developed on larger scale

- **Instant Provisioning – Takes Few Minutes**

  Its quick, in most popular PaaS providers like Google App Engine and Cloud Foundry, it takes seconds to get the environment development ready.

- **Inherent Dynamic Scalability**

  As it's in Clouds, applications can scale to any extent without any delay or discontinuity in application presence.

- **Eliminates the Complexities of Hardware and Software Dependencies**

  In PaaS, developer is only need to deploy the code in cloud, so that can be achieved through simple desktop with commodity hardware. As the code will be running on provider platform, this eliminates the complexities of hardware and software dependencies.

Challenges of PaaS

- **Risk of Vendor Lock-in**

  Vendor lock-in poses a big challenge when the application needs to be migrated to a different PaaS provider/platform, since platform is proprietary of to the vendor and not standardized.

- **Interoperability and Connectivity with Existing On-premises Applications**

  Computation platform changes from vendor to vendor. So its difficult to have an integrate Pass and an application which is running on traditional computation logic as the PaaS application will be running at provider's premise and normal application will be in-premise

- **Has to rely on 3rd party performance and scalability SLAs**

  When we deploy an application on PaaS provider's platform, we loose control on it and we have to be dependent on their system's performance. Consider a scenario where there is PaaS provider, developer company and service consuming company, here the Service Level Agreement just cannot be between Service consuming company and developer company, we have consider the PaaS provider for its SLAs.

- **Potential Security Risk and Loss of Control Over the Data since it's Located Out of Premises**

  As we are deploying code on Public Cloud, sometimes it can be a threat to the sensitive data. Also, complete data, though produced by user, is owned by PaaS provider and the end user won't be having any control over it.

- **Currently supported too few Programming Languages like java, python, .NET, ruby etc.**

Some PaaS Providers

- Google App Engine
- Cloud Foundry
- Hereko
- Rails Engine

1.5.3 Infrastructure as a Service (IaaS)

Infrastructure as a service is to take the servers on rent instead of buying them directly and pay for the use.

IaaS is,

- The Computer Infrastructure comprising of Servers, Storage and Network is delivered as a service
- Rather than buying and owning the infrastructure, clients can buy this as a fully outsourced service
- Clients pay only for the resources they consume on a **Utility Computing** basis. Similar to public utility services such as Electricity, Public Transport etc.
- IaaS has the ability to provide single server up to entire data centers

- With IaaS the processing, storage, network capacity and other fundamental computing resources are rented out on need basis.

Benefits of IaaS

- **Effective Infrastructure Utilization**

  It's been found that, on an average a server just uses 30%-40% of its capacity in a year when it comes to computation and storage. In IaaS, resources are used on shared basis as in 2-3 applications are deployed on a single server. By using shared pool of resources we are actually saving the energy and other expenses. If a sudden demand comes, cloud applications can be scaled up in no time.

- **Highly Automated Resulting in Faster Provisioning of Resources**

  To get a server for development is just a matter of few clicks. Most of IaaS providers gives template for servers required. Also, to use the server space, neither you actually need to buy the floor space for server nor you have to buy the expensive hardware.

- **Cab Quickly and Easily Meet the Changing Dynamic Demand for Consumption**

  There is one device called Load balancer so when a Load balancer comes to know that server has met the threshold capacity (70% or more) it triggers an event to add a new server to the service. So when needed service is available.

- **Reduced cost due to**

  - Less hardware resources.
  - Less real estate space for on-premise.
  - Less power consumption.
  - Less manual work and hence lesser administration.

Challenges in IaaS

- **Integration outside the enterprise firewall across the cloud boundary for consuming resources from the public cloud IaaS.**

  Use of Public cloud to store the sensitive data is threat. In public cloud, as control over data is lost, we have to be dependent on IaaS provider's availability. It's difficult to make a gateway when we are trying to integrate in-premise, firewall protected application with application hosted on public cloud.

- **Migration of applications in terms of assessing the fitment from dimensions such as Technology, Security etc.**

  As we have seen in case of PaaS and SaaS, it's difficult to migrate an application, hosted on traditional devices to an IaaS cloud as there is no standardized process followed.

- **Vendor reliability and potential security risk when the service are consumed from public cloud IaaS providers.**

  As there is no control over data, we have to be dependent on vendor for the availability of the application.

- **Need of good connectivity in terms of network bandwidth and internet availability IaaS Providers**
  - Amazon Web services
  - Rackspace Cloud Hosting

Fig. 1.4 : Software as a Service (SaaS)

Cloud Services Brokerage

These brokerages will use several types of brokers and platforms to enhance service delivery and, ultimately service value. According to Gartner, before these scenarios can be enabled, there is a need for brokerage business to use these brokers and platforms. According to Gartner, the following types of Cloud Service Brokerages (CSB) are foreseen :

- **Cloud Service Intermediation**. An intermediation broker providers a service that directly enhances a given service delivered one or more service consumers, essentially on top of a given service to enhance a specific capability.

- **Aggregation.** An aggregation brokerage service combines multiple services into one or more new services.

- **Cloud Service Arbitrage.** These services will provide flexibility and opportunistic choices for the service aggregator.

1.6 ADMINISTRATING AND MAINTAINING THE CLOUD SERVICES

Administration of Cloud services are similar to traditional way of administrating the servers and data centers, only difference here is cloud administrating requires less manpower than as compared to traditional data center administration.

1.7 BENEFITS AND LIMITATIONS OF CLOUD COMPUTING

Traditional Vs. Cloud Computing

Parameter	Traditional Computing	Cloud Computing
Resource Provisioning	Weeks	Minutes
Scalability	Add resources manually	On-Demand scalability
Delivery Model	Buy Assets	Buy Service
Flexibility	Traditional procurement	Self Service
Cost	Additional Yearly CAPEX	Pay Per Use

Limitations of Cloud Computing

- **Network Connection**

  The concept assumes that the client has reliable network connection. If there are problems of network connectivity, accessing the cloud also becomes a problem. Performance of the cloud applications also depend on the performance of network at client's side. Upload and download speeds are slower as compared to that of a local server.

- **Security and Privacy**

The biggest concerns about cloud computing are security and privacy. Users might not be comfortable handing over their data to a third party. This is an even greater concern when it comes to companies that wish to keep their sensitive information on cloud servers. While most service vendors would ensure that their servers are kept free from viral infection and malware, it is still a concern considering the fact that a number of users from around the world are accessing the server. Privacy is another issue with cloud servers. Ensuring that a client's data is not accessed by any unauthorized users is of great importance for any cloud service. To make their servers more secure, cloud service vendors have developed password protected accounts, security servers through which all data being transferred must pass and data encryption techniques. After all, the success of a cloud service depends on its reputation, and any sign of a security breach would result in a loss of clients and business.

- **Dependency (Loss of Control)**
  - Quality problems with CSP (Cloud Service Providers). No influence on maintenance levels and fix frequency when using cloud services from a CSP.
  - No or little insight in CSP contingency procedures. Especially backup, restore and disaster recovery.
  - No easy migration to another CSP.
  - Measurement of resource usage and end user activities lies in the hands of the CSP.
  - Tied to the financial health of another company.

- **Cost**

  Higher Costs : While in the long run, cloud hosting is a lot cheaper than traditional technologies, the fact that it's currently new and has to be researched and improved actually makes it more expensive. Data centers have to buy or develop the software that will run the cloud, rewire the machines and fix unforeseen problems (which are always there). This makes their initial cloud offers more expensive. Like in all other industries, the first customers pay a higher price and have to deal with more issues than those who switch later (although it would be very hard to create and improve new technologies without these initial adopters).

- **Decreased Flexibility**

  This is only a temporary problem (as the others on this list), but current technologies are still in the testing stages, so they don't really offer the flexibility they promise. Of course, that will change in the future, but some of the current users might have to deal with the facts that their cloud server is difficult or impossible to upgrade without losing some data, for example.

- **Knowledge and Integration**

  Knowledge : More and deeper knowledge is required for implementing and managing SLA contracts with CSP's. Since all knowledge about the working of the cloud (e.g. hardware, software, virtualization, and deployment) is concentrated at the CSP, it is hard to get grip on the CSP.

  Integration : Integration with equipment hosted in other data centers is difficult to achieve. Peripherals integration. Printers (Bulk) and local security IT equipment (e.g. access systems) is difficult to integrate. But also (personal) USB devices or smart phones or groupware and email systems are difficult to integrate.

1.8 DEPLOY APPLICATIONS OVER CLOUD

- Before deploying an application over cloud, we have to first do the analysis of our requirements, we have to see :
    - What is the purpose of this applications ?
    - What are the target users?
    - Is this a new marketing product?
    - What is the duration of use?
    - What kind of content is expected?
    - What is the time to market?
    - Any specific programming language requirements?
    - What is the budget?
- After we get this requirement, we have to finalize on what cloud model we are going to work on, means if the application contains sensitive information of an organization then Private Cloud can be a good option, if not so, then can opt for cheap cloud i.e. Public Cloud.
- Once we decide on this, we have to finalize on what services we have to buy means SaaS, PaaS or IaaS. In case of generalized applications like Survey Tools or CRM tools.
- SaaS is a best option to go with. If we have any specific requirement and have developers to work on application then PaaS can be a good option. If we have some requirement which is out of scope of PaaS we should be going with IaaS.

- Once we decide on Cloud Deployment model and Cloud Service Offering, we have choose a best in class vendor, which gives facilities to in our budget and then we have sign the SLAs.
- Once the requirements and structural designing is done, actual development can be done and at the end of it, we have our cloud application ready for deployment.

1.9 COMPARISON OF SaaS, PaaS AND IaaS

Parameter	SaaS	PaaS	IaaS
Definition	Software as Service	Platform as a Service	Infrastructure as a Service
Deployment Model	Public Cloud	Public Cloud	Public/Private/Hybrid Cloud
Time to Market	Very Less	More than SaaS	More than SaaS
Flexibility in Specifications	Very Less	Good	Most Flexible
End User	Common People	Developers	Administrators
Cost	Cheaper	Free of cost upto certain threshold	Expensive
Data Control	Very Less	Better than SaaS	More controlled
Maintenance	Maintained by Provider	Maintained Partially by Developer and Partially by Provider	Completely maintained by developing organization or individual
Suitable For	Common Business apps like mails, CRMs etc.	Any application	Any application, mostly application with huge data.

1.10 PRIMARY CLOUD DEPLOYMENT MODEL

(A) Public Cloud

- The public cloud, offer applications, storage and other services to the general public by a service provider. This is based on "pay-as-you-go" model. A public cloud is constructed with a view to offer unlimited storage space and increased bandwidth via Internet to all businesses.
- Public clouds are owned, hosted and operated by third-party service providers. A public cloud caters to all kind of requirements from small, medium or big businesses.
- A public cloud is the most simplest to setup as it liberates that subscriber from woes of hardware, application and bandwidth expenses. Enterprises pay for only those condiments which they are utilizing.

- Users have to pay a monthly bill for public cloud services. Public cloud functions on the prime principle of storage demand scalability, which means it requires no hardware device.
- Popular examples of public clouds include Amazon Elastic Cloud Compute, Google App Engine, and Blue Cloud by IBM and Azure services Platform by Windows.

Public cloud caters to four basic characteristics that are as follows :

- **Flexible and Elastic Environment :** Public clouds like Google App engine or Amazon elastic cloud compute offers its users highly flexible cloud environment. They enable users to share and store data as per their personal capacities. They can decide what to share and what not to share with their clients.
- **Freedom of Self-Service :** Public clouds encourage users to create a cloud on their own without taking anyone's help. These are pre-configured clouds existing on Internet. The only thing businesses that wish to opt for public cloud need to do is to visit public cloud portals and get started with it. You don't have to depend upon on any third party help to create or run this type of cloud. It will be managed and handled by you as you will be the prime proprietor of it.
- **Pay for what You Use :** This particular characteristic enables cloud technology more accessible for businesses to work in a synchronized fashion. The more you use cloud services, better will be the future business prospects. However, payment is charged on the basis of cloud services used by users.
- **Availability and Reliability :** Yet another feature of public cloud is that, it is available to all and believes inability. You can catch up with your work any time you wish and from any corner of the globe. Not only users become more independent in running important business tasks but also more efficient in strengthening customer relations across the globe.

(B) Private Cloud

- Private cloud is a cloud infrastructure build exclusively for a single organization, deployed within certain boundaries like fire wall settings whether managed internally or by a third-party and hosted internally or externally.
- Users are charged on the basis of per Gigabyte usage along with bandwidth transfer fees.
- Data stored in the private cloud can only be shared amongst users of an organization and third party sharing depends upon trust they build with them.
- Popular examples of private cloud include Amazon Virtual Private Cloud (Amazon VPC), Eucalyptus Cloud Platform, IBM Smart Cloud Foundation and Microsoft Private Cloud There are two variations of private clouds :
- **On-Premise Private Cloud :** This format, also known as an "internal cloud," is hosted within an organization's own data centre. It provides a more standardized process and protection, but is often limited in size and scalability. Also, a firm's IT department would incur the capital and operational costs for the physical resources with this model. On-premise private clouds are best used for applications that require complete control and configurability of the infrastructure and security.

- **Externally-Hosted Private Cloud :** This private cloud model is hosted by an external cloud computing provider. The service provider facilitates an exclusive cloud environment with full guarantee of privacy. This format is recommended for organizations that prefer not to use a public cloud infrastructure due to the risks associated with the sharing of physical resources :

Some of the characteristics of private cloud are :

- **Enhanced Security Measures :** Security has become one of the primary concerns for many organizations especially for financial institutions. Let's take a bank or a mortgage company, the confidentiality and security of their critical data is the utmost concern. Virtual private cloud computing comes equipped with a customizable and thorough firewall and a plethora of security tools which ensure maximum protection against unauthorized use, hacking and other such malicious attempts.
- **Dedicated Resources :** The essence of private cloud is "no compromise". As a subscriber to private cloud computing an enterprise has its own dedicated resources such as processor time and data buses which ensure optimum performance.
- **Greater Customization :** Private cloud services are acquiescent and customizable so they can be molded to suit the exact requirements of an enterprise. This in turns bestows the enterprise with more control over their data.

(C) Hybrid Cloud

- Hybrid clouds combine the advantages of private and public clouds, offer flexibility, control and security of multiple deployment models as shown in the Fig. 1.5. IT organizations use hybrid clouds to employ cloud bursting for scaling across clouds.
- Cloud bursting is an application deployment model in which an application runs in a private cloud or data centre and "bursts" to a public cloud when the demand for computing capacity increases.
- A primary advantage of cloud bursting and a hybrid cloud model is that an organization only pays for extra compute resources when they are needed. Hybrid cloud architecture requires both on-premises resources and off-site (remote) server-based cloud infrastructure.

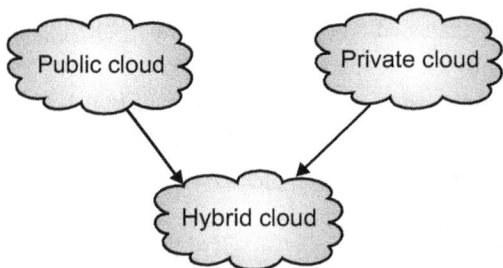

Fig. 1.5 : Hybrid Cloud as a Combination of Public Cloud and Private Cloud

Some of the characteristics of hybrid clouds are :

- **Optimal Utilization :** The available server resources in typical data centers are actually used from 5-20%. This is because of peak loads which are ten times higher than that of the average load. Hence, servers are mostly idle, generating unnecessary costs. Hybrid clouds can increase server utilization by scaling out to public resources to handle crowds.

- **Data Centre Consolidation :** Instead of providing the capacity to cope for worst-case scenarios, a private cloud only needs resources in average cases. The option to burst out allows server consolidation and hence resulting in reduction of operating costs. In particular, this includes the costs for hardware, power, cooling, maintenance, and administration.

- **Risk Transfer :** The companies themselves are responsible for keeping up and running their data centre and private cloud. The public cloud provider has to ensure a high uptime for their service. Using a hybrid cloud model, "the risk of misestimating work load is shifted to the cloud vendor from the service operator". Most of the cloud providers have service level agreements which ensure an uptime of more than 99.9% per year, i.e., a downtime of maximum of 9 hours per year.

- **Availability :** The high availability in the corporate data centre is difficult and expensive, because it requires redundancy, backups, and geographic dissemination. Especially in companies where IT is not the core business, the expertise in this area is rather limited. In a hybrid cloud environment, the public cloud can scale up or take over operations completely if the company's data centre is unavailable due to failures or Distributed Denial of Service (DDoS) attacks.

(D) Community Cloud

- The cloud infrastructure is shared between the organizations with similar interests and requirements whether managed internally or by a third-party and hosted internally or externally.

- The costs are spread over fewer users than a public cloud (but more than a private cloud), so only some of the cost savings potential of cloud computing are realized.

- This may help limit the capital expenditure costs for its establishment as the costs are shared among the organizations.

- For example, all the government agencies in a city can share the same cloud but not the non government agencies.

1.10.1 Public Cloud versus Private Cloud

Public Cloud and Private Cloud have their own distinct characteristics. We compare the Public Cloud and Private Cloud as shown in the Fig. 1.6, to get a clearer understanding of using one over the other.

- **Accessibility :** A private cloud, functions independently for an organization and that too behind firewall settings does prove to be accessible. By stating this, we mean that a private cloud cannot be accessed from anywhere and at any point of time. It is completely managed by the users working for an organization. Public Cloud architecture is built with the view to create an accessible business environment that can be shared and accessed from any part of the globe and at any time of the hour using internet.

- **Scalability** : Private cloud gives scalable business environment, public cloud infrastructures is that they are typically larger in scale than a private cloud, which provides clients with seamless, on-demand scalability.

- **Data Security Risks** : Security of data is utmost priority of cloud providers so that they offer customers a reliable and flexible cloud environment. Data security risks of private cloud are less as compared to the one stored in public cloud.

- **Initial Cost** : Private cloud initial cost is expensive, but gets minimal at later stages of using it as a service. In a public cloud, initial cost is minimal, but if data is stored for a long period of time, it proves to be expensive.

- **Availability and Reliability** : These are the two factors that make public cloud computing service more popular. The reason being, it is available to users via web installed at a given server off-premises.

- **Data Storage** : Larger amounts of data can be stored in the private cloud for a lower cost. Many different types of data can be stored in the public cloud however large amounts stored for long periods tend to get pricey.

- **Public Clouds have Better Utilization Rates** : With private cloud, your organization still has to build and maintain all kinds of servers to meet spikes in demand across various divisions or functions. Public cloud offers the same spare demand on a pay-as-you-need-it basis.

- **Public Clouds Offer Greater Elasticity** : An organization will never consume all the capacity of a public cloud, but organizations private cloud is another matter entirely. Public cloud offers greater elasticity compared to private cloud

- **Private Clouds Tend to Use Older Technology than Public Clouds** : You may have spent hundreds of thousands of dollars on new hardware and software for a private cloud, but try getting your organization to agree to that every year. Hence private clouds tend to use older technology compared to a public cloud.

- **Public Clouds get Enterprises out of the "Datacenter Business"** : establishing private cloud probably gets you in deeper into the DC business than with traditional on-premises servers. For instance, the public cloud is like an apartment building filled with multiple tenants while a private cloud is like an apartment building you have to yourself.

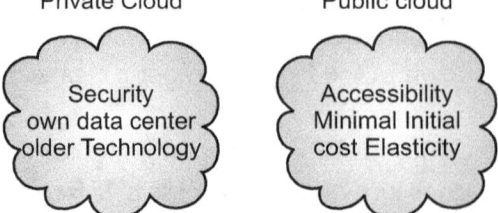

Fig. 1.6 : Comparison between Public Cloud and Private Cloud

1.10.2 Which Deployment Model to Choose Among Public, Private and Hybrid Cloud

A public cloud is the obvious choice when

- Public Cloud Computing is the easiest of cloud solutions to setup and maintain and is the preferred choice of most small scale and start-up enterprises, that don't require high data security measures. These companies often don't have much capital and have less risk in losing information due to theft or security breaches.
- Your standardized workload for applications is used by lots of people, such as e-mail.
- You need to test and develop application code.
- You have SaaS (Software as a Service) applications from a vendor who has a well-implemented security strategy.
- You need incremental capacity (the ability to add computer capacity for peak times).
- You are doing collaboration projects.
- You are doing an ad-hoc software development project using a Platform as a Service (PaaS) offering cloud.

A private cloud is the obvious choice when

- Private cloud has been adopted by industries when security is something of primary concern such as finance and health care which have some of the most rigorous compliance requirements. Your business is your data and your applications. Therefore, control and security are paramount.
- Your business is part of an industry that must conform to strict security and data privacy issues.
- Your company is large enough to run a next generation cloud data center efficiently and effectively on its own.

A hybrid environment is best choice when.

- Your company wants to use a SaaS application but is concerned about security. Your SaaS vendor can create a private cloud just for your company inside their firewall. They provide you with a virtual private network (VPN) for additional security.
- Your company offers services that are tailored for different vertical markets. You can use a public cloud to interact with the clients but keep their data secured within a private cloud.
- The management requirements of cloud computing become much more complex when you need to manage private, public, and traditional data centers all together. You will need to add capabilities for federating these environments.
- Using the private cloud for mission-critical applications and using public clouds for non-critical applications. A firm, for example, may use a private cloud for production deployment and a public cloud for test and development of lower-tier applications.
- Another example is non-destructive Disaster Recovery (DR) testing. Organizations can test if their production environment is DR-ready by tapping the public clouds without any disruption.

1.11 CLOUD COMPUTING PLATFORMS

1.11.1 The Eucalyptus Open-Source Private Cloud

- Eucalyptus is a Linux-based open-source software architecture that implements efficiency-enhancing private and hybrid clouds within an enterprise's existing IT infrastructure. Eucalyptus is an acronym for "Elastic Utility Computing Architecture for Linking Your Programs to Useful Systems."

- A Eucalyptus private cloud is deployed across an enterprise's "on premise" data center infrastructure and is accessed by users over enterprise intranet. Thus, sensitive data remains entirely secure from external intrusion behind the enterprise firewall.

- Initially, developed to support the high performance computing (HPC) research of Professor Rich Wolski's research group at the University of California, Santa Barbara. Eucalyptus is engineered according to design principles that ensure compatibility with existing Linux-based data center installations.

- Eucalyptus can be deployed without modification on all major Linux OS distributions, including Ubuntu, RHEL, Centos, and Debian.

- And Ubuntu distributions now include the Eucalyptus software core as the key component of the Ubuntu Enterprise Cloud.

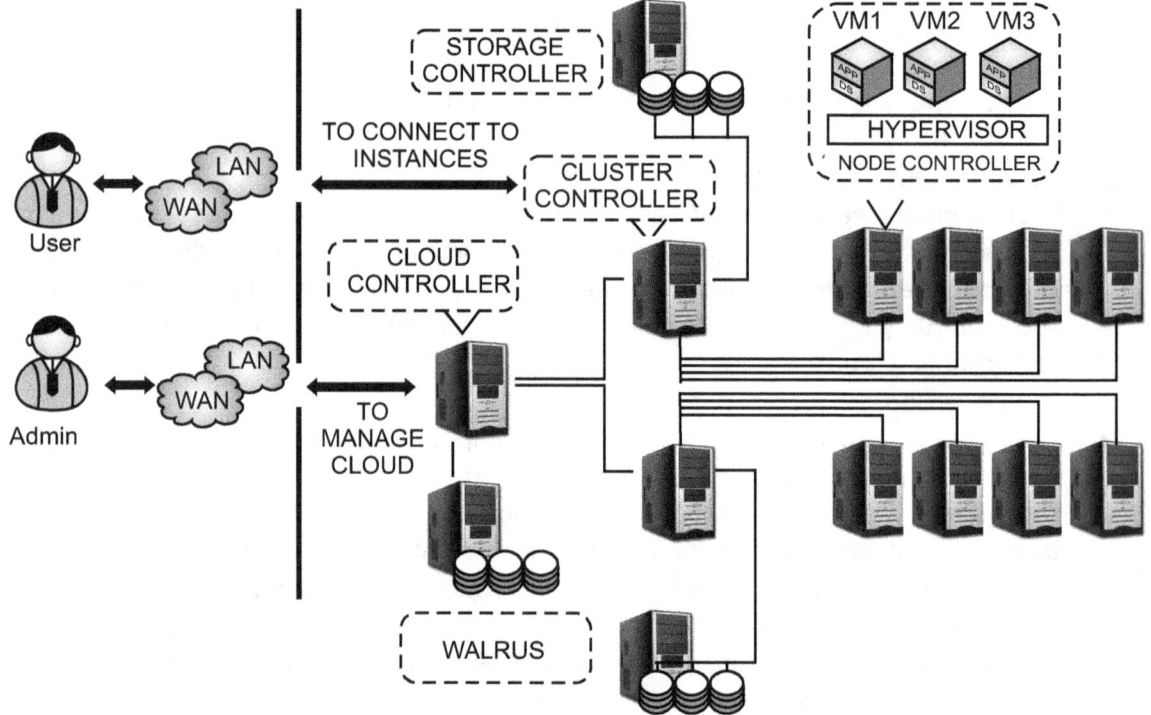

Fig. 1.7 : Eucalyptus components

1.11.2 Eucalyptus Components

- Each Eucalyptus service component exposes a well-defined language agnostic API in the form of a WSDL document containing both the operations that the service can perform and the input/output data structures.
- Inter-service authentication is handled via standard WS-Security mechanisms. There are five high-level components, each with its own Web-service interface, that comprise a Eucalyptus installation (Fig. 1.7).

A brief description of the components within the Eucalyptus system follows.

1. Cloud Controller

- Cloud Controller (CLC) is the entry-point into the cloud for administrators, developers, project managers, and end-users. The CLC is responsible for querying the node managers for information about resources, making high level scheduling decisions, and implementing them by making requests to cluster controllers.
- The CLC is also the interface to the management platform. In essence, the CLC is responsible for exposing and managing the underlying virtualized resources (servers, network, and storage) via a well-defined industry standard API (Amazon EC2) and a Web-based user interface.

Functions :

1. Monitor the availability of resources on various components of the cloud infrastructure, including hypervisor nodes that are used to actually provision the instances and the cluster controllers that manage the hypervisor nodes.
2. Resource arbitration : deciding which clusters will be used for provisioning the instances.
3. Monitoring the running instances.

In short, CLC has a comprehensive knowledge of the availability and usage of resources in the cloud and the state of the cloud.

2. Cluster Controller

- Cluster Controller (CC) generally executes on a cluster front-end machine or any machine that has network connectivity to both the nodes running NCs and to the machine running the CLC. CCs gather information about a set of VMs and schedules VM execution on specific NCs.
- The CC also manages the virtual instance network and participates in the enforcement of SLAs as directed by the CLC. All nodes served by a single CC must be in the same broadcast domain (Ethernet).

Functions

1. To receive requests from CLC to deploy instances.
2. To decide which NCs to use for deploying the instances on.
3. To control the virtual network available to the instances.
4. To collect information about the NCs registered with it and report it to the CLC.

3. Node Controller

- Node Controller (NC) is executed on every node that is designated for hosting VM instances. A UEC node is a VT-enabled server capable of running KVM as the hypervisor. UEC automatically installs KVM when the user chooses to install the UEC node.
- The VMs running on the hypervisor and controlled by UEC are called instances. Eucalyptus supports other hypervisors like Xen apart from KVM, but Canonical has chosen KVM as the preferred hypervisor for UEC.
- The NC runs on each node and controls the life cycle of instances running on the node. The NC interacts with the OS and the hypervisor running on the node on one side and the CC on the other side.
- NC queries the operating system running on the node to discover the node's physical resources, the number of cores, the size of memory, and the available disk space. It also learns about the state of VM instances running on the node and propagates this data up to the CC.

Functions

1. Collection of data related to the resource availability and utilization on the node and reporting the data to CC.
2. Instance life cycle management.

4. Storage Controller

- Storage Controller (SC) implements block-accessed network storage (e.g., Amazon Elastic Block Storage - EBS) and is capable of interfacing with various storage systems (NFS, iSCSI, etc.).
- An elastic block store is a Linux block device that can be attached to a virtual machine but sends disk traffic across the locally attached network to a remote storage location. An EBS volume cannot be shared across instances but does allow a snapshot to be created and stored in a central storage system such as Walrus, the Eucalyptus storage service.

Functions

1. Creation of persistent EBS devices.
2. Providing the block storage over AoE or iSCSI protocol to the instances.
3. Allowing creation of snapshots of volumes.

Walrus

- Walrus (put/get storage) allows users to store persistent data, organized as eventually-consistent buckets and objects. It allows users to create, delete, list buckets, put, get, and delete objects, and set access control policies.
- Walrus is interface compatible with Amazon's S3, and supports the Amazon Machine Image (AMI) image-management interface, thus providing a mechanism for storing and accessing both the virtual machine images and user data.
- Using Walrus, users can store persistent data, which is organized as buckets and objects. WS3 is a file-level storage system, as compared to the block-level storage system of Storage Controller.

- For using Walrus to manage Eucalyptus VM images, you can use Amazon's tools to store/register/delete them from Walrus. Other third-party tools can also be used to interact with Walrus directly.

Third-Party Tools for Interacting with Walrus

1. S3curl : a command line tool that is a wrapper around curl.
   http ://open.eucalyptus.com/wiki/s3curl
2. S3cmd : a tool that allows command line access to storage that supports the S3 API.
   http ://open.eucalyptus.com/wiki/s3cmd
3. S3fs : a tool that allows users to access S3 buckets as local directories.
   http ://open.eucalyptus.com/wiki/s3fs

Management Platform

Management Platform provides an interface to various Eucalyptus services and modules. These features can include VM management, storage management, user/group management, accounting, monitoring, SLA definition and enforcement, cloud-bursting, provisioning, etc.

Euca2ool

Euca2ools are command-line tools for interacting with Web services that export a REST/Query-based API compatible with Amazon EC2 and S3 services. The tools can be used with both Amazon's services and with installations of the Eucalyptus open-source cloud-computing infrastructure. The tools were inspired by command-line tools distributed by Amazon (api-tools and ami-tools) and largely accept the same options and environment variables. However, these tools were implemented from scratch in Python, relying on the Boto library and M2Crypto toolkit.

Features

1. Query of availability zones (i.e., clusters in Eucalyptus).
2. SSH key management (add, list, delete).
3. VM management (start, list, stop, reboot, get console output).
4. Security group management.
5. Volume and snapshot management (attach, list, detach, create, bundle, delete).
6. Image management (bundle, upload, register, list, deregister).
7. IP address management (allocate, associate, list, release).

Key Benefits

- Build and manage self-service heterogeneous on-premise IaaS clouds using either existing infrastructure or dedicated compute, network and storage resources.
- Support high-availability IaaS for the most demanding cloud deployments.
- Gain precise control of private cloud resources via enterprise-ready user and group identity management along with resource quotas.
- Pool dynamic resources with built-in elasticity, allowing organizations to scale up and down virtual compute, network and storage resources.
- Integrate robust storage, enabling IT to easily connect and manage existing storage systems from within Eucalyptus clouds.

- Build hybrid clouds between on-premise Eucalyptus clouds and AWS and AWS-compatible public clouds.
- Run Eucalyptus or Amazon Machine Images as virtual cloud instances on Eucalyptus and AWS-compatible clouds.
- Leverage vibrant AWS ecosystem and management tools to manage Eucalyptus IaaS clouds.

1.12 OPENSTACK

- OpenStack is a collection of open source software projects that can be collectively utilized to operate a cloud network infrastructure in order to provide IaaS. The OpenStack project began as a collaboration of Rackspace Hosting and NASA as an open source project.
- NASA was a user of the Eucalyptus open source cloud project before scalability issues in their Nebula project meant that they needed to develop their own technologies in this space. A contribution of their Cloud Files platform by Rackspace, combined with the Nebula computing software from NASA led to the initial birth of OpenStack.
- In the time since it's inception, the OpenStack consortium has managed to bring in over 100 members, including high profile industry names such as Citrix, Canonical and Dell.
- Since Amazon's AWS was the first majorly used cloud service, OpenStack also makes its services available via Amazon EC2 and S3 compatible APIs. This ensures that all the existing tools that work with Amazon's cloud offerings, can work with deployments of OpenStack as well.

The OpenStack project is combination of three main components :

- OpenStack Compute (Nova) : It is used to orchestrate, manage and offer virtual machines upon many hypervisors, including QEMU and KVM. This is analogous to the Amazon Elastic Compute Cloud (EC2).
- OpenStack Object Store (Swift) : Provides redundant storage for static objects. This serviceis scalable to massive data sizes and theoretically can provide infinite storage. It is analogous to the Amazon Simple Storage Service (S3).
- OpenStack Image Service (Glance) : Provides storage for virtual disk, kernel and images. Glance is also used to provide image registration and querying services. It is able to accept images in many formats, including the popular Amazon Machine Image (AMI), Amazon Kernel Image (AKI) and Amazon Ramdisk Image (ARI).
- Installing, configuring and working with Nova and Glance are covered as part of this tutorial. However, Swift is beyond the scope. Nonetheless, setting up Swift should not be a hard task for anyone who completes this tutorial.
- It should also be noted that this tutorial is based upon the OpenStack Diablo release and uses an Ubuntu 11.10 Oneiric Ocelot server environment to setup all necessary packages. However, this is only because Ubuntu provides prebuilt packages for OpenStack Diablo. As such, the configuration of OpenStack can be performed on any flavor of Linux by using this tutorial as a basic guide.

1.12.1 OpenStack Compute (Nova)

Nova takes up the role of providing computing services within the OpenStack cloud. As such, any activity needed to support the life cycle of a virtual machine instance within the cloud is handled by Nova.

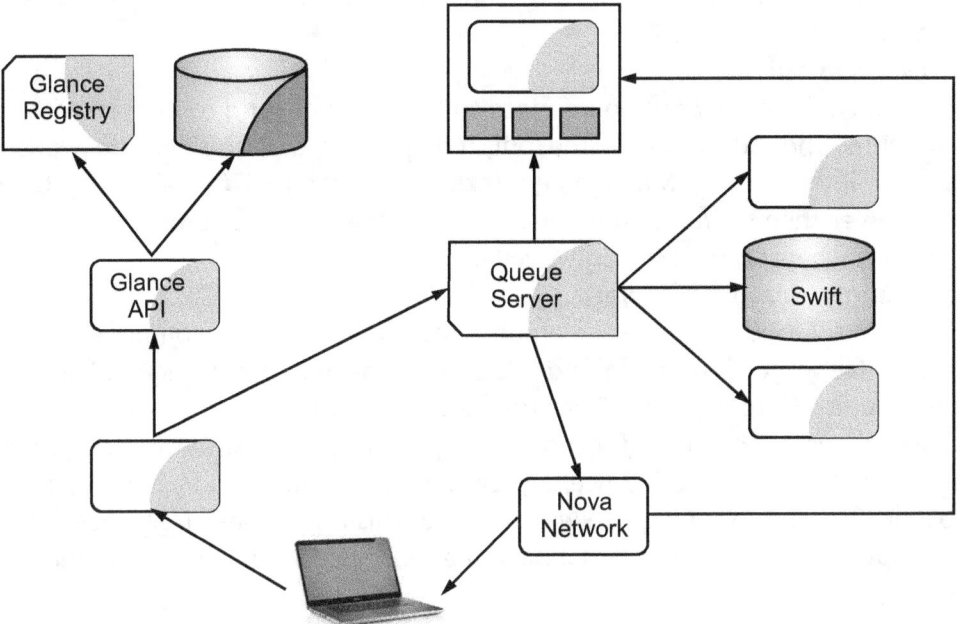

Fig. 1.8 : OpenStack architecture

- An overview of the OpenStack architecture is shown as in Fig. 1.8. The client interacts with Nova API services. This uses Glance API for image registration and retrieval. All other requests are sent to the queue server, which passes them off to the Compute, Volume, Schedule or Network nodes, as the need be.

- This includes things like managing block storage, networking, scheduling, computing resources, authorization and hypervisors.

- However, Nova does not provide any virtualization capabilities by itself. It is designed to use libvirt APIs to interact with any supported hypervisors.

- This means that Nova is hypervisor agnostic and provides support for Xen, XenServer/XCP, KVM, UML, VMware vSphere and Hyper-V amongst others.

- All services provided by Nova are accessible via an API that is compatible with the AWS EC2. The main components of Nova are nova-api, rabbitmq-server, nova-compute, nova-network, nova-volume and nova-scheduler.

- An overview of the OpenStack architecture can be seen in Fig. 1.8. As can be seen, the client interacts with the Nova API server. In case requests dealing with registration or querying of images are sent, the API forwards these requests to the Glance API, which can perform queries within the Glance registry (stored in a SQL database).

- However, if the request deals with managing an instance, then this is forwarded to the queue server, which in turn distributes the requests to appropriate components. Network address allocation, association and deallocation requests are handled by nova-network.
- On the other hand, block storage creation, deletion and association requests are handled by nova-volume. Similarly, virtual machine instance related queries are processed by nova-compute.

API Services (nova-api)

- The nova-api service provides an interface to the outside world to interact with the cloud infrastructure. The API server is the only component that the outside world uses to manage the infrastructure. Management is done through RESTful calls using the EC2 API. The API server then, in turn, communicates with the relevant components of the cloud infrastructure by using the Message Queue.

Message Queuing (rabbitmq-server)

- The OpenStack Cloud Controller communicates with other nova components such as the Scheduler, Network Controller, and Volume Controller by using AMQP (Advanced Message Queue Protocol). OpenStack uses the rabbitmq-server for this purpose.
- Nova uses asynchronous calls for request-response, with a call-back that gets triggered once a response is received. Since asynchronous communication is used, none of the user actions get stuck for long in a waiting state. This is especially true since many actions expected by the API calls such as launching an instance or uploading an image are time consuming.

Computing Services (nova-compute)

- Servers providing computing services via nova-compute deal with instance management life cycle. They receive requests for life cycle management via the Message Queue and carry out appropriate operations.
- There are several servers providing computing services in a typical production cloud deployment. An instance is deployed on any of the available compute workers based on the scheduling algorithm used by Nova.

Network Services (nova-api)

- The network services provided by nova-api deals with the network configuration of host machines. It does operations like allocating IP addresses, configuring VLANs for projects, implementing security groups and configuring networks for compute nodes.

Block Storage Services (nova-volume)

- Block storage services performed by nova-volume include creation, deletion, attaching a volume to an instance, and detaching a volume from an instance.
- Volumes provide a way of providing persistent storage for use by instances, as the main disk attached to an instance is non-persistent and any changes made to it are lost when the volume is detached or the instance is terminated.
- When a volume is detached from an instance or when an instance, to which the volume is attached, is terminated, it retains the data that was stored on it when it was attached to an instance earlier.

- This data can be accessed by reattaching the volume to the same instance or by attaching it to another instances.
- As such, any valuable data that gets accumulated during the life cycle of an instance should be written to a volume, so that it can be accessed later.

Scheduling Services (nova-scheduler)

- The nova-scheduler maps API calls to the appropriate OpenStack components. It picks a server from a pool depending upon the scheduling algorithm in place. A scheduler can base its decisions on various factors such as load, memory, physical distance of the availability zone, CPU architecture, etc.

1.12.2 OpenStack Image Service (Glance)

- OpenStack Imaging Service is a lookup and retrieval system for virtual machine images. While it can be configured to use Swift or S3 storage to store the images, it normally uses a regular filesystem on the host for the glance service.
- The information regarding registered images is stored in an SQL database, which can be either MySQL, PostgreSQL, SQLite or many other varieties as well.

Installation and Configuration

- The distributed architecture of OpenStack means that all components can be installed on either a single or multiple systems. This means that a single computer could be used to provide API, Scheduler, Network, Compute, Volume, Message Queuing and Glance services.
- On the other hand, any of these services could be installed on separate hosts as well. In fact, some services, like Volume and Compute, can be installed on multiple servers for load balancing purposes.
- In this tutorial, installation on a single server will be covered, however, by simple extension of the configuration file this can be extended to any configuration necessary. An Ubuntu 11.10 server install with OpenSSH and Virtual Machine Host tasks is used as the base.
- In case you miss choosing OpenSSH and/or Virtual Machine Host tasks, make sure to install the openssh and qemu packages before proceeding. This can be done by using apt-get :

```
$ sudo apt-get install openssh-server qemu libvirt0
```

- It is assumed that the host has a single network interface named eth0 with an IP address 172.16.4.10.
- In order to work with nova-volume, the host also has two hard drives; the first contains the base OS installation, while the second one will be used to create LVM volumes used by virtual machine instances.

1. Install MySQL

- The Nova installation uses a SQL database to store all metadata and operation information. We will use MySQL, however, you may use any other flavor as well.

Install MySQL server and set the root password as "nova".

```
$ sudo apt-get install mysql-server
```

- Open /etc/mysql/my.cnf and change the bind-address property to look like :
  bind-address = 0.0.0.0

Now restart the server.

```
$ sudo restart mysql
```

- Once this is done, you must create the Nova database and give permissions to the root user to access this database from any connecting IP address, so that if you decide to add more nodes or create a multi-node setup, it will still work without any troubles.

```
$ mysqladmin -u root -p create nova Enter password :
$ mysql -u root -p -e "GRANT ALL PRIVILEGES ON *.* TO 'root'@'%' WITH GRANT OPTION;" Enter password :
$ mysql -uroot -p -e "SET PASSWORD FOR 'root'@'%' = PASSWORD('nova');" Enter password :
```

- Now that MySQL is setup and ready for Nova, we can proceed with installing the other services.

2. Install RabbitMQ

- Before installing RabbitMQ, make sure that your hostname is set to your correct IP address in your /etc/hosts file. Without this correctly entered, RabbitMQ will refuse to start.

Once this is done, install RabbitMQ.

```
$ sudo apt-get install rabbitmq-server
```

3. Install Glance

- Nova can use Glance service to manage Operating System images that it needs for bringing up instances. Installing this is also easy.

```
$ sudo apt-get install glance
```

- There is no need to make any further configuration changes since we are going to let Glance use the local file system for storing images and a default SQLite database for metadata.

4. Setup the Nova Cloud Controller

- The cloud controller is responsible for the API, Scheduling and Network services. As such, install these along with some other dependencies.

```
$ sudo apt-get install nova-common nova-doc nova-api
$ sudo apt-get install nova-network nova-objectstore nova-scheduler $ sudo apt-get install python-nova unzip
```

- These install commands added all the packages needed on the cloud controller, along with a large number of dependencies. In addition, the package installation scripts have added a system user nova and added it to the appropriate groups.

- A minimal configuration file for Nova is also created during the installation procedure, but this needs to be edited in order to suit our installation environment. As such, edit the /etc/nova/nova.conf file to reflect the following :

```
--daemonize=1
--dhcpbridge_flagfile=/etc/nova/nova.conf       --dhcpbridge=/usr/bin/nova-dhcpbridge       --logdir=/var/log/nova --state_path=/var/lib/nova
```

```
--verbose --libvirt_type=qemu

--sql_connection=mysql ://root :nova@172.16.4.10/nova --s3_host=172.16.4.10
--rabbit_host=172.16.4.10 --ec2_host=172.16.4.10 --ec2_dmz_host=172.16.4.10

--ec2_url=http ://172.16.4.10 :8773/services/Cloud --fixed_range=10.0.0.0/8

--network_size=64   --num_networks=1   --FAKE_subdomain=ec2   --public_interface=eth0   --
state_path=/var/lib/nova --lock_path=/var/lock/nova --glance_host=172.16.4.10
--image_service=nova.image.glance.GlanceImageService --glance_api_servers=172.16.4.10 :9292 -
-vlan_start=100

--vlan_interface=eth0 --iscsi_ip_prefix=172.16.4 --iscsi_helper=tgtadm
```

- Please note that in our single-node setup the IP address of the host node is 172.16.4.10, however, this may differ in your case. As such, substitute this with your cloud controller's IP address.
- As is evident from the above, we are instructing Nova to use QEMU as the hypervisor of choice. It is then instructed to use the nova MySQL database sitting on the cloud controller.
- The --s3_host configuration parameter is used to instruct Nova where the Swift services are installed (omitted in this tutorial). The --rabbit_host parameter tells Nova where the RabbitMQ server is installed; in our case it is on the cloud controller. The 2_host parameter is used to configure the target API server, as are all the other ec2 parameters.
- Nova is then instructed to use the 10.0.0.0/8 network for its private network between the instances. This network is referred to the fixed network by Nova.
- A network size of 64 means that Nova should use up to 64 IPs from the 10.0.0.0/8 network and it is also instructed to create only a single network.
- There is only one interface on the host interface, which provides access to the public network. As such, Nova is instructed to use the eth0 interface for all public traffic via the--public_interface option.
- It is also essential for Nova to know where Glance is installed, so that it can successfully register and retrieve images when necessary. In our case, this is the same as the cloud controller, and Nova is instructed to use the Glance image service located on the cloud controller via the Glance related switches, i.e. glance_host, image_service and glance_api_servers.
- Nova uses VLANs to setup communication between the nova-network host and the virtual machine instances. The vlan_start option instructs Nova to start numbering the VLANs at 100. Please note that this is the minimum number recommended. The

vlan_interface option should be set to the interface that can provide connectivity between the cloud controller, volume host and compute host. In our case, this is eth0.

- Lastly, since it is essential to have persistent storage in the virtual machine instances, nova-volume is used and must be configured. The nova-volume service uses ISCSI to export LVM volumes and attach these to instances. These may then be used for block storage inside instances. The --iscsi_prefix option must be set to the IP prefix of the network which can be used to reach the volume host. The--iscsi_helper option instructs nova-volume and nova-compute to use the tgtadm package for administering the ISCSI volumes.

- Please note that in a multi-host setup, the nova.conf file must be existent on every host that has any Nova services on it.

5. Setup the Volume Host

- The volume host provides block storage services to the virtual machine instances by installing the nova-compute package along with the ISCSI tools.

```
$ sudo apt-get install nova-volume iscsitarget iscsitarget-dkms tgt
```

Once these are installed, you must enable the iscsitarget service to start by default.

```
$ sudo sed -i 's/false/true/g' /etc/default/iscsitarget
```

- It is advisable for the volume host to have an additional hard drive that can be used to setup the necessary LVM volumes. In our single node environment, the cloud controller is the volume host as well and has a second hard drive, which is visible to the system at /dev/sdb. As such, a physical volume and volume group named nova-volumes must be created on /dev/sdb.

```
$ sudo pvcreate /dev/sdb
$ sudo vgcreate nova-volumes /dev/sdb
```

6. Setup the Compute Host

- The compute host uses the nova-compute package to provide virtual machine instantiation services. It is also uses the ISCSI tools to discover available appropriate targets and attach them to relevant virtual machines. As such, install the following packages on the compute host.

```
$ sudo apt-get install nova-compute qemu
$ sudo apt-get install iscsitarget iscsitarget-dkms tgt open-iscsi
```

- It is also important to note that when working along with the tgt ISCSI packages, which are the default as well, Nova has a bug that causes it to fail attaching ISCSI volumes to a virtual machine instance. This can be fixed by editing the /usr/lib/python2.7/dist-packages/nova/volume/driver.py file.

  Change the following line :

```
mount_device = ("/dev/disk/by-path/ip-%s-iscsi-%s-lun-0" %
```

To :

```
mount_device = ("/dev/disk/by-path/ip-%s-iscsi-%s-lun-1" %
```

This should be located on, or around, line 536.

7. Create Network Schema

- It is recommended that you now reboot all your Nova hosts, before setting up the networking schema necessary to instantiate virtual machines. After rebooting, create the schema on the cloud controller :

```
$ sudo nova-manage db sync
```

- Now that the basic database schema has been created, it is important for all services to be restarted. Since there are too many services to restart by hand, reboot all your Nova hosts once again. After the reboot, check if all the nova services have started up correctly :

  ```
  $ sudo nova-manage service list
  ```

Binary	Host	Zone	Status		State Updated_At	
nova-compute	cloud-controller	nova	enabled	:-)	2012-06-02 15 :05 :14	
nova-volume	cloud-controller	nova	enabled	:-)	2012-06-11	08 :40 :21
nova-scheduler	cloud-controller	nova	enabled	:-)	2012-06-11	08 :40 :21
nova-network	cloud-controller	nova	enabled	:-)	2012-06-11	08 :40 :21

- If you see smiley faces, " :-)", against all service names, it means that all services started up correctly after the reboot. If not, you should wait for some time and try to check the service list once again, since sometimes it can take a little while before a service comes up.
- However, even after waiting, if a service does not get a smiley face next to it, but only "XXX", then a manual start of that particular service can at times help. For example, if the nova-network service is the one that has not started, then restart it manually with "/etc/init.d/nova-network restart".
- After a few moments, you should now see a smiley face. If, however, this too does not work, it is recommended that you check the nova.conf configuration file and log files located in

/var/log/nova/.

Once all the services have started up correctly, you can create the network schema :

```
$ sudo nova-manage network create vmnet --fixed_range_v4=10.0.0.0/8 \
```

```
--network_size=64   --bridge_interface=eth0   $   sudo   nova-manage   floating   create
ip_range=172.16.4.224/27
```

- The vmnet (or fixed network) is the VLAN created for use between the Nova network host and the virtual machines on the compute node. The parameters used here are the same as in the nova.conf file.
- On the other hand, the floating network is the block of public IP addresses that are reachable on the eth0 interface and can be handed out to virtual machines on demand.
- At this point your basic OpenStack Nova and Glance setup is complete. The following section will cover some important details regarding working with OpenStack. Registering and uploading images to Glance, creating VM instances, configuring network firewall

policies, associating public IP addresses, creating persistent block storage and attaching it to VMs is covered.

```
$ sudo    nova-manage user create aimsuser
export    EC2_ACCESS_KEY=d77406c3-cea1-45af-bbd9-acfd16ff49e3
export    EC2_SECRET_KEY=b9c6ab50-65d7-4185-a1a9-267a2afe30f9
```

- At this point, it is important to note that a minor bug in the way the nova-manage command works, causes the environment variables to be setup incorrectly.
- As such, it is important for you to make a note of the value the EC2_ACCESS_KEY shell variable has after the above command is issued. Once you have made a note of it, you can continue assigning roles to the user and creating associated projects :

```
$ sudo nova-manage role add aimsuser cloudadmin
$ sudo nova-manage project create aimsproj aimsuser $ sudo nova-manage project zipfile
aimsproj aimsuser
```

- You shall now have a nova.zip file, which contains the credentials necessary to work with the Nova. Copy this zip file to your client machine and expand it.
- Once expanded, you will need to open the novarc file in an editor, with super-user privileges, and change the following line :

```
export EC2_ACCESS_KEY="aimsuser :aimsproj"
```

- Instead of the user name, aims user, which is currently in this line, you must replace it with the value of the variable that you noted before.
  As such, in our example, this will change to :

```
export EC2_ACCESS_KEY="d77406c3-cea1-45af-bbd9-acfd16ff49e3 :aimsproj"
```

- On your client machines, once the zip file is expanded and the above mentioned edit to the novarc file made, setup the environment variables included in the novarc file.

```
$ source ./novarc
```

- You might want to add it to your shell profile to have it automatically sourced on login.

8. Uploading Images

- Before you can actually instantiate a virtual machine, you will need to upload and register an image with Glance. For the purposes of our test server setup, let's use Ubuntu's Enterprise Cloud images.

```
$ wget \
http ://uec-images.ubuntu.com/releases/lucid/release/\
ubuntu-10.04-server-cloudimg-i386.tar.gz
```

- Once this is done, you can upload the image to Glance.

```
$ cloud-publish-tarball ubuntu-10.04-server-cloudimg-i386.tar.gz images
Sun May 5 15 :48 :19 PDT 2012 : ====== extracting image ======
Warning : no ramdisk found, assuming '--ramdisk none' kernel  : natty-server-uec-amd64-
vmlinuz-virtual ramdisk : none
image : natty-server-uec-amd64.img
Sun May 5 15 :48 :45 PDT 2012 : ====== bundle/upload kernel ======
```

Sun May 5 15 :49 :52 PDT 2012 : ====== bundle/upload image ======
Sun May 5 15 :54 :19 PDT 2012 : ====== done ======
emi="ami-00000002"; eri="none"; eki="aki-00000001";

- Once you have the ami number, then you are ready to start instances.

9. Launching Instances

- With the ami number available, you can not have ami number, you can use the images. euca-describe-images use the euca2ools package to launch instances. In case, you do command to get a list of all available.
- However, before launching an instance, it is useful to create your keypair so that you can later access this instance via ssh.

```
$ euca-add-keypair aimsuser > aimsuser.pem; chmod 600 aimsuser.pem
```

- Now launch an instance by using the euca-run-instances command, your keypair and providing a system type.

```
$ euca-run-instance -k aimsuser -t m1.tiny ami-00000002
```

- You can view a list of running instances using the euca-describe-instances command. If an instance has not been marked as running after 10-15 minutes, it is likely that something has gone awry and you should look at Nova log files.

10. Network Connectivity

- Configuring network access to the virtual machine is important since that makes it usable. By default Nova sets up the iptables firewall to not allow access to the machine in any form. It makes sense to enable at least ICMP and SSH traffic.

```
$ euca-authorize default -P tcp -p 22 -s 0.0.0.0/0 $ euca-authorize default -P icmp -t -1 :-1
```

- Once the traffic is permitted to the instance, you can allocate and associate an address with the instance. The example below associates the allocated IP with instance i-00000001.

```
$ euca-allocate-address
ADDRESS            172.16.4.224
$ euca-associate-address        -i i-00000001 172.16.4.224
ADDRESS            172.16.4.224 i-00000001
```

To access the instance via SSH, just use the created keypair and the recently associated floating IP address.

```
$ ssh -i aimsuser.pem  ubuntu@172.16.4.224
```

- It is important to note that the initially assigned fixed address is not routeable from outside the Nova hosts, as such you must associate a floating address with an instance before it is reachable.
- It is important to turn on IPv4 forwarding on the **nova-network** and **nova-compute** hosts so that the virtual machines can reach the public Internet.

Attaching Volumes

- Before a volume can be attached to an instance, it must be created. Volumes should be created in the zone named nova.

```
$ euca-create-volume -s 1 -z nova
```

- Once the volume is successfully created, you can get a list of all volumes and their status using the euca-describe-volumes command. Use the euca-attach-volume command to associate an available volume to an instance.
- In the example below, the volume vol-00000001 is attached to instance i-00000001 as a raw block device at /dev/vdb.

```
$ euca-attach-volume vol-00000001 -i i-00000001 -d /dev/vdb
```

- Once the volume is attached, you can use fdisk to format it. Following that you may mount it and store files for persistent storage.
- If you encounter troubles, you can use the euca-describe-availability-zones verbose command to get an overview of which servers are running without problems.

1.13 OPENNEBULA

- OpenNebula is an open-source cloud computing toolkit for managing heterogeneous distributed data center infrastructures. The OpenNebula toolkit manages a data center's virtual infrastructure to build private, public and hybrid IaaS (Infrastructure as a Service) clouds.
- OpenNebula orchestrates storage, network, virtualization, monitoring, and security technologies to deploy multi-tier services (e.g. compute clusters) as virtual machines on distributed infrastructures, combining both data center resources and remote cloud resources, according to allocation policies.
- According to the European Commission's report about the future of cloud computing from a group of experts "... only few cloud dedicated research projects in the widest sense have been initiated – most prominent amongst them probably OpenNebula ...".
- The toolkit includes features for integration, management, scalability, security and accounting.
- It also emphasizes standardization, interoperability and portability, providing cloud users and administrators with a choice of several cloud interfaces (EC2 Query, OGF OCCI and vCloud) and hypervisors (Xen, KVM and VMware), and a flexible architecture that can accommodate multiple hardware and software combinations in a data center.
- OpenNebula was a mentoring organization in Google Summer of Code 2010. OpenNebula is sponsored by C12G.

1.13.1 OpenNebula Features

Powerful User Security Management

- Secure and efficient Users and Groups Subsystem for authentication and authorization of requests with complete functionality for user management : create, delete, show...
- Pluggable authentication and authorization based on passwords, ssh rsa keypairs, X509 certificates or LDAP
- Special authentication mechanisms for SunStone (OpenNebula GUI) and the Cloud Services (EC2 and OCCI)

- Authorization framework with fine-grained ACLs that allows multiple-role support for different types of users and administrators, delegated control to authorized users, secure isolated multi-tenant environments, and easy resource (VM template, VM image, VM instance, virtual network and host) sharing

Advanced Multi-tenancy with Group Management

Administrators can groups users into organizations that can represent different projects, division...

- Each group have configurable access to shared resources so enabling a multi-tenant environment with multiple groups sharing the same infrastructure.
- Configuration of special users that are restricted to public cloud APIs (e.g. EC2 or OCCI).
- Complete functionality for management of groups : create, delete, show

On-Demand Provision of Virtual Data Centers

- A Virtual Data Centers (VDC) is a fully-isolated virtual infrastructure environment where a group of users, under the control of the VDC administrator, can create and manage compute, storage and networking capacity
- Advanced multi-tenancy with complete functionality for management of VDCs : create, delete, show...

Advanced Control and Monitoring of Virtual Infrastructure

- Image Repository Subsystem with catalog and complete functionality for VM image management : list, publish, unpublish, show, enable, disable, register, update, saveas, delete...
- Template Repository Subsystem with catalog and complete functionality for VM template management : add, delete, list...
- Full control of VM instance life-cycle and complete functionality for VM instance management : submit, deploy, migrate, livemigrate, stop, save, resume, cancel, shutdown, restart, delete, monitor, list...
- Broad network virtualization capabilities with traffic isolation, ranged or fixed networks, definition of generic attributes to define multi-tier services consisting of groups of inter-connected VMs, and complete functionality for virtual network management to interconnect VM instances : create, delete, monitor, list...
- Configurable system usage statistics to visualize and report resource usage data, to allow their integration with chargeback and billing platforms, or to guarantee fair share of resources among users
- Tagging of users, VM images and virtual networks with arbitrary metadata that can be later used by other components.

Virtual Machine Configuration

- Complete definition of VM attributes and requirements.
- Support for automatic configuration of VMs with advanced contextualization mechanisms.
- Hook Manager to trigger administration scripts upon VM state change.

- Wide range of guest operating system including Microsoft Windows and Linux.
- Flexible network definition.
- Configuration of firewall for VMs to specify a set of black/white TCP/UDP ports.

Advanced Control and Monitoring of Physical Infrastructure

- Configurable to deploy public, private and hybrid clouds.
- Host Management Subsystem with complete functionality for management of physical hosts : create, delete, enable, disable, monitor, list.
- Dynamic creation of logical clusters to serve different types of service workloads.
- Powerful and extensible built-in monitoring subsystem.

Broad Commodity and Enterprise Platform Support

- Hypervisor agnostic Virtualization Subsystem with broad hypervisor support (Xen, KVM and VMware), centralized management of environments with multiple hypervisors, and support for multiple hypervisors within the same physical box.
- Storage Subsystem supporting any backend configuration, from non shared file systems with image transferring with SSH to shared file systems (NFS, GlusterFS, Lustre...) or LVM with CoW, and any storage server, from using commodity hardware to enterprise-grade solutions.
- Flexible Network Subsystem with integration with Ebtable, Open vSwitch and 802.1Q tagging.
- Optional integration with datacenter monitoring tools like Ganglia.

Distributed Resource Optimization

- Powerful and flexible requirement/rank matchmaker scheduler providing automatic initial VM placement for the definition of workload and resource-aware allocation policies such as packing, striping, load-aware, affinity-aware...
- Resource quota management to allocate, track and limit resource utilization.

Centralized Management of Multiple Zones

- Single access point and centralized management for multiple instances of OpenNebula.
- Federation of multiple OpenNebula zones for scalability, isolation or multiple-site support.
- Complete functionality for management of zones : create, delete, show, list...

High Availability

- Persistent database backend with support for high availability configurations.
- Configurable behavior in the event of host, VM, or OpenNebula instance failure to provide an easy to use and cost-effective failover solution.
- Support for high availability architectures.

Hybrid Cloud Computing and Cloudbursting

- Extension of the local private infrastructure with resources from remote clouds.
- Support for Amazon EC2 and for simultaneous access to multiple remote clouds.

Interfaces for Cloud Consumers

- Transform your local infrastructure into a public cloud by exposing REST-based interfaces.
- OGF OCCI service, the emerging cloud API standard, and client tools.
- AWS EC2 API service, the de facto cloud API standard, with compatibility with EC2 ecosystem tools and client tools.
- Support for simultaneously exposing multiple cloud APIs.
- Easily-customizable self-service portal.

Rich Operation Interfaces and User Self-Service Portal

- Unix-like Command Line Interface to manage all resources : users, VM images, VM templates, VM instances, virtual networks, zones, VDCs, physical hosts, accounting, authentication, authorization...
- Easy-to-use Sunstone Graphical Interface providing usage graphics and statistics with cloudwatch-like functionality, VNC support, different system views for different roles, catalog access, multiple-zone management...

Deployment Options

- Easy to install with packages for most common Linux distributions.
- Available in most popular Linux distributions.
- Optional building from source code.
- System features a small footprint, less than 10Mb.
- Detailed log files for the different components that maintain a record of significant changes.

Extension and Integration

- Modular and extensible architecture to fit into any existing datacenter.
- Customizable drivers for the main subsystems to easily leverage existing IT infrastructure and system management products : Virtualization, Storage, Monitoring, Image Repository, Network, Auth and Hybrid Cloud.
- New drivers can be easily written in any language.
- Plugin support to easily extend SunStone Graphical Interface with additional tabs to better integrate Cloud and VM management with each site own operations and tools.
- Easily customizable self-service portal for cloud consumers.
- Configuration and tuning parameters to adjust behavior of the cloud management instance to the requirements of the environment and use cases.
- Fully open-source technology available under Apache license.
- Well-documented database schema for accounting.
- Powerful and extensible low-level cloud API in Ruby and JAVA and XMLRPC API.
- A Ruby API to build applications on top of the Zones/VDC component ZONA, the ZONes Api.

- OpenNebula ecosystem with experimental components enhancing the functionality provided by OpenNebula.

Reliability, Efficiency and Massive Scalability

- Automated testing process for functionality, scalability, performance, robustness and stability.
- Technology matured through an active and engaged community.
- Proven on large scale infrastructures consisting of tens of thousands of cores and VMs.
- Highly scalable database back-end with support for MySQL and SQLite.
- Virtualization drivers adjusted for maximum scalability.
- Very efficient core developed in C++ language.

1.14 CLOUD MULTI-TENANCY

- The term Multi-tenancy has gotten significant attention after the rise of cloud computing in the global market. Most of the time, the term is misused when describing cloud computing.
- A few of us may relate multi-tenancy with a database or application architecture, while others think it has something to do with virtualization. Both views are correct, depending on the context.
- Should we proceed with the tried and tested path of single-tenant application, or use the unknown, and less travelled but more challenging, multi-tenant SaaS? The development team was more enthusiastic to get the application architected as a multi-tenant SaaS.
- But how could we design the application (and the database) so that a single instance of it (and the database) could be shared by all the member institutes? This led us to brainstorm the idea of multi-tenancy.
- And designing a multi-tenant application is definitely not child's play, especially if you are designing it on a traditional platform (ASP.NET, SQL Server etc). It may be a bit easier to architect a multi-tenant SaaS on a cloud PaaS.

What is Multi-tenancy?

Think of *tenants* as customers (clients) of a service. Before we discuss more about tenants let us understand the following :

SaaS can have two broad categories.

1. Line-of-Business (LOB) : Services like CRM and Project management solutions are meant for enterprise customers. A few examples are :

- Salesforce CRM
- Google Apps for business
- DeskAway
- Impel CRM
- Freshdesk

2. Consumer-Oriented : Services are meant for the general public and may be offered free of cost. Examples are :

- Dropbox (Now they are also offering *Dropbox for teams* : enterprise version)
- Microsoft SkyDrive
- Gmail, Google Apps (Free), Google Analytics.

Multitenancy is fundamental technology that clouds use to share IT resources cost-efficiently and securely. Just like in an apartment building, where many tenants cost-efficiently share the common infrastructure of the building but have walls and doors that give them privacy from other tenants, a cloud uses multitenancy technology to share IT resources securely among multiple applications and tenants (businesses, organizations, etc.) that use the cloud. Some clouds use virtualization-based architectures to isolate tenants, others use custom software architectures to get the job done.

1.14.1 Multi-Tenancy Implementation Based on Service Models

1. Infrastructure as a Service (IaaS) :

- Tenants on a multi-tenant application share infrastructure resources like servers and storage devices. Here multi-tenancy is achieved using Virtual Machines (VMs).

What are Virtual Machines (VMs)?

- In simple words, your application will be executed on a virtual computer (also known as an instance). You have your choice of virtual computer, meaning that you can select a configuration of CPU, memory and storage that is optimal for your application.
- The following diagram depicts a simplified illustration of multi-tenant implementation in IaaS. The image shows a cloud provider that has a number of Virtual Machines (VMs) available that it can allocate to clients; block A shows vm_4, vm_5, ... , vm_n. Block A shows 2 clients – A and B.
- Client A can access and use vm_1 and vm_2. Client B can access vm_3. Block B shows entry of a new client C who has access to vm_4, vm_5 and vm_6.

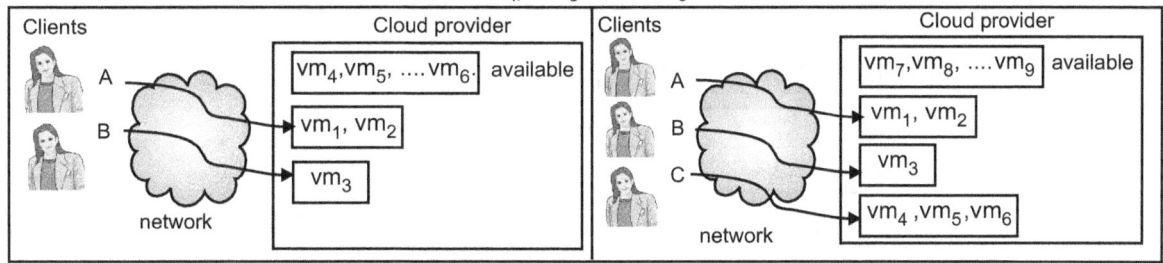

Fig. 1.9 : Cloud Providers and Virtual Machines

2. Platform as a Service (PaaS) :

- Here different processes may share an operating system and networking services.
- PaaS multi-tenancy means that, like a Heroku or a Cloud Bees, the platform can isolate code from different apps/vendors on the same OS instance (usually by commingling processes and databases on OS instances).
- This removes the need to allocate a whole VM per application stack component, improving efficiency.

- The following diagram is a simplified illustration of a multi-tenant PaaS. The PaaS provider has an inventory of applications, namely A, B, C, D.
- Here a tenant can be a developer, or a customer (C_1 in the Fig. 1.10). As shown in the following Fig. 1.10 the developer is creating applications and the customer is consuming them $B \rightarrow exr_1$ and $B \rightarrow exr_2$. In brief, multiple developers and customers are sharing the resources provided by PaaS. PaaS can also use the services of an IaaS.

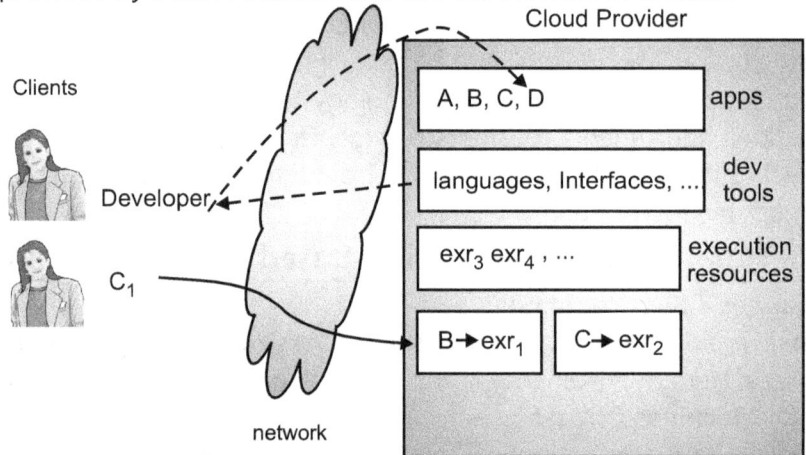

Fig. 1.10 : Interaction : Cloud Provider and Developer

3. Software as a Service (SaaS) :

- Here multi-tenancy is marked by a single application instance (i.e. code base) and single database instance for supporting multiple customers.
- Customers are sharing the same code base and the data is stored on the same set of tables distinguished by Tenant ID. Stated simply : The separation of data is logical and not physical. In a database table records can be saved in the following format

TenantID			CustName	Address	
4	TenantID		ProductID	ProductName	
1	4	TenantID	Shipment	Data	
6	1	4711	324965	2006-02-21	
4	6	132	115468	2006-04-08	
	4	680	654109	2006-03-27	
		4711	324956	2006-02-23	

Fig. 1.11 : Sample Database Table

A unique TenantID will distinguish between the records of different customers. In reality it's not as simple as we are assuming here, because, if it's a line-of-business (i.e. enterprise) application we again need to distinguish between the records of multiple users of the same customer.

- Also, the presentation layer (User Interface) needs to be provided with settings / configuration options which can offer unique user experience to each customer.

- The following simplified illustration depicts how three customers C_1, C_2 and C_3 are sharing a single application on a single database.

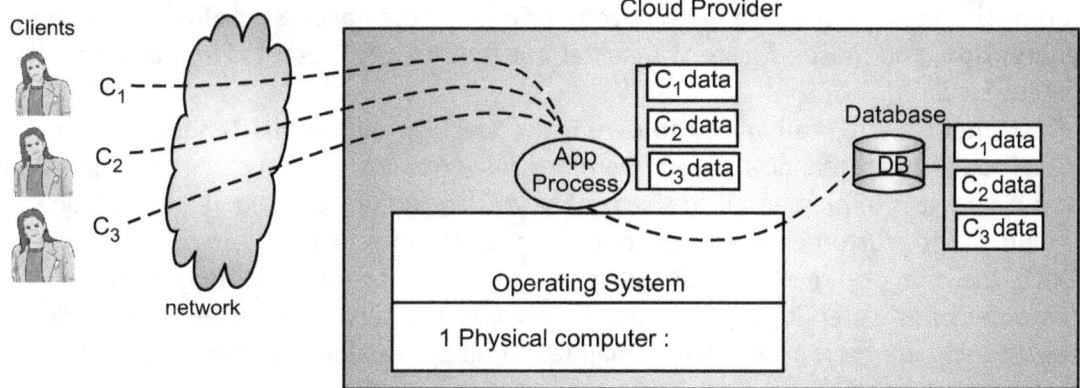

Fig. 1.12 : Client Accessing App Over Cloud

- A Microsoft document on multi-tenant SaaS architecture proposes SaaS architecture which is more mature than the model described above, also known as *SaaS at maturity level iv*. Check the following Fig. 1.13.

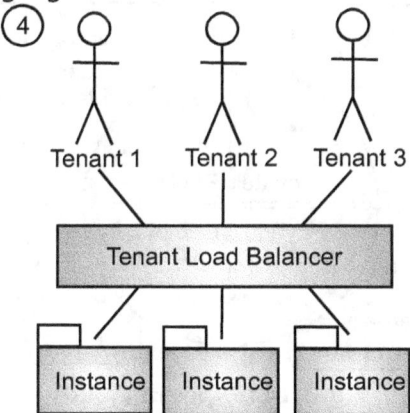

Fig. 1.13 : Saas at Maturity Level

- The above Fig. 1.13 shows the most matured multi-tenant SaaS model. This is somewhat similar to the hybrid of Fig. 1.5 and Fig. 1.6. In simple words, a multi-tenant SaaS architecture making use of virtualization based multi-tenant IaaS.
- The cloud provider hosts multiple clients on a load-balanced farm of *identical instances*, with each customer's data kept separate.

1.14.2 Multi-Tenancy Risk

- In a multi-tenant SaaS architecture a single application and database instance is shared with multiple customers.
- This simply means that the same database and same set of tables can be used to store the records of multiple customers. It is very rare but it may happen that a flaw in the software while querying the data can lead your adversary (who may be a customer of the same service) to access your record.

- At the IaaS level Virtual Machines (VMs) can be attacked by other VMs residing on the same physical host.
- Although these risks are minimized using robust **access policies** and strong **encryption,** you must educate yourself about the security measures in place for a multi-tenant SaaS.

As a Customer do you really need to care if the SaaS is really multi-tenant?

- Yes. Though multi-tenancy is cloud vendor's responsibility you must care to know a little about how it is implemented in the service you are going to use. Everything's fine until the number of customers your provider is supporting increases.
- Once the number grows, it becomes very difficult to manage upgrades on a per customer basis. Later, it may increase the price of the service because the provider may need to engage more resources to maintain multiple versions of code and database per customer.

1.15 TYPES OF CLOUD COMPUTING : PRIVATE, PUBLIC AND HYBRID CLOUDS

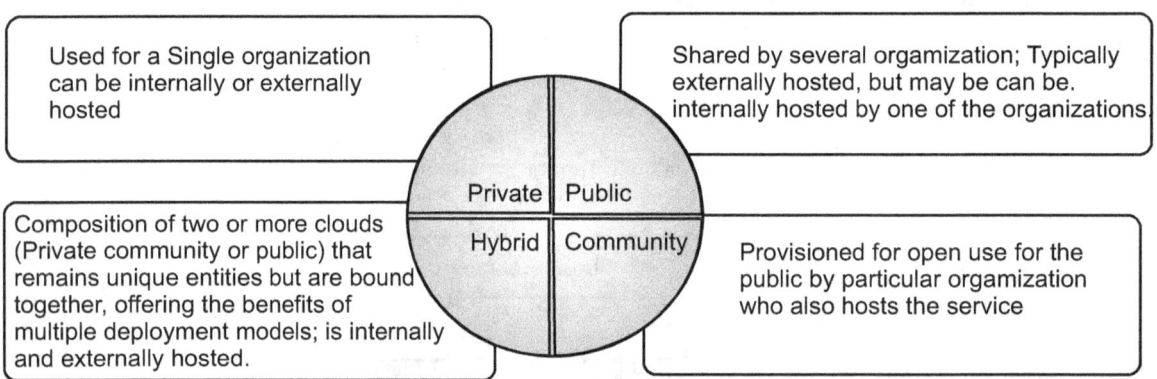

Fig. 1.14 : Types of Clouds

- A recent study conducted by KPMG found that 81% of businesses were either evaluating cloud services, planned a cloud implementation or had already implemented a cloud strategy. Fewer than one in 10 said they had no immediate plans to start using the cloud. No matter how businesses decide to move to the cloud, one thing's clear : they are moving to the cloud.
- With cloud computing technology, large pools of resources can be connected through private or public networks. This technology simplifies infrastructure planning and provides dynamically scalable infrastructure for cloud based applications, data, and file storage. Businesses can choose to deploy applications on Public, Private, Hybrid clouds or the newer Community Cloud.
- What are the differences between these types of cloud computing, and how can you determine the right cloud path for your organization? Here are some fundamentals of each to help with the decision-making process.

1.15.1 Public Clouds

- Public clouds are made available to the general public by a service provider who hosts the cloud infrastructure. Generally, public cloud providers like Amazon AWS, Microsoft and Google own and operate the infrastructure and offer access over the Internet. With this model, customers have no visibility or control over where the infrastructure is located. It is important to note that all customers on public clouds share the same infrastructure pool with limited configuration, security protections and availability variances.
- Public Cloud customers benefit from economies of scale, because infrastructure costs are spread across all users, allowing each individual client to operate on a low-cost, "pay-as-you-go" model.
- Another advantage of public cloud infrastructures is that they are typically larger in scale than an in-house enterprise cloud, which provides clients with seamless, on-demand scalability.
- These clouds offer the greatest level of efficiency in shared resources; however, they are also more vulnerable than private clouds.

A public cloud is the obvious choice when :

- Your standardized workload for applications is used by lots of people, such as e-mail.
- You need to test and develop application code.
- You need incremental capacity (the ability to add compute resources for peak times).
- You are doing collaboration projects.

1.15.2 Private Clouds

- Private cloud is cloud infrastructure dedicated to a particular organization. Private clouds allow businesses to host applications in the cloud, while addressing concerns regarding data security and control, which is often lacking in a public cloud environment.
- It is not shared with other organizations, whether managed internally or by a third-party, and it can be hosted internally or externally.

There are two variations of private clouds :

- **On-Premise Private Cloud :** This type of cloud is hosted within an organization's own facility. A businesses IT department would incur the capital and operational costs for the physical resources with this model. On-Premise Private Clouds are best used for applications that require complete control and configurability of the infrastructure and security.
- **Externally Hosted Private Cloud :** Externally hosted private clouds are also exclusively used by one organization, but are hosted by a third party specializing in cloud infrastructure. The service provider facilitates an exclusive cloud environment with full guarantee of privacy. This format is recommended for organizations that prefer not to use a public cloud infrastructure due to the risks associated with the sharing of physical resources.

- Undertaking a private cloud project requires a significant level and degree of engagement to virtualize the business environment, and it will require the organization to reevaluate decisions about existing resources.
- Private clouds are more expensive but also more secure when compared to public clouds. An Info-Tech survey shows that 76% of IT decision-makers will focus exclusively on the private cloud, as these clouds offer the greatest level of security and control.

When is a Private Cloud for you?
- You need data sovereignty but want cloud efficiencies.
- You want consistency across services.
- You have more server capacity than your organization can use.
- Your data center must become more efficient.
- You want to provide private cloud services.

1.15.3 Hybrid Clouds

- Hybrid Clouds are a composition of two or more clouds (private, community or public) that remain unique entities but are bound together offering the advantages of multiple deployment models. In a hybrid cloud, you can leverage third party cloud providers in either a full or partial manner; increasing the flexibility of computing. Augmenting a traditional private cloud with the resources of a public cloud can be used to manage any unexpected surges in workload.
- Hybrid cloud architecture requires both on-premise resources and off-site server based cloud infrastructure. By spreading things out over a hybrid cloud, you keep each aspect of your business in the most efficient environment possible. The downside is that you have to keep track of multiple cloud security platforms and ensure that all aspects of your business can communicate with each other.

Here are a couple of situations where a hybrid environment is best :
- Your company wants to use a SaaS application but is concerned about security.
- Your company offers services that are tailored for different vertical markets. You can use a public cloud to interact with the clients but keep their data secured within a private cloud.
- You can provide public cloud to your customers while using a private cloud for internal IT.

1.15.4 Community Clouds

- A community clouds is a is a multi-tenant cloud service model that is shared among several or organizations and that is governed, managed and secured commonly by all the participating organizations or a third party managed service provider.
- Community clouds are a hybrid form of private clouds built and operated specifically for a targeted group. These communities have similar cloud requirements and their ultimate goal is to work together to achieve their business objectives.
- The goal of community clouds is to have participating organizations realize the benefits of a public cloud with the added level of privacy, security, and policy

compliance usually associated with a private cloud. Community clouds can be either on-premise or off-premise.

Here are a couple of situations where a community cloud environment is best :

- Government organizations within a state that need to share resources.
- A private HIPAA compliant cloud for a group of hospitals or clinics.
- Telco community cloud for telco DR to meet specific FCC regulations.

Cloud computing is about shared IT infrastructure or the outsourcing of a company's technology. It is essential to examine your current IT infrastructure, usage and needs to determine which type of cloud computing can help you best achieve your goals. Simply, the cloud is not one concrete term, but rather a metaphor for a global network and how to best utilize its advantages depends on your individual cloud focus.

1.16 SERVICE SCALABILITY OVER THE CLOUD

1.16.1 Understanding Performance, Scale and Throughput

Because the terms *performance*, *scale*, and *throughput* are used in a variety of ways when discussing computing, it is useful to examine their typical meanings in the context of cloud computing infrastructures.

- **Performance :** Performance is generally tied to an application's capabilities within the cloud infrastructure itself. Limited bandwidth, disk space, memory, CPU cycles, and network connections can all cause poor performance. Often, a combination of lack of resources causes poor application performance. Sometimes poor performance is the result of an application architecture that does not properly distribute its processes across available cloud resources.

- **Throughput :** The effective rate at which data is transferred from point A to point B on the cloud is throughput. In other words, throughput is a measurement of raw speed. While speed of moving or processing data can certainly improve system performance, the system is only as fast as its slowest element. A system that deploys ten gigabit Ethernet yet its server storage can access data at only one gigabit effectively has a one gigabit system.

- **Scalability :** The search for continually improving system performance through hardware and software throughput gains is defeated when a system is swamped by multiple, simultaneous demands. That 10 gigabit pipe slows considerably when it serves hundreds of requests rather than a dozen. The only way to restore higher effective throughput (and performance) in such a "swamped resources" scenario is to scale, add more of the resource that is over loaded.

For this reason, the ability of a system to easily scale when under stress in a cloud environment is vastly more useful than the overall throughput or aggregate performance of individual components. In cloud environments, this scalability is usually handled through either horizontal or vertical scaling.

1.16.2 Horizontal and Vertical Scalability

- When increasing resources on the cloud to restore or improve application performance, administrators can scale either horizontally (out) or vertically (up), depending on the nature of the resource constraint.
- Vertical scaling (up) entails adding more resources to the same computing pool, for example, adding more RAM, disk, or virtual CPU to handle an increased application load.
- Horizontal scaling (out) requires the addition of more machines or devices to the computing platform to handle the increased demand. This is represented in the transition from Fig. 1.15 to Fig. 1.16 below.

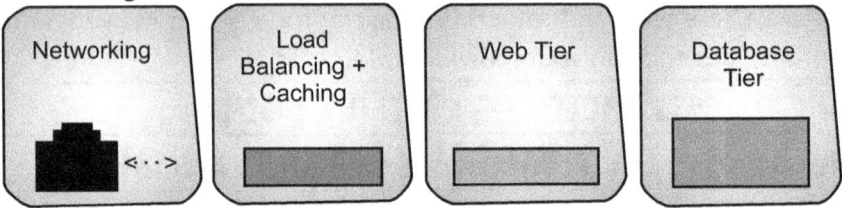

Fig. 1.15 : Basic, Single Silo, n-tier architecture

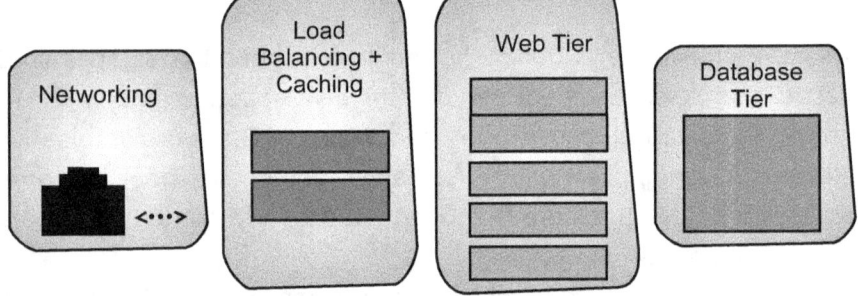

Fig. 1.16 : Horizontally scaled load balancing and web-tier. Vertically scaled database tier

- Vertical scaling can handle most sudden, temporary peaks in application demand on cloud infrastructures since they are not typically CPU-intensive tasks.

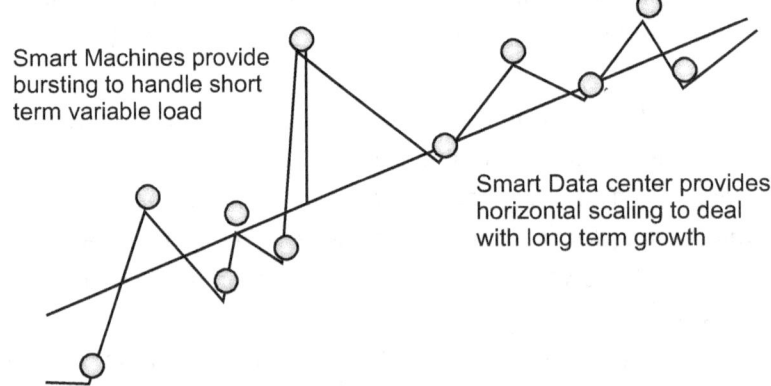

Fig. 1.17 : Horizontal Scaling

- Sustained increases in demand, however, require horizontal scaling and load balancing to restore and maintain peak performance. Horizontal scaling is also manually intensive and time consuming, requiring a technician to add machinery to the customer's cloud configuration.

- Manually scaling to meet a sudden peak in traffic may not be productive, traffic may settle to its pre-peak levels before new provisioning can come on line.
- Businesses may also find themselves experiencing more gradual increases in traffic. Here, provisioning extra resources provides only temporary relief as resource demands continue to rise and exceed the newly provisioned resources.

1.16.3 Administrative and Geographical Scalability

- While adding computing components or virtual resources is a logical means to scale and improve performance, few companies realize that the increase in resources may also necessitate an increase in administration, particularly when deploying horizontal scaling.
- In essence, a scaled increase in hard or virtual resources often requires a corresponding increase in administrative time and expenses.
- This administrative increase may not be a one-time configuration demand as more resources require continual monitoring, backup, and maintenance.
- Companies with critical cloud applications may also consider geographical scaling as a means to more widely distribute application load demands or as a way to move application access closer to dispersed communities of users or customers.
- Geographical scaling of resources in conjunction with synchronous replication of data pools is another means of adding fault tolerance and disaster recovery to cloud-based data and applications.
- Geographical scaling may also be necessary in environments where it is impractical to host all data or applications in one central location.

1.16.4 Practical and Theoretical Limits of Scale

While scalability is the most effective strategy for solving performance issues in cloud infrastructures, practical and theoretical limits prevent it from ever becoming an exponential, infinite solution.

- Practically speaking, most companies cannot commit an infinite amount of money, people, or time to improving performance.
- Cloud vendors also may have a limited amount of experience, personnel, or bandwidth to address customer application performance.
- Every computing infrastructure is bound by a certain level of complexity and scale, not the least of which is power, administration, and bandwidth, necessitating geographical dispersal.

1.16.5 Addressing Application Scalability

- For a cloud computing platform to effectively host business data and applications, however, it must accommodate a wide range of performance characteristics and network demands. Storage, CPU, memory, and network bandwidth all come into play at various times during typical application use.

- Application switching, for example, places demands on the CPU as one application is closed, flushed from the registers, and another application is loaded. If these applications are large and complex, they put a greater demand on the CPU.

- Serving files from the cloud to connected users stresses a number of resources, including disk drives, drive controllers, and network connections when transferring the data from the cloud to the user.

- File storage itself consumes resources not only in the form of physical disk space, but also disk directories and metafile systems that consume RAM and CPU cycles when users either access or upload files into the storage system.

- As these examples illustrate, applications can benefit from both horizontal and vertical scaling of resources on demand, yet truly dynamic scaling is not possible on most cloud computing infrastructures. Therefore, one of the most common and costly responses to scaling issues by vendors is to over-provision customer installations to accommodate a wide range of performance issues.

1.16.6 Application Development to Improve Scalability

- One practical means for addressing application scalability and to reduce performance bottlenecks is to segment applications into separate silos. Web-based applications are theoretically stateless, and therefore theoretically easy to scale, all that is needed is more memory, CPU, storage, and bandwidth to accommodate them, as was depicted in Fig. 1.18. However, in practice Web-based applications are not stateless.

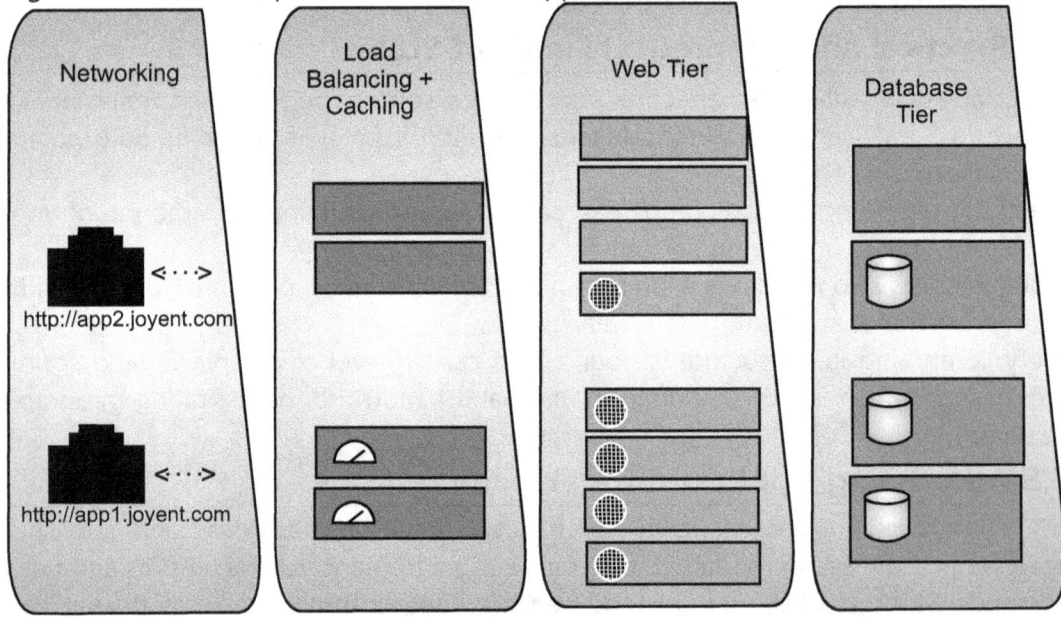

Fig. 1.18 : Scalability Improvement

- They are accessed through a network connection(s) that requires an IP address (es) that is fixed and therefore stateful, and they connect to data storage (either disk or database) which maintains logical state as well as requiring hardware resources to execute.
- Balancing the interaction between stateless and stateful elements of a Web application requires careful architectural consideration and the use of tiers and silos to allow some form of horizontal resource scaling.
- To leverage the most from resources, application developers can break applications into discrete tiers, state or stateless processes, that are executed in various resource silos. Fig. 1.18 depicts breaking an application into two silos identified by their DNS name.
- By segregating state and stateless operations and provisioning accordingly, applications and systems can run more efficiently and with higher resource utilization than under a more common scenario.

1.17 THE GREENFIELD AND BROWNFIELD DEPLOYMENT OPTIONS

In networking, a Greenfield deployment is the installation and configuration of a network where none existed before, for example in a new office. A brownfield deployment, in contrast, is an upgrade or addition to an existing network and uses some legacy components. The terms come from the building industry, where undeveloped land (and especially unpolluted land) is described as *Greenfield* and previously developed (often polluted and abandoned) land is described as *brownfield*.

In software development, Greenfield is a project which doesn't have to obey constraints imposed by prior work. In a Greenfield environment there is no need to remodel or demolish an existing structure. Brownfield describes the deployment of existing physical and virtual servers workloads into new cloud environments.

Greenfield

20% of applications are delivered on Greenfield sites, while the rest of 80% are Brownfield. There are many challenges when performing Greenfield migrations and any Greenfield development is to become a Brownfield one in couple of months. Greenfield development don't need to go through a lengthy IT process to locate available enterprise resources and lay claim to them, or for that matter endure a corporate procurement process. Greenfield is a popular way to describe all-new infrastructure built with no regard for legacy compatibility. In networking, a Greenfield deployment is the installation and configuration of a network where one did not exist before. Greenfield developments happen when you start a brand new project; no legacy code to maintain and you are able to start fresh, with no restrictions. Although it may seem easier to rip out and replace existing systems, companies would see the benefit in continuity with existing infrastructure, which means redeveloping applications.

Brownfield

Most businesses already have a significant and complex IT environment. Many already have some type of server or cloud infrastructure in place, meaning they fall into the Brownfield category. A Brownfield deployment is an upgrade or an addition to an existing structure. Brownfield development refers to the deployment of systems, servers and applications in the presence of other existing software applications / systems. This implies that any new architecture must take into account and coexist with already existent software. This requires a detailed knowledge of the systems, services and data in the immediate vicinity of the application under construction.

1.18 CHALLENGES IN CLOUD NIST GUIDELINES

- The terms of traditional information technology outsourcing contracts, particularly those involving sensitive data, can serve as guidelines for cloud computing initiatives.
- Three main security and privacy issues in service contracts have been identified previously and are relevant to outsourcing public cloud computing services :

Inadequate Policies and Practices : The security policies and practices of the cloud provider might not be adequate or compatible with those of the organization. The same issue applies to privacy as well. This can result in complications such as the following :

- Undetected intrusions or violations due to insufficient auditing and monitoring policies by the cloud provider.
- Lack of sufficient data and configuration integrity due to a mismatch between the organization's and the cloud provider's policies for separation of duty (i.e., clear assignment of roles and responsibilities) or redundancy (i.e., having sufficient checks and balances to ensure an operation is done consistently and correctly).
- Loss of privacy due to the cloud provider handling sensitive information less rigorously than the organization's policy dictates.

Weak Confidentiality and Integrity Sureties

- Insufficient security controls in the cloud provider's platform could affect negatively the confidentiality and privacy, or integrity of the system.
- For example, use of an insecure method of remote access could allow intruders to gain unauthorized access, modify, or destroy the organization's information systems and resources; to deliberately introduce security vulnerabilities or malware into the system; or to launch attacks on other systems from the organization's network, perhaps making the organization liable for the damages incurred.

Weak Availability Sureties

- Insufficient safeguards in the cloud provider's platform could negatively affect the availability of the system. Besides the applications directly affected, a loss of system availability may cause a conflict for key resources that are required for critical organizational operations.

- For example, if disruptive processing operations (e.g., load rebalancing due to site failure or emergency maintenance) are performed by the cloud provider at the same time as peak organizational processing occurs, a denial of service condition could arise.
- A denial of service attack targeted at the cloud provider could also affect the organization's applications and systems operating in the cloud or at the organization's data center.
- Assurances furnished to the organization by the cloud provider to support security claims, or by a certification and compliance review entity paid by the cloud provider, should be verified whenever possible through independent assessment by the organization.
- Moreover, a third-party certification or other assurances from the cloud provider do not necessarily grant a tenant application or system that same level of certification or compliance; those elements would likely require a separate certification assessment for that specific cloud environment. Other noteworthy concerns, which are indirectly related to security and privacy, also exist with outsourcing to public clouds.
- One of the most prevalent and challenging concerns is called the principal-agent problem. Another is the attenuation of an organization's technical expertise.

Principal-Agent Problem

- The principal-agent problem occurs when the incentives of the agent (i.e., the cloud provider) are not aligned with the interests of the principal (i.e., the organization). Because it can be difficult to determine the level of effort a cloud provider is exerting towards security and privacy administration and remediation, the concern is that the organization might not recognize if the service level is dropping or has dropped below the extent required.
- One confounding issue is that increased security efforts are not guaranteed to result in noticeable improvements (e.g., fewer incidents), in part because of the growing amounts of malware and new types of attacks.

Attenuation of Expertise

- Outsourced computing services can, over time, diminish the level of technical knowledge and expertise of the organization, since management and staff no longer need to deal regularly with technical issues at a detailed level.
- As new advancements and improvements are made to the cloud computing environment, the knowledge and expertise gained directly benefit the cloud provider, not the organization.
- Unless precautions are taken, an organization can lose its ability to keep up to date with technology advances and related security and privacy considerations, which in turn can affect its ability to plan and oversee new information technology projects effectively and to maintain accountability over existing cloud-based systems.

QUESTIONS

1. Define cloud computing and explain the characteristics of cloud computing.
2. Explain cloud service models in short.
3. How applications are deployed over cloud?
4. Explain the following
   (a) Public cloud
   (b) Private cloud
   (c) Hybrid cloud
5. Explain the term cloud multi-tenancy in detail.
6. Write short note on multi-tenancy implementation based on service models.
7. Explain the benefits of cloud computing.
8. Write short note on service scalability over the cloud.
9. Write short note on Greenfield and Brownfield deployment options in cloud computing
10. Explain following cloud computing platforms
    (a) Openstack
    (b) Opennimbus
    (c) Eucalyptus
11. Differentiate between Grid computing and Utility computing

VIRTUALIZATION

2.1 INTRODUCTION

- The IT industries focus on virtualization technology has increased considerably in the past few years.
- The concept of virtualization has its origins in the mainframe days in the late 1960s and early 1970s, when IBM invested a lot of time and effort in developing robust time-sharing solutions.
- At that time main intention behind virtualization was to allow large expensive mainframes to be easily shared among different application environments.
- Time-sharing refers to the shared usage of computer resources among a large group of users, aiming to increase the efficiency of both the users and the expensive computer resources they share.
- This model represented a major breakthrough in computer technology : The cost of providing computing capability dropped considerably and it became possible for organizations, and even individuals, to use a computer without actually owning one.
- IT industry is constantly searching for a way to utilize the resources in most efficient way.
- The best way to improve resource utilization, and at the same time simplify data center management, is through virtualization.
- Data centers today use virtualization techniques to make abstraction of the physical hardware, create large pools of logical resources consisting of CPUs, memory, disks, file storage, applications, networking, and offer those resources to users or customers in the form of agile, scalable, consolidated virtual machines.
- The core meaning of virtualization is to enable a computing environment to run multiple independent systems at the same time.
- Virtualization is an industry-changing movement that will touch all aspects of IT infrastructure and drive new levels of flexibility and dynamism in IT.

2.2 OVERVIEW OF VIRTUALIZATION

- Virtualization is a technique for hiding the physical characteristics of computing resources from the way other systems, applications or end users interact with them.
- Virtualization is a framework or methodology of dividing the resources of a computer into multiple execution environments, by applying one or more concepts or technologies such as hardware and software partitioning, time-sharing, partial or complete machine simulation, emulation, quality of service, and many others.

- We all are aware of the simple mechanism that one physical machine runs one operating system at any given time.
- By virtualizing the machine, we are able to run several operating systems (and all of their applications) at the same time.
- Virtualization provides the following two functionalities :
  1. Making multiple physical resources appear to function as a single logical resource. Refer Fig. 2.1.

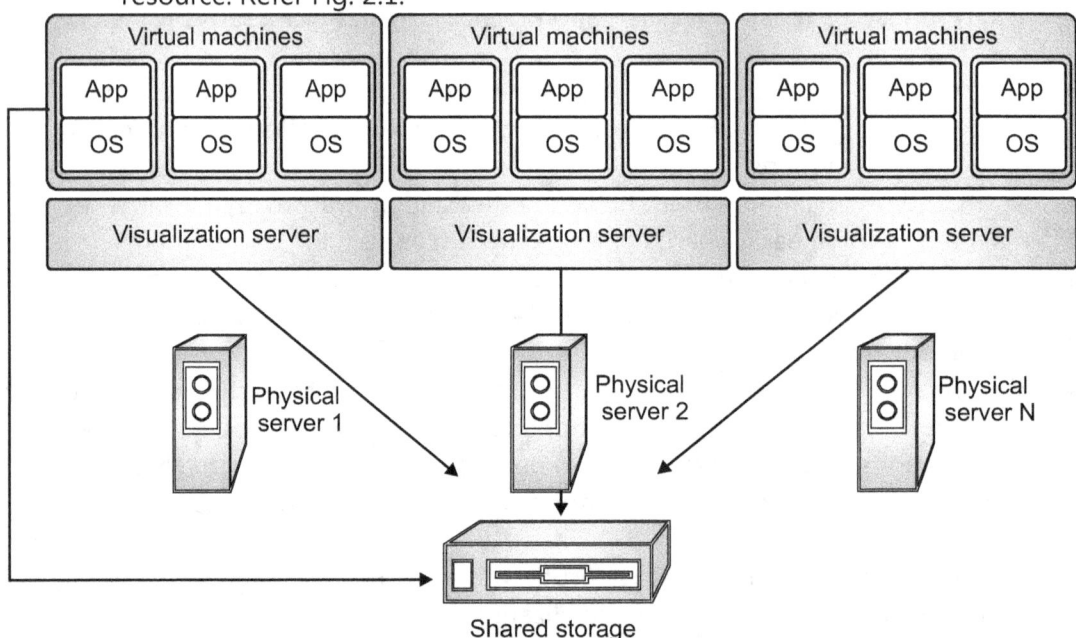

Fig. 2.1 : Multiple Physical Resources as a Single Logical Resource

  1. Making a single physical resource appear to function as multiple logical resources. Refer Fig. 2.2.

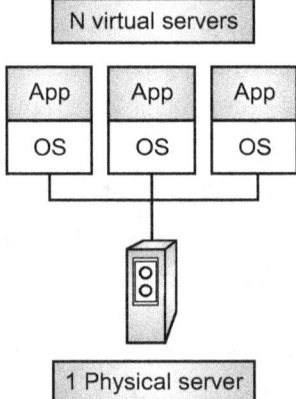

Fig. 2.2 : Single Physical Resource as a Multiple Logical Resources

- Now let's understand the difference between multitasking, multithreading and virtualization.

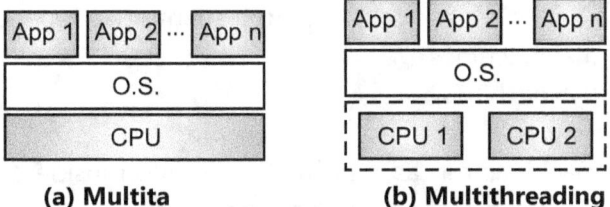

(a) Multita   **(b) Multithreading**

Fig. 2.3

- In case of multitasking, there is only one Central Processing Unit (CPU) and one operating system which can be used for running several applications. Refer Fig. 2.3 (a)
- Whereas in case of multithreading there can be two or more physical as well as logical instances of CPU, called as threads which can be used for running several applications. Refer Fig. 2.3 (b).
- Parallel processing is made possible by letting the number of applications to run on multiple cores.
- Virtualization describes a process which enables the sharing of resources of one or more computers, namely its CPU, memory or hard disk, through the creation of virtual hardware platforms, operating systems, storage devices or network resources.
- This improves the performance existing system, allowing users to run more software and applications without the need to install new hardware or appliances. Refer Fig. 2.4.
- With the virtualization it is possible to create several instances of CPUs, called as virtual CPU and operating systems.
- Each instance (CPU + Operating System) is treated as separate entity and it is responsible for running number of applications.

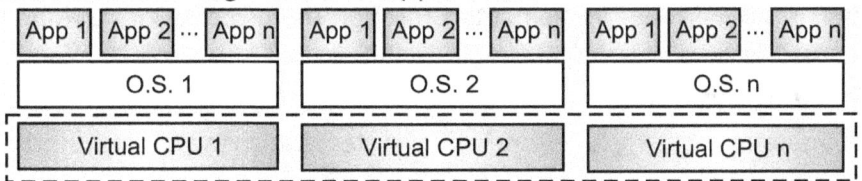

Fig. 2.4 : Virtualization

- Till now we have seen the virtualization and what can be done using virtualization. Now let's turn towards the basic entities which are used for creating virtual environment.

1. Virtual Machines

- Virtual machines are presentation of a real machine using software that provides an operating environment which can run or host a guest operating system. Virtual machines are created and managed by virtual machine monitors.

- Virtual machines are simply implementation of a machine that executes programs as if it is a real machine.
- These virtual machines are basically categorized into two types :
  (a) Process virtual machines.
  (b) System virtual machines.

(a) Process Virtual Machines

- Process virtual machines run as a normal application inside an operating system to abstract away the details of the underlying hardware.
- These are designed to provide a platform-independent environment to a single process (i.e., program).
- The environment is created when its associated process is started and destroyed when that process exits.
- Process virtual machines allow program to execute in the same way regardless of the physical platform it is running on.
- They are implemented using an interpreter.
- The programmer's code is not compiled, but the interpreter requires compilation before providing the processing environment.

(b) System Virtual Machine

- System virtual machines allow multiplexing (time sharing) of the underlying hardware between different operating systems.
- These are designed to provide a complete platform which can support the execution on multiple, and different, operating systems.
- They allow time-sharing of underlying hardware between virtual machines.
- In system virtual operating systems remain isolated from one another.
- The Instruction Set Architecture (ISA) provided by the virtual machine can be different from that of the real machine.
- System virtual machines implemented through the use of a Virtual Machine Monitor (VMM) also-known-as a Hypervisor.

2. Guest Operating System

- Guest operating system is an operating system which is running inside the created virtual machine.

3. Hypervisor

- Hypervisor is a thin layer of software that generally provides virtual partitioning capabilities, which runs directly on hardware, but below the higher-level virtualization services.
- Hypervisors are classified into two categories.

(a) Native Hypervisor (Hardware-Level)

- Native hypervisor is a software which runs directly on top of a given hardware platform as a control program for operating systems. Refer Fig. 2.5.

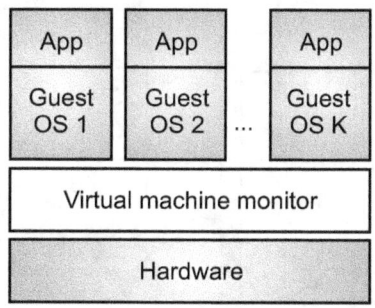

Fig. 2.5 : Native Hypervisor

- It is where actual virtualization begins.

(b) Hosted Hypervisor (OS-Level)

- Hosted hypervisor is software which runs within an operating system environment as a control program for other operating systems.
- Virtual Machine Monitor layer is moved one level higher as compared to Native VMs.
- Hosted hypervisor runs within a Host operating system environment.
- An operating system is installed first; as usual, on top of Hardware.
- A Virtual Machine Monitor is then installed within the Host OS.
- Guest operating systems can be installed on top of the VMM layer.
- Host OS sees the VMM as a process.
- VMM controls the allocation of time between Guest operating systems.
- Guest operating system is segregated from the rest of the environment. Refer Fig. 2.6.

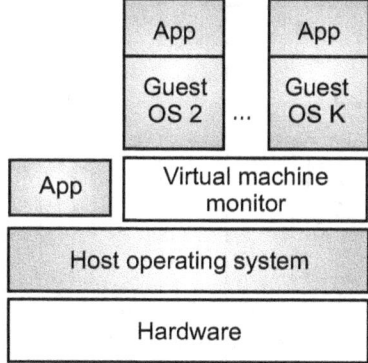

Fig. 2.6 : Hosted Hypervisor

4. Virtual Machine Monitor

- Above entities use the terms like hypervisor and virtual machine monitor, but they are conceptually different.
- Virtual Machine Monitor (VMM) is a software that runs in a layer between host operating system and one or more virtual machines that provides the virtual machine abstraction to the guest operating systems. Refer Fig. 2.7.

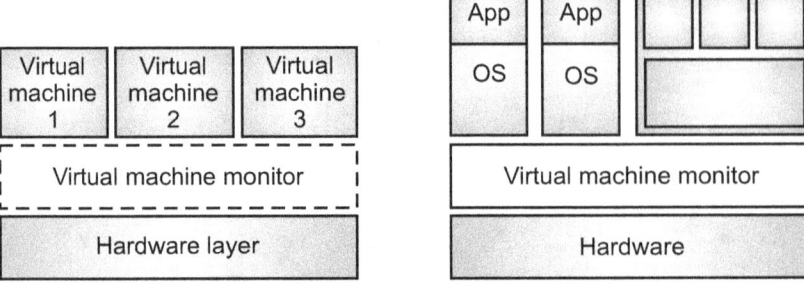

Fig. 2.7 : Role of Virtual Machine Monitor in Virtualization

- With full virtualization, the virtual machine monitor exports a virtual machine abstraction identical to a physical machine, so that standard operating systems can run just as they would on physical hardware.

2.3 THE VIRTUAL SERVER

- Before directly moving to the virtual server concept, first we must understand the traditional server concept.

- Servers can be considered as a whole unit that includes the hardware, the OS, the storage, and the applications.

- Servers are often referred to by their function i.e. the Web server, the SQL server, the file server, etc. Refer Fig. 2.8.

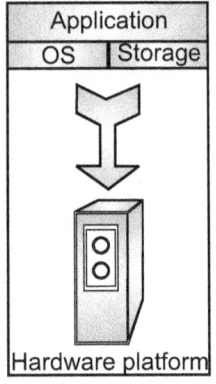 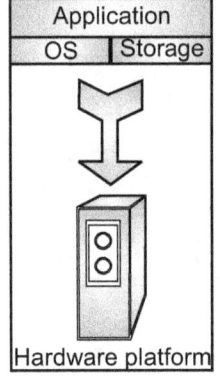 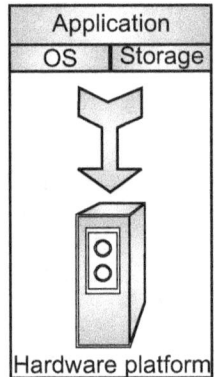 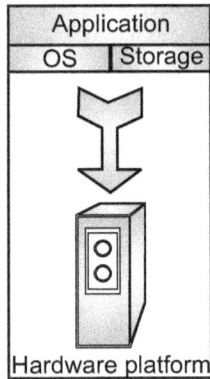

Fig. 2.8 : Traditional Servers

- If the any of the server is overloaded or that server fills up then the system administrators must add in a new server.

- If there are no multiple servers and if a service experiences a hardware failure, then the service is down completely. Refer Fig. 2.9.

- It is also possible to implement clusters of servers to make them more fault tolerant. However, even clusters have limits on their scalability, and not all applications work in a clustered environment.

- Although traditional servers mentioned above provide many advantages such as easy deployment, easy to backup, less complexity we must not ignore disadvantages such as expenses to maintain hardware, limited scaling, difficulty in replication, difficulty in maintaining redundancy, under utilization of processor etc.

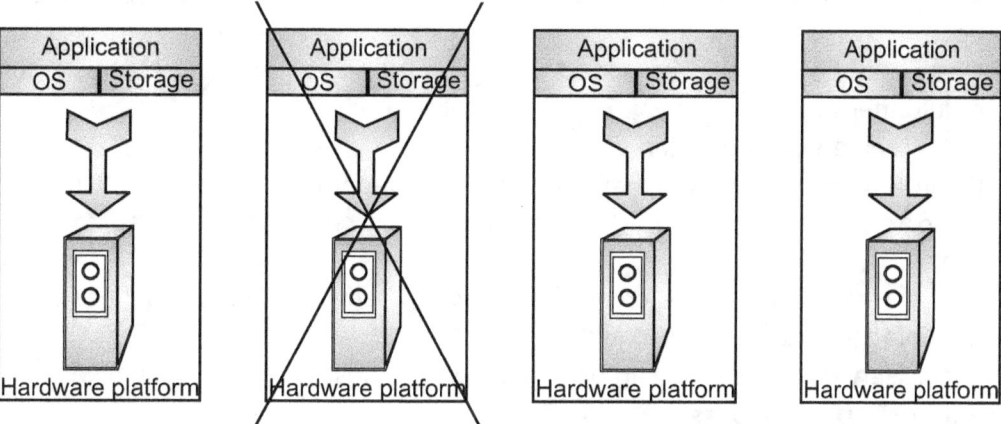

Fig. 2.9 : Service is Completely Down if Server Fails

- Virtual servers are implemented using virtualization to overcome the disadvantages of traditional servers mentioned above.

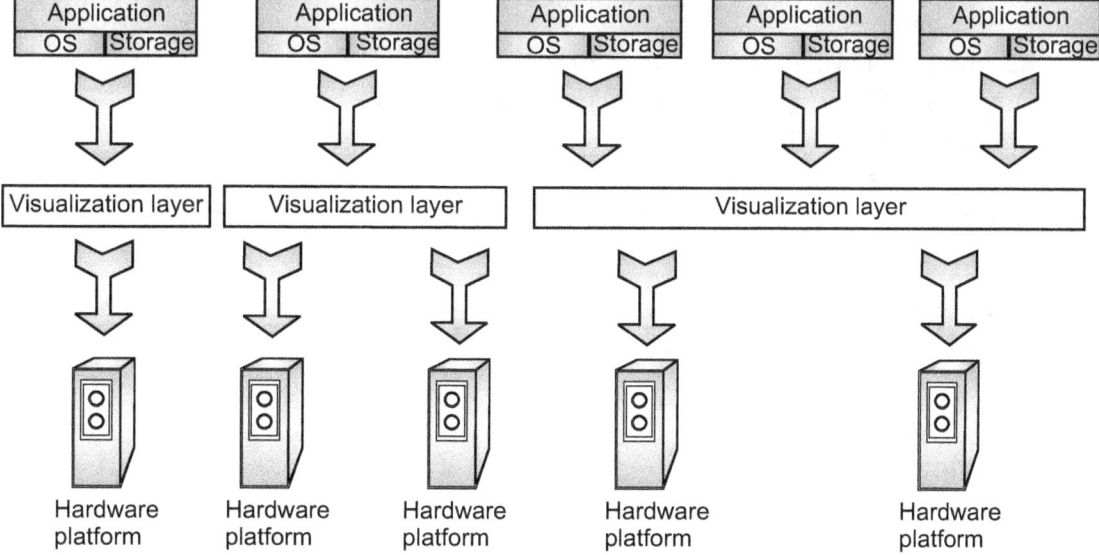

Fig. 2.10 : Virtual Server

- Virtual servers seek to encapsulate the server software away from the hardware.
- This includes the OS, the applications, and the storage for that server.
- Servers end up as mere files stored on a physical box, or in enterprise storage.

- A virtual server can be serviced by one or more hosts, and one host may contain more than one virtual server. Refer Fig. 2.10.
- Virtual servers can still be referred to by their function i.e. email server, database server, etc.
- If the environment is built correctly, virtual servers will not be affected by the loss of a host.
- Hosts may be removed or added at any time and as per requirement to fulfill the requirements.
- Virtual servers can be scaled out easily.
- If the administrators find that the resources supporting a virtual server are being taxed too much, they can adjust the amount of resources allocated to that virtual server.
- Server templates can be created in a virtual environment to be used to create multiple, identical virtual servers.
- Virtual servers themselves can be migrated from host to host almost at will.

Advantages of Virtual Servers
- Resource pooling.
- Highly redundant.
- Highly available.
- Rapidly deploy new servers.
- Easy to deploy.
- Reconfigurable while services are running.
- Optimizes physical resources by doing more with less.

Disadvantages of Virtual Servers
- Slightly harder to conceptualize.
- Slightly more costly (must buy hardware, OS, Apps and now the abstraction layer).

2.4 TYPES OF VIRTUALIZATION

- Virtualization approaches are classified into the following five types :
1. Emulation
2. Full Virtualization
3. Para Virtualization
4. Operating System Level Virtualization
5. Application Level Virtualization

2.4.1 Emulation

- In this approach, virtual machine simulates the entire hardware set needed to run unmodified guests for completely different hardware architectures.
- It is used to create new operating systems for the hardware which is in design phase and not in physical form.

- Virtual Machine provides a "guest" operating system the (simulated) hardware environment it expects.
- Software is unaware that it is really talking to a virtualized device. Refer Fig. 2.11.

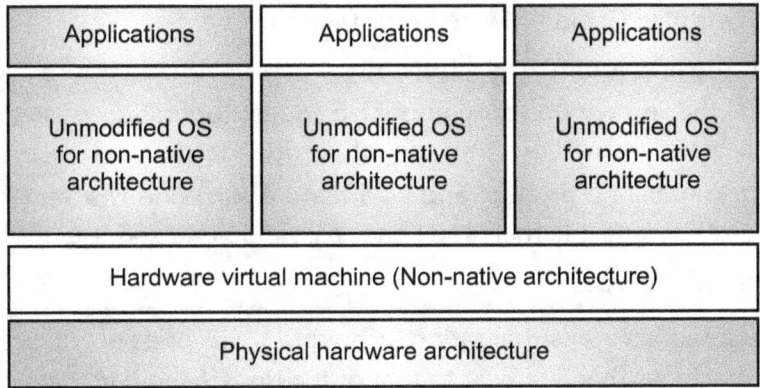

Fig. 2.11 : Emulation

- Each interaction between Guest device driver with the emulated device hardware requires transaction with VMM.
- The real hardware does its job as usual, but the VMM must now translate the result for the guest.
- **Advantage :** Guest Software need not be modified
- **Disadvantage :** Must pay Performance Penalty.

2.4.2 Full Virtualization

- Full virtualization is a native kind of virtualization in which hypervisor runs directly on top of a given hardware platform as a control program for operating systems.
- It is similar to emulation except it is designed to simulate the underlying hardware which is physically available.

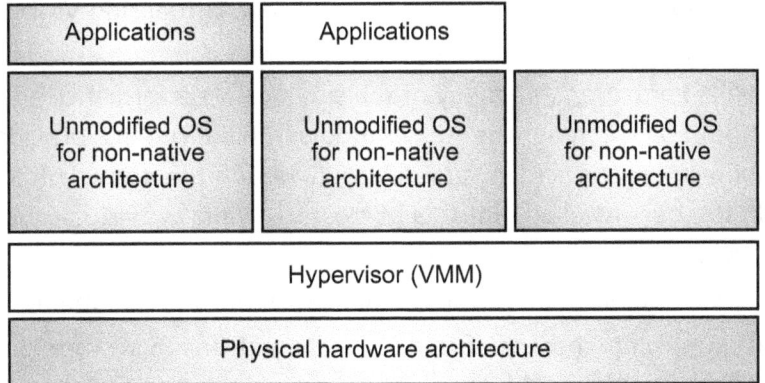

Fig. 2.12 : Full Virtualization

- It runs unmodified guests on a physical machine.

- It gives the flexibility to move entire virtual machines from one host to another host very easily, but for the cost of performance due to the overhead added by the emulator Layer. Refer Fig. 2.12.

- Examples : Virtual PC and VMware Workstation.

- VMware is the first commercial virtualization product provider for x86 architecture.

- It enables the execution of unmodified guest operating systems through the translation of x86 instructions that cannot be virtualized.

- Hyper-V, a standalone product and as a feature for Windows Server 2008, windows edition translates guest kernel mode and real mode into x86 user mode.

2.4.3 Para Virtualization

- Para virtualization is a virtualization technique that presents a software interface to virtual machines that is similar to that of the underlying hardware.

- Application Programming Interface (API) is provided to the Guest OS by the VMM so the guest may utilize the hardware.

- The hypervisor exports a modified version of the underlying physical hardware.

- The intent of the modified interface is to reduce the portion of the guest's execution time spent performing operations which are substantially more difficult to run in a virtual environment compared to a non-virtualized environment.

- A successful para virtualized platform may allow the Virtual Machine Monitor (VMM) to be simpler (by relocating execution of critical tasks from the virtual domain to the host domain), and/or reduce the overall performance degradation of machine-execution inside the virtual-guest.

- Para virtualization requires the guest operating system to be explicitly ported for the para-API. This is because a conventional OS distribution that is not para virtualization-aware cannot be run on top of a para virtualizing VMM.

- However, even in cases where the operating system cannot be modified, components may be available that enable many of the significant performance advantages of para virtualization. For example, the Xen Windows GPLPV project provides a kit of para virtualization-aware device drivers, licensed under the terms of the GPL, that are intended to be installed into a Microsoft Windows virtual-guest running on the Xen hypervisor.

- Thus with para virtualization guest interacts with VMM at a higher level of abstraction

- Instead of supplying the specifics of how to use the hardware, software provides general requests to the VMM.

- Para virtualization decreases the number of interactions between Guest and VMM for a specific operation. Refer Fig. 2.13.

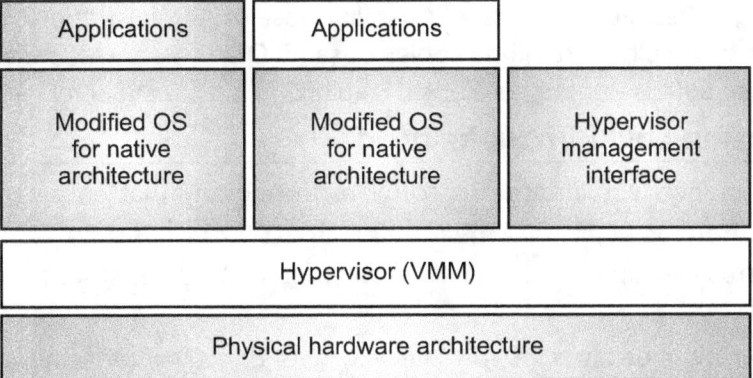

Fig. 2.13 : Para Virtualization

- **Advantage :** Better Performance.
- **Disadvantage :** Guest OS must be modified to use API.

2.4.4 Operating System Level Virtualization

- With operating system level virtualization virtual machine monitor software is not required.
- With this technique of virtualization single OS image handles all the guest images in different isolated containers.
- There is host OS that handles all other guest OS images present in respective containers.
- OS level virtualization does not support running different operating systems (Specifically, different kernel) at a time.
- With OS level virtualization instead of virtualizing the hardware, it is possible to run multiple virtual instances of same OS on single hardware.
- Thus with OS level virtualization only single kernel runs at a time.
- Single kernel means very low overhead (1 to 3%) compared to standalone server.
- Containers are the entities which provide isolation between processes.
- Each process appears as separate OS. Refer Fig. 2.14.

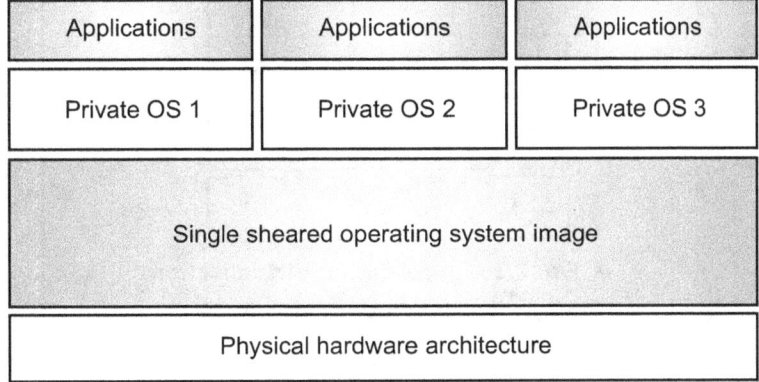

Fig. 2.14 : OS Level Virtualization

- **Advantage :** Best Performance / Scalability, Ease of Administration.
- **Disadvantage :** Only virtualizes copies of same OS.
- **Examples :** Solaris Containers/Zones, FreeBSD Jails, Linux VServers and OpenVZ.

2.4.5 Application Level Virtualization

- Application level virtualization is software technology that encapsulates application software from the underlying operating system on which it is executed.
- A fully virtualized application is not installed in the traditional sense, although it is still executed.
- The application behaves at runtime like it is directly interfacing with the original operating system and all the resources managed by it, but can be isolated or sandboxed to varying degrees.
- In this context, the term "virtualization" refers to the object being encapsulated (application), which is quite different from its meaning in hardware virtualization, where it refers to the object being abstracted (physical hardware).
- Application level virtualization is also known as process virtualization.
- Application virtualization is the approach of running applications inside a virtual execution environment.
- The virtual execution environment provides a standard API for cross platform execution and manages the consumption of application's local resources such as threading model, environment variables, user interface libraries and objects.
- Modern operating systems such as Windows and Linux can include limited application virtualization.
- For example, Windows 7 provides Windows XP Mode that enables older Windows XP application to run unmodified on Windows 7.

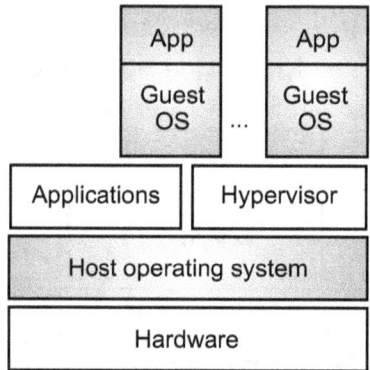

Fig. 2.15 : Application Virtualization

- Full application virtualization requires a virtualization layer.
- Application virtualization layers replace part of the runtime environment normally provided by the operating system.

- The layer intercepts all disk operations of virtualized applications and transparently redirects them to a virtualized location, often a single file.
- The application remains unaware that it accesses a virtual resource instead of a physical one.
- Since the application is now working with one file instead of many files spread throughout the system, it becomes easy to run the application on a different computer and previously incompatible applications can be run side-by-side.

2.5 NEED AND ADVANTAGES OF VIRTUALIZATION

2.5.1 Need of Virtualization

- We have already learnt about virtualization concepts, virtual machine and types of virtualization.
- Still we are not really sure of why there is need of virtualization.
- Most of the businesses often use a combination of a number of application servers, web servers, image servers, audio-video servers, document servers and database servers.
- Above mentioned hardware infrastructure is not being used well almost all the time.
- If the 75% of the hardware appears as being used at any point of time on the basis of average number of server requests recorded, the servers are still largely under-utilized.
- The servers typically take only about 1-10 ms to service each request. However it should be much faster.
- Given this extremely short amount of time taken to service the request, the amount of time the server machine is kept up and running relative to the actual time spent by it servicing the requests, is much higher.
- This clearly indicates that a significant amount of energy is wasted per server in the process of keeping the servers up and ever-ready to service requests upon their arrival.
- Cumulative energy wasted is actually high considering the fact that we use not one server for each purpose, but a number of them for different purposes.
- Maximizing the server utilization is limited by the number of incoming server requests.
- Even if we have done our best to ensure that server spends a good fraction of time servicing requests, this equivalent to the number of requests the server receives at any point of time.
- Virtualization is the technique for eliminating this wastage and maximizing the profit.
- We already know that virtualization essentially means to create multiple, logical instances of software or hardware on a single physical hardware resource.

- This technique simulates the available hardware and gives every application running top of it, the feeling that it is the unique holder of the resource.
- The details of the virtual, simulated environment are kept transparent from the application.
- Organizations use this technique to perform the tasks away from many of their physical servers and map these functions onto one robust, evergreen physical server.
- This is beneficial in terms of cost of maintenance and reduced energy wastage.
- Since we have fewer physical servers, we need only their maintenance and therefore maintenance becomes much easier and cheaper.
- Also the amount of energy wasted is a function of the number of physical servers which is clearly much lower in virtualized environment.

2.5.2 Advantages of Virtualization

- Allows applications to run in environments that do not suit the native application :
    1. Wine allows some Microsoft_Windows applications to run on Linux.
    2. CDE, a lightweight application virtualization, allows Linux applications to run on another platform.
- May protect the operating system and other applications from poorly written or buggy code and in some cases provide memory protection and IDE style debugging features.
- Uses fewer resources than a separate virtual_machine.
- Run applications that are not written correctly, for example applications that try to store user data in a read-only system-owned location.
- Run incompatible applications side-by-side, at the same time and with minimal regression testing against one another.
- Reduce system integration and administration costs by maintaining a common software baseline across multiple diverse computers in an organization.
- Implement the security principle of least privilege by removing the requirement for end-users to have Administrator privileges in order to run poorly written applications.
- Simplified operating system migrations.
- Improved security, by isolating applications from the operating system.
- Allows applications to be copied to portable media and then imported to client computers without need of installing them, so called Portable software.

2.5.3 Limitations of Virtualization

- Not all software can be virtualized. Some examples include applications that require a device driver and 16 bit applications that need to run in shared memory space.
- Some types of software such as anti-virus packages and applications that require heavy OS integration are difficult to virtualize.
- Only file and registry-level compatibility issues between legacy applications and newer operating systems can be addressed by application virtualization.

- For example, applications that don't manage the heap correctly will not execute on Windows Vista as they still allocate memory in the same way, regardless of whether they are virtualized or not.
- For this reason, specialist application compatibility fixes (shims) may still be needed, even if the application is virtualized.
- Moreover, in software licensing, application virtualization bears great licensing pitfalls mainly because both the application virtualization software and the virtualized applications must be correctly licensed.

2.6 XEN OVERVIEW

2.6.1 Introduction to XEN

- Virtualization of operating systems is used in many different computing areas. It finds its applications in server consolidation, energy saving efforts, or the ability to run older software on new hardware.
- Number of systems have been designed which use virtualization to subdivide the many resources of a modern computer.
- Some require specialized hardware, or cannot support commodity operating systems.
- Some target 100% binary compatibility at the expense of performance. Others sacrifice security or functionality for speed.
- Few offer resource isolation or performance guarantees; most provide only best effort provisioning, risking denial of service.
- Xen, an x86 virtual machine monitor which allows multiple commodity operating systems to share conventional hardware in a safe and resource managed fashion, but without sacrificing either performance or functionality.
- Xen is a virtualization system supporting both para-virtualization (PV)and hardware assistant full virtualization (HVM).
- The name XEN has evolved from ne**X**t g**EN**eration virtualization.
- This is achieved by providing an idealized virtual machine abstraction to which operating systems such as Linux, BSD and Windows, can be ported with minimal effort.

2.6.2 Basic Components of XEN Environment

- A Xen virtual environment consist of several items that work together to deliver the virtualization environment.
- The basic components of a Xen-based virtualization environment are the Xen hypervisor, the Domain0, any number of other VM Guests, and the tools, commands, and configuration files that let you manage virtualization.
- Collectively, the physical computer running all these components is referred to as a virtual machine host because together these components form a platform for hosting virtual machines.
- Xen virtualization environment consists of following components :

1. Xen Hypervisor.
2. Domain 0 Guest.
3. Domain Management and Control (Xen DM&C).
4. Domain U Guest (Dom U).
5. PV Guest.
6. HVM Guest.

The diagram below shows the basic organization of these components.

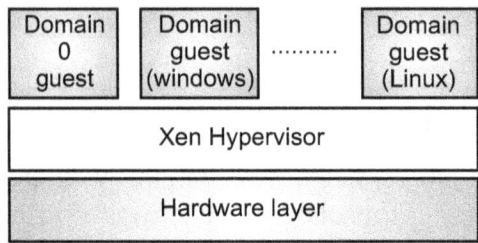

Fig. 2.16 : Block diagram of Xen virtualization Environment

1. The Xen Hypervisor

- The Xen hypervisor sometimes referred to generically as a virtual machine monitor, is an open-source software program that coordinates the low-level interaction between virtual machines and physical hardware.
- The Xen hypervisor is the basic abstraction layer of software that sits directly on the hardware below any operating systems. It is responsible for CPU scheduling and memory partitioning of the various virtual machines running on the hardware device.
- The hypervisor not only abstracts the hardware for the virtual machines but also controls the execution of virtual machines as they share the common processing environment.
- It has no knowledge of networking, external storage devices, video, or any other common I/O functions found on a computing system.

2. The Domain 0

- The virtual machine host environment, also referred to as domain0 or controlling Domain.
- The term "Domain 0" refers to a special domain that provides the management environment. This may be run either in graphical or in command line mode.
- Domain 0, a modified Linux kernel, is a unique virtual machine running on the Xen hypervisor that has special rights to access physical I/O resources as well as interact with the other virtual machines (Domain U : PV and HVM Guests) running on the system.
- All Xen virtualization environments require Domain 0 to be running before any other virtual machines can be started.

- Two drivers are included in Domain 0 to support network and local disk requests from Domain U PV and HVM Guests; the Network Backend Driver and the Block Backend Driver. Refer Fig. 2.17.

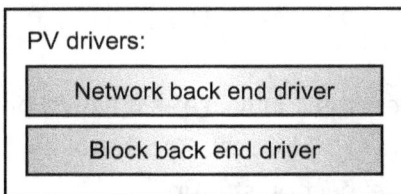

Fig. 2.17 : Drivers of Domain 0

- The Network Backend Driver communicates directly with the local networking hardware to process all virtual machines requests coming from the Domain U guests.
- The Block Backend Driver communicates with the local storage disk to read and write data from the drive based upon Domain U requests.

3. **Domain U**

- Domain U guests have no direct access to physical hardware on the machine as a Domain 0 Guest does and is often referred to as unprivileged.
- All para-virtualized virtual machines running on a Xen hypervisor are referred to as Domain U PV Guests and are modified Linux operating systems, Solaris, FreeBSD, and other UNIX operating systems.
- All fully virtualized machines running on a Xen hypervisor are referred to as Domain U **HVM Guests** and run standard Windows or any other unchanged operating system.

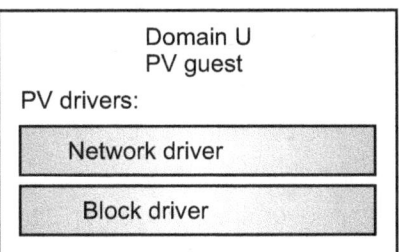

Fig. 2.18 : Divers of Domain U

- The Domain U PV Guest virtual machine is aware that it does not have direct access to the hardware and recognizes that other virtual machines are running on the same machine.
- The Domain U HVM Guest virtual machine is not aware that it is sharing processing time on the hardware and that other virtual machines are present.
- A Domain U PV Guest contains two drivers for network and disk access, PV Network Driver and PV Block Driver. Refer Fig. 2.18.

- A Domain U HVM Guest does not have the PV drivers located within the virtual machine; instead a special daemon is started for each HVM Guest in Domain 0.

4. Qemu-DM

- Qemu-DM supports the Domain U HVM Guest for networking and disk access requests.
- The Domain U HVM Guest must initialize as it would on a typical machine so software is added to the Domain U HVM Guest, Xen virtual firmware, to simulate the BIOS an operating system would expect on startup.
- Every HVM Guest running on a Xen environment requires its own Qemu daemon.
- This tool handles all networking and disk requests from the Domain U HVM Guest to allow for a fully virtualized machine in the Xen environment.
- Qemu-DM must exist outside the Xen hypervisor due to its need for access to networking and I/O and is therefore found in Domain 0. Refer Fig. 2.19.
- A new tool, Stub-dm, is in development for future versions of Xen that will remove the need for a Qemu-DM running for every Domain U HVM Guest and will instead provide a set of services available to every Domain U HVM Guest.

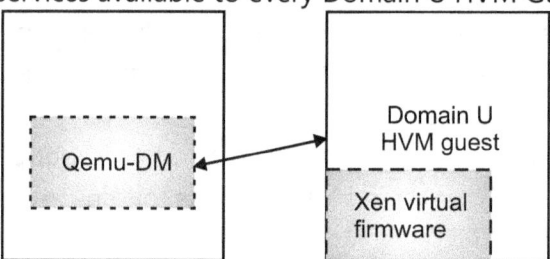

Fig. 2.19 : Qemu-DM

5. Domain Management and Control

- A series of Linux daemons are classified as Domain Management and Control by the open source community.
- These services support the overall management and control of the virtualization environment and exist within the Domain 0 virtual machine.

6. Xend

- The Xend daemon is a python application that is considered the system manager for the Xen environment.
- It leverages the libXenctrl library to make requests of the Xen hypervisor.
- All requests processed by the Xend are delivered to it via an XML RPC interface by the Xm tool. Refer Fig. 2.20.
- The Xend daemon (Xend) stores configuration information about each virtual machine and controls how virtual machines are created and managed.

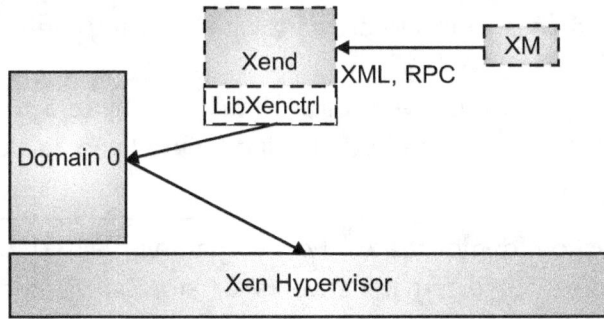

Fig. 2.20 : Xend Daemon

7. Xm

- Xm is the command line tool that takes user input and passes to Xend via XML RPC.

8. Xenstored

- The Xenstored daemon maintains a registry of information including memory and event channel links between Domain 0 and all other Domain U Guests.

- The Domain 0 virtual machine leverages this registry to setup device channels with other virtual machines on the system.

9. LibXenctrl

- LibXenctrl is a C library that provides Xend the ability to talk with the Xen hypervisor via Domain 0.

- A special driver within Domain 0, privcmd delivers the request to the hypervisor. Refer Fig. 2.21.

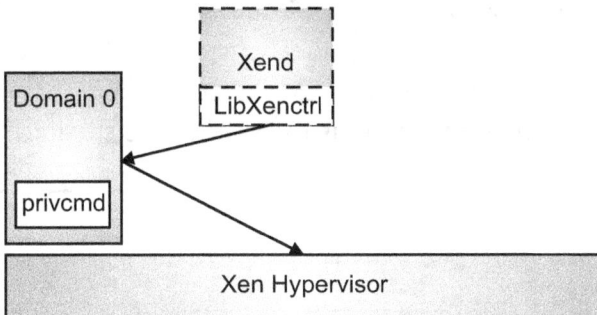

Fig. 2.21 : LibXenctrl

10. Xen Virtual Firmware

- The Xen Virtual Firmware is a virtual BIOS that is inserted into every Domain U HVM Guest to ensure that the operating system receives all the standard start-up instructions it expects during normal boot-up providing a standard PC-compatible software environment.

11. Xen PCI Passthru

- A new feature in Xen designed to improve overall performance and reduce the load on the Domain 0 Guest is PCI Passthru which allows the Domain U Guest to have direct access to local hardware without using the Domain 0 for hardware access.

- The Domain U Guest is given rights to talk directly to a specific hardware device instead of the previous method of using Fronted and Backend drivers.

2.6.3 Xen Operation

- This subsection demonstrates how a para-virtualized Domain U is able to communicate with external networks or storage via the Xen hypervisor and Domain 0.

2.6.3.1 Domain 0 to Domain U Communication

- As stated earlier, the Xen hypervisor is not written to support network or disk requests thus a Domain U PV Guest must communicate via the Xen hypervisor with the Domain 0 to accomplish a network or disk request.
- The example shown below shows a Domain U PV Guest writing data to the local hard disk.
- The Domain U PV Guest PV block driver receives a request to write to the local disk and writes the data via the Xen hypervisor to the appropriate local memory which is shared with Domain 0.
- An event channel exists between Domain 0 and the Domain U PV Guest that allows them to communicate via asynchronous inter-domain interrupts in the Xen hypervisor.
- Domain 0 will receive an interrupt from the Xen hypervisor causing the PV Block Backend Driver to access the local system memory reading the appropriate blocks from the Domain U PV Guest shared memory.
- The data from shared memory is then written to the local hard disk at a specific location.

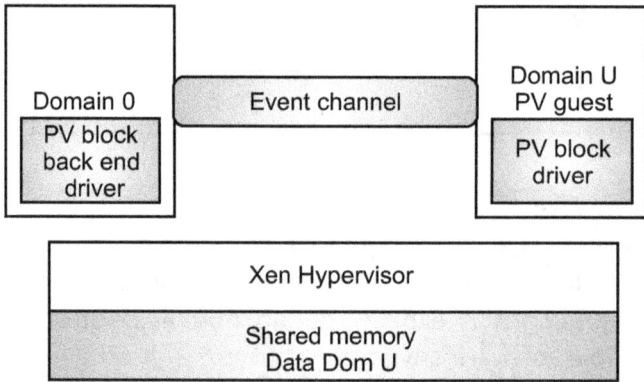

Fig. 2.22 : Domain 0 to Domain U Communication

- The event channel is shown in Fig. 2.22 as a direct link between Domain 0 and Domain U PV Guest which is a simplified view of the way the system works.

- In fact, the event channel runs through the Xen hypervisor with specific interrupts registered in Xenstored allowing both the Domain 0 and Domain U PV Guest to quickly share information across local memory.

2.6.4 Understanding Virtualization Modes

- Guest operating systems are hosted on virtual machines in either full virtualization mode or para-virtual mode.(Refer 2.4)
- There are several ways to implement virtualization.
- Two leading approaches are full virtualization and para-virtualization. Each virtualization mode has advantages and disadvantages.
- Full virtualization is designed to provide total abstraction of the underlying physical system and creates a complete virtual system in which the guest operating systems can execute.
- No modification is required in the guest OS or application; the guest OS or application is not aware of the virtualized environment so they have the capability to execute on the VM just as they would on a physical system.
- This approach can be advantageous because it enables complete decoupling of the software from the hardware.
- As a result, full virtualization can streamline the migration of applications and workloads between different physical systems.
- Full virtualization also helps provide complete isolation of different applications, which helps make this approach highly secure.
- However, full virtualization may incur a performance penalty. The VM monitor must provide the VM with an image of an entire system, including virtual BIOS, virtual memory space, and virtual devices.
- The VM monitor also must create and maintain data structures for the virtual components, such as a shadow memory page table.
- These data structures must be updated for every corresponding access by the VMs.
- In contrast, para-virtualization presents each VM with an abstraction of the hardware that is similar but not identical to the underlying physical hardware.
- Para-virtualization techniques require modifications to the guest operating systems that are running on the VMs.
- As a result, the guest operating systems are aware that they are executing on a VM allowing for near-native performance.
- Para-virtualization methods are still being developed and thus have limitations; including several insecurities such as the guest OS cache data, unauthenticated connections, and so forth.

2.6.5 The Virtual Machine Interface

- Table 2.1 presents an overview of the para-virtualized x86 interface, classified into three broad aspects of the system : memory management, the CPU, and device I/O.

Table 2.1 : Virtual Machine Interfaces

Memory Management	
Segmentation	Cannot install fully-privileged segment descriptors and cannot overlap with the top end of the linear address space.
Paging	Guest OS has direct read access to hardware page tables, but updates are batched and validated by the hypervisor. A domain may be allocated discontinuous machine pages.
CPU	
Protection	Guest OS must run at a lower privilege level than Xen.
Exceptions	Guest OS must register a descriptor table for exception handlers with Xen. A side from page faults, the handlers remain the same.
System Calls	Guest OS may install a 'fast' handler for system calls, allowing direct calls from an application into its guest OS and avoiding in directing through Xen on every call.
Interrupts	Hardware interrupts are replaced with a lightweight event system.
Time	Each guest OS has a timer interface and is aware of both `real' and `virtual' time.
Device I/O	
Network, Disk, etc.	Virtual devices are elegant and simple to access. Data is transferred using asynchronous I/O rings.
	An event mechanism replaces hardware interrupts for notifications.

2.6.5.1 Memory Management

- Virtualizing memory is the most difficult part of para-virtualizing an architecture in terms of the mechanisms required in the hypervisor and modifications required to port each guest OS.

- The task is easier if the architecture provides a software managed TLB as these can be efficiently virtualized in a simple manner.

- Associating an address-space identifier tag with each TLB entry allows the hypervisor and each guest OS to efficiently coexist in separate address spaces because there is no need to flush the entire TLB when transferring execution.

- Unfortunately, x86 does not have a software managed TLB; instead TLB misses are serviced automatically by the processor by walking the page table structure in hardware.

- Thus to achieve the best possible performance, all valid page translations for the current address space should be present in the hardware-accessible page table.
- Moreover, because the TLB is not tagged, address space switches typically require a complete TLB flush.
- Given these limitations, two decisions are made :
  - (a) Guest OSs are responsible for allocating and managing the hardware page tables, with minimal involvement from Xen to ensure safety and isolation; and
  - (b) Xen exists in a 64MB section at the top of every address space, thus avoiding a TLB flush when entering and leaving the hypervisor.
- Each time a guest OS requires a new page table, for example a new process is being created, it allocates and initializes a page from its own memory reservation and registers it with Xen.
- At this point the OS must give up direct write privileges to the page-table memory : All subsequent updates must be validated by Xen.
- This restricts updates in a number of ways, including only allowing an OS to map pages that it owns, and disallowing writable mappings of page tables.
- Guest OSes may batch update requests to pay back the overhead of entering the hypervisor.
- The top 64MB region of each address space, which is reserved for Xen, is not accessible or remappable by guest OSs.
- This address region is not used by any of the common x86 architectures.
- So this restriction does not break application compatibility.
- Segmentation is virtualized in a similar way, by validating updates to hardware segment descriptor tables. The only restrictions on x86 segment descriptors are :
  - (a) They must have lower privilege than Xen.
  - (b) They may not allow any access to the Xen reserved portion of the address space.

2.6.5.2 CPU

- Virtualizing the CPU has several implications for guest OSs.
- Principally, the insertion of a hypervisor below the operating system violates the usual assumption that the OS is the most privileged entity in the system.
- In order to protect the hypervisor from OS misbehavior (and domains from one another) guest OSs must be modified to run at a lower privilege level.
- Many processor architectures only provide two privilege levels.
- In these cases the guest OS would share the lower privilege level with applications.
- The guest OS would then protect itself by running in a separate address space from its applications, and indirectly pass control to and from applications via the hypervisor to set the virtual privilege level and change the current address space.
- Again, if the processor's TLB supports address-space tags then expensive TLB flushes can be avoided.

- Efficient virtualizing of privilege levels is possible on x86 because it supports four distinct privilege levels in hardware.
- The x86 privilege levels are generally described as rings, and are numbered from zero (most privileged) to three (least privileged). Refer Fig. 2.23.

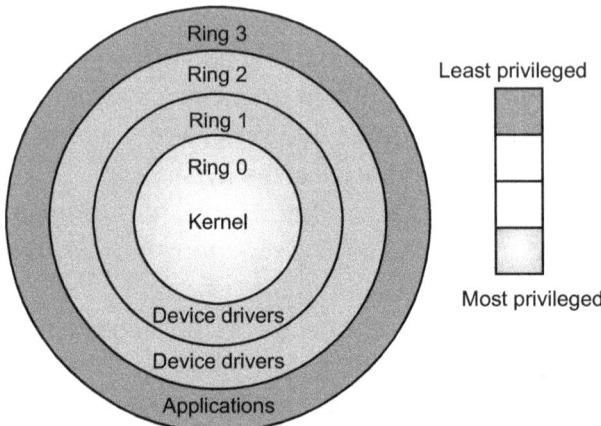

Fig. 2.23 : x86 Privilege Rings

- OS code typically executes in ring 0 because no other ring can execute privileged instructions, while ring 3 is generally used for application code. To our knowledge, rings 1 and 2 have not been used by any well-known x86 OS.
- Any OS which follows this common arrangement can be ported to Xen by modifying it to execute in ring 1. This prevents the guest OS from directly executing privileged instructions, yet it remains safely isolated from applications running in ring 3.
- Privileged instructions are para-virtualized by requiring them to be validated and executed within Xen. This applies to operations such as installing a new page table, or yielding the processor when idle.
- Any guest OS attempt to directly execute a privileged instruction is failed by the processor, either silently or by taking a fault, since only Xen executes at a sufficiently privileged level.
- Exceptions, including memory faults and software traps, are virtualized on x86 very straightforwardly.
- A table describing the handler for each type of exception is registered with Xen for validation.
- The handlers specified in this table are generally identical to those of real x86 hardware. This is possible because the exception stack frames are unmodified in our para-virtualized architecture. The sole modification is to the page fault handler, which would normally read the faulting address from a privileged processor register (CR2); since this is not possible, we write it into an extended stack frame2.
- When an exception occurs while executing outside ring 0, Xen's handler creates a copy of the exception stack frame on the guest OS stack and returns control to the appropriate registered handler.

- Typically only two types of exception occur frequently enough to affect system performance : System calls (which are usually implemented via a software exception), and page faults.
- Performance of system calls can be improved by allowing each guest OS to register a 'fast' exception handler which is accessed directly by the processor without indirecting via ring 0; this handler is validated before installing it in the hardware exception table.
- Unfortunately it is not possible to apply the same technique to the page fault handler because only code executing in ring 0 can read the faulting address from register CR2; page faults must therefore always be delivered via Xen so that this register value can be saved for access in ring 1.
- Safety is ensured by validating exception handlers when they are presented to Xen. The only required check is that the handler's code segment does not specify execution in ring 0.
- Since no guest OS can create such a segment, it suffices to compare the specified segment selector to a small number of static values which are reserved by Xen.

2.6.5.3 Device I/O

- Rather than emulating existing hardware devices, as is typically done in fully-virtualized environments, Xen exposes a set of clean and simple device abstractions.
- This allows us to design an interface that is both efficient and satisfies requirements for protection and isolation. To this end, I/O data is transferred to and from each domain via Xen, using shared-memory, asynchronous buffer descriptor rings.
- These provide a high-performance communication mechanism for passing buffer information vertically through the system, while allowing Xen to efficiently perform validation checks (for example, checking that buffers are contained within a domain's memory reservation).
- Similar to hardware interrupts, Xen supports a lightweight event delivery mechanism which is used for sending asynchronous notifications to a domain. These notifications are made by updating a bitmap of pending event types and, optionally, by calling an event handler specified by the guest OS.

2.6.6 Xen Architecture

- Xen is open source virtualization software based on para-virtualization technology. This subsection provides an overview of the Xen architecture.
- Fig. 2.24 shows the architecture of Xen hosting four VMs (Domain 0, VM 1, VM 2, and VM 3). This architecture includes the Xen Virtual Machine Monitor (VMM), which abstracts the underlying physical hardware and provides hardware access for the different virtual machines.

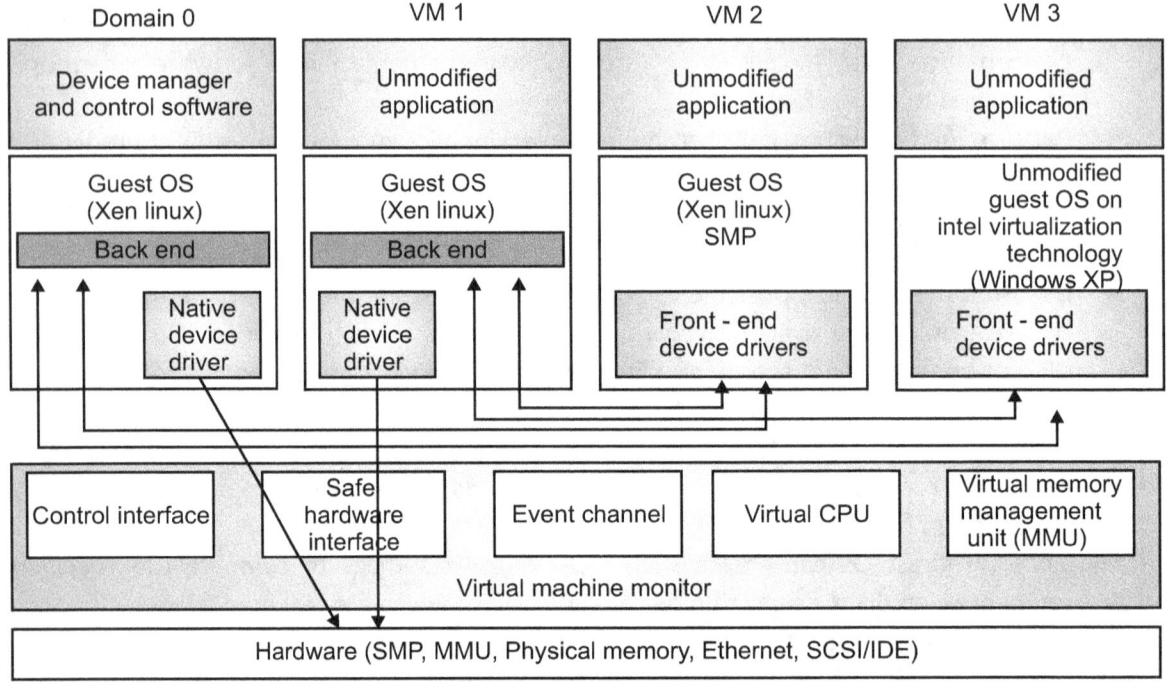

Fig. 2.24 : Xen Architecture

- Fig. 2.24 also shows the special role of the VM called Domain 0. Only Domain 0 can access the control interface of the VMM, through which other VMs can be created, destroyed, and managed.
- Management and control software runs in Domain 0.
- Administrators can create virtual machines with special privileges such as VM 1 that can directly access the hardware through secure interfaces provided by Xen.
- Administrators can create other virtual machines that can access the physical resources provided by Domain 0's control and management interface in Xen.

2.6.6.1 CPU Operations

- The Intel x86 architecture provides four levels of privilege modes. These modes, or rings, are numbered 0 to 3, with 0 being the most privileged.
- In a non-virtualized system, the OS executes at ring 0 and the applications at ring 3. Rings 1 and 2 are typically not used.
- In Xen para-virtualization, the VMM executes at ring 0, the guest OS at ring 1, and the applications at ring 3. This approach helps to ensure that the VMM processes the highest privilege, while the guest OS executes in a higher privileged mode than the applications and is isolated from the applications.
- Privileged instructions issued by the guest OS are verified and executed by the VMM.

2.6.6.2 Memory Operations

- In a non-virtualized environment, the OS expects contiguous memory.

- Guest operating systems in Xen para-virtualization are modified to access memory in a non-contigious manner.
- Guest operating systems are responsible for allocating and managing page tables. However, direct writes are intercepted and validated by the Xen VMM.

2.6.6.3 I/O Operations

- In a fully virtualized environment, hardware devices are emulated.
- Xen para-virtualization exposes a set of clean and simple device abstractions. For example, I/O data to and from guest operating systems is transferred using shared memory ring architecture (memory is shared between Domain 0 and the guest domain) through which incoming and outgoing messages are sent.
- Modifying the guest OS is not feasible for non–open source platforms Windows operating systems.
- As a result, such operating systems are not supported in a para-virtualization environment.

2.7 X86 VIRTUALIZATION

2.7.1 Introduction to x86 Virtualization

- x86 virtualization refers to hardware virtualization for the x86 architecture.
- It allows multiple operating systems to simultaneously share x86 processor resources in a safe and efficient manner.
- In the early days of x86 virtualization, all CPUs were implemented essentially the same 32-bit architecture and the virtual machine monitor (VMM) always used software techniques to run guest operating systems.
- Later uniformity no longer exists. CPUs today come in 32 and 64 bit variants. Some CPUs have hardware support for virtualization; others do not. Moreover, this hardware support comes in multiple forms for virtualizing different aspects of the x86 architecture.
- This subsection provides description of x86 architecture from virtualization point of view along with the understanding of :
  (a) Which CPU features are required.
  (b) Which CPU features can be utilized (but are not required).
  (c) Which CPU features can be virtualized that is, made available to software running in the virtual machine.
- With a better understanding of how CPU features are required, used, and virtualized we can more precisely talk about what can be virtualized, what performance levels may result for a given combination of CPU, guest operating system, and how workloads may respond to adjusting configuration parameters both for software running in the virtual machine and at the underlying hardware level.

2.7.2 x86 Architecture- History

- The x86 architecture has roots that link back to 8 bit processors built by Intel in the late 1970s.
- As manufacturing capabilities improved and software demands increased, Intel extended the 8-bit architecture to 16 bits with the 8086 processor.
- With the arrival of the 80386 CPU in 1985, Intel extended the architecture to 32 bits known as IA-32, but the vendor use the generalized term as x86 .
- From the last two decades, the basic 32-bit architecture remained the same, although successive generations of CPUs added many new features such as chip floating point unit, support for large physical memories and vector instructions.
- In 2003, AMD introduced a 64-bit extension to the x86 architecture, after that Intel announced its own 64-bit architectural extension of IA-32 known as IA-32e. The AMD and Intel 64-bit extensions are extremely similar, with some minor differences which is crucial for virtualization.

2.7.3 VMware ESX

- VMware released the first version of VMware Workstation in 1999. It ran on, and virtualized, 32 bit x86 CPUs.
- Later VMware switched to the ESX Server product. This ESX server used a custom built kernel instead of workstation which relies on either Linux or Windows.
- The custom built kernel also known as VMkernel is designed to be scalable and efficiently run a workload that consists primarily of virtual machines while providing strong information and performance isolation among the virtual machines.
- The VMkernel row in Table 2.2 shows the architectural requirements for running the VMkernel itself in different versions of ESX.

Table 2.2 : Physical and Virtual CPU Options

	ESX 1.0-2.5	ESX 3.0	ESX 3.5	ESX 4.0
VMkernel	32 bit	32 bit	32 bit	64 bit
Virtual CPU	32 bit	32-64 bit	32-64 bit	32-64 bit

- All versions of ESX before 4.0 can run on the 32-bit x86 architecture. They also can run on x64 CPUs but do not take advantage of the 64-bit architectural extensions.
- With VMware ESX 4.0, a 64-bit CPU is required to run the VMkernel. However this requirement causes a slight loss of hardware compatibility.
- After 2009 the majority of server CPUs implements the x64 architecture, making it desirable to use the large 64 bit address space and other architectural advances to improve performance and scalability.

2.7.4 Virtualizing 32- and 64-bit CPUs

- The VMkernel does not run virtual machines directly. Instead, it runs a VMM that in turn is responsible for execution of the virtual machine.
- Each VMM is dedicated to one virtual machine. To run multiple virtual machines, the VMkernel starts multiple VMM instances.
- Because the VMM decouples the virtual machine from the VMkernel, it is possible to run 64 bit guest operating systems on a 32 bit VMkernel (and vice versa) as long as the underlying physical CPUs have all the required features.
- VMM can also be designed which can take advantage of a 64-bit physical CPU to run a 64-bit guest operating system efficiently, even if the underlying VMkernel runs in 32-bit mode.
- The Virtual CPU row in Table 2.2 shows which versions of ESX can run just 32-bit virtual machines and which can run both 32- and 64-bit virtual machines.

2.7.5 Execution Modes

- The VMM implements the virtual hardware on which the virtual machine runs. This hardware includes a virtual CPU, virtual I/O devices, timers, and other devices.
- The virtual CPU has three important features :
  a. The virtual instruction set.
  b. The virtual memory management unit (MMU).
  c. The virtual interrupt controller (PIC or APIC).
- The VMM can implement each of these aspects using either software techniques or hardware techniques. The combination of techniques used to virtualize the instruction set and memory determines an execution mode.

2.7.5.1 Instruction Set Virtualization

- In order to run one or more virtual machines safely on a single host, ESX must isolate the virtual machines so that they can not interfere with each other or with the VMkernel.
- In particular, it must prevent the virtual machines from directly executing privileged instructions that could affect the state of the physical machine as a whole. Instead, it must intercept such instructions and emulate them so their effect is applied to the virtual machine's hardware, not the physical machine's hardware. For example, issuing the reboot command in a virtual machine should reboot just that virtual machine, not the entire host.
- Now we will see some software and hardware techniques for x86 virtualization.

Software Technique : Binary Translation

- The original approach to virtualizing the 32 bit x86 instruction set is just-in-time binary translation (BT).

- This approach is implemented in all versions of VMware ESX, and it is the only approach used in VMware ESX 1.x and 2.x. This approach is actually called as BT32 as this technique virtualizes the 32-bit architecture.
- When running a virtual machine's instruction stream using binary translation, the virtual machine instructions must be translated before they can be executed. Refer Fig. 2.25.
- When a virtual machine is about to execute a block of code for the first time, ESX sends this code through a just-in-time binary translator, much like a Java virtual machine (JVM) which translates Java byte code on the fly into native instructions.

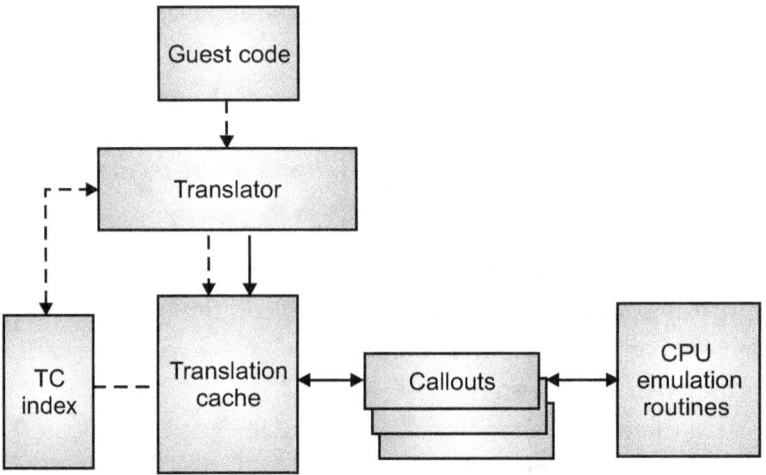

Fig. 2.25 : Binary Translation

- The translator in the VMM does not perform a mapping from one architecture to another, but instead translates from the full unrestricted x86 instruction set to a subset that is safe to execute. In particular, the binary translator replaces privileged instructions with sequences of instructions that perform the privileged operations in the virtual machine rather than on the physical machine.
- This translation enforces encapsulation of the virtual machine while preserving the x86 semantics as seen from the perspective of the virtual machine.
- To keep translation overheads low, the VMM translates virtual machine instructions the first time they are about to execute, placing the resulting translated code in a translation cache.
- If the same virtual machine code executes again in the future, the VMM can reuse the translated code from the translation cache, thereby amortizing the translation costs over all future executions.
- To reduce translation cost further and to minimize memory usage by the translation cache, the VMM combines binary translation of kernel code running in the virtual machine with direct execution of user mode code running in the virtual machine. This is safe because user mode code cannot execute privileged instructions.

- A Binary Translation-based VMM must enforce a strict boundary between the part of the address space that is used by the virtual machine and the part that is used by the VMM. The VMware VMM enforces this boundary using segmentation.
- Segmentation is a hardware feature of the x86 CPU that links back to its 16 bit ancestors. A segment is a consecutive range of memory, identified by a base (the starting address) and a limit (the length of the segment).
- Whenever an x86 instruction accesses memory, it does so with respect to a particular segment.
- The segmentation hardware checks the memory address against the segment limit. If it is within the limit, the base address is added and the access is permitted to proceed. If the address exceeds the limit, the memory access is aborted and the processor raises a protection fault.
- Since most of the modern operating systems, including Windows, Linux make limited use of segmentation, it is possible for the VMM to use segmentation to enforce the boundary between virtual machine and VMM.
- In rare cases when the uses of segmentation by the virtual machine and the VMM conflict, the VMM can perform software segmentation checks again, causing a slight loss of performance.
- In 2003, when AMD extended the x86 architecture from 32 to 64 bits, it eliminated segment limit checks for 64-bit code although 32 bit code still retained segment limit checks for backwards compatibility. This change meant that a BT-based VMM could not use segmentation to protect the VMM from a 64-bit virtual machine. In other words, BT32 could virtualize the 32-bit x86 architecture efficiently, but BT64 could not virtualize the 64-bit architecture efficiently.
- To overcome this AMD added segment limits back into 64-bit code. Thus, all 64-bit AMD CPUs can run virtual machines with BT64.
- The Intel 64-bit extensions to the x86 architecture also omitted support for segment limit checks for 64-bit code. Unlike AMD, however, Intel has not added support for segment limit checks in subsequent processors. This limitation makes it inefficient to run 64-bit virtual machines using BT64 on Intel CPUs.

Table 2.3 : Support for Binary Translation (BT)

	ESX 1.0-2.5	ESX 3.0	ESX 3.5	ESX 4.0
AMD	BT32	BT32 , BT64	BT32, BT64	BT32, BT64
Intel	BT32	BT32	BT32	BT32

Hardware Technique : VT-x and AMD-V

- During the transition from 32-bit to 64-bit hardware, both Intel and AMD recognized the importance of virtualization. Both companies began designing hardware that made it easier for a VMM to run virtual machines.

- The first hardware designs by both of them focused on how to virtualize the 32- and 64-bit x86 instruction set.
- The Intel design, called VT-x got the importance because it provided a way to virtualize 64-bit virtual machines efficiently. (BT64 is not efficient because of the lack of segment limit checks in 64 bit mode on Intel CPUs.)
- AMD subsequently introduced AMD-V to provide hardware support for instruction set virtualization (virtualization of 64 bit virtual machines using BT64 was possible already for AMD CPUs).
- VT-x and AMD-V are similar in aim. Both designs allow a VMM to do away with binary translation while still being able to fully control the execution of a virtual machine by restricting which kinds of (privileged) instructions the virtual machine can execute without intervention by the VMM.
- VT-x and AMD-V both allow a VMM to give the CPU to a virtual machine for direct execution (an action called a VM entry) up until the point when the virtual machine tries to execute a privileged instruction.
- At that point, the virtual machine execution is suspended and the CPU is given back to the VMM (an action called a VM exit). The VMM then follows the inspection of the virtual machine instruction that caused the exit as well as other information provided by the hardware in response to the exit.
- With the relevant information collected, the VMM emulates the virtual machine instruction against the virtual machine state and then resumes execution of the virtual machine with another VM entry.

Table 2.4 : Support for Hardware Instruction Set Virtualization

	ESX 1.0-2.5	ESX 3.0	ESX 3.5	ESX 4.0
AMD	-	AMD-V32, AMD-V64	AMD-V32, AMD-V64	AMD-V32, AMD-V64
Intel	-	VT-x64	VT-x64	VT-x64

2.7.5.2 Memory and MMU Virtualization

- All modern x86 CPUs implement virtual memory, which is a technique for flexibly mapping multiple virtual address spaces (typically one per process) into a possibly smaller amount of physical memory.
- However, for the x86 architecture, the mapping is specified using a set of memory-resident hierarchical 4KB page tables. A tree of such page tables, identified by a root page table, specifies the entire mapping of a virtual address space into physical memory.
- The x86 MMU contains two main structures : a page table walker and a content-addressable memory called a Translation Lookaside Buffer (TLB) to accelerate address translation lookups.

- When an instruction accesses a virtual address, segmentation hardware converts the virtual address to a linear address by adding the segment base. Then the page table walker receives the logical address and traverses the page table tree to produce the corresponding physical address. Refer Fig. 2.26.

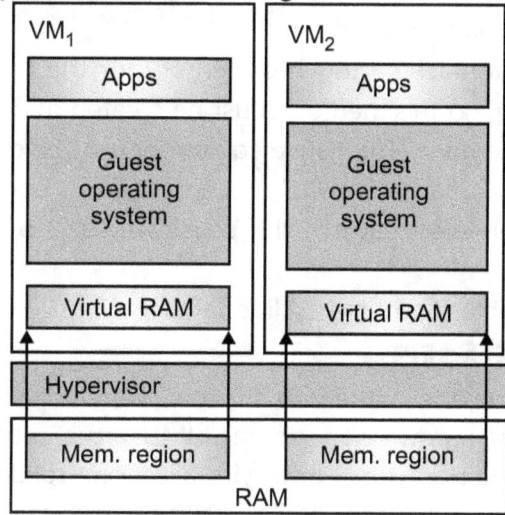

Fig. 2.26 : Memory virtualization

- When the page table walk completes, the pair is inserted into the TLB to accelerate future accesses to the same address.
- Accordingly, the task of the VMM is not only to virtualize memory but to virtualize virtual memory so that the guest operating system can use virtual memory.
- To accomplish this task, the VMM must virtualize the x86 MMU. It does so by having the VMM remap addresses a second time, below the virtual machine, from physical address to machine address, to confine the virtual machine to the machine memory that the VMM and VMkernel have allowed it to use.

Software Technique : Shadow Page Tables

- To virtualize memory without special hardware support, the VMM creates a shadow page table for each primary page table that the virtual machine is using.
- The VMM populates the shadow page table with the composition of two mappings :
    a. The Logical Address : Physical Address mapping specified by the guest operating system, obtained from the primary page tables.
    b. The Physical Address : Logical Address mapping defined by the VMM and VMkernel.
- By building shadow page tables that capture this composite mapping, the VMM can point the hardware MMU directly at the shadows, allowing the virtual machine's memory accesses to run at native speed while being assured that the virtual machine cannot access machine memory that does not belong to it.

- However, shadow page tables incur overheads in following situations.
    a. When the virtual machine updates a primary page table, the VMM must trap the update and propagate the change into the corresponding shadow page table or tables. This slows down memory mapping operations as well as creation of new processes in virtual machines.
    b. When the virtual machine touches memory for the first time, the shadow page table entry mapping this memory must be created on demand, slowing down the first access to memory. (The native equivalent is a TLB miss.)
    c. When the virtual machine switches context from one process to another, the VMM must intervene to switch the physical MMU to the new process' shadow page table root.
    d. Shadow page tables consume additional memory.

Hardware Technique : RVI and EPT

- To address the overheads inherent in shadow page tables, both AMD and Intel now build special purpose hardware to support MMU virtualization.
- AMD introduced support for MMU virtualization, called RVI, in the quad-core Opteron CPU. Intel introduced similar functionality, called EPT, in its "Nehalem" generation of CPUs.
- Just as AMD-V and VT-x are similar in their aim, so are RVI and EPT. Both designs permit the two levels of address mapping to be performed in hardware by pointing the physical MMU at two distinct sets of page tables.
- The first is defined by the virtual machine and the second, invisible to the virtual machine, is controlled by the VMM.
- Given these two mappings, the physical CPU's page walker can walk the two sets of page tables to produce pairs that are cached in the TLB.
- This arrangement does away with shadow page tables at the cost of a single set of nested or extended page tables that map from physical address to machine address.
- Because the nested or extended page tables are largely static and need no update whenever the virtual machine creates or modifies page tables, the VMM need not interfere when virtual machine page tables are updated. Moreover, the VMM does not need to be involved in virtual machine context switches. The virtual machine can change the page table root on its own.
- Although RVI and EPT have compelling advantages, there is one potential downside : A TLB miss is now more expensive because it must be serviced by a two-level page walker.
- For most workloads, RVI or EPT provides an overall performance win over shadow page tables.
- For workloads that suffer frequent TLB misses or perform few context switches or page table updates RVI or EPT does not perform well.

Table 2.5 : Support RVI and EPT

	ESX 1.0-2.5	ESX 3.0	ESX 3.5	ESX 4.0
AMD	-	-	yes	yes
Intel	-	-	-	yes

2.7.5.3 Monitor Modes

- This subsection describes a two way choice between software and hardware techniques for instruction set virtualization (BT on one hand and AMD-V or VT-x on the other hand) and for memory virtualization (shadow page tables on one hand and RVI or EPT on the other hand).

- However the two forms of hardware support are not orthogonal. RVI is inseparable from AMD-V and EPT is inseparable from VT-x. This leaves only three valid combinations :

  a. BT(software) and MMU - binary translation and shadow page tables.

  b. HV(software) MMU - AMD-V or VT-x and shadow page tables.

  c. HV(hardware) MMU - AMD-V with RVI or VT-x with EPT.

  (HV stands for hardware support for instruction virtualization)

- Above three options are called as monitor modes because they describe the way the VMM runs a particular virtual machine on a given physical CPU.

Choice of Monitor Mode

- When a virtual machine is powering on, the VMM inspects the physical CPUs features and the guest operating system type to determine the set of possible execution modes.

- On ESX 3.0 and earlier only one monitor mode can be executed. Refer tables 2.2, 2.3, 2.4, 2.5.

- However from ESX 3.5, and especially with ESX 4.0, there are cases in which more than one execution mode is possible.

- In such a case VMM first finds the set of modes allowed. Then it restricts the allowed modes by configuration file settings. Finally, among the remaining sets, it chooses the "preferred" mode. The following examples illustrate the process :

  a. ESX 3.5 on an AMD CPU and a 64 bit virtual machine - The allowed modes are BT-(software) + MMU and HV-(hardware) + MMU (AMD-V with RVI). The preferred option for a 64 bit virtual machine is HV(hardware) + MMU, so the VMM chooses this mode at power on time.

  b. ESX 3.5 on an Intel Nehalem CPU and a 64 bit virtual machine - Run with HV(software) + MMU (because ESX 3.5 does not support EPT).

  c. ESX 4.0 on an AMD CPU and a 64-bit virtual machine - The choice is among BT-(software) + MMU, HV-(software) + MMU, and HV-(hardware) MMU. HV-(hardware) + MMU wins.

  d. ESX 4.0 on an older Opteron CPU and a 64-bit virtual machine - Only one option is available : BT-(software) + MMU (because ESX cannot use AMD-V on this CPU).

  e. ESX 4.0 on an Intel Nehalem CPU and a 64-bit virtual machine - The allowed modes are HV-(software) + MMU and HV-(hardware) + MMU (BT is not allowed for 64-bit virtual machines on Intel CPUs because segment limit checks are missing). The VMM chooses HV-(hardware) + MMU.

- Certain features may restrict the available modes. For example, VMware Fault Tolerance cannot use RVI or EPT because of their lack of determinism, and it avoids BT, thus only choice left is HV-(software) + MMU.

- When multiple choices remain, a prioritization algorithm runs to choose the best mode :

  a. For ESX 3.5, the only case in which there is a choice is on AMD CPUs on which BT-(software) + MMU and HV-(hardware) + MMU might both be available. The default choice for 32-bit virtual machines is BT-(software) + MMU. For 64-bit virtual machines, it is HW-(hardware) + MMU.

  b. For ESX 4.0, many more situations can result in multiple allowable execution modes.

  c. The general priority for CPUs that have hardware support for APIC virtualization is : HV-(hardware) + MMU, followed by HV- (software) + MMU, followed by BT-(software) + MMU.

  d. For CPUs without hardware support for APIC virtualization, the order for 32-bit Windows guest operating systems is : HV- (hardware) + MMU, followed by BT-(software) + MMU, followed by HV-(software) + MMU.

Specifying the Preferred Monitor Mode

- In some cases, an explicit specification of monitor mode preference may be needed.

- Although this situation is rare, the complexity of workloads and virtual machine configurations makes a manual approach more desirable in cases in which the default choice leads to less than optimal performance.

- In virtual machine configuration files, we can restrict the set of modes by setting one or both of the following options :

 monitor.virtual_mmu = software | hardware | automatic

 monitor.virtual_exec = software | hardware | automatic

- Choose from software, hardware, or automatic can be made for each variable. Both ESX 3.5 and ESX 4.0 recognize the monitor.virtual_mmu setting. Only ESX 4.0 recognizes monitor.virtual_exec.

- We can express all possible ESX 3.5 mode choices with the monitor.virtual_mmu option alone.

- If a setting is not specified, the effect is the same as automatic. If it is set to hardware, it forces the use of the given form of hardware support if the feature is available and supported. Likewise, if the setting is software, the VMM attempts to run the virtual machine without the given form of hardware support, if allowed.
- Although the configuration file settings are flexible enough to express all of the 2×2 possible combinations, only three of the four combinations are valid. Valid combinations are used to select one of the three execution modes.
- If the CPU does not support the requested execution mode, the settings are ignored. In addition, the settings are ignored if the CPU implements the execution mode but the version of ESX does not support it.

2.8 INSTALLATION AND CONFIGURATION

- Xen is an open-source para-virtualizing Virtual Machine Monitor (VMM), or "hypervisor", for a variety of processor architectures including x86. Xen can securely execute multiple virtual machines on a single physical system with near native performance.
- Xen can be used for
a. **Server Consolidation**
   Move multiple servers onto a single physical host with performance and fault isolation provided at the virtual machine boundaries.
b. **Hardware Independence**
   Allow legacy applications and operating systems to exploit new hardware.
c. **Multiple OS Configurations**
   Run multiple operating systems simultaneously, for development or testing purposes.
d. **Cluster Computing**
e. Management at VM granularity provides more flexibility than separately managing each physical host, but better control and isolation than single-system image solutions, particularly by using live migration for load balancing.
f. **Hardware Support for Custom OSes.**
   Allow development of new OSes while benefiting from the wide-ranging hardware support of existing OSes such as Linux.

2.8.1 Installation

- The Xen distribution includes three main components : Xen itself, ports of Linux and NetBSD to run on Xen, and the user-space tools required to manage a Xen-based system.
- The following is a full list of basic items. Items marked '†' are required by the xend control tools, and hence required if you want to run more than one virtual machine; items marked '*' are only required if you wish to build from source.
1. A working Linux distribution using the GRUB boot loader and running on a P6- class or newer CPU.

2. The iproute2 package.
3. The Linux bridge-utils1 (e.g., /sbin/brctl).
4. The Linux hotplug system2 (e.g., /sbin/hotplug and related scripts). On newer distributions, this is included alongside the Linux udev system3.
- All above mentioned tools are required by the xend control tools.
1. Build tools (gcc v3.2.x or v3.3.x, binutils, GNU make).
2. Development installation of zlib (e.g., zlib-dev).
3. Development installation of Python v2.2 or later (e.g., python-dev).
4. LaTex and transFig. are required to build the documentation.
- Above mentioned tools are required only if user wish to build virtual machine from source.
- Once these prerequisites are satisfied, it is possible to install either a binary or source distribution of Xen.

2.8.2 Installing from Binary Tarball

- Pre-built tarballs are available for download from the XenSource downloads page :
  http://www.xensource.com/downloads/
- Once user has downloaded the tarball, simply unpack and install :
  # tar zxvf xen-3.0-install.tgz
  # cd xen-3.0-install
  # sh ./install.sh
- Once the binaries are installed user need to configure your system.

2.8.3 Installing from RPMs

- Pre-built RPMs are available for download from the XenSource downloads page :
  http://www.xensource.com/downloads/
- Once user has downloaded the RPMs, he typically install them via the RPM commands :
  rpm -iv rpmname

2.8.4 Installing from Source

This part describes how to obtain, build and install Xen from source.

2.8.4.1 Obtaining the Source

- The Xen source tree is available as either a compressed source tarball or as a clone of master Mercurial repository.
- **Obtaining the Source Tarball**
  Stable versions and daily snapshots of the Xen source tree are available from the Xen download page :
  http://www.xensource.com/downloads/

- **Obtaining the Source via Mercurial**

  The source tree may also be obtained via the public Mercurial repository at : http://xenbits.xensource.com

2.8.4.2 Building from Source

The top-level Xen Makefile includes a target "world" that will perform following functionalities :

- Build Xen.
- Build the control tools, including xend.
- Download (if necessary) and unpack the Linux 2.6 source code, and patch it for use with Xen.
- Build a Linux kernel to use in domain 0 and a smaller unprivileged kernel, which can be used for unprivileged virtual machines.
- After the build has completed top-level directory is created called dist/ in which all resulting targets will be placed. Two XenLinux kernel images are very important one with a "-xen0" extension which contains hardware device drivers and drivers for Xen's virtual devices, and one with a "-xenU" extension that just contains the virtual ones.
- These are found in dist/install/boot/ along with the image for Xen itself and the configuration files used during the build.
- To customize the set of kernels built user needs to edit the top-level Makefile.

  KERNELS ?= linux-2.6-xen0 linux-2.6-xenU. This can be changed to include any set of operating system kernels which have configurations in the top-level buildconfigures/ directory.

2.8.4.3 Custom Kernels

- If you wish to build a customized XenLinux kernel (e.g. to support additional devices or enable distribution-required features), you can use the standard Linux configuration mechanisms, specifying that the architecture being built for is xen, e.g :

```
# cd linux-2.6.12-xen0
# make ARCH=xen xconfigure
# cd..
# make
```

- It is also possible to copy an existing Linux configuration (.configure) into e.g. linux-2.6.12-xen0 and execute :

```
# make ARCH=xen oldconfigure
```

- Only difference between the two types of Linux kernels that are built is the configuration file used for each. The "U" suffixed (unprivileged) versions don't contain any of the physical hardware device drivers, leading to a 30% reduction in size; hence you may prefer these for your non-privileged domains. The "0" suffixed privileged versions can be used to boot the system, as well as in driver domains and unprivileged domains.

2.8.4.4 Installing Generated Binaries

- The files produced by the build process are stored under the dist/install/ directory.
- To install them in their default locations, use the coomand :

  # make install

- Alternatively, users with special installation requirements may wish to install them manually by copying the files to their appropriate destinations.
- The dist/install/boot directory will also contain the configure files used for building the XenLinux kernels, and also versions of Xen and XenLinux kernels that contain debug symbols such as (xen-syms-3.0.0 and vmlinux-syms-2.6.12.6-xen0) which are essential for interpreting crash dumps.

2.8.5 Configuration

- Once you have built and installed the Xen distribution, it is simple to prepare the machine for booting and running Xen.

2.8.5.1 GRUB Configuration

- An entry should be added to grub.conf (often found under /boot/ or /boot/grub/) to allow Xen / XenLinux to boot. This file is sometimes called menu.lst, depending on your distribution. The entry should look something like the following :

  title Xen 3.0 / XenLinux 2.6

  kernel /boot/xen-3.0.gz dom0_mem=262144

  module /boot/vmlinuz-2.6-xen0 root=/dev/sda4 ro console=tty0

- The kernel line tells GRUB where to find Xen itself and what boot parameters should be passed to it (setting the domain 0 memory allocation in kilobytes and the settings for the serial port).
- The module line of the configuration describes the location of the XenLinux kernel that Xen should start and the parameters that should be passed to it. These are standard Linux parameters, identifying the root device and specifying it be initially mounted read only and instructing that console output be sent to the screen.
- When installing a new kernel, it is recommended that you do not delete existing menu options from menu.lst, as you may wish to boot your old Linux kernel in future, particularly if you have problems.

2.8.5.2 Serial Console

- Serial console access allows you to manage, monitor, and interact with your system.
- This can allow access from another nearby system via a null modem ("LapLink") cable or remotely via a serial concentrator.

- System's BIOS, bootloader (GRUB), Xen, Linux, and login access must each be individually configured for serial console access. It is not strictly necessary to have each component fully functional, but it can be quite useful.

a. Serial Console BIOS Configuration

- Enabling system serial console output neither enables nor disables serial capabilities in GRUB, Xen, or Linux, but may make remote management of your system more convenient by displaying POST and other boot messages over serial port and allowing remote BIOS configuration.
- It is advised to refer your hardware vendor's documentation for capabilities and procedures to enable BIOS serial redirection.

b. Serial Console GRUB Configuration

- Enabling GRUB serial console output neither enables nor disables Xen or Linux serial capabilities, but may made remote management of your system more convenient by displaying GRUB prompts, menus, and actions over serial port and allowing remote GRUB management.
- Adding the following two lines to your GRUB configuration file, typically either /boot/grub/menu.lst or /boot/grub/grub.conf will enable GRUB serial output.

  serial --unit=0 --speed=115200 --word=8 --parity=no --stop=1

  terminal --timeout=10 serial console

- Note that when both the serial port and the local monitor and keyboard are enabled, the text "Press any key to continue" will appear at both. Pressing a key on one device will cause GRUB to display to that device. The other device will see no output. If no key is pressed before the timeout period expires, the system will boot to the default GRUB boot entry.

2.8.5.3 Serial Console Xen Configuration

- Enabling Xen serial console output neither enables nor disables Linux kernel output or logging in to Linux over serial port. It does however allow you to monitor and log the Xen boot process via serial console and can be very useful in debugging.
- In order to configure Xen serial console output, it is necessary to add a boot option to your GRUB configure; e.g. kernel / boot / xen.gz dom0_mem = 131072 com1 = 115200, 8n1 console=com1,vga This configures Xen to output on COM1 at 115,200 baud, 8 data bits, no parity and 1 stop bit.
- It is also possible to configure XenLinux to share the serial console; to achieve this append "console=ttyS0" to your module line.

2.8.5.4 Serial Console Linux Configuration

- Enabling Linux serial console output at boot neither enables nor disables logging in to Linux over serial port. It does however allow you to monitor and log the Linux boot process via serial console and can be very useful in debugging.

- To enable Linux output at boot time, add the parameter console=ttyS0 (or ttyS1, ttyS2, etc.) to your kernel GRUB line. Under Xen, this might be :

  module /vmlinuz-2.6-xen0 ro root=/dev/VolGroup00/LogVol00 \

  console=ttyS0, 115200to enable output over ttyS0 at 115200 baud.

2.8.5.5 Serial Console Login Configuration

- Logging in to Linux via serial console, under Xen or otherwise, requires specifying a login prompt be started on the serial port. To permit root logins over serial console, the serial port must be added to /etc/securetty.
- To automatically start a login prompt over the serial port, add the line :

  c:2345:respawn:/sbin/mingetty ttyS0 to /etc/inittab. Run init q to force a reload of your inttab and start getty.

- To enable root logins, add ttyS0 to /etc/securetty if not already present.

2.8.5.6 TLS Libraries

- Users of the XenLinux kernel should disable Thread Local Storage (TLS) (e.g. by doing a mv /lib/tls /lib/tls.disabled) before attempting to boot a Xen- Linux kernel4.
- It is always possible to run TLS by restoring the directory to its original location (i.e. mv /lib/tls.disabled /lib/tls). The reason for this is that the current TLS implementation uses segmentation in a way that is not permissible under Xen. If TLS is not disabled, an emulation mode is used within Xen which reduces performance substantially. To ensure full performance you should install a 'Xen-friendly' (nosegneg) version of the library.

2.8.6 Booting Xen

- It should now be possible to restart the system and use Xen. Reboot and choose the new Xen option when the Grub screen appears.
- It should look much like a conventional Linux boot. The first portion of the output comes from Xen itself, supplying low level information about itself and the underlying hardware. The last portion of the output comes from XenLinux.
- You may see some error messages during the XenLinux boot. These are not necessarily anything to worry about—they may result from kernel configuration differences between your XenLinux kernel and the one you usually use.
- When the boot completes, you should be able to log into your system as usual. If you are unable to log in, you should still be able to reboot with your normal Linux kernel by selecting it at the GRUB prompt.

- Booting the system into Xen will bring you up into the privileged management domain, Domain0. At that point you are ready to create guest domains and "boot" them using the xm create command.
- The first step in creating a new domain is to prepare a root filevsystem for it to boot. Typically, this might be stored in a normal partition, an LVM or other volume manager partition, a disk file or on an NFS server.
- A simple way to do this is simply to boot from your standard OS install CD and install the distribution into another partition on your hard drive.
- To start the xend control daemon, type
  # xend start
- Once the daemon is running, you can use the xm tool to monitor and maintain the domains running on your system.

2.8.7 Booting Guest Domains

2.8.7.1 Creating a Domain Configuration File

- Before you can start an additional domain, you must create a configuration file.
- Two example files are provided here which you can use as a starting point :
  /etc/xen/xmexample1 is a simple template configuration file for describing a single VM.
  /etc/xen/xmexample2 file is a template description that is intended to be reused for multiple virtual machines.
  Setting the value of the vmid variable on the xm command line fills in parts of this template.
- Copy one of these files and edit it as appropriate. Typical values you may wish to edit include :
  kernel
  Set this to the path of the kernel you compiled for use with Xen
   (e.g. kernel ="/boot/vmlinuz-2.6-xenU").
  memory
  Set this to the size of the domain's memory in megabytes (e.g. memory = 64).
  disk
  Set the first entry in this list to calculate the offset of the domain's root partition, based on the domain ID. Set the second to the location of /usr if you are sharing it between domains (e.g. disk = ['phy:your hard drive%d,sda1,w' % (base partition number + vmid), 'phy:your usr partition,sda6,r'].
  dhcp
  Uncomment the dhcp variable, so that the domain will receive its IP address from a DHCP server (e.g. dhcp="dhcp").
- You may also want to edit the **vif** variable in order to choose the MAC address of the virtual ethernet interface yourself. For example: vif = ['mac=00:16:3E:F6:BB:B3'] If you do not set this variable, xend will automatically generate a random MAC address

from the range 00:16:3E:xx:xx:xx, assigned by IEEE to XenSource as an OUI (organizationally unique identifier). XenSource Inc. gives permission for anyone to use addresses randomly allocated from this range for use by their Xen domains.

2.8.7.2 Booting the Guest Domain

- The xm tool provides a variety of commands for managing domains. Use the create command to start new domains. Assuming you've created a configuration file myvmconf based around /etc/xen/xmexample2, to start a domain with virtual machine ID 1 you should type :

  # xm create -c myvmconf vmid=1

- The -c switch causes xm to turn into the domain's console after creation. The vmid=1 sets the vmid variable used in the myvmconf file.
- Now you should be able to see the console boot messages from the new domain appearing in the terminal in which you typed the command, culminating in a login prompt.

2.8.7.3 Starting / Stopping Domains Automatically

- It is possible to have certain domains start automatically at boot time and to have dom0 wait for all running domains to shutdown before it shuts down the system.
- To specify a domain is to start at boot-time, place its configuration file under /etc/xen/auto/.
- You can then enable it in the appropriate way for your distribution.
- For instance, on Red Hat :

  # chkconfigure --add xendomains.

- By default, this will start the boot-time domains in runlevels 3, 4 and 5. You can also use the service command to run this script manually,

  e.g : # service xendomains start- Starts all the domains with configure files under / etc / xen / auto/.

- # service xendomains stop - Shuts down all running Xen domains.

2.8.8 Domain Management Tools

2.8.8.1 Xend

- The Xend node control daemon performs system management functions related to virtual machines. It forms a central point of control of virtualized resources, and must be running in order to start and manage virtual machines.
- Xend must be run as root because it needs access to privileged system management functions. An initialization script named /etc/init.d/xend is provided to start Xend at boot time.
- Use the tool appropriate (i.e. chkconfigure) for your Linux distribution to specify the run levels at which this script should be executed, or manually create symbolic links in the correct run level directories.

- Xend can be started on the command line as well, and supports the following set of parameters :

  # xend start start xend, if not already running
  # xend stop stop xend if already running
  # xend restart restart xend if running, otherwise start it
  # xend status indicates xend status by its return code

  A SysV init script called xend is provided to start xend at boot time make install installs this script in /etc/init.d. To enable it, you have to make symbolic links in the appropriate run level directories or use the chkconfigure tool, where available. Refer Fig. 2.27.

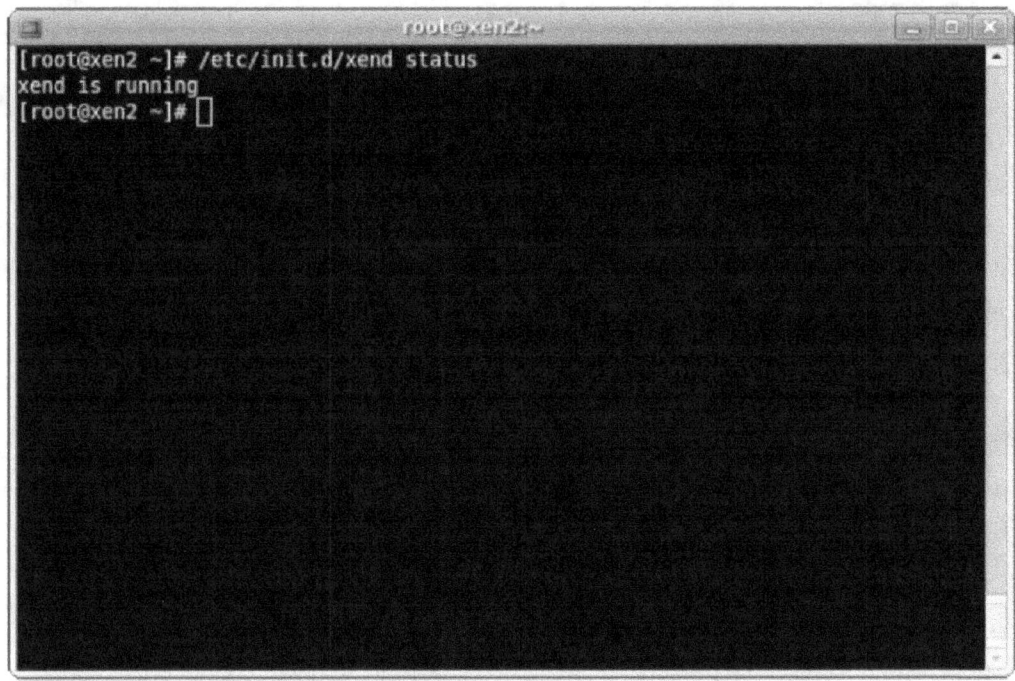

Fig. 2.27 : Status Message Showing Xend is Running

- Once xend is running, administration can be done using the xm tool.
- As xend runs, events will be logged to /var/log/xen/xend.log and (less frequently) to /var/log/xen/xend-debug.log. These, along with the standard syslog files, are useful when troubleshooting problems.

2.8.8.2 Configureuring Xend

- Xend is written in Python. At startup, it reads its configuration information from the file /etc/xen/xend-configuresxp.
- The Xen installation places an example xend-configuresxp file in the /etc/xen subdirectory which should work for most installations.

- Some of the most important parameters are discussed below.
- An HTTP interface and a Unix domain socket API are available to communicate with Xend. This allows remote users to pass commands to the daemon. By default, Xend does not start an HTTP server. It does start a Unix domain socket management server, as the low level utility xm requires it.
- For support of cross-machine migration, Xend can start a relocation server. This support is not enabled by default for security reasons.
- Here important point to note that xend configuration file modifies the defaults and starts up Xend as an HTTP server as well as a relocation server.
- From the file :

  #(xend-http-server no)

  (xend-http-server yes)

  #(xend-unix-server yes)

  #(xend-relocation-server no)

  (xend-relocation-server yes)

  Comment or uncomment lines in that file to disable or enable features that you require.

  Connections from remote hosts are disabled by default :

  # Address xend should listen on for HTTP connections.

  # Specifying 'localhost' prevents remote connections.

  # Specifying the empty string " (the default) allows all connections.

  #(xend-address ")

  (xend-address localhost)

- It is recommended that if migration support is not needed, the xend-relocation-server parameter value be changed to "no".

2.8.8.3 Xm

- The xm tool is the primary tool for managing Xen from the console. The general format of an xm command line is :

  # xm command [switches] [arguments] [variables]

- The available switches and arguments are dependent on the command chosen. The variables may be set using declarations of the form variable=value and command line declarations override any of the values in the configuration file being used, including the standard variables described above and any custom variables (for instance, the xmdefconfigure file uses a vmid variable).

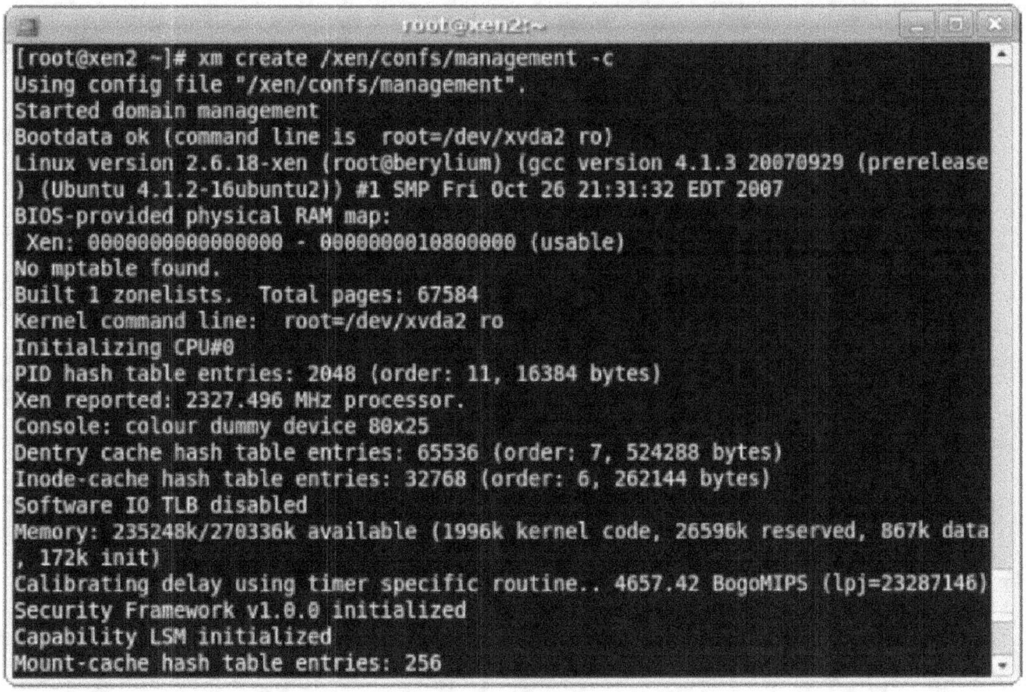

```
[root@xen2 ~]# xm create /xen/confs/management -c
Using config file "/xen/confs/management".
Started domain management
Bootdata ok (command line is  root=/dev/xvda2 ro)
Linux version 2.6.18-xen (root@berylium) (gcc version 4.1.3 20070929 (prerelease
) (Ubuntu 4.1.2-16ubuntu2)) #1 SMP Fri Oct 26 21:31:32 EDT 2007
BIOS-provided physical RAM map:
 Xen: 0000000000000000 - 0000000010800000 (usable)
No mptable found.
Built 1 zonelists.  Total pages: 67584
Kernel command line:  root=/dev/xvda2 ro
Initializing CPU#0
PID hash table entries: 2048 (order: 11, 16384 bytes)
Xen reported: 2327.496 MHz processor.
Console: colour dummy device 80x25
Dentry cache hash table entries: 65536 (order: 7, 524288 bytes)
Inode-cache hash table entries: 32768 (order: 6, 262144 bytes)
Software IO TLB disabled
Memory: 235248k/270336k available (1996k kernel code, 26596k reserved, 867k data
, 172k init)
Calibrating delay using timer specific routine.. 4657.42 BogoMIPS (lpj=23287146)
Security Framework v1.0.0 initialized
Capability LSM initialized
Mount-cache hash table entries: 256
```

Fig. 2.28 : Xm Create Command

2.8.8.4 Basic Management Commands

- One useful command is # xm list which lists all domains running in rows of the following format :

  name domid memory vcpus state cputime

- The meaning of each field is as follows :

  name - The descriptive name of the virtual machine.

  domid - The number of the domain ID this virtual machine is running in.

  memory - Memory size in megabytes.

  vcpus - The number of virtual CPUs this domain has.

  state - Domain state consists of 5 fields :

  r - running

  b - blocked

  p - paused

  s - shutdown

  c - crashed

  cputime - How much CPU time (in seconds) the domain has used so far. Refer Fig. 2.29.

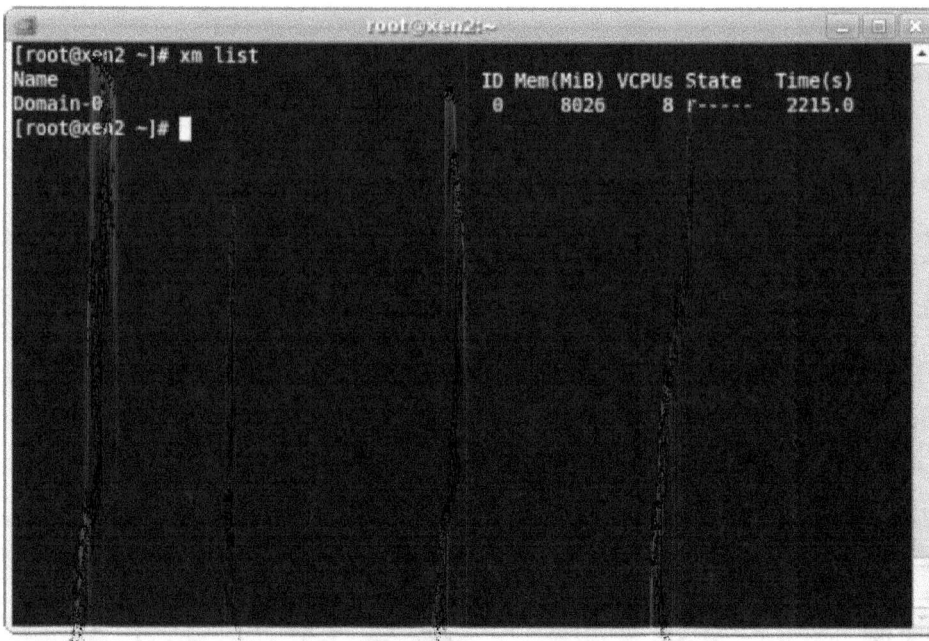

Fig. 2.29 : Xm List On A Machine With No Guest Running

- The xm list command also supports a long output format when the - 1 switch is used. This outputs the full details of the running domains in xend's SXP configuration format. Refer Fig. 2.30.

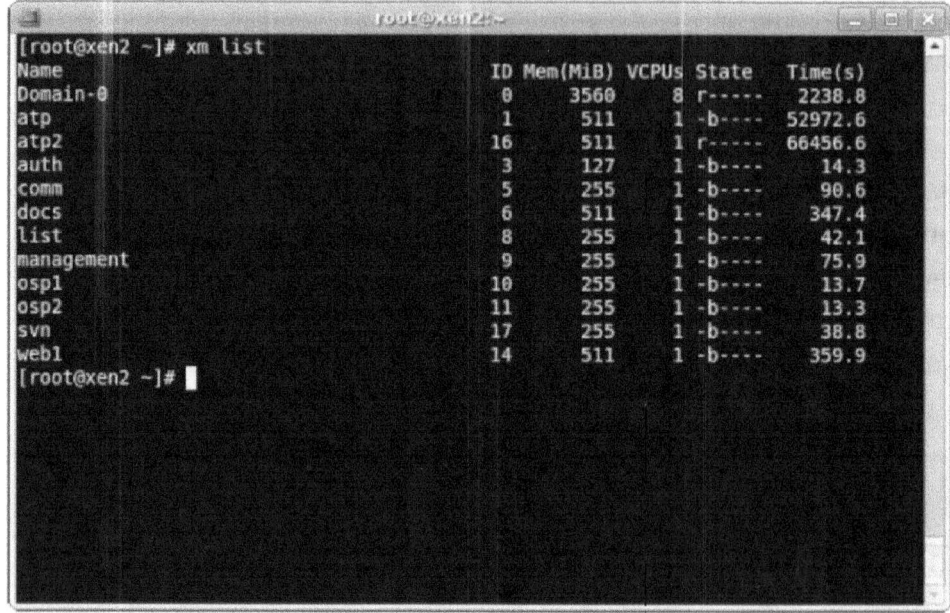

Fig. 2.30 : Xm List Showing Several Vms Running

- If you want to know how long your domains have been running for, then you can use the # xm uptime command.
- You can get access to the console of a particular domain using the # xm console command (e.g. # xm console myVM).

2.8.8.5 Domain Scheduling Management Commands

- The credit CPU scheduler automatically load balances guest VCPUs across all available physical CPUs on an SMP host. The user need not manually pin VCPUs to load balance the system. However, user can restrict which CPUs a particular VCPU may run on using the xm vcpu-pin command.
- Each guest domain is assigned a weight and a cap. A domain with a weight of 512 will get twice as much CPU as a domain with a weight of 256 on a contended host. Legal weights range from 1 to 65535 and the default is 256.
- The cap optionally fixes the maximum amount of CPU a guest will be able to consume, even if the host system has idle CPU cycles. The cap is expressed in percentage of one physical CPU : 100 is 1 physical CPU, 50 is half a CPU, 400 is 4 CPUs and so on. The default, 0, means there is no upper cap.
- When you are running with the credit scheduler, you can check and modify your domain's weights and caps using the xm sched-credit command :

  xm sched-credit -d <domain> lists weight and cap.

  xm sched-credit -d <domain> -w <weight> sets the weight.

  xm sched-credit -d <domain> -c <cap> sets the cap.

2.9 VIRTUAL MACHINE BOOTING AND CONFIGURATION

- Virtual machine configuration is the arrangement of resources assigned to a virtual machine. The resources allocated to a virtual machine (VM) typically include allocated processors, memory, disks, network adapters and the user interface.
- Before you can use virtualization, the virtualization packages must be installed on your computer. Virtualization packages can be installed either during the host installation sequence or after host installation using Subscription Manager.
- Many users install Virtualization Workstation on a dual-boot or multiple-boot computer so they can run one or more of the existing operating systems in a virtual machine. Sometimes you may want to use the existing installation of an operating system rather than reinstall it in a virtual machine.
- To support such installation virtual machine booting makes it possible for you to use a physical IDE disk or partition, also known as a raw disk, inside a virtual machine.

- You may sometimes want to run an operating system inside a virtual machine and at other times want to run that same installation of the operating system by booting the host computer directly into that operating system. If you want to use this approach, you must be aware of some special considerations.

- The issues arise because the virtual hardware that the operating system sees when it is running in a virtual machine is different from the physical hardware it sees when it is running directly on the host computer. It is as if you were removing the boot drive from one physical computer and running the operating system installed there in a second computer with a different motherboard, video card and other peripherals - then moving it back and forth between the two systems.

- The general approach for resolving these issues is to set up platforms for each of the two operating environments - the virtual machine and the physical computer. You can then choose the appropriate platform when you start the operating system. On some hardware, however, booting a previously installed operating system within a virtual machine may not work.

- Virtual machine uses description files to control access to each raw IDE device on the system. These description files contain access privilege information that controls a virtual machine's access to certain partitions on the disks. This mechanism prevents users from accidentally running the host operating system again as a guest or running a guest operating system that the virtual machine was not configured to use. The description file also prevents accidental corruption of raw disk partitions by badly behaved operating systems or applications.

- If a boot manager is installed on the computer system, the boot manager runs inside the virtual machine and presents you with the choice of guest operating systems to run. You must manually choose the guest operating system that this configuration was intended to run.

- If an operating system is installed directly into a virtual machine, the operating system properly detects all the virtual devices by scanning the hardware. However, if an operating system is already installed on the physical computer (for example, in a dual-boot configuration), the operating system already is configured to use the physical hardware devices. In order to boot such a preinstalled operating system in a virtual machine, you need to create separate hardware profiles in order to simplify the boot process.

2.9.1 Creating Up Hardware Profiles in Virtual Machines

- Certain operating systems use hardware profiles to load the appropriate drivers for a given set of hardware devices. If you have a dual-boot system and want to use a virtual machine to boot a previously installed operating system from an existing partition, you must set up "physical" and "virtual" hardware profiles.

- Each virtual machine provides a platform that consists of the following set of virtual devices :

- Virtual DVD/CD-ROM

- Virtual hard disk drives

- Standard PCI graphics adapter

- Standard floppy disk drive

- PCI Bus Master IDE controller

  (includes primary and secondary IDE controllers)

- BusLogic BT-958 compatible SCSI host adapter

- Standard 101/102-key keyboard

- Mouse

- Ethernet adapter

- Serial ports (COM1-COM4)

- Parallel ports (LPT1-LPT2)

- Two-port USB hub

- Sound card compatible with the Sound Blaster AudioPCI

- This set of virtual devices is different from the set of physical hardware devices on the host computer and is independent of the underlying hardware with a few exceptions (the processor itself is such an exception).

- This feature provides a stable platform and allows operating system images installed within a virtual machine to be migrated to other physical machines, regardless of the configuration of the physical machine.

QUESTIONS

1. Explain functionalities provided by Virtualization.

2. Explain difference between multitasking, multithreading and virtualization.

3. Explain XEN Architecture with suitable diagram.

4. Write short note on :

   (a) Virtual machines

   (b) Hypervisor

   (c) Virtual machine monitor

5. Why virtual servers are used ? State its advantages and disadvantages ?

6. State types of virtualization and explain any three of them.

7. Explain Need, Advantages and Limitations of virtualization.

8. What is XEN ? What are the components of XEN Environment ?

9. Explain software and hardware techniques for X86 virtualization.

Unit - III

STORAGE IN CLOUD

3.1 STORAGE SYSTEM ARCHITECTURE

Cloud storage is based on highly virtualized infrastructure and is like broader cloud computing in terms of accessible interfaces, near-instant elasticity and scalability, multi-tenancy, and metered resources. Cloud storage services can be utilized from an off-premises service (Amazon S3) or deployed on-premises (ViON Capacity Services).

Cloud storage typically refers to a hosted object storage service, but the term has broadened to include other types of data storage that are now available as a service, like block storage.

Object storage services like Amazon S3 and Microsoft Azure Storage, object storage software like Openstack Swift, object storage systems like EMC Atmos, EMC ECS and Hitachi Content Platform, and distributed storage research projects like OceanStore and VISION Cloud are all examples of storage that can be hosted and deployed with cloud storage characteristics.

Cloud storage is a model of data storage where the digital data is stored in logical pools, the physical storage spans multiple servers (and often locations), and the physical environment is typically owned and managed by a hosting company. These cloud storage providers are responsible for keeping the data available and accessible, and the physical environment protected and running. People and organizations buy or lease storage capacity from the providers to store user, organization, or application data.

Cloud storage services may be accessed through a co-located cloud computer service, a web service Application Programming Interface (API) or by applications that utilize the API, such as cloud desktop storage, a cloud storage gateway or Web-based content management systems.

Cloud Storage is:
- Made up of many distributed resources, but still acts as one - often referred to as federated storage clouds.
- Highly fault tolerant through redundancy and distribution of data.
- Highly durable through the creation of versioned copies.
- Typically eventually consistent with regard to data replicas.

3.1.1 Three Layer Storage System Architecture

Most cloud storage providers generally follow three-layer architecture. Refer Fig. 3.1.

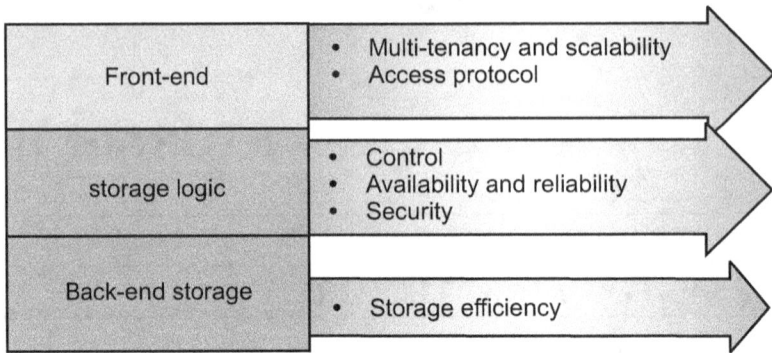

Fig. 3.1 : Three layer storage system architecture

The front end is in charge of the communication between the clients and the servers. There will be different APIs to access the actual storage. This layer is also about achieving results such as *multi-tenan*cy. In addition, it provides the means for different types of scalability through various methods.

The storage logic layer handles a variety of features, and is in charge of certain administrative procedures such as ensuring a high level of availability and reliability for instance. It is also a form of security perimeter. Furthermore, it acts like a controller for cloud storage.

The back-end focuses on the actual implementation of the physical storage of data with protocols such as the GFS (Google File System). It involves the use of various ways to increase storage efficiency and in a way to drive the infrastructure costs down.

The front end and the back end are connected to each other through a network, usually the Internet. The front end is the side the computer user, or client, sees. The back end is the "cloud" section of the system. The front end includes the client's computer (or computer network) and the application required to access the cloud computing system. Not all cloud computing systems have the same user interface. Services like Web-based e-mail programs leverage existing Web browsers like Internet Explorer or Firefox. Other systems have unique applications that provide network access to clients. On the back end of the system are the various computers, servers and data storage systems that create the "cloud" of computing services. In theory, a cloud computing system could include practically any computer program you can imagine, from data processing to video games. Usually, each application will have its own dedicated server. A central server administers the system, monitoring traffic and client demands to ensure everything runs smoothly. It follows a set of rules called protocols and uses a special kind of software called middleware. Middleware allows networked computers to communicate with each other. Most of the time, servers don't run at full capacity. That means there's unused processing power going to waste. It's possible to fool a physical server into thinking it's actually multiple servers, each running with its own independent operating system. The technique is called server virtualization. By maximizing the output of individual servers, server virtualization reduces the need for more physical machines. If a cloud computing company has a lot of clients, there's likely to be a high demand for a lot of storage space. Some companies require hundreds of digital storage devices. Cloud computing systems need at least twice the number of storage devices it requires to keep all its client's information stored. That's because these devices, like all computers, occasionally break down. A cloud computing system must make a copy of all its clients' information and store it on other devices. The copies enable the central server to access backup machines to retrieve data that otherwise would be unreachable. Making copies of data as a backup is called redundancy.

3.1.2 Database in the Cloud

Database is a key component in most computing infrastructures. Database allows users to store data in an organized manner and retrieve them easily.

Relational and Non-Relational Databases

Many cloud computing providers offer users both relational and non-relational databases. Both types of database are scalable in the cloud and can be highly available. However relational cloud databases perform create, update and delete operations faster than non-relational cloud databases. However, for read operations, non-relational cloud databases do perform better than relational cloud databases. Usage-wise, both relational and non-relational cloud databases are as easy to use as the other. This is because cloud computing providers take on most of the burden of database administration, especially for relational databases, as relational databases usually come with heavy database administration workload compared to non-relational databases.

Non-relational databases are commonly referred to by the term NoSQL. They are made up of individual tables and these tables cannot have defined relationships between them, unlike in relational databases. With these databases one can retrieve the account balance of a specific Customer given the Customer's name through table joins using SQL due to the Primary Key/Foreign Key relationship. In a non-relational database for the same schema, without the relationship, the developer has to use application code to obtain the Customer's account number and then access the Account table and match the account number obtained previously to retrieve the balance.

Cloud-based Database

- **Amazon Relational Database Service**

Amazon Relational Database Service (Amazon RDS) is a service from Amazon (among Amazon Web Services), which provides cloud-based relational database service. Since it support Oracle and MySQL (two popular relational database system), many users can transfer their existing relational database to the cloud easily. Amazon provides several types of pre-configured database instance (a dedicated cloud instance to store database, with either MySQL or Oracle database system installed), with sensible parameters to help user launching their database easier.

The database instance can range from small one (which is comparable to a regular computer), to high end one, which could be as powerful as 20-30 regular computers. For any instance, user can select a storage capacity from 5 Gb to 1 TB and if user need more, they can easily launch more instances. After the user transfers their database to Amazon RDS, Amazon will take care of storing and back up the data, and help user recover the data if any bad things could happen. Amazon RDS also provides metrics about the database instance's health through Amazon Cloud Watch, just like a normal EC2 instance.

As a Cloud Services, Amazon RDS takes care of the infrastructure works required, and gives developers the ability to scale their resources and storage capacity easily, so that they can handle more requests from clients. Developer can also take advantage of some functions that Amazon RDS offers, such as : Multi A-Z deployment and Read replicas (for MySQL database), to enhance availability and scalability for their database.

- **Amazon Dynamo Database**

Amazon DynamoDB is a service from Amazon that provide NoSQL database service with seamless scalability. It allows user to launch a new Amazon DynamoDB database table, and scale up or down their request capacity for the table without downtime or performance degradation. Similar to Amazon RDS and many other cloud services, it also provides monitoring information about resource utilization and performance.

Amazon DynamoDB stores data in key-value fashion: Database consists of multiple tables of data. In each table, there are multiple items (the rows), each item has multiple attributes. As a NoSQL Database, Amazon DynamoDB does not has any schema (except the restriction that there need to be a primary key for the table). Each items can have any number of attribute (doesn't need to be the same among different items), but the item size need to be smaller than 64 KB. Each attribute, can be a single value or multi-valued set, is stored as a name-value pair. However, the attribute cannot has null or empty string value.

Amazon DynamoDB is an evolution from the earlier NoSQL Database service from Amazon (Amazon SimpleDB). It inherits the most prominent features of SimpleDB: that is the simplicity in database administration. Yet, it brings a lot of improvements from Amazon's Dynamo technology (a powerful, ultra-scalable NoSQL database system that is used internally at Amazon). Amazon takes care of the underlying technology (spread the data and traffic over many servers) to provide high availability and scalability for the database.

- **Google Datastore**

Google Datastore (App Engine Datastore) is the main data storage service for Google App Engine applications. It's a NoSQL database system, built on top of Google's own Big table database structure. As a NoSQL database system, Google Datastore is a schema-less database. It stores data in data objects known as entities. Each entity is categorized into some categories known as its kind (for query purpose), and it keeps a key (which is not mutable) to identifies itself from other entities of the same kind. Each entity has one or more properties, which is a named value of some supported data types.

Google Datastore offers two data storage options: High Replication Datastore (HRD), which makes use of Paxos architecture to enhance reliability and availability, and Master/Slave Datastore, which makes use of Master-slave architecture to ensure strong consistency for database operations.

As a Cloud database service, in particularly a NoSQL database system, Google Datastore uses a distributed architecture to help increase the scalability for the database system. It can scale easily to extremely large data sets, while still maintaining good performance.

- **Google Cloud SQL**

Google Cloud SQL is a web services from Google that provides relational database service for Application deployed on Google App Engine. This is a new feature from Google App Engine and it's currently in limited preview phase. Google Cloud SQL supports MySQL database, with feature to import or export from existing MySQL database into and out of the cloud. As Google Cloud SQL is designed to ensure reliability and availability, it supports replication of data in different availability regions.

Currently, Google Cloud SQL only support Java-based and Python-based application. To use it, developers need to use JDBC (Java Database Connectivity) to connect to the database if their application is a Java-based application, or DB-API if their application is a Python-based application.

Similar to Amazon Relational Database service, the underlying database system in Google Cloud SQL is fully managed by Google, so user can be saved from redundant and tiring tasks such as patch management for the database. On top of it, a rich GUI is provided to help user to managing, monitoring and configuring their database system easily.

3.1.3 Architectures of Cloud Databases

Cloud databases providers often let users choose from multiple database architectures. Since these different architectures have different levels of database consistency, latency and costs, you need to understand the architectures to have a better idea of which service suits your application's needs. We will discuss two different architectures which are being used by major cloud service providers here - the Master/Slave architecture and the architecture based on the Paxos algorithm.

In the Master/Slave database architecture (see Fig. 3.2), a database server acts as the *Master*. When the user sends in a write/delete request to his database, the request goes to the *Master* database server. The *Master* database server checks against and updates its own database and then asynchronously replicates the update in other *Slave* database servers.

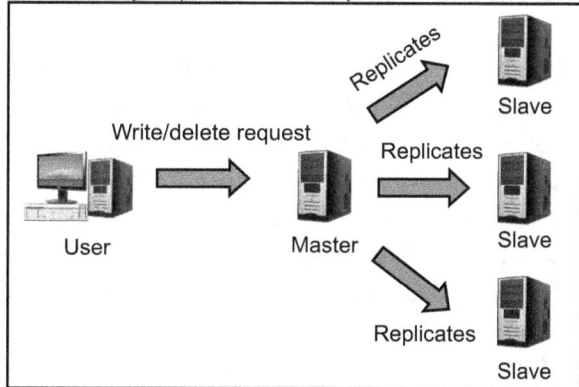

Fig. 3.2 : Master / Salave architecture

For the Paxos architecture (see Fig. 3.3), when the user sends a write/delete request, this request goes to a network of several database servers. The different database servers will check the requests against their own databases and states and then communicate with each other to affirm the request. There are numerous pros and cons of using one database architecture over the other.

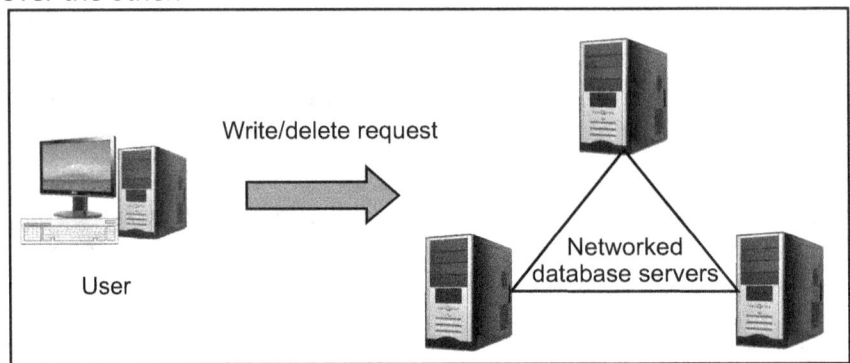

Fig. 3.3 : Paxos architecture

Master/Slave Architectures uses Lesser Write/Delete CPU Time :

Databases built on the Paxos architecture use more write CPU time than databases built on the Master/Slave architecture due to the servers needing to communicate with each other to affirm the write/delete request, unlike in the Master/Slave database architecture, where the Master itself affirms the request and sends the affirmed changes to the Slaves.

Master/Slave Architecture has Lower Write/Delete Latency : It is higher for the databases built on the Paxos architecture as the affirming of requests between the various servers takes time.

Master/Slave Architectures have Stronger Query Consistency : Query consistency of databases built on Paxos architecture is "eventual" as they require time to process certain tricky requests among the data centres - a read request might come in before the processing of a previous write/delete request can be completed, resulting in the read request not getting the most up-to-date results.

Paxos Architectures have Higher Availability and Reliability : Databases built on Paxos architecture do not suffer from downtimes like their counterparts built on Master/Slave architecture. For example, if the Master data centre for a certain database built on Master/Slave architecture goes down for maintenance, write/delete requests will not be processed. However for databases built on the Paxos architecture, the user's database can still be updated even if a data centre goes down, as long as there are other data centres that remain operational, since any of the data centres can process the write/delete request.

The overview of the two different architectures should now give you a better understanding of why some databases offered by cloud computing providers are more costly than others or why there is higher consistency for some types of database over the others for example. Moreover, the two types of architectures covered can also serve as examples for you to make use of infrastructures offered by cloud computing providers to model and build your very own cloud database architecture.

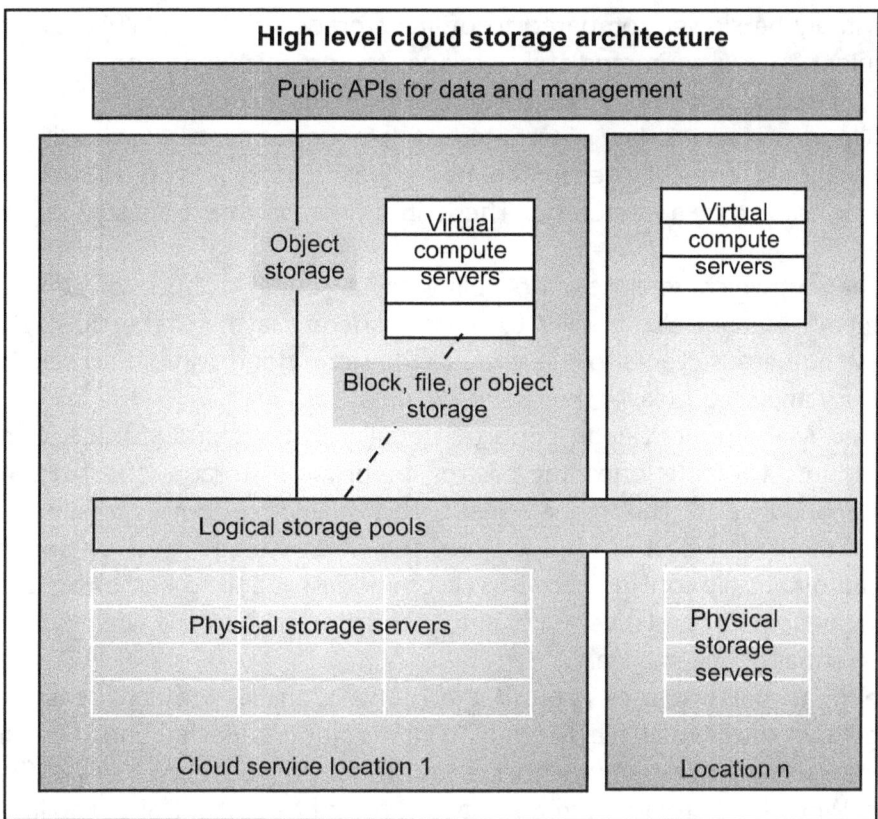

Fig. 3.4 : High level cloud storage architecture

3.1.4 Cloud Storage Characteristics

- **Integration**

Before utilizing the cloud storage, an organization will need to integrate the cloud storage into their existing work-flow or other forms of offline storage facilities. The fact is normal file servers and cloud storage services do not use the same file access protocols. Servers use block protocol access to their storage, but cloud storage services generally only provides web protocol access such as REST-based APIs, SOAP-based APIs which are APIs designed on-top of the HTTP protocol to provide access with better efficiency. Each of the major providers has their separate set of APIs to handle the operations. This complicates things a little.

Mature organizations generally have more complicated existing file storage workflows. A considerable amount of time, money and attention will have to be spent to integrate the use of cloud storage into their existing workflows. On the other hand, a younger organization with a less complex infrastructure will not face the same problem because it will certainly be easier to integrate cloud storage into a workflow that is not so developed yet.

- **Performance and Latency**

Cloud storage may be used by organizations for periodic backups of massive amounts of data. These back-up operations will involve sending data to a geographically distant location.

This will inevitably be slower compared to offline storage solutions. While cloud storage is more convenient to use, is immediately scalable for organizations and more reliable, but unfortunately speed-wise it still trails behind offline storage solutions.

In general, cloud storage today is targeted at less performance demanding operations. Organizations should generally leave the operations having a stringent requirement for performance outside of cloud-storage. These include real-time transactions in banks for example.

- **Multi-tenancy**, which refers to the ability for a single instance of services to serve multiple clients or tenants, also applies to several different layers of the cloud storage stack and this allows numerous clients to subscribe to the same cloud computing capabilities while retaining privacy and security over their sensitive data.

- **Automated Management** is an important quality of the cloud storage. Generally, cost can be divided into two categories: the cost of the physical storage infrastructure itself and the cost of managing it. The management cost is hidden but is really a substantial component of the overall cost in the long run. The cloud storage must be able to add new storage and automatically conFig. 3.itself to accommodate it and to find errors automatically. Automated management is relatively critical to cloud storage because what cloud computing is selling is essentially convenience.

- **Consistency in performance around the globe** is one of the core reasons to choose cloud storage over traditional file hosting. With traditional file hosting, files are typically stored on one server hence clients who are far away from that server will suffer from bad performance. With cloud storage, there are two levels of geographical scalability. Firstly, the file is distributed around multiple servers in the region where your original data is stored at. Secondly, there are on-demand CDNs (Content Delivery Networks). These are networks that have servers distributed globally to allow fast content delivery to clients anywhere in the world. By using CDNs, cloud storage can also achieve the same high level of consistency in performance all around the world and also make your data more mobile because it is available and highly accessible at all parts of the world.

- **Unique access methods** are also one of the main differences between cloud storage and traditional storage. Many cloud storage providers now implement multiple access methods but the most prevalent one is still the Web-Service API. These are implemented by following the REST (Representational State Transfer) architecture. The architecture is used to develop protocols over the layer of HTTP to harness HTTP as a transport utility. By following this architecture, APIs are stateless and therefore relatively efficient. Bigger cloud storage providers such as Amazon (S3) and Microsoft Azure are both currently using this approach. There are also other forms of access methods such as file based APIs such as NFS and FTP and these two APIs are adopted by IBM Smart Business Storage Cloud.

- **High Reliability** is one of the cornerstones of cloud storage. One might think that with the technological advances today, hard-disk failures and mass information losses are no longer common. On the contrary, hardware failures are inevitable and could be devastating if backups were not adequate. Cloud providers generally use two different approaches to ensure reliability.

- **Replication :** Big cloud service providers generally have the same information stored on multiple machines. In the case of Google, their cloud back-end storage is typically split into huge clusters and entirely broken into chunks of 64 MB each. Each of these chunks is uniquely identifiable and they are replicated to multiple servers in their data centers. Furthermore, these machines are run on different power supplies. That way, even if one power supply fails, clients will still have access to their data.

- **Reconstruction :** Some service providers also use data-reconstruction algorithms to help with lost or damaged data. One of these algorithms is IDA (Information Dispersal Algorithm). This algorithm is able to construct a full set of data from multiple parts of the data that has been distributed before-hand. For example, if the data is divided into four parts, it can still be reconstructed if one site holding one part of the data is lost. Different ratios are possible to implement as well. E.g. 20 parts will allow eight failed sites. These pieces of data are usually distributed at different geographical locations to reduce the chances of all parts of the data being lost at one time.

- **Good cost-to-storage ratio** is another characteristic of cloud storage that is worth mentioning. To reduce cost, more data must be stored with the same hardware resources. One common way to do this is to use data-reduction algorithms to reduce the resources data take up. There are notably two different approaches to this: *compression*- the encoding of the data in another more economical representation to achieve data reduction, *de-duplication* the removal of any identical copies of data found through the scanning of data signatures.

- **High levels of security** are essential to cloud storage, in particular, when storing sensitive data on the cloud.

3.1.5 Cloud Storage Providers

Amazon Elastic Block System (EBS)

Amazon Elastic Block System, referred to as Amazon EBS, allows you to attach storage volumes ranging from 1 GB to 1 TB onto EC2 instances.

One of the most important feature that EBS has is its snapshot function. Snapshots, as the name implies lets you store the current status of the EBS, allowing you to restore data, or replicate the data easily. If granted access, such snapshots can also be shared with other users, allowing other users to access the same basis towards your EBS, making working together much easier.

New users are provided with 30 GB of EBS storage, 2 million I/O and 1 GB of snapshot storage for each month for one year.

- **Amazon Simple Storage Service (Amazon S3)1**

Amazon Simple Storage Service, or more commonly known as S3, refers to a storage that Amazon provides for users. These storage are usually referred to as buckets. S3 allows you to store countless objects of each consisting up to 5 TB in size. This is mainly used to store your data and to work alongside EC2 or other services. To ensure durability and reliability, S3 copies the data provided by you in multiple facilities in your chosen region to ensure your data is safe and retrievable. Amazon also provides a Amazon S3 Encryption Client library should you want to encrypt your data for security reasons.

An additional option, called the Reduced Redundancy Storage (RRS) tries to lower costs further by replicating the data in less locations. However, this option is for less important data, as it is in a slightly more risky situation as compared to S3 itself.

For new users, they are given 5 GB of Amazon S3 storage, 20,000 Get Requests, 2,000 Put Requests, and 15 GB of data transfer out each month for one year.

- **Amazon Import/Export**

Amazon Import/Export is a service that Amazon provides, where you may ship a storage device to the address they give you so that they can directly transfer the large amounts of data in your storage device into or out of S3 or EBS. Such a direct transfer is much faster than having to go through the internet, though it might cost more with regards to the shipping costs. You may then quickly obtain the required data that you may need to perhaps retrieve some data, or share it with other business associates.

- **Amazon Storage Gateway**

Currently, Amazon Storage Gateway is still under beta testing. However, this feature allows you to shift data from your on-premises storage onto S3 to ensure its availability and durability. To make things even more efficient, these data are stored as EBS snapshots within S3, allowing you to easily retrieve these snapshots with EBS replication and EC2 commands to attach the EBS storage. The transfer speed can be further improved with AWS Direct Connect where a private connection is established between you and AWS just for the transfer of files.

Some popular Cloud Storage providers includes Microsoft Azure, JustCloud, zipCloud and livedrive. The providers I have just mentioned differs slightly from what a simple user might want, to simply store some of their files on their hardisk on Cloud. These providers allow us to access the files via methods that can be used in sites or web development. New users may not be so familiar with Cloud and may want to test Cloud out before joining the community. In that case, we recommend Amazon Web Services, that is both user friendly, a year with limited free usage, as well as many functionalities that help you start up.

3.1.6 Characteristics of Cloud Databases

- **Portability**

Moving to a Cloud-based database system means the user needs to transfer their existing data from their current database to the cloud. Especially with organizations who currently use traditional relational database and have lots of existing data, portability is really needed. For these organization, choosing some relational database systems on the cloud, such as Amazon Relational Database services (which support Oracle and MySQL database, with import, export feature), or Google Cloud SQL (which is currently in limited preview phase, which also support import, export existing data) is a sensible solution.

In addition, the migration possibility of database from one cloud-computing provider to another, or even from a cloud-computing provider to your own server, matters. There might be unexpected circumstances that occur, forcing the user to drop the current cloud-computing provider and moving to another one. Therefore, before actually settling on a particular database from a particular cloud-computing provider, the user needs to consider if they can easily port their application and its database code after they have implemented it.

- **Reliability and Availability**

For database that requires high reliability and availability, a cloud-based database that offer replication of data is really important.

For example, Amazon Relation Database Services offer a feature that could help to ensure reliability for the data: Multi AZ deployment. When user enable this and run their instance as a Multi AZ instance, Amazon RDS will automatically create and manage a "standby" replica in a different Availability Zone. Database updates are performed to both primary and standby database at the same time. The standby database cannot be used to serve read traffic, but it can be used to replace the primary one in case of database maintenance or database instance failure. It helps to ensure reliability and availability for the database system in case of any incident.

Google Cloud SQL is also designed to cater for database with high replication application, because it is designed with inherent support for replication of data in different availability regions. Google Datastore (a NoSQL db system) offers the model High-Replication Datastore (HRD), using Paxos architecture to increase reliability and availability for the database sytem.

However, with database that does not require high replication of data, using database service with these feature could badly affects the performance of the application.

- **Scalability**

Scalability is one of the main reasons why companies should consider using cloud-based database system, because most cloud-based database systems are designed to offer users with easier scalability than traditional database systems.

For users with some existing database systems, who just want to improve their database performance, and take advantage of a cloud solution, but at the same time requires complex transaction operations (such as join query) and complex relations among data in their database, the solution of moving their existing database system to a cloud service like Amazon Relational Database Service or Google Cloud SQL is a great option to consider.

However, for applications that really demands performance and scalability instead of complex database operation, or the data stored is not well-structured, any relational database system, due to the innate nature of relational database, will not perform as good as NoSQL database system for extremely large amount of data. Therefore, a NoSQL database solution on the Cloud such as DynamoDB (from Amazon), or Google Datastore (used for Google App Engine), is much more suitable. For Amazon DynamoDB, all the users need to do is specify the level of traffic they wish to serve, and Amazon will take care of all the works of scaling up the system to ensure the application could serve the desired traffic level.

3.2 BIG DATA

Organizations are increasingly generating large volumes of data as result of business processes, monitoring of user activity, web site tracking, sensors, finance, accounting, among other reasons. With the advent of social network Web sites, users create records of their lives by daily posting details of activities they perform, events they attend, places they visit, pictures they take, and things they enjoy and want. This data flood is often referred to as Big Data.

Big data is a term utilized to refer to the increase in the volume of data that are difficult to store, process, and analyze through traditional database technologies. The nature of big data is indistinct and involves considerable processes to identify and translate the data into new insights. The term "big data" is relatively new in IT and business. However, several researchers and practitioners have utilized the term in previous literature. For instance, big data can be referred as a large volume of scientific data for visualization. Several definitions of big data currently exist. For instance, defined big data as "the amount of data just beyond technology's capability to store, manage, and process efficiently." Meanwhile, and defined big data as characterized by three Vs: volume, variety, and velocity. The terms volume, variety, and velocity were originally introduced by Gartner to describe the elements of big data challenges. IDC also defined big data technologies as "a new generation of technologies and architectures, designed to economically extract value from very large volumes of a wide variety of data, by enabling the high velocity capture, discovery, and/or analysis." specified that big data is not only characterized by the three Vs mentioned above but may also extend to four Vs, namely, volume, variety, velocity, and value. This 4V definition is widely recognized because it highlights the meaning and necessity of big data.

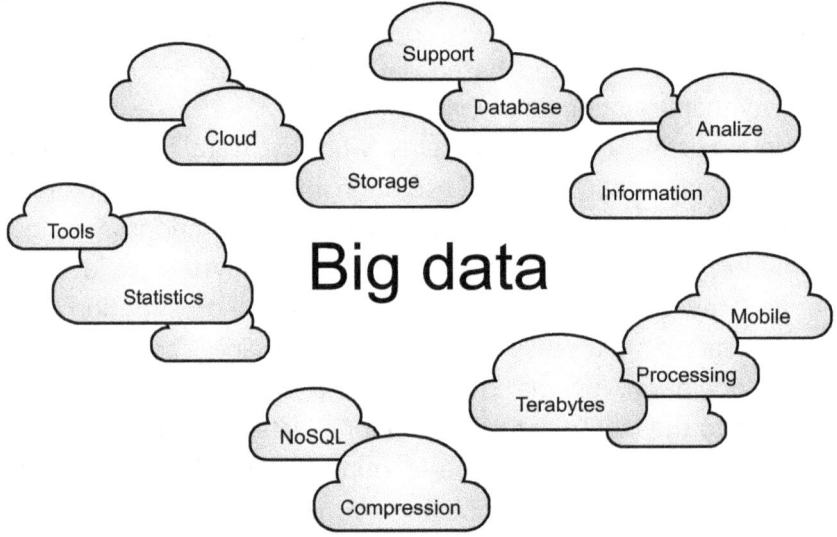

Fig. 3.5 : Big Data

Big data is an evolving term that describes any voluminous amount of structured, semi-structured and unstructured data that has the potential to be mined for information.

Although big data doesn't refer to any specific quantity, the term is often used when speaking about petabytes and exabytes of data.

In other way, big data is the realization of greater business intelligence by storing, processing, and analyzing data that was previously ignored due to the limitations of traditional data management technologies.

The Four Dimensions of Big Data :

- Volume : Large volumes of data
- Velocity : Quickly moving data
- Variety : Structured, unstructured, images, etc.
- Veracity : Trust and integrity is a challenge and a must and is important for big data just as for traditional relational Data Base. (Refer Fig. 3.5)

3.2.1 Big Data Mining

Big Data mining is the capability of extracting useful information from these large datasets or streams of data, that due to its volume, variability, and velocity, it was not possible before to do it.

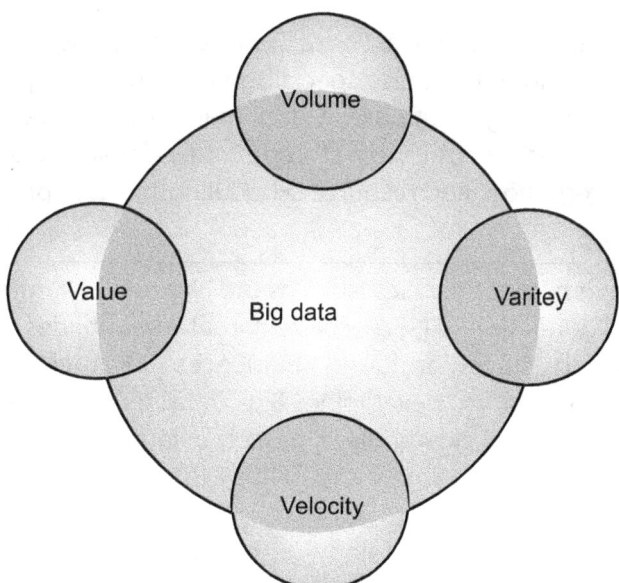

Fig. 3.6 : Four dimensions of big data

Big data is a term that presents the challenges it poses on existing infrastructure with respect to storage, management, interoperability, governance, and analysis of the data.

In today's competitive market, being able to explore data to understand customer behavior, segment customer base, offer customized services, and gain insights from data provided by multiple sources is key to competitive advantage. Although decision makers would like to base their decisions and actions on insights gained from this data, making sense of data, extracting non obvious patterns, and using these patterns to predict future behavior become very common. Knowledge Discovery in Data (KDD) aims to extract non obvious information using careful and detailed analysis and interpretation. Data mining more specifically, aims to discover previously unknown interrelations among apparently unrelated attributes of data sets by applying methods from several areas including machine learning, database systems, and statistics. Analytics comprises techniques of KDD, data mining, text mining, statistical and quantitative analysis, explanatory and predictive models, and advanced and interactive visualization to drive decisions and actions.

Data from various sources, including databases, streams, marts, and data warehouses, are used to build models. The large volume and different types of the data can demand pre-processing tasks for integrating the data, cleaning it, and filtering it. The prepared data is used to train a model and to estimate its parameters. Once the model is estimated, it should be validated before its consumption. Normally this phase requires the use of the original input data and specific methods to validate the created model. Finally, the model is consumed and applied to data as it arrives. This phase, called model scoring, is used to generate predictions, prescriptions, and recommendations. The results are interpreted and evaluated, used to generate new models or calibrate existing ones, or are integrated to pre-processed data.

To achieve economies of scale and elasticity, Cloud-enabled Big Data analytics needs to explore means to allocate and utilize these specialized resources in a proper manner. The rest of this section discusses existing solutions on data management irrespective of where data experts are physically located, focusing on storage and retrieval of data for analytics; data diversity, velocity and integration; and resource scheduling for data processing tasks.

3.2.2 Opportunities

Recently, several US government agencies, such as the National Institutes of Health (NIH) and the National Science Foundation (NSF), ascertain that the utilities of Big Data to data-intensive decision-making have profound influences in their future developments. Consequently, they are trying to developing Big Data technologies and techniques to facilitate their missions after US government passed a large-scale Big Data initiative. This initiative is very helpful for building new capabilities for exploiting informative knowledge and facilitate decision-makers.

From the Networking Information Technology Research and Development (NITRD) program which is recently recognized by President's Council of Advisors on Science and Technology (PCAST), we know that the bridges between Big Data and knowledge hidden in it are highly crucial in all areas of national priority. This initiative will also lay the groundwork for complementary Big Data activities, such as Big Data infrastructure projects, platforms development, and techniques in settling complex, data-driven problems in sciences and engineering. Finally, they will be put into practice and benefit society.

According to the report from McKinsey institute, the effective use of Big Data has the underlying benefits to transform economies, and delivering a new wave of productive growth. Taking advantages of valuable knowledge beyond Big Data will become the basic competition for today's enterprises and will create new competitors who are able to attract employees that have the critical skills on Big Data. Researchers, policy and decision makers have to recognize the potential of harnessing Big Data to uncover the next wave of growth in their fields. There are many advantages in business section that can be obtained through harnessing Big including increasing operational efficiency, informing strategic direction, developing better customer service, identifying and developing new products and services, identifying new customers and markets, etc.

3.2.3 Challenges

Opportunities are always followed by challenges. On the one hand, Big Data bring many attractive opportunities. On the other hand, we are also facing a lot of challenges when handle Big Data problems, difficulties lie in data capture, storage, searching, sharing, analysis, and visualization. If we cannot surmount those challenges, Big Data will become a gold ore but we do not have the capabilities to explore it, especially when information surpass our capability to harness. One challenge is existing in computer architecture for several decades, that is, CPU-heavy but I/O-poor. This system imbalance still restrain the development of the discovery from Big Data.

The CPU performance is doubling each 18 months following the Moore's Law, and the performance of disk drives is also doubling at the same rate. However, the disk's rotational speed has slightly improved over the last decade. The consequence of this imbalance is that random I/O speeds have improved moderately while sequential I/O speeds increase with density slowly. Moreover, information is increasing at exponential rate simultaneously, but the improvement of information processing methods is also relatively slower. In a lot of important Big Data applications, the state-of-the-art techniques and technologies cannot ideally solve the real problems, especially for real-time analysis. So partially speaking, until now, we do not have the proper tools to exploit the gold ores completely. Typically, the knowledge is discovered in data mining. Challenges in Big Data analysis include data inconsistence and incompleteness, scalability, timeliness and data security. As the prior step to data analysis, data must be well-constructed. However, considering variety of data sets in Big Data problems, it is still a big challenge for us to purpose efficient representation, access, and analysis of unstructured or semi-structured data in the further researches. How can the data be preprocessed in order to improve the quality data and the analysis results before we begin data analysis? As the sizes of data set are often very huge, sometimes several gigabytes or more, and their origin from heterogeneous sources, current real-world databases are severely susceptible to inconsistent, incomplete, and noisy data. Therefore, a number of data preprocessing techniques, including data cleaning, data integration, data transformation and date reduction, can be applied to remove noise and correct inconsistencies.

3.3 VIRTUALIZE DATA CENTER (VDC) ARCHITECTURE AND ENVIRONMENT

Today almost all the operational organizations and their units cannot work without automated machines or computers. The dependency over the computer systems developed dramatically. The desire for the very perfect, highly speedy and less error-prone calculations of humans, made the computer systems famous and deployable in almost every sector of the business and its intelligence. Today we can observe the long distant but a reliable connectivity between different computer systems has been faithfully accepted. Human interventions have been reduced. A single data storage source has made the remote and distributed businesses connected. But somewhere down the line, each of these operational scenarios has to be monitored and controlled by a ultra-mega-super System a collection of multiple server systems gathered at a common place for a special purpose A DATA CENTER. Data Center is critical for corporal operations, monitoring networks and keeping control over all business intelligence activities. Businesses bloom over the operations of data center today. Data Center systems are like building or a portion of building whose primary function is to house a computer system and its support areas. This paper aims to introduce the concept of Virtualized data centers that can play a vital role in today's very challenging domain of Cloud Computing.

A dramatic transformation in the way Information Technology (IT) departments operate has put their directors and managers at crossroads. On one side, they're under pressure to deliver higher levels of service and be more responsive to enabling competitive business objectives. On the other side, IT departments are equally pressured to constrain their budgets, "do a lot more with a lot less," and reflect ROI that is as positive as possible from optimization initiatives. Savvy IT leaders have begun to resolve both sides of this conflict by rethinking their virtualization strategies. Originally considered a way to improve utilization of physical servers, virtualization has since been expanded to turn entire data centers into dynamic, agile, services-oriented architectures. These architectures can now accelerate business objectives and competitiveness.

Data center virtualization is a rare chance for IT. The cost savings are remarkable to a great extent. The efficient sharing of servers, storage space and network assets translate into far lower capital purchases and operating expenses. Wasteful application "silos" are eliminated. With virtualization at the data center level, it can now be compatible with more applications, get them implemented quicker, and stick to higher levels of service. It also provides IT managers powerful new tools for scheduling, protection and recovery.

Now, with the prospect of cloud computing on the near horizon, IT organizations also face another transformative landscape :

How best to use data center virtualization as a springboard to either access third-party cloud services to build their own private cloud platform with many of the same economies and efficiencies touted by third-party cloud providers.

For some organizations, full data center virtualization offers the most benefit. While some others take data center virtualization even further and develop a highly automated and standardized "cloud model."

Either way, IT must become more efficient and agile to meet increasing business demands and remain relevant and strategic to the organization. It also risks creating operational challenges as virtualization scales up.

Virtualization was originally a way to improve utilization of physical servers. Now it's being expanded to turn entire data centers into a more dynamically, service-centered architecture ones that accelerate business objectives and competitiveness.

3.3.1 Challenges for IT

In most companies, IT departments are cost centers. It caters the support required for increasing revenue and profits, certainly, but its operations still weigh on the expense side of the spreadsheet. IT directors and managers are under constant pressure to deliver more services and resources to the organization while reducing both capital outlays and expenses. Here are some challenges they face:

- **Low Utilization**

Server virtualization has highlighted the traditionally low utilization of applications running on physical servers sometimes as low as five to ten percent. The tremendous growth of applications and their supporting infrastructure put IT under pressure to optimize physical resources storage and internal networks.

- **Energy and Environmental Costs**

A data center full of hardware consumes a lot of energy to both power the systems and keep them cool. Energy costs can add up to a significant percentage of the IT budget, while utility rates typically increase every year. In some communities, additional power does not exist. To top it up, some companies have adopted "green" operating principles that put extra pressure on IT departments to conserve energy at the same time they're asked to provide more services.

- **Complex Operations**

Application-centric data center architectures can lead to silos of architecture of the infrastructure. These arrays of resources are provably redundant and not so efficient, prevent resource sharing, and add complexity to the number of environments that must be managed.

- **Lack of Agility**

Every new enterprise application takes time to install, configure, patch, debug and put into production. Meanwhile, almost every smart-phone user has become accustomed to downloading and installing applications in minutes.

Business owners recognize that new delivery models can significantly reduce the time required to provision applications thus increasing competitiveness and profits. Organizations simply can't afford to waste time building whole new infrastructures every time somebody wants a new tool. Delivering applications much more efficiently than in the past is a major IT challenge.

- **Economic Impact**

In the era of Return on Investment, even cost centers such as IT are expected to show an immediate return on their expenditures. This is especially difficult given the typically low utilization of existing systems, plus the fact that most of the IT budget is dedicated to be under the limelight. As companies take incremental steps toward data center virtualization, they should expect positive returns with operational improvements.

Data Center is a facility used to house computer systems and is associated with the components, such as telecommunications and storage systems. Cloud computing is a method of delivering computing services from a large, highly virtualized data center to many independent end users, using shared applications and pooled resources. While there are many different definitions for cloud computing, it is typically distinguished by the following attributes: on-demand self-service, broad network access, resource pooling, rapid and elastic resource provisioning, and metered service at various quality levels. Implementation of these attributes as part of a large enterprise-class cloud computing service that provides continuous availability to a large number of users typically requires significantly more server, networking, and storage resources than conventional data centers. This is only achievable through extensive use of virtualization. This is achievable only through extensive use of virtualization. While server virtualization has existed since the 1960s, when it was first implemented on IBM mainframes, it has only become widely available on affordable commodity x86 servers within the last decade or so.

In recent years, many equipment vendors have contributed to the hardware and software infrastructure, which has made enterprise-class virtualization widely available. This, in turn, enables new designs for cloud computing, including hosting multiple independent tenants on a shared infrastructure, rapid and dynamic provisioning of new features, and implementing advanced load balancing, security, and business continuity functions (including multisite transaction mirroring). This has brought about profound changes in many aspects of data center design, including new requirements for the data center network. Data Center generally includes redundant or backup power supplies, redundant data communications connections, environmental controls (e.g., air conditioning, fire suppression) and security devices. Also known as the server farm or the computer room, and is deployed where the majority of an enterprise servers and storage are located, operated and managed. For Example, The National Climatic Data Center (NCDC) is a public data center that maintains the world's largest archive of weather information. A private data center may exist within an organization's facilities or may be maintained as a specialized facility. Every organization has a data center, although it might be referred to as a server room or even a computer closet. Functionality a restricted access area containing automated systems that constantly monitor server activity, Web traffic, and network performance, etc. To cope up with above mentioned problems, taking consideration of dedicated virtualizations and its inter-related technology to design high end systems like Data Center is the only sensible solution to the problem. Every time we cannot compete with the hardware, in fact whatever the advancement in the software be made, we just cannot match the pace of dedicated hardware units which are designed for a special purpose, ex; RAID (Redundant Array of Independent Disks). But still, today even the desktop home PC processors have been developed and advanced enough to serve this motto. They are capable to produce multithreaded programs and run them, so we can certainly choose for this solution of Virtualized Data Center.

Basic motives that we must have a data center in today's era of computing: Today each and every business thrives on data and internet and IT operations are a crucial aspect of most organizational operations. When we have many servers to take care of, bringing them together and keeping them at a centralized location so that their maintenance and monitoring becomes easier is the only option. i.e. The purpose of data center Important for any organization that owns a number of servers, since datacenters bring everything at one place. They can be proved very effective against initial errors such as manual intervention with data, software or hardware failures.

When there is centralized location of all critical hardware of a business group. A data plan of an enterprise should be able to work against all the odds such as manual errors, application failures, natural and man-made disasters such as fire, theft, floods etc.

The data center stores not only servers but also routers and switches that help the servers to communicate with one another at one place. It offers high availability and business continuity. When one server fails, the others take over, providing you a seamless experience. It accommodates all the changes as a business grows.

You can maximize the usage of your own networking assets to improve company internal network operations and many other technical and non-technical benefits.

3.3.2 Architecture of Virtual Data Centers

At present the technology era attempts for Tier-III architecture when it come to the moment of designing a high performance, scalable and dependable data center; which indeed has become a critical issue because of the increasing use of the Internet in supporting various Web-based services.

As the network bandwidth continues to increase faster than the server capacity, data centers are anticipated to be bottleneck in hosting network based services. It has been observed that the data centers contribute, to approximately 40% of the overall Fig. 3.shows a typical three-tier architecture of data center. This architecture is a SOA i.e. Service Oriented Architecture. In this architecture, the frontend Web server is the closest to the edge of a data center and is responsible for handling the static requests. The middle tier, called the *application server,* is responsible for handling the dynamic Web contents, while the back-end *database server* is dedicated for complex database contents, while the back-end database server is dedicated for complex database transactions. Almost all cluster based web servers/data centers use TCP/IP over Ethernet for supporting inter/intra cluster communication.

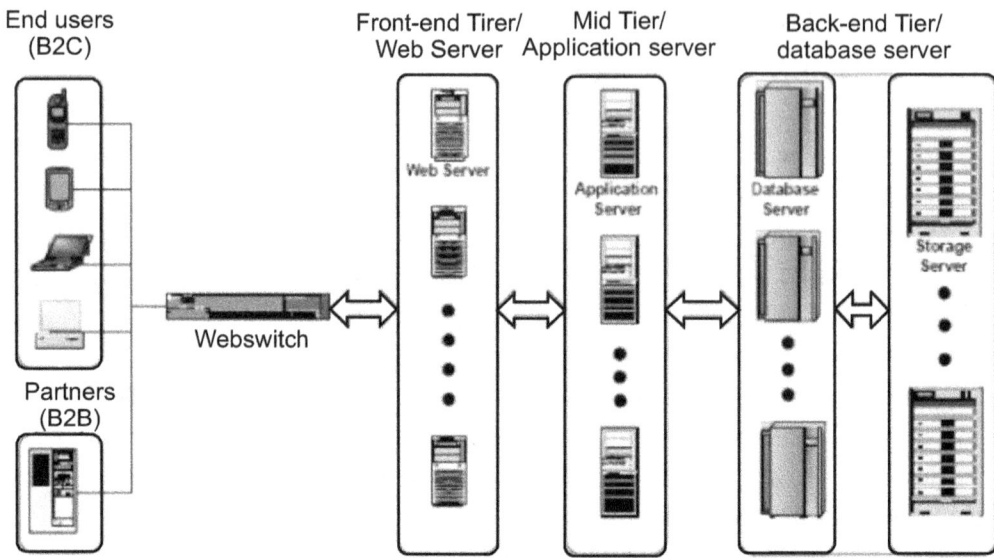

Fig. 3.7 : Three tier VDC architecture

Very few of them have exploited the advantage of switching to a user-level communication so as to enhance the communication performance. So this actually suits more to cloud. In the area of high-performance scientific computing employing clusters, it has been demonstrated that user-level communication mechanisms such as the Virtual Interface Architecture (VIA) can significantly reduce the communication overhead by minimizing the kernel involvement in message transfer. Basically this architecture is just a part of cores of architecture, as depicted in Fig. 3.7.

Basically in the proposed architecture, there is a main super-server that actually acts as a main management server and all the servers are consolidated inside this. The advantage of consolidating these many servers is that we can get maximum throughput from this and we also have mathematically well-improved percentage of overall performance. For this purpose virtualize the server. That means try to build maximum number of the servers virtually in a single powerful hardware, but all of them should be virtual. The advantage of virtualized servers is that we can restore them very easily and successfully by the feature called "Snapshots" of the systems this feature is available with almost every single Hypervisor such as KVM, Virtual Box, VMware, etc.

Using well defined interfaces facilitates independent subsystem development by both hardware and software design teams.

The simplifying abstractions hide lower-level implementation details, thereby reducing the complexity of the design process. Along with these, there also floats one hidden objective and that is to realize Virtual Power. The goals of this virtual power management are :

1.   To support the isolated and independent operation by guest Virtual Machines (VMs) running on virtualized platforms.

2.   To make it possible to control and globally coordinate the effect of the diverse power management policies applied by these VMs to virtualized resources.

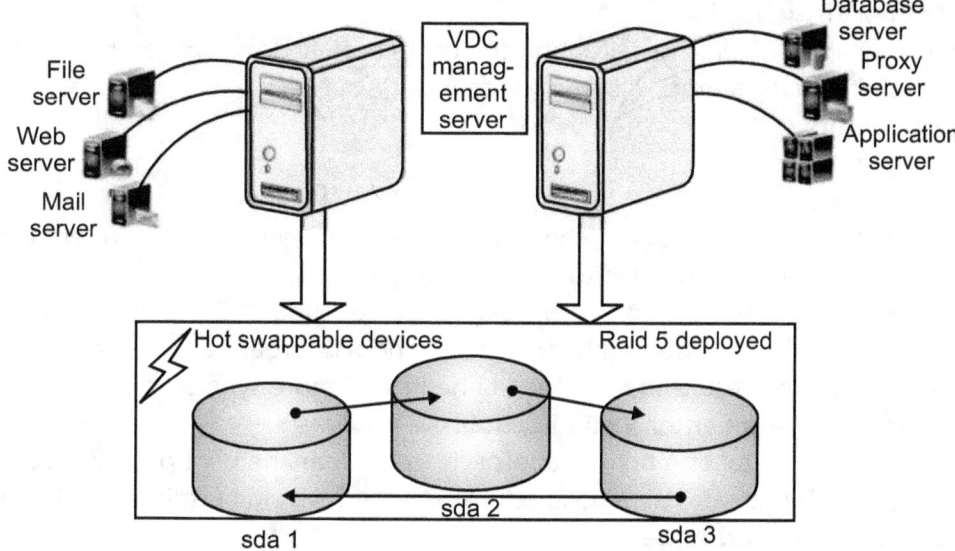

Fig. 3.8 : Data center

Fig. 3.8 elaborates how the build of a Data Center should look like.

The architecture contains a super server that manages all the virtual machines and server that are consolidated in your single bare hardware. This contains file server, web server, mail server, application server, database server, etc.

3.3.3 Data Center Virtualization

Virtualization across the data center can provide spectacular savings on floor space, power, cooling costs, as well as utilization of existing assets across network, storage devices, and servers. While the financial benefits alone are compelling, the largest gains can be obtained by reducing complexity and streamlining the speed at which IT accelerates the business.

These benefits cannot be maximized with server virtualization alone.

3.3.3.1 Defining Different Types of Virtualization

- **Virtualization**

This technology allows multiple logical units to operate "virtually" on one physical unit or resource. Alternately, virtualization technology can also allow multiple physical units or resources to appear and act as one "virtual" or logical unit or resource.

- **Server Virtualization**

Server virtualization Software is used to make the most of the physical resources of a server. In server virtualization, a software-based "hypervisor" (such as VMware or Microsoft Hyper-V) partitions one physical server into multiple virtual servers. Virtual servers are also often known as virtual machines. Each virtual server typically uses its native operating system and its own set of resources. Each virtual server can also operate its own application stack separately from the operation of other applications and other virtual servers on the same core machine.

- **Data Center Virtualization**

Extends the concept of server virtualization to consolidate and maximize other key physical resources inside the data center. This goes on to include :

Server virtualization

Network virtualization

Storage virtualization

Data center virtualization abstracts the relationship between services offered and the underlying physical hardware needed to make them run.

It consolidates each resource into a virtual resource "pool." By then integrating and coordinating each virtual pool with the other pools, organizations can go beyond virtualization "silos." This results in multiplied benefits and more synergies.

The Advantages Of Data Center Virtualization

A virtualized data center takes a holistic approach to the management of server, storage and network processes. This creates an infrastructure with the following attributes or benefits :

- **Dynamic, Efficient and Agile**

More efficient resource sharing (thanks to virtual pooling).

Reduced complexity that now means fewer things to manage.

Deeper gains in degree of consolidation, better resource planning and sharing and simplified management of a unanimous infrastructure.

This last set of benefits produce the largest gains in efficiency and productivity. Such benefits can be gained by applying advances in virtualization infrastructure management and unified infrastructures. These technologies offer greater virtualization management capabilities and deeper integration that let organizations develop and leverage virtual resources at multiple levels simultaneously from compute through to storage, networks and management and security resources.

The power of virtualization thus becomes multiplied as integration with compute, storage, network, management and security technologies create a synergistic approach.

The opportunity is to expand from islands of virtualization with virtualized servers for some applications and virtualized storage for others to a more coordinated virtualization strategy. This is where servers, storage and network strategies are combined.

Virtualized Applications Platform

Instead of building separate infrastructures according to the needs of individual applications, data center virtualization lets you build a dynamic platform of infrastructure that supports all (or most) apps. Abstracting applications from physical resources gives you management capabilities that you can't get from hardware. This would include :

The competencies required to migrate from one physical server to another without disruption.

- Increased availability for applications during hardware failure.
- Resource scheduling and load balancing across existing infrastructure.
- Improved backup and disaster recovery.
- Increased performance, scale and security.

- Integration with storage and network infrastructures.

The result is a platform that will support many if not most IT applications. The availability, performance, and security are provided by the platform, which reduce the need to build those services into each individual application. The resulting common shared infrastructure is much more flexible and agile.

3.4 DESKTOP AND APPLICATION VIRTUALIZATION TECHNIQUES AND BENEFITS

Virtualization Technology Overview

Virtualization has revolutionized data center's technology through a set of techniques and tools that facilitate the providing and management of the dynamic data center's infrastructure. It has become an essential and enabling technology of cloud computing environments. Virtualization can be defined as the abstraction of the four computing resources (storage, processing power, memory, and network or I/O). It is conceptually similar to emulation, where a system pretends to be another system, whereas virtualization is a system pretending to be two or more of the same system.

Virtualization approaches are classified into following five types.

3.4.1 Emulation

- In this approach virtual machine simulates the entire hardware set needed to run unmodified guests for completely different hardware architectures.
- It is used to create new operating systems for the hardware which is in design phase and not in physical form.
- Virtual Machine provides a "guest" operating system the (simulated) hardware environment it expects.
- Software is unaware that it is really talking to a virtualized device. Refer Fig 3.9.

Applications	Applications	Applications
Unmodified OS for Non-native architecture	Unmodified OS for Non-native architecture	Unmodified OS for Non-native architecture
Hardware virtual machine (Non-native architecture)		
Physical Hardware Architecture		

Fig. 3.9 : Emulation

- Each interaction between Guest device driver with the emulated device hardware requires transaction with VMM.
- The real hardware does its job as usual, but the VMM must now translate the result for the guest.
- **Advantage :** Guest Software need not be modified.
- **Disadvantage :** Must pay Performance Penalty.

3.4.2 Full Virtualization

- Full virtualization is a native kind of virtualization in which hypervisor runs directly on top of a given hardware platform as a control program for operating systems.
- It is similar to emulation except it is designed to simulate the underlying hardware which is physically available.
- It runs unmodified guests on a physical machine.
- It gives the flexibility to move entire virtual machines from one host to another host very easily, but for the cost of performance due to the overhead added by the emulator Layer. Refer Fig. 3.10.

Applications	Applications	
Unmodified OS for native architecture	Unmodified OS for native architecture	Hypervisor management interface
Hypervisor (VMM)		
Physical Hardware Architecture		

Fig. 3.10 : Full Virtualization

- **Examples :** Virtual PC and VMware Workstation.
- VMware is the first commercial virtualization product provider for x86 architecture.
- It enables the execution of unmodified guest operating systems through the translation of x86 instructions that cannot be virtualized.
- Hyper-V, a standalone product and as a feature for Windows Server 2008, windows edition translates guest kernel mode and real mode into x86 user mode.

3.4.3 Para Virtualization

- Para virtualization is a virtualization technique that presents a software interface to virtual machines that is similar to that of the underlying hardware.
- Application Programming Interface (API) is provided to the Guest OS by the VMM so the guest may utilize the hardware
- The hypervisor exports a modified version of the underlying physical hardware.
- The intent of the modified interface is to reduce the portion of the guest's execution time spent performing operations which are substantially more difficult to run in a virtual environment compared to a non-virtualized environment.
- A successful para virtualized platform may allow the Virtual Machine Monitor (VMM) to be simpler (by relocating execution of critical tasks from the virtual domain to the host domain), and/or reduce the overall performance degradation of machine-execution inside the virtual-guest.
- Para virtualization requires the guest operating system to be explicitly ported for the para-API. This is because a conventional OS distribution that is not para virtualization-aware cannot be run on top of a para virtualizing VMM.

- However, even in cases where the operating system cannot be modified, components may be available that enable many of the significant performance advantages of para virtualization. For example, the Xen Windows GPLPV project provides a kit of para virtualization-aware device drivers, licensed under the terms of the GPL, that are intended to be installed into a Microsoft Windows virtual-guest running on the Xen hypervisor.
- Thus with para virtualization guest interacts with VMM at a higher level of abstraction.
- Instead of supplying the specifics of how to use the hardware, software provides general requests to the VMM.
- Para virtualization decreases the number of interactions between Guest and VMM for a specific operation. Refer Fig. 3.11.

Applications	Applications	
Modified OS for native Architecture	Modified OS for native Architecture	Hypervisor Management Interface
Hypervisor (VMM)		
Physical Hardware Architecture		

Fig. 3.11 : Para virtualization

Advantage : Better Performance.

Disadvantage : Guest OS must be modified to use API.

3.4.4 Operating System Level Virtualization

- With operating system level virtualization virtual machine monitor software is not required.
- With this technique of virtualization single OS image handles all the guest images in different isolated containers.
- There is host OS that handles all other guest OS images present in respective containers.
- OS level virtualization does not support running different operating systems (Specifically, different kernel) at a time.
- With OS level virtualization instead of virtualizing the hardware, it is possible to run multiple virtual instances of same OS on single hardware.
- Thus with OS level virtualization only single kernel runs at a time.
- Single kernel means very low overhead (1 to 3%) compared to standalone server.
- Containers are the entities which provide isolation between processes.
- Each process appears as separate OS. Refer Fig. 3.12.

Applications	Applications	Applications
Private OS1	Private OS2	Private OS3
Single shared operating system image		
Physical Hardware Architecture		

Fig. 3.12 : OS level virtualization

Advantage : Best Performance / Scalability, Ease of Administration.

Disadvantage : Only virtualizes copies of same OS.

Examples : Solaris Containers/Zones, FreeBSD Jails, Linux VServers and OpenVZ.

3.4.5 Application Level Virtualization

- Application virtualization is software technology that encapsulates application software from the underlying operating system on which it is executed.
- A fully virtualized application is not installed in the traditional sense, although it is still executed as if it were.
- The application behaves at runtime like it is directly interfacing with the original operating system and all the resources managed by it, but can be isolated or sandboxed to varying degrees.
- In this context, the term "virtualization" refers to the object being encapsulated (application), which is quite different from its meaning in hardware virtualization, where it refers to the object being abstracted (physical hardware).
- Application level virtualization is also known as process virtualization.
- Application virtualization is the approach of running applications inside a virtual execution environment.
- The virtual execution environment provides a standard API for cross platform execution and manages the consumption of application's local resources such as threading model, environment variables, user interface libraries and objects.
- Modern operating systems such as Windows and Linux can include limited application virtualization.
- For example, Windows 7 provides Windows XP Mode that enables older Windows XP application to run unmodified on Windows 7.

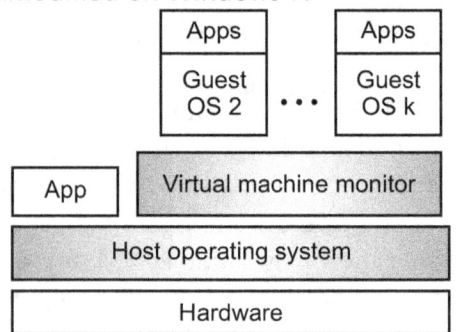

Fig. 3.13 : Application virtualization

- Full application virtualization requires a virtualization layer.
- Application virtualization layers replace part of the runtime environment normally provided by the operating system.
- The layer intercepts all disk operations of virtualized applications and transparently redirects them to a virtualized location, often a single file.
- The application remains unaware that it accesses a virtual resource instead of a physical one.

- Since the application is now working with one file instead of many files spread throughout the system, it becomes easy to run the application on a different computer and previously incompatible applications can be run side-by-side.

3.5 NEED AND ADVANTAGES OF VIRTUALIZATION

3.5.1 Need of Virtualization

- We have already learnt about virtualization concepts, virtual machine and types of virtualization.
- Still we are not really sure of why there is need of virtualization.
- Most of the businesses often use a combination of a number of application servers, web servers, image servers, audio-video servers, document servers and database servers.
- Above mentioned hardware infrastructure is not being used well almost all the time.
- If the 75% of the hardware appears as being used at any point of time on the basis of average number of server requests recorded, the servers are still largely under-utilized.
- The servers typically take only about 1-10 ms to service each request. However it should be much faster.
- Given this extremely short amount of time taken to service the request, the amount of time the server machine is kept up and running relative to the actual time spent by it servicing the requests, is much higher.
- This clearly indicates that a significant amount of energy is wasted per server in the process of keeping the servers up and ever-ready to service requests upon their arrival.
- Cumulative energy wasted is actually high considering the fact that we use not one server for each purpose, but a number of them for different purposes.
- Maximizing the server utilization is limited by the number of incoming server requests.
- Even if we have done our best to ensure that server spends a good fraction of time servicing requests, this equivalent to the number of requests the server receives at any point of time.
- Virtualization is the technique for eliminating this wastage and maximizing the profit.
- We already know that virtualization essentially means to create multiple, logical instances of software or hardware on a single physical hardware resource.
- This technique simulates the available hardware and gives every application running top of it, the feeling that it is the unique holder of the resource.
- The details of the virtual, simulated environment are kept transparent from the application.
- Organizations use this technique to perform the tasks away from many of their physical servers and map these functions onto one robust, evergreen physical server.
- This is beneficial in terms of cost of maintenance and reduced energy wastage.

- Since we have fewer physical servers, we need only their maintenance and therefore maintenance becomes much easier and cheaper.
- Also the amount of energy wasted is a function of the number of physical servers which is clearly much lower in virtualized environment.

3.5.2 Advantages of Virtualization

Allows applications to run in environments that do not suit the native application :

- Wine allows some Microsoft Windows applications to run on Linux.
- CDE, a lightweight application virtualization, allows Linux applications to run on another platform.
- May protect the operating system and other applications from poorly written or buggy code and in some cases provide memory protection and IDE style debugging features.
- Uses fewer resources than a separate virtual machine.
- Run applications that are not written correctly, for example applications that try to store user data in a read-only system-owned location.
- Run incompatible applications side-by-side, at the same time and with minimal regression testing against one another.
- Reduce system integration and administration costs by maintaining a common software baseline across multiple diverse computers in an organization.
- Implement the security principle of least privilege by removing the requirement for end-users to have Administrator privileges in order to run poorly written applications.
- Simplified operating system migrations.
- Improved security, by isolating applications from the operating system.
- Allows applications to be copied to portable media and then imported to client computers without need of installing them, so called Portable software.

3.5.3 Limitations of Virtualization

- Not all software can be virtualized. Some examples include applications that require a device driver and 16-bit applications that need to run in shared memory space.
- Some types of software such as anti-virus packages and applications that require heavy OS integration are difficult to virtualize.
- Only file and registry-level compatibility issues between legacy applications and newer operating systems can be addressed by application virtualization.
- For example, applications that don't manage the heap correctly will not execute on Windows Vista as they still allocate memory in the same way, regardless of whether they are virtualized or not.
- For this reason, specialist application compatibility fixes (shims) may still be needed, even if the application is virtualized.
- Moreover, in software licensing, application virtualization bears great licensing pitfalls mainly because both the application virtualization software and the virtualized applications must be correctly licensed.

3.6 VIRTUAL MACHINE COMPONENTS AND PROCESS OF CONVERTING PHYSICAL TO VMS

- Virtualization is a technique for hiding the physical characteristics of computing resources from the way other systems, applications or end users interact with them.
- Virtualization is a framework or methodology of dividing the resources of a computer into multiple execution environments, by applying one or more concepts or technologies such as hardware and software partitioning, time-sharing, partial or complete machine simulation, emulation, quality of service, and many others.
- We all are aware of the simple mechanism that one physical machine runs one operating system at any given time.
- By virtualizing the machine, we are able to run several operating systems (and all of their applications) at the same time.

3.6.1 Virtual Desktop Infrastructure

A Virtual Desktop Infrastructure (VDI) complements virtual and physical servers, providing similar value propositions as VMs. These value propositions include simplified management and a reduction in hardware, software, and support services at the desktop or workstation, shifting them to a central or consolidated server. Benefits include simplified software management (installation, upgrades, repairs), data protection (backup/ restore, HA, BC, DR) and security. Another benefit of VDI similar to VMs is the ability to run various versions of a specific guest operating system at the same time, similar to server virtualization. In addition to different versions of Windows, other guests, such as Linux, may also coexist. For example, to streamline software distribution, instead of rolling images out to physical desktops, applications are installed into a VM that is cloned, individually configured if necessary, and made accessible to the VDI client. From a cloud perspective, VDIs are also referred to as Desktop as a Service (DaaS) (not to be confused with Disk as a Service or Data as a Service). VDI vendors include Citrix, Microsoft, and VMware, and various platform or client suppliers ranging from Dell to Fujitsu, HP, IBM, and Wyse.

The VDI client can be a zero device that essentially functions as a display, such as an iPad, Droid, or other smart phone or tablet. Another type of VDI client is a thin device that has less compute and expansion capabilities, with or without a HDD, requiring less maintenance as there are no moving parts or dedicated installed software images that result in a lower cost. Normal workstations, desktops, and laptops can also be used as thick clients where more capabilities are needed or for mobile workers who can benefit from the enhanced capabilities of such devices. By moving the applications and their associated data files to a central server, local storage demands are reduced or eliminated, depending on the specific configuration. However, this means that, with applications running in part or in whole on a server, there is a trade-off of local storage and I/O on a workstation or desktop with increased network traffic. Instead of the desktop doing I/O to a local HDD, HHDD, or SSD, I/Os are redirected over the network to a server.

Fig. 3.14 shows a resilient VDI environment that also supports non-desktop VMs. In addition to supporting thin and zero VDI clients, mobile desktops are also shown, along with E2E management tools. The shared storage contains the VM images stored as VHD, VMDK, or OVF on shared storage that is also replicated to another location. In addition, some VMs and VDIs are protected as well as accessible via a cloud.

Depending on how the VDI is being deployed for example, in display mode less I/O traffic will go over the network, with activity other than during workstation boot mainly being display images. On the other hand, if the client is running applications in its local memory and making data requests to a server, then those I/Os will be placed on the network. Generally speaking, and this will vary with different types of applications, most workstations do not generate a large number of IOPS once they are running. During boot or start-up, there is a brief flurry of activity that should not be too noticeable, depending on your specific configuration and network.

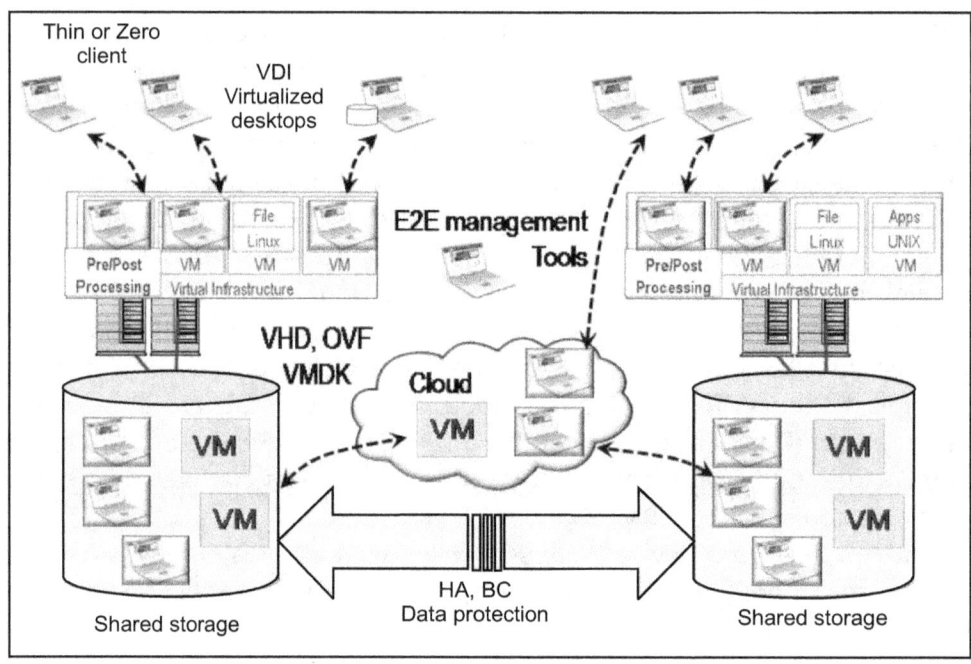

Fig. 3.14 : Virtual desktop infrastructures (VDIs).

If many clients boot up at the same time, such as after a power failure, maintenance, upgrade, or other event, a boot storm could occur and cause server storage I/O and network bottlenecks. For example, if a single client needs 30 IOPS either in a normal running state when it is busy or during boot, most servers and networks should support that activity. If the number of clients jumps from 1 to 100, the IOPS increases from 30 to 3000, well in excess of a single server HDD capability and requiring a faster storage system. Going further to 1000 clients needing 30 IOPS, the result is 30,000 IOPS of storage I/O performance. IOPS can be read or write and will vary at different times, such as more reads during boot or writes during updates. While this simple example does not factor in caching and other optimization techniques, it does point to the importance of maintaining performance during abnormal situations as well as normal running periods Part of a VDI assessment and planning should be to understand the typical storage I/O and networking characteristics for normal, boot, and peak processing periods to size the infrastructure appropriately.

VDI can also help streamline backup/restore and data protection along with antivirus capabilities, by centralizing those functions instead of performing them on an individual desktop basis. VDI considerations in addition to server, storage, I/O and networking resource performance, availability, and capacity should include looking at application availability requirements, as well as verification of which versions of guest operations systems work with various hypervisor or virtualization solutions. This includes verifying support for 32 bit and 64 bit modes, USB device support for encryption or authorization key, biometric security access control, video graphic driver capabilities, and management tools. Management tools include the ability to capture video screens for playing to support training or troubleshooting purposes, pausing or suspending running VDIs, and resource monitoring or accounting tools. Licensing is another consideration for VDIs, for the hypervisor and associated server side software and any updates to guest applications.

Virtualization provides following two functionalities :

1. Making multiple physical resources appear to function as a single logical resource. Refer Fig. 3.15.

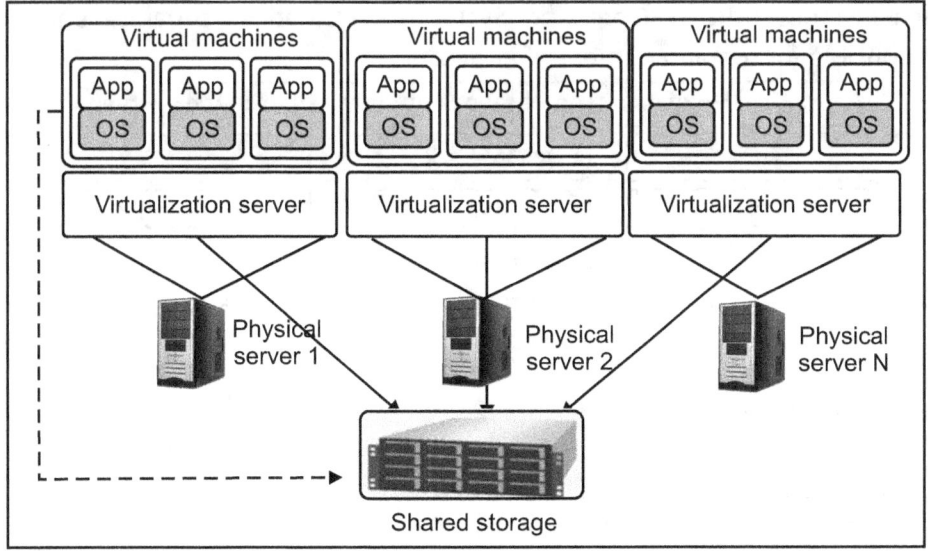

Fig. 3.15 : Multiple physical resources as a single logical resource

2. Making a single physical resource appear to function as multiple logical resources.

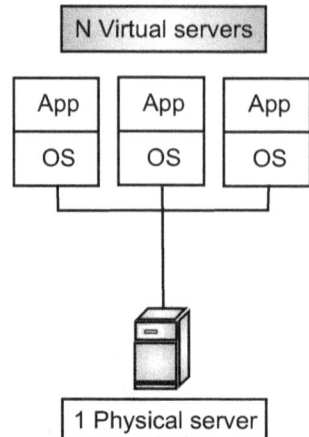

Fig. 3.16 : Single physical resource as a multiple logical resources

- Virtualization describes a process which enables the sharing of resources of one or more computers, namely its CPU, memory or hard disk, through the creation of virtual hardware platforms, operating systems, storage devices or network resources.
- This improves the performance existing system, allowing users to run more software and applications without the need to install new hardware or appliances. Refer Fig. 3.16.
- With the virtualization it is possible to create several instances of CPUs, called as virtual CPU and operating systems.
- Each instance (CPU + Operating System) is treated as separate entity and it is responsible for running number of applications.

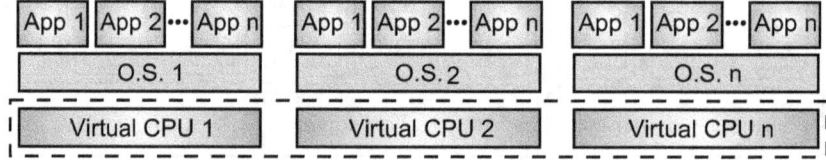

Fig. 3.17 : Virtualization

- Till now we have seen the virtualization and what can be done using virtualization. Now let's turn towards the basic entities which are used for creating virtual environment.

1. Virtual Machines :

- Virtual machines are presentation of a real machine using software that provides an operating environment which can run or host a guest operating system. Virtual machines are created and managed by virtual machine monitors.
- Virtual machines are simply implementation of a machine that executes programs as if it were a real machine.
- These virtual machines are basically categorized into two types.
    - (a) Process virtual machines
    - (b) System virtual machines

Process Virtual Machines

- Process virtual machines run as a normal application inside an operating system to abstract away the details of the underlying hardware.
- These are designed to provide a platform-independent environment to a single process (i.e., program).
- The environment is created when its associated process is started and destroyed when that process exits.
- Process virtual machines allow program to execute in the same way regardless of the physical platform it is running on.
- They are implemented using an interpreter.
- The programmer's code is not compiled, but the interpreter requires compilation before providing the processing environment.

System Virtual Machine

- System virtual machines allow multiplexing (time sharing) of the underlying hardware between different operating systems.
- These are designed to provide a complete platform which can support the execution on multiple, and different, operating systems.
- They allow time-sharing of underlying hardware between virtual machines.
- In system virtual operating Systems remain isolated from one another.
- The Instruction Set Architecture (ISA) provided by the virtual machine can be different from that of the real machine.
- System virtual machines implemented through the use of a Virtual Machine Monitor (VMM) also-known-as a Hypervisor.

1. Guest Operating System

Guest operating system is an operating system which is running inside the created virtual machine.

2. Hypervisor

- Hypervisor is a thin layer of software that generally provides virtual partitioning capabilities, which runs directly on hardware, but below the higher-level virtualization services.
- Hypervisors are classified into two categories.

(a) Native Hypervisor (Hardware-Level)

- Native hypervisor is a software which runs directly on top of a given hardware platform as a control program for operating systems. Refer Fig. 3.18.

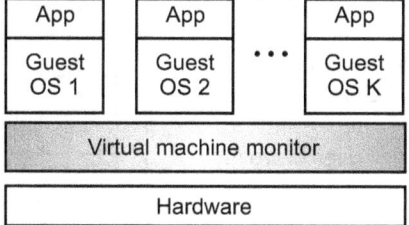

Fig. 3.18 : Native Hypervisor

- It is where actual virtualization begins.

(b) Hosted Hypervisor (OS-Level)
- Hosted hypervisor is software which runs within an operating system environment as a control program for other operating systems.
- Virtual Machine Monitor layer is moved one level higher as compared to Native VMs.
- Hosted hypervisor runs within a Host operating system environment.
- An operating system is installed first; as usual, on top of Hardware.
- A Virtual Machine Monitor is then installed within the Host OS.
- Guest operating systems can be installed on top of the VMM layer.
- Host OS sees the VMM as a process.
- VMM controls the allocation of time between Guest operating systems.
- Guest operating system is segregated from the rest of the environment. Refer Fig. 3.19.

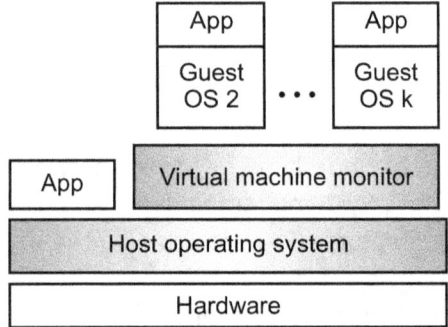

Fig. 3.19 : Hosted Hypervisor

1. Virtual Machine Monitor
- Above entities use the terms like hypervisor and virtual machine monitor, but they are conceptually different.
- Virtual Machine Monitor (VMM) is a software that runs in a layer between host operating system and one or more virtual machines that provides the virtual machine abstraction to the guest operating systems. Refer Fig. 3.20.

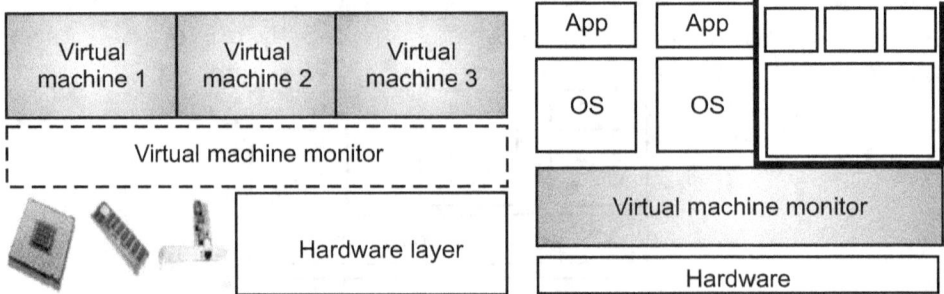

Fig. 3.20 : Role of Virtual Machine Monitor in virtualization

- With full virtualization, the virtual machine monitor exports a virtual machine abstraction identical to a physical machine, so that standard operating systems can run just as they would on physical hardware.

3.6.2 The Virtual Server

- Before directly moving to the virtual server concept, first we must understand the traditional server concept.
- Servers can be considered as a whole unit that includes the hardware, the OS, the storage, and the applications.
- Servers are often referred to by their function i.e. the Web server, the SQL server, the File server, etc. Refer Fig. 3.21.

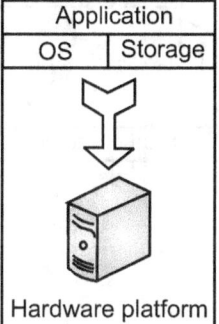 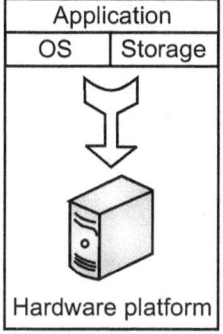 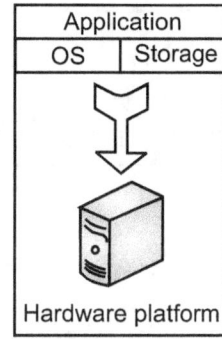 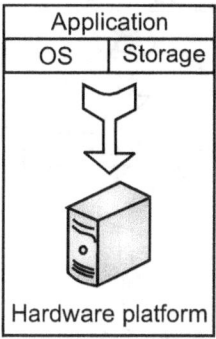

Fig. 3.21 : Traditional servers

- If the any of the server is overloaded or that server fills up then the system administrators must add in a new server.
- If there are no multiple servers and if a service experiences a hardware failure, then the service is down completely. Refer Fig. 3.22.

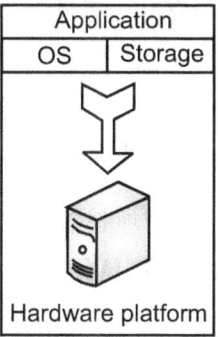 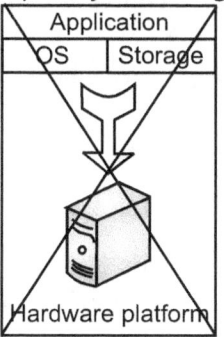 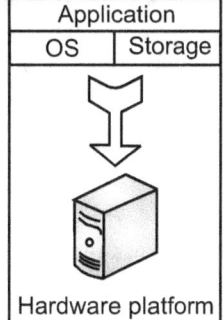 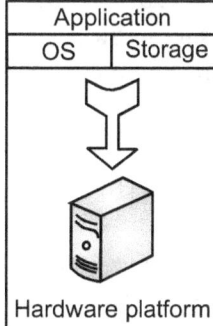

Fig. 3.22 : Service is completely down if server fails

- It is also possible to implement clusters of servers to make them more fault tolerant. However, even clusters have limits on their scalability, and not all applications work in a clustered environment.
- Although traditional servers mentioned above provide many advantages such as easy deployment, easy to backup, less complexity we must not ignore disadvantages such

as expenses to maintain hardware, limited scaling, difficulty in replication, difficulty in maintaining redundancy, under utilization of processor etc.

- Virtual servers are implemented using virtualization to overcome the disadvantages of traditional servers mentioned above.
- Virtual servers seek to encapsulate the server software away from the hardware.
- This includes the OS, the applications, and the storage for that server.
- Servers end up as mere files stored on a physical box, or in enterprise storage.
- A virtual server can be serviced by one or more hosts, and one host may contain more than one virtual server. Refer Fig. 3.23.

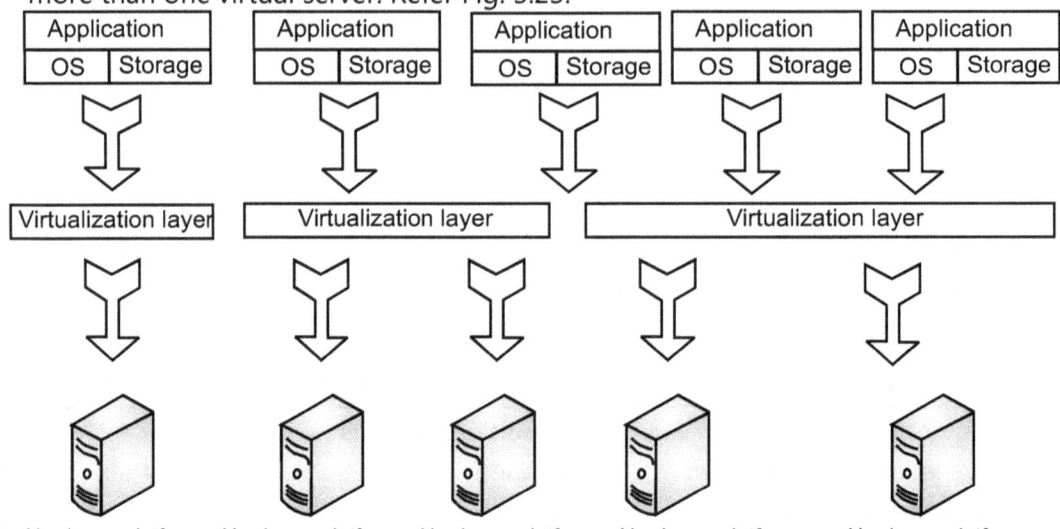

Fig. 3.23 : Virtual server

- Virtual servers can still be referred to by their function i.e. email server, database server, etc.
- If the environment is built correctly, virtual servers will not be affected by the loss of a host.
- Hosts may be removed or added at any time and as per requirement to fulfill the requirements.
- Virtual servers can be scaled out easily.
- If the administrators find that the resources supporting a virtual server are being taxed too much, they can adjust the amount of resources allocated to that virtual server.
- Server templates can be created in a virtual environment to be used to create multiple, identical virtual servers.

3.6.3 Cloud and Virtual Servers

Virtual servers and clouds (public and private) are complementary and can rely on each other or be independent. For example, VMs can exist without accessing public or private cloud resources, and clouds can be accessed and used by non-virtualized servers. While clouds and virtualization can be independent of each other, like many technologies they work very well together. VMs and VDIs can exit on local PMs or on remote HA and BC or DR systems. VMs and VDIs can also be hosted for BC and DR purposes or accessible for daily use via public and private clouds. Many public services, including Amazon, Eucalyptus, GoGrid, Microsoft, and Rackspace, host VMs. Types of VMs and formats (VMDK, VHD, OVF) will vary by service, as will functionality, performance, availability, memory, I/O, and storage capacity per hour of use. The benefit of using a cloud service for supporting VMs is to utilize capacity on demand for elasticity or flexibility to meet specific project activities such as development, testing, research, or surge seasonal activity. Some environments may move all of their VMs to a service provider, while others may leverage them to complement their own resources.

3.6.4 Can and Should All Servers or Desktops Be Virtualized?

The primary question should not be whether all servers, workstations, or desktops can or should be virtualized. Rather, should everything be consolidated? While often assumed to mean the same thing, and virtualization does enable consolidation, there are other aspects to virtualization. Aggregation has become well known and a popular approach to consolidate underutilized IT resources including servers, storage, and networks. The benefits of consolidation include improved efficiency by eliminating underutilized servers or storage to reduce electrical power, cooling requirements, floor space, and management activity, or to reuse and repurpose servers that have been made surplus to enable growth or support new application service capabilities.

For a variety of reasons, including performance, politics, finances, and service-level or security issues, not all servers or other IT resources, including storage and networking, lend themselves to consolidation. For example, an application may need to run on a server at a low CPU utilization to meet performance and response-time objectives or to support seasonal workload changes. Another example is that certain applications, data, or even users of servers may need to be isolated from each other for security and privacy concerns.

Political, financial, legal, or regulatory requirements also need to be considered with regard to consolidation. For example, a server and application may be owned by different departments or groups and, thus, managed and maintained separately. Similarly, regulatory or legal requirements may dictate, for compliance or other purposes, that certain systems are kept away from other general-purpose or mainstream applications, servers, and storage. Another reason for separation of applications may be to isolate development, test, quality assurance, back-office, and other functions from production or online applications and systems and to support business continuance, disaster recovery, and security.

For applications and data that do not lend themselves to consolidation, a different use of virtualization is to enable transparency of physical resources to support interoperability and coexistence between new and existing software tools, servers, storage, and networking technologies for example, enabling new, more energy- efficient servers or storage with improved performance to coexist with existing resources and applications.

Another form of virtualization is emulation or transparency providing abstraction to support integration and interoperability with new technologies while preserving existing technology investments and not disrupting software procedures and policies. Virtual tape libraries are a commonly deployed example of storage technology that combines emulation of existing tape drives and tape libraries with disk-based technologies. The value proposition of virtual tape and disk libraries is to coexist with existing backup software and procedures while enabling new technology to be introduced.

3.7 DESKTOP VIRTUALIZATION

Desktop virtualization can be used to create a more robust, flexible, secure and easier-to-operate desktop computing environment. This is significant for a number of reasons. Devices that present users with a personal electronic desktop or workspace are integral to IT service delivery. Whether it's a desktop PC, laptop, ultrabook, tablet or other type of device such as a 'thinclient' terminal, the 'desktop client' represents the primary point of access for users into business systems and information. How well it performs and the experience it delivers has a big impact on user productivity, as well as significantly influencing business user perception of how well IT is being managed. Modernizing the desktop computing environment can, therefore, be a good way of enhancing business performance and user satisfaction. Conversely, allowing your infrastructure to drift out of date leads to escalating cost and risk as older desktop hardware and software are more expensive to maintain, more prone to failure, more hassle to support and more difficult to secure. Beyond these general considerations, the traditional ways in which desktops have been implemented and managed are being challenged by broader trends and developments that are changing needs and expectations. Increasingly pervasive connectivity and a growing richness of device choice/capability is enabling ever more flexible working, e.g. from home, hot-desks, conference rooms, hotels, airports, client sites, and so on.

Put this together with a trend towards users employing multiple devices for work purposes, including personally owned equipment (the 'consumerization' phenomenon), and the result is a need for a rethink of how end user computing is enabled and managed from an IT perspective. In particular, the model in which all software is installed and managed locally on each physical desktop or device is looking increasingly less likely to cope with future needs.

What is desktop virtualization?

Many readers will be aware of virtualization in the context of x86 servers, where it has been used as the basis for consolidating server estates, streamlining operations and increasing flexibility.

An enabling component is the 'hypervisor', which allows multiple 'virtual machines' (VMs) to run on a single physical computer, breaking the traditional tight coupling between software and hardware. This basic idea of 'uncoupling' previously dependent components can also be applied to desktop computing, but here it is extended to provide even greater flexibility. In the traditional desktop model, the desktop computer runs an operating system upon which applications are executed, with their user interface displayed on the computer screen. By introducing virtualization into this mix, we break the bindings between physical hardware, operating systems, applications and displays, meaning that some or all of the software components can be run or managed from a remote server instead of locally.

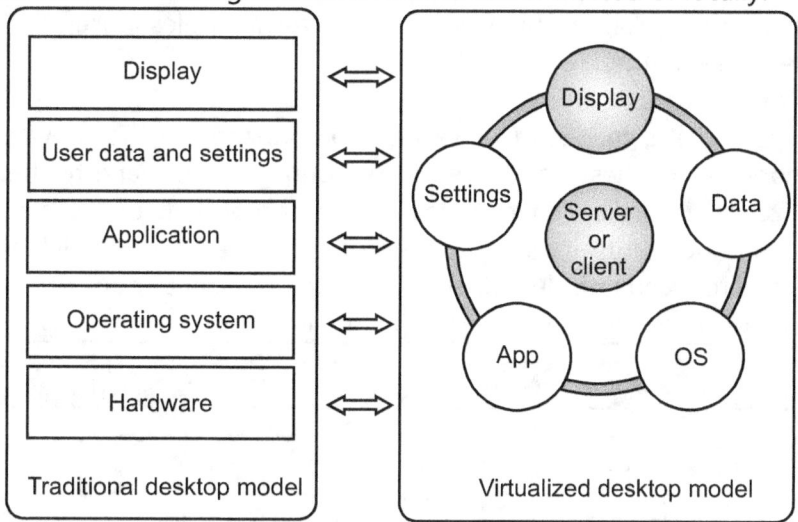

Fig. 3.24 : Breaking the traditional bindings between layers

As shown in this Fig. 3.24 in addition to having a choice about where the operating system and individual applications reside, we can also choose whether user information such as application data and configuration settings are stored locally or on the server. The latest generation of desktop virtualization solutions allows all of these options (and more) to be freely mixed and matched, according to what's going on at any particular moment in time. The way the operating system and applications are served up to a user may be different, for example, depending on whether they are logging in from their desk PC over the corporate network, from their laptop over a hotel WiFi service, or from their home PC over a domestic broadband connection.

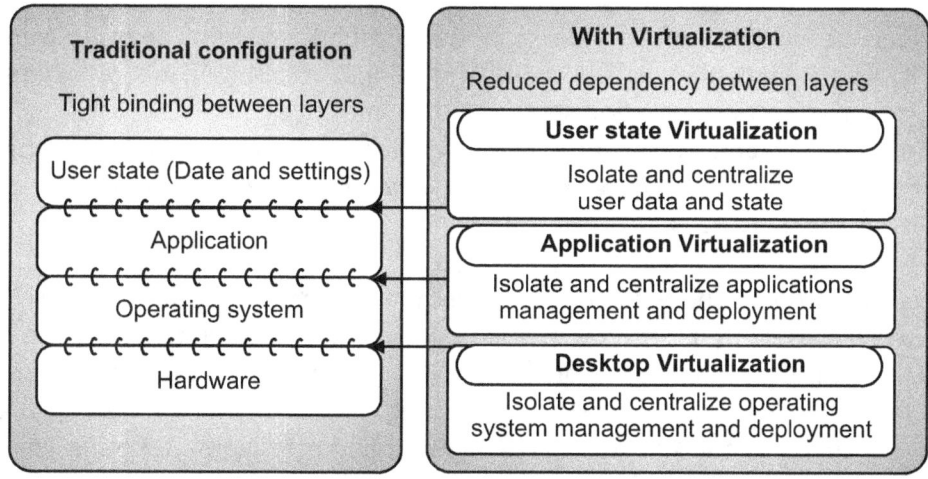

Fig. 3.25 (a) : Configuration : Tradition vs. Virtualization

Virtualization is the act of decoupling one computing resource from others without impacting the usability across these resources. Rather than locking the various layers together the Operating System (OS) to the hardware, the application to the OS, and the user interface and data to the local machine virtualization technologies loosen the direct reliance these parts have on each other.

Defining Desktop Virtualization :

The desktop experience is made up of several components. In the prevalent desktop or laptop for all model, all of these components are bound together and to the access device. Desktop virtualization is the act of decoupling one component of the desktop from the others and from the device itself without compromising the ability to deliver the end user experience. It is this reduced interdependency, this flexibility, that opens the door to many of the benefits commonly associated with desktop virtualization.

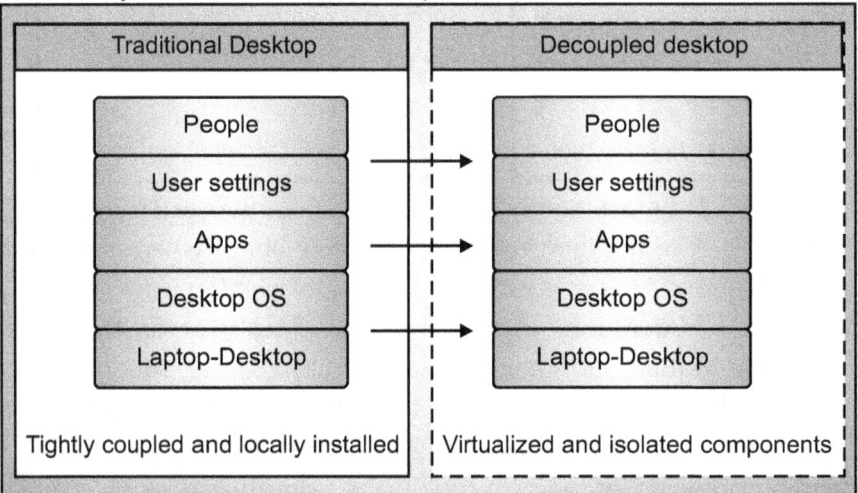

Fig. 3.25 (b) : Defining Desktop Virtualization: Decoupling the Desktop

3.7.1 Formulating a Desktop Virtualization Strategy

If we consider the question of 'why desktop virtualization?' to have been answered at the outset of this document, there are four key questions that should be considered before embarking on a desktop virtualization strategy:

"**A combination of technology and market developments means that enterprises face significantly more choices in how they work with user devices and how they deliver applications to those devices.**

Who?

The first step is to understand the end user landscape. An organization will typically comprise many different types of users, each with their own needs and requirements. The variety of solutions falling under the umbrella of desktop virtualization and the differences between them dictate that, in the majority of cases, no single solution will be appropriate for the entire end user environment. As such, an end user profiling study that assesses work patterns and roles is an essential part of building the comprehensive view required to identify how, where and what type of desktop virtualization technology should be deployed across the end user landscape. Here are some examples of roles that will be common

- Or at least familiar
- To most businesses.

Information Worker

For example, a customer service assistant. This user is typically desk-based, has little exposure to sensitive data and requires access to just a handful of applications.

Offline Information Worker

This could be a shift supervisor or field engineer. This user's daily tasks require little interaction with IT access to voice communication tools is the primary IT requirement.

Knowledge Worker

For example, an engineer or software developer. This user is primarily deskbound but requires access from both the office and home. Duties require rich, sophisticated applications and 'read and write' access to corporate data and processes. This user will have a large peer network and so access to a wide range of communications tools is a must.

Mobile Knowledge Worker

This might be a sales agent who spends most of the working day on the road or at client locations. Anytime, anywhere access to IT services is a prerequisite, as is access to a variety of communication tools. Once a comprehensive understanding of the different users across the organization has been established and user groups, or families, have been identified, the next steps should be to look at the different forms of desktop virtualization and begin considering which solutions, or combination of solutions, provide the best fit for the users while addressing IT and business objectives.

What?

Desktop virtualization can be separated into three distinct layers :

User State Virtualization is the simplest layer of virtualization. Here, user data and user settings are separated from the end user device. Data is stored centrally and is accessible from any end user device.

Operating System Virtualization is the adoption of hypervisor technology to abstract the operating system from underlying hardware.

Application Virtualization refers to the adoption of application virtualization technologies that enable applications to run in their own specific environments.

The benefits of desktop virtualization are both clear and compelling – the wealth of options available, though potentially overwhelming, renders the existing 'one size fits all' approach to end user IT services sub-optimal and, ultimately, tant amount to competitive disadvantage.

However, as with any emerging technology, there is much to consider before implementation and the following steps should be followed to ensure maximum benefit :

Assess the End user Landscape

An end user assessment or user profiling exercise should be seen as a 'must do' task when considering desktop virtualization. Only by understanding the needs and characteristics of the different user families can the correct delivery methods be chosen.

Understand the Technology

Understand the differences between the various types of desktop virtualization technologies and how they fit or do not fit with business and IT objectives.

Despite apparent similarities, each of the solutions falling under the banner of desktop virtualization has its own advantages and drawbacks poorly informed deployment decisions can prove costly.

Develop a Roadmap

A road map, that incorporates where and when to deploy each technology option identified should be generated. Any such roadmap needs to consider the existing IT estate and be sufficiently flexible to accommodate some of the uncertainties of working with emerging technologies.

Desktop virtualization holds the promise of bringing management, security and control back to IT, while generating efficiencies through a centralized, virtualized infrastructure and delivering a highly satisfying

- and productive
- user experience.

Simply put, it presents organizations with the opportunity to change the way the end user experience is provisioned, paid for and operated.

Benefits and Practicalities

Two common threads run through all of the models we have been discussing: centralized management and the minimization of dependencies between components and activities. Let's take a look at the benefits that arise from these, then go on to consider the individual pros and cons of each specific desktop virtualization model.

Benefits of Centralized Management

From an IT perspective, central control can simplify operational challenges such as asset management, patch management and license management, as well as enabling desktop policies to be defined and implemented more straightforwardly, a welcome benefit for often overstretched IT professionals Better central control is also the basis for improved security and compliance. It helps to ensure user environments are as up to date (and therefore secure) as possible, and offers an opportunity to lock down elements of the desktop to prevent user mishaps, misuse and abuse. The centralization of storage can then facilitate enhanced data protection. The other big benefit is improved support. Flexibility for the user is enabled in a more controlled and consistent manner, with enhanced visibility of what has been deployed and how it is being used. This makes troubleshooting and remedial work much easier, further reducing IT overheads, as well as providing a better service to users.

Benefits of Minimizing Dependencies

Breaking the bond between hardware components, software components and user data underpins many of the benefits to do with flexibility. Users can access applications and data wherever it's most convenient, including running the work environment on a home PC or an internet kiosk. They can receive new and updated applications more quickly, and can even benefit from self-service application provisioning. Separating applications from each other minimizes conflicts, which means fewer interruptions because of crashes and machine instability. Business continuity and flexible working practices in general are also enhanced, e.g. if a local desktop or even the entire office becomes unavailable, users can access their work from other (appropriately configured) machines, including from home.

Virtual Application Streaming

All users see increased stability, and those using multiple devices enjoy broad, flexible access to their applications from any compatible physical or virtual desktop. IT sees a reduction in time spent on testing, rollout, maintenance and support, and where vendor terms permit, licensing costs may be reduced through on-demand software deployment.

3.7.2 Application Virtualization

Application virtualization is software technology that encapsulates computer programs from the underlying operating system on which it is executed. A fully virtualized application is not installed in the traditional sense, although it is still executed as if it were. The application behaves at runtime like it is directly interfacing with the original operating system and all the resources managed by it, but can be isolated or sandboxed to varying degrees.

In this context, the term "virtualization" refers to the artifact being encapsulated (application), which is quite different from its meaning in hardware virtualization, where it refers to the artifact being abstracted (physical hardware).

Full application virtualization requires a virtualization layer. Application virtualization layers replace part of the runtime environment normally provided by the operating system. The layer intercepts all disk operations of virtualized applications and transparently redirects them to a virtualized location, often a single file. The application remains unaware that it accesses a virtual resource instead of a physical one. Since the application is now working with one file instead of many files spread throughout the system, it becomes easy to run the application on a different computer and previously incompatible applications can be run side-by-side. Examples of this technology for the Windows platform include :

- 2X Software
- Cameyo
- Ceedo
- Citrix XenApp
- InstallFree
- Microsoft App-V
- Numecent Application Jukebox
- Oracle Secure Global Desktop
- Sandboxie
- Spoon (formerly Xenocode)
- Symantec Workspace Virtualization
- Systancia
- VMware ThinApp

Benefits
- Application virtualization allows applications to run in environments that do not suit the native application. For example, Wine allows some Microsoft Windows applications to run on Linux. CDE allows Linux applications to run on Linux distros in distro-agnostic way.
- Application virtualization reduces system integration and administration costs by maintaining a common software baseline across multiple diverse computers in an organization. Lesser integration protects the operating system and other applications from poorly written or buggy code. In some cases, it provides memory protection, IDE-style debugging features (as in IBM OLIVER) and may even run applications that are not written correctly, for example applications that try to store user data in a read-only system-owned location. (This feature assist in the implementation of the principle of least privilege by removing the requirement for end-users to have administrative privileges in order to run poorly written applications). It allows incompatible applications to run side-by-side, at the same time and with minimal regression testing against one another.Isolating applications from the operating system has security benefits as well, as the exposure of the application does automatically entail the exposure of the entire OS.
- Application virtualization also enables simplified operating system migrations. Applications can be transferred to removable media or between computers without the need of installing them, becoming portable software.
- Application virtualization uses fewer resources than a separate virtual machine.

Limitations
- Not all computer programs can be virtualized. Some examples include applications that require a device driver (a form of integration with the OS) and 16-bit applications that need to run in shared memory space. Anti-virus programs and applications that require heavy OS integration, such as WindowBlinds or StyleXP are difficult to virtualize.
- Moreover, in software licensing, application virtualization bears great licensing pitfalls mainly because both the application virtualization software and the virtualized applications must be correctly licensed.
- While application virtualization can address file and Registry-level compatibility issues between legacy applications and newer operating systems, applications that don't manage the heap correctly will not execute on Windows Vista as they still allocate memory in the same way, regardless of whether they are virtualized or not. For this reason, specialist application compatibility fixes (shims) may still be needed, even if the application is virtualized.
- software without modifying the host computer or making any changes to the local operating system, file system, or registry. Using this virtualization technology, organizations can deploy custom and commercial software across the enterprise without installation conflicts, system changes, or any impact on stability or security.

- Virtualized applications eliminate nearly all of the complexities and support issues associated with delivering and accessing traditional applications for both fat- and thin-client deployments. The time and regression testing required to successfully deliver applications and updates is shortened to hours instead of weeks. Virtualized applications from VMware ThinApp can be run without any modifications or additions to a PC, including administrative security permissions. Applications virtualized with ThinApp operate exclusively in user mode; therefore the host operating system and other applications are protected from potential corruption by installation modifications.

The Market for Virtualization Solutions

- Despite highly publicized consolidated applications, the number of applications that businesses are supporting is growing. As they are stacked on top of each other, applications need to operate simultaneously and communicate seamlessly with each other. Over time, the systems supporting such a complex web of intertwined software become increasingly fragile, forcing the cost of software deployments to rise as more support and time is needed. IT staff face months of multi-application regression testing, end-user support, and downtime caused by unforeseen application conflicts. Traditionally, reliable and readily accessible software requires constant planning and a great deal of ongoing support. For rester Research reports that companies typically spend more than $500 per year, per desktop, just managing applications.

- Enter Application Virtualization. According to Michael Rose, associate research analyst for enterprise virtualization software at IDC, "The market will increasingly implement virtualization in a growing set of use cases, in order to help customers create much more agile Service-Oriented Infrastructures (SOIs). Corporations are looking for virtualization solutions that are easily managed, reduce costs, and provide a stable, secure program that is easily implemented. VMware ThinApp is providing a dynamic solution to meet a range of user demands."

The Benefits of Virtualized Applications

Virtualizing applications ensures faster software deployment with a more seamless end-user experience :

- **Full Portability :** Virtualized applications can stream from any network share without a local client or a backend server.
- **Increased Efficiency of Application Deployments :** Agentless virtual applications enable administrators to confidently deploy or de-commission applications on the fly with little or no regression testing, even for the most secure desktops.
- **No Runtime Conflicts :** Deploying virtual applications reduces lengthy QA and regression testing.
- **Supportability :** Single application packages can be supported by any Windows platform. Virtualized applications can run without requiring any modification of administrative security permissions, which protects the host operating system from possibly corruptive installation modifications.

3.8 BLOCK AND FILE LEVEL STORAGE VIRTUALIZATION

Storage virtualization is a process of presenting a logical view of physical storage resources to hosts. Logical storage appears and behaves as physical storage directly connected to host. Storage virtualization separates logical and physical storage resources in the same manner as that of separation of logical and physical resources.

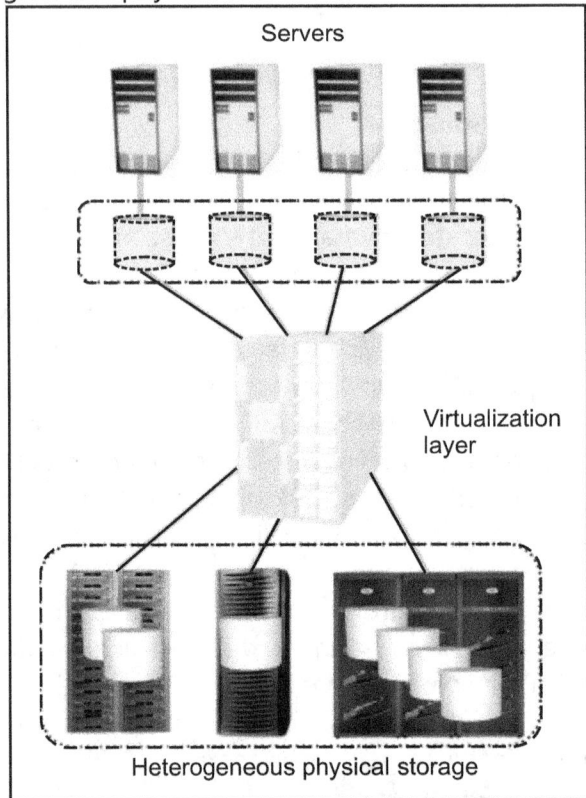

Fig. 3.26 : Basic storage virtualization

Storage can be virtualized at the block level (SAN storage) and at the file level (NAS storage). Storage virtualization is basically used to resolve application growth issue. As the data stores continue to grow, migrating data without production downtime is its important benefit. Data growth has reached to a point where using a specific time period to perform data migration is not sufficient.

Maximum data migration depends on the number of servers moving data. However most of the organizations store terabytes of data and migrating such huge amount over specific period of time is very slow.

With storage virtualization, data migration can be part of daily infrastructure management and optimization technique with very little or almost no downtime.

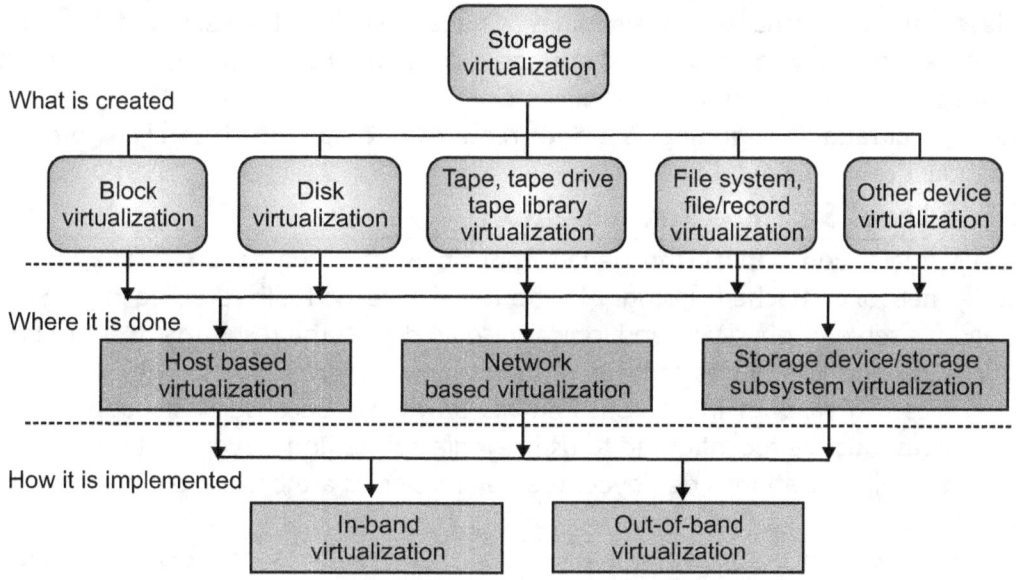

Fig. 3.27 : Storage virtualization

In out of band virtualization, the virtualized environment configuration is stored external to the data path, where as in in-band virtualization implementation places the virtualization function in the data path.

There are two types of storage virtualization : block level and file level.

3.8.1 Block Level Virtualization

Block level storage virtualization enables a Storage Area Network (SAN) to present multiple storage arrays as a single virtual array. Mapping within the storage network redirects I/Os to the underlying physical arrays, providing non disruptive data mobility and data migration.

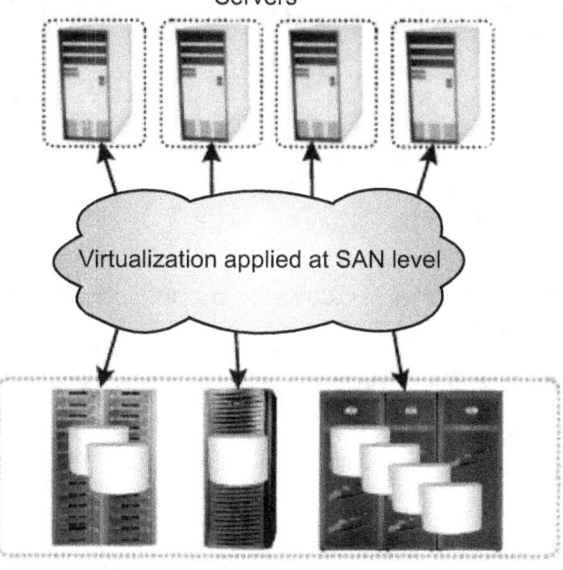

Fig. 3.28 : Block level virtualization

Block level storage virtualization simplifies data access for the user and provides non disruptive data mobility to replace old storage, add additional storage or leverage multiple tiers of storage without affecting service levels.

Without virtualization, migrating storage requires storage to be taken offline; with virtualization it can remain online.

3.8.2 File Level Storage Virtualization

File level virtualization applies the general principles of virtualization to the file storage, specifically network attached storage. Without file level virtualization, each NAS storage device and file server is physically and logically isolated, with the result that files are bound to a specific file server. This causes capacity problems and underutilized storage.

Migrating files to deal with these issues entails downtime because hosts, applications and storage devices must be reconfigured to use new file names and server locations.

When file level virtualization is deployed, the dependencies are broken between data and its physical location.

File level virtualization optimizes storage virtualization, enables non disruptive migrations and support file sharing across multiple organizational boundaries.

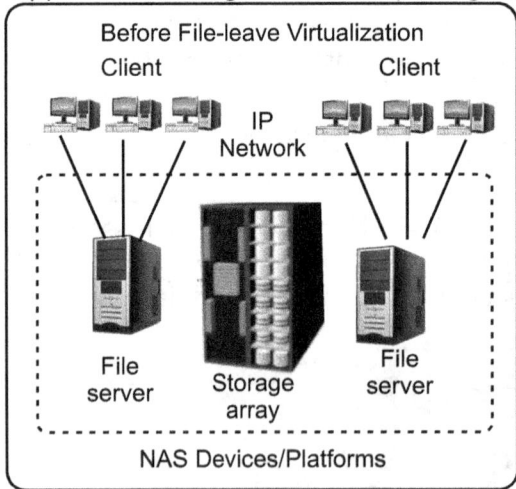 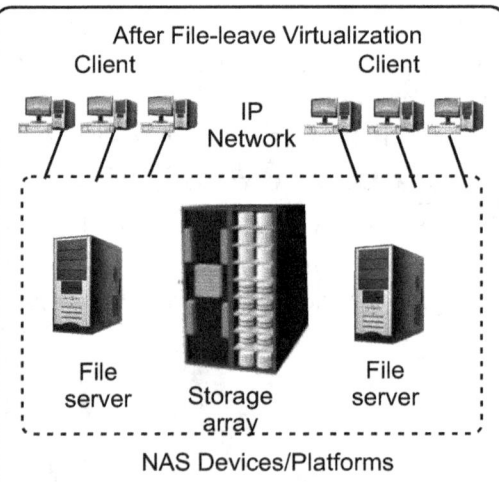

Fig. 3.29 : File level storage virtualization

Benefits of Storage Virtualization:
- Increased storage utilization.
- Adding or deleting storage without affecting application's availability.
- Non-disruptive data migration.

3.9 VIRTUAL PROVISIONING

Virtual provisioning is a strategy for efficiently managing space in a Storage Area Network (SAN) by allocating physical storage on an "as needed" basis. This strategy is also called thin provisioning.

Virtual provisioning is designed to simplify storage administration by allowing storage administrators to meet requests for capacity on-demand. Virtual provisioning gives a host, application or file system the illusion that it has more storage than is physically provided. Physical storage is allocated only when the data is written, rather than when the application is initially configured.

Virtual provisioning can reduce power and cooling costs by cutting down on the amount of idle storage devices in the array. As a result, virtual provisioning has become a part of green computing and green data center initiatives. The caveat for virtual provisioning is that it requires administrators to carefully monitor the usage of virtually provisioned resources to ensure that no virtual disks become full, resulting in storage errors for mission-critical applications.

Green computing, also called green technology, is the environmentally responsible use of computers and related resources. Such practices include the implementation of energy-efficient Central Processing Units (CPUS), SERVERS AND PERIPHERALS AS WELL AS REDUCED RESOURCE CONSUMption and proper disposal of electronic waste (e-waste).

One of the earliest initiatives toward green computing in the United States was the voluntary labeling program known as Energy Star. It was conceived by the Environmental Protection Agency (EPA) in 1992 to promote energy efficiency in hardware of all kinds. The Energy Star label became a common sight, especially in notebook computers and displays. Similar programs have been adopted in Europe and Asia.

Government regulation, however well-intentioned, is only part of an overall green computing philosophy. The work habits of computer users and businesses can be modified to minimize adverse impact on the global environment. Here are some steps that can be taken :

- Power-down the CPU and all peripherals during extended periods of inactivity.
- Try to do computer-related tasks during contiguous, intensive blocks of time, leaving hardware off at other times.
- Power-up and power-down energy-intensive peripherals such as laser printers according to need.
- Use Liquid-Crystal-Display (LCD) monitors rather than Cathode-Ray-Tube (CRT) monitors.
- Use notebook computers rather than desktop computers whenever possible.
- Use the power-management features to turn off hard drives and displays after several minutes of inactivity.
- Minimize the use of paper and properly recycle waste paper.
- Dispose of e-waste according to federal, state and local regulations.
- Employ alternative energy sources for computing workstations, servers, networks and data centers.

A green data center is a repository for the storage, management, and dissemination of data in which the mechanical, lighting, electrical and computer systems are designed for maximum energy efficiency and minimum environmental impact. The construction and operation of a green data center includes advanced technologies and strategies. Here are some examples :

- Minimizing the footprints of the buildings.

- The use of low-emission building materials, carpets and paints.
- Sustainable landscaping.
- Waste recycling.
- Installation of catalytic converters on backup generators.
- The use of alternative energy technologies such as photovoltaics, heat pumps, and evaporative cooling.
- The use of hybrid or electric company vehicles.

Building and certifying a green data center or other facility can be expensive up front, but long-term cost savings can be realized on operations and maintenance. Another advantage is the fact that green facilities offer employees a healthy, comfortable work environment. In addition, green facilities enhance relations with local communities.

There is growing pressure from environmentalists and, increasingly, the general public for governments to offer green incentives: monetary support for the creation and maintenance of ecologically responsible technologies.

Virtual provisioning is a Virtual Storage Network (VSAN)-based technology in which storage space is allocated on demand to devices. This process allows virtualized environments to control the allocation and management of physical disk storage connected with Virtual Machines (VM).

Virtual provisioning is also known as thin provisioning. However, virtual provisioning is more relevant to a virtual environment, while thin provisioning is more relevant to physical computing implementations.

Virtual provisioning presents but does not actually assign higher storage capacity to VMs. The underlying host allocates physical storage to each VM, based on actual requirements and as needed.

For example, a collective VSAN pool may contain 30 GB. A connected VM device may be presented with a logical space of 10 GB, but in actuality, the space may be smaller. Therefore, when the VM requests storage space, storage capacity up to 5 GB or more, if required and available, is allocated.

3.10 AUTOMATED STORAGE TIERING

Automated Storage Tiering (AST) is a storage software management feature that dynamically moves information between different disk types and RAID levels to meet space, performance and cost requirements.

Automated storage tiering features use policies that are set up by storage administrators. For example, a data storage administrator can assign infrequently used data to slower, less-expensive SATA storage but allow it to be automatically moved to higher-performing SAS or Solid-State Drives (SSDs) as it becomes more active (and vice versa).

Automated tiered storage (also **automated storage tiering**) is the automated progression or demotion of data across different tiers (types) of storage devices and media. The movement of data takes place in an automated way with the help of a software and is assigned to the related media according to performance and capacity requirements. Here, the intelligence is driven by a software and so Automated Tiered Storage can be tagged as a characteristic of a Software Defined Storage.

A software based example of automated tiering which can work across SSDs, Flash Memory devices, different types of storage devices and arrays and Cloud storage is available from DataCore and is a feature of their storage hypervisor software. An example of automated tiered storage in a hardware storage array is a feature called Data Progression from Compellent Technologies. Data Progression has the capability to transparently move blocks of data between different drive types and RAID groups such as RAID 10 and RAID 5. The blocks are part of the "same virtual volume even as they span different RAID groups and drive types. Compellent can do this because they keep metadata about every block which allows them to keep track of each block and its associations."

Fusion Drive combines the high storage capacity of a traditional hard drive with the high performance of flash storage. Disk-intensive tasks from booting up to launching apps to importing photos are faster and more efficient because frequently used items are kept at the ready on speedy flash storage, while infrequently accessed items go to the hard drive.

In a caching solution files live on the hard disk drive and are temporarily mirrored to the SSD cache as needed. In an enterprise auto-tiering situation, and with Fusion Drive, the data is moved from one tier to another, rather than only being temporarily cached there.

Application workloads are hard to predict. Auto-Tiering is a real-time intelligent mechanism that continuously positions data on the appropriate class of storage based on how frequently the data is accessed. The result is superior application performance and lower TCO across the entire storage architecture.

Auto-Tiering leverages any combination of Flash and traditional disk technologies, whether it is internal or array based, with support up to 15 different storage tiers.

Tier	Details	% of total production
1	Ultra-High-Speed Disk (Flash)	15%
2	High Speed Disk (SAS 15k)	25%
3	Capacity Disk (SAS 7.2k NL)	60%
4	Test/Dev Disk (SATA)	As Needed
5	Archival Cloud Disk	As Needed

As more advanced disk technologies become available, existing tiers can be modified as necessary and additional tiers can be added to further diversify the architecture. Auto-tiering will move frequently accessed data to the faster tier and less frequently access data to the slower tier. The Automated Storage Tiering feature (also known as Auto-tiering) continually calculates the frequency that data in disk pools is accessed and migrates data based on the frequency or "temperature". The initial temperature assigned to an SAU is the average temperature of data in the tier to which it is stored. Auto-tiering identifies access patterns in Storage Allocation Units (SAUs) and either promotes the data to a higher priority tier or demotes the data to a lower priority tier based on usage relative to other data within the pool. The most frequently and consistently accessed data will be migrated to higher priority tiers and the least-accessed data will be migrated to lesser priority tiers. The tiers used for storage are also effected by the storage profile of a virtual disk, as described in the next section. Automated Storage Tiering is a licensed option.

The default behavior of auto-tiering is to migrate data based on the frequency of read operations only. Data can also be monitored for the frequency of both read and write operations by enabling a custom storage profile setting and applying the storage profile to virtual disks. The write-aware auto-tiering setting, when enabled, gives auto-tiering the ability to migrate data based on both reads and writes equally. This setting could be useful when very few read operations occur to the back-end storage used by a virtual disk. In this case, read operations alone might not present a true picture of how frequently the data is accessed. This could occur with some applications where most operations are performed in memory. See Storage Profiles for important information about write-aware auto-tiering and creating custom storage profiles.

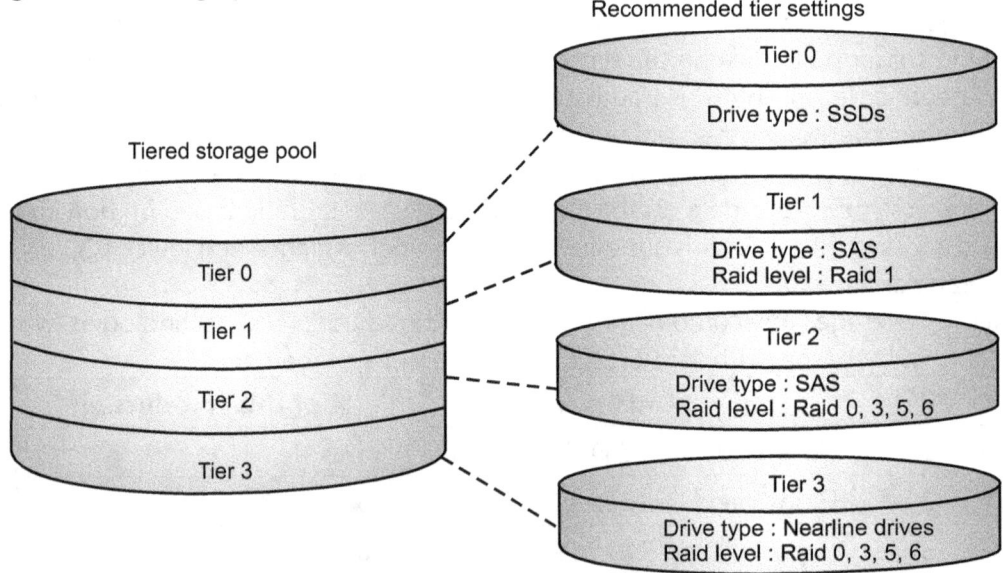

Fig. 3.30 : Storage tiering

A disk pool is comprised of a number of tiers that are used to separate physical disks of different speeds and performance within the same pool. Each pool can have from one to 15 tiers; the default setting is three. The number of tiers in a pool is assigned when it is created, but can be changed at any time. See Changing the Number of Tiers in a Disk Pool in this topic.

When calculating the number of tiers in a disk pool, be aware that there should be a significant difference in performance between tiers in order to justify the migration of data between the tiers. Data migration will affect the disk pool performance.

When physical disks are initially added to a pool, they are assigned (by default) to a tier which falls in the middle of the top and bottom tiers. To implement the auto-tiering scheme, after adding disks to the pool, the user should change the tier number assigned to the disks to reflect the speed and performance of the disks. For instance, if the disk pool has three tiers, Tier 1 should consist of the fastest physical disks in the pool or the disks that should be used the most often. Tier 3 should consist of the slowest disks or disks that should be used the least. See Changing Physical Disk Tier Numbers in this topic. In this manner, frequently accessed data will utilize the fastest disks in the highest priority tiers, while infrequently accessed data can be relegated to the slowest disks in the lowest priority tiers. Automated Storage Tiering can improve performance by decreasing response time when data is being read from physical disks.

Benefits	
Features	By assigning applications to different tiers consisting of different drive types and RAID levels, users can easily meet wide variety of service level requirements
Fine-tuning storage deployment	SSDs are used most efficiently in an automated storage tiering architecture to optimize performance by up to 150% at no additional costs compared to a non-tiered configuration
Optimized storage performance	Optimized performance available at no additional costs or lower costs By precisely meeting service level requirements, storage can be efficiently utilized Efficient storage utilization increases lifespan
Enhanced ROI	While enjoying higher performance and reduced costs, capacity can be increased by deploying high-capacity nearline drives in lower tiers
Flexible capacity deployment	Based on data usage patterns, migration ensures optimized distribution of data in storage pools Sub-volume tiering ensures highly granular data movement Scheduling options ensure data migration can be conducted based on actual user requirements Ensures SSDs have the necessary space to serve mission-critical applications
Highly efficient data migration	Doing more with less reduces storage footprint and lowers power consumption SSDs feature low power consumption levels
Efficient storage utilization	Automated features help IT managers spend much less time on assigning applications to storage media and migrating data
Simplified management	

3.11 VLAN

Virtual LAN (Local Area Network) is a Local Area Network configured by software and not by hardware (i.e. not by physical wiring).

Thus, same switched LAN divided into VLANs is shown in Fig. 3.31.

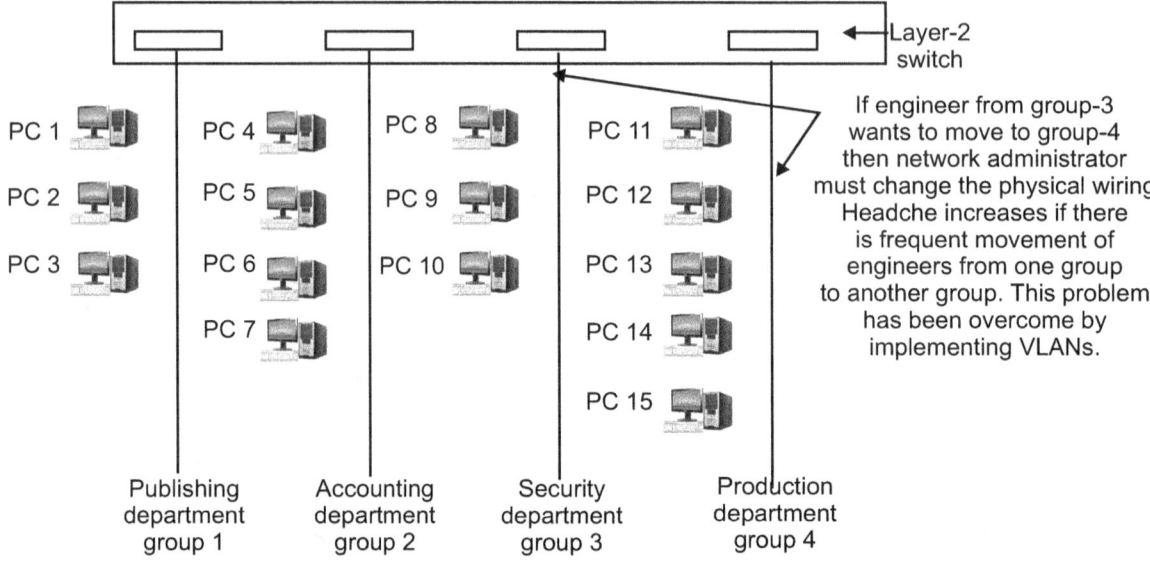

If engineer from group-3 wants to move to group-4 then network administrator must change the physical wiring Headche increases if there is frequent movement of engineers from one group to another group. This problem has been overcome by implementing VLANs.

Fig. 3.31 : Layer-2 switch connecting four LANs in a company

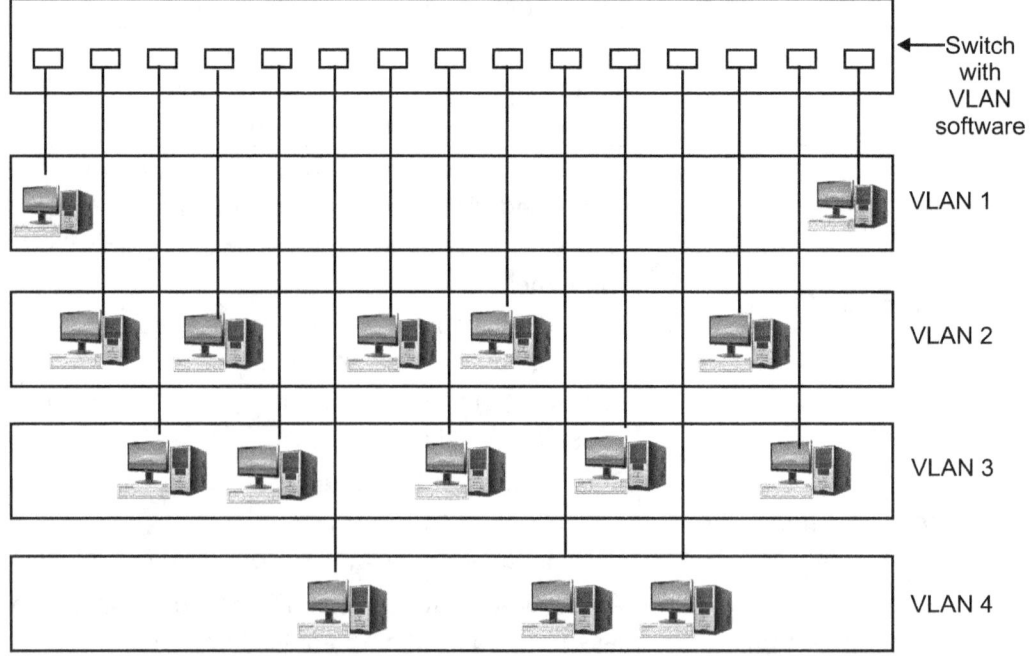

Fig. 3.32 : VLAN network using switch with VLAN software

- VLAN is completely logical configuration using software known as VLAN software.

- VLAN membership is defined by software, not by hardware (or physical wiring).
- Thus, all members belonging to a respective VLAN (i.e. VLAN1 or VLAN2 or VLAN3 or VLAN4) can receive broadcast messages sent to that specific/particular VLAN only.
- This means if PC station moves from VLAN3 to VLAN4, it receives broadcast messages sent to VLAN4, but will no longer receive broadcast messages sent to VLAN3.
- Thus, if engineers working in company in publishing department group 1 move to production department group 4, through the VLAN software, it is easier than changing the configuration of the physical network (i.e. physical wiring etc.).

3.11.1 Practical Virtual Lans

- A switch can have number of ports from 12 ports to 80 or more, and by default all hosts connected to that switch are going to be in the same broadcast domain. Let's say we have an 80-port switch. If one host connected to that switch sends a broadcast, by default, all of the other 79 hosts are going to receive the broadcast. That will unnecessarily take-up network's available bandwidth.
- It gets worse. For some network services and protocols, a broadcast received by a host results in that same host transmitting the received broadcast as well as broadcast of its own. When all the hosts receive that broadcast, they all end up transmitting even more broadcasts. Pretty soon, all these broadcasts have snowballed into a broadcast storm, which can take-up most of a network's bandwidth and make normal network operations almost impossible.
- Most likely, only a few hosts on each switch really need to communicate with each other. Let's take a eight-port switch for example, where three of the hosts are in the security department, another three in the accounting department, and the other two in the publishing department.
- If any of these PC's sends a broadcast, every other host attached to that switch is going to receive it, and may well generate a broadcast of its own in response. That's what we want to guard against, and we can do so through the creation of Virtual LAN's, or VLAN's.
- Physically, these hosts all reside on the same Local Area Network, but we can conFig. 3.the switch to place them in different logical (Virtual) LAN's. When a switch is configured with VLAN's, the switch will forward a broadcast only to those hosts in the same VLAN as the host that originated it. By creating three VLAN's on this switch, we now have three smaller broadcast domains, which helps to limit the impact of a broadcast on network operations.

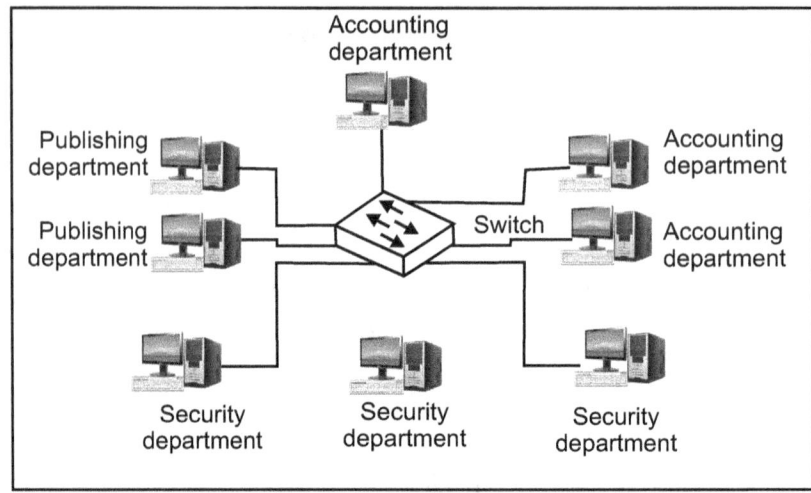

Fig. 3.33 : Switch connecting three departments in a company

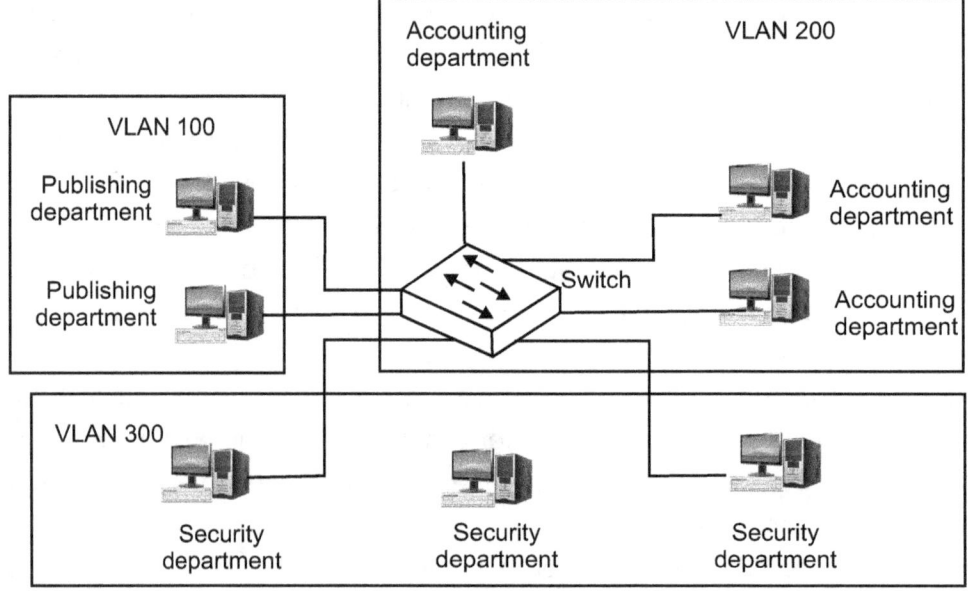

Fig. 3.34 : VLAN network using switch VLAN software

- After placing the security hosts in their own VLAN, and then doing the same for the accounting and publishing hosts, broadcasts are now limited to being forwarded throughout their own VLAN. If a host in the security department sends a broadcast, only other hosts in that same VLAN will receive it.

- Most switches require to assign a number to a VLAN when it is created, so here VLAN 100 was assigned to the Publishing VLAN, VLAN 200 to the Accounting VLAN, and VLAN 300 to the Security VLAN.

3.11.2 Pre-Requisites Of VLAN

*   These are special purpose devices and computers that just transfer messages from one network to another. Before we look deep into the topic Virtual LANs, let us see the basic devices used in the network backbone. They are :
*   Bridges
*   Switches
*   Routers
*   Gateways
*   Hubs.
*   **Bridges :** Bridges operate at the data link layer. They connect two LAN segments that use the same data link and network protocols.
*   **Switches :** Like bridges, switches operate at the data link layer. Switches connect two or more computers or network segments that use the same data link and network protocols.
*   **Routers :** Routers operate at the network layer. Routers connect two or more LANs that use the same or different data link protocols, but it does the basic system interconnection and the necessary translation between the protocols in both directions.
*   **Hubs :** Physical layer devices are really just multiple port repeaters. When an electronic digital signal is received on a port, the signal is reamplified or regenerated and forwarded out to all segments except the segment from which the signal was received.
*   In a broadcast environment, a broadcast is sent out by a host on a single segment that would propagate to all segments, saturating the bandwidth of the entire network. Also, without forcing some method of checking at an upper layer, all devices in the broadcast domain would be able to communicate via layer-2. This severely limits the amount of security that could be enforced on the network. Before the introduction of switches and VLANs, networks were divided into multiple broadcast domains by connectivity through a router. Because routers do not forward broadcasts, each interface is in a different broadcast domain. Each segment is an individual IP subnet and regardless of a workstation's function, its subnet is defined by its physical location.
*   A VLAN is logical broadcast domain that can span multiple physical LAN segments. A VLAN can be designed to provide independent broadcast domains for station logically segmented by functions, project teams, or applications, regardless to the physical location of users. Each switch port can be assigned to only one VLAN. Ports in a VLAN share broadcasts. Ports that do not belong to the same VLAN do not share broadcasts. This control of broadcast improves the overall performance of network.
*   A group of devices on one or more logically segmented LANs (configured by use of software), enabling devices to communicate as if attached to the same physical medium, when they are actually located on numerous different LAN segments.

VLANs are based on logical instead of physical connections and thus are tremendously flexible.

VLANs enable switches to create multiple broadcast domains within a switched network. Any user in this VLAN would receive a broadcast from any other member of the VLAN; users of other VLANs would not receive these broadcasts. Each of the users in a given VLAN would also be in the same IP subnet.

3.11.3 Definitions Of VLAN

- **Definition 1 :** A Virtual LAN, commonly known as a VLAN, is a group of hosts with a common set of requirements that communicate as if they were attached to the broadcast domain, regardless of their physical location. A VLAN has the same attributes as a physical LAN, but it allows for end stations to be grouped together even if they are not located on the same network switch. Network reconfiguration can be done through software instead of physically relocating the devices.
- **Definition 2 :** A VLAN acts like an ordinary LAN, but connected devices do not have to be physically connected to the same segment. While clients and servers may be located anywhere on a network, they are grouped together by VLAN technology, and broadcasts are sent to devices within the VLAN.
- **Definition 3 :** A LAN is a Local Area Network and is defined as all devices in the same roadcast domai n. If you remember, routers stop broadcasts, switches just forward them. VLAN is a virtual LAN. In technical terms, a VLAN is a broadcast domain created by switches. Normally, it is a router creating that broadcast domain. With VLANs, a switch can create the broadcast domain.
- **Definition 4 :** Virtual Local Area Networks (VLAN or virtual LAN) allow multiple logical Local Area Networks (LANs) to exist within a single physical LAN. In other words, the LANs are defined in software rather than hardware.
- **Definition 5 :** A VLAN is a network that is logically segmented on an organizational basis, by functions, project teams, or applications rather than on a physical or a geographical basis. The network can be reconfigured through software rather than by physically unplugging and moving devices or wires. Stations are connected by switches and routers to form broadcast domains.
- **Definition 6 :** Virtual Local Area Network also called a "VLAN," it is a logical subgroup within a local area network that is created via software rather than manually moving cables in the wiring closet. It combines user stations and network devices into a single unit regardless of the physical LAN segment they are attached to and allows traffic to flow more efficiently within populations of mutual interest.
- **Definition 7 :** Virtual LANs (VLANs) are used to break up broadcast domains in a layer-2 switched internetwork.
- **Definition 8 :** A local area network (LAN) is a private network usually confined to one plant. Virtual LANs (VLANs) allow a single physical LAN to be partitioned into several smaller logical LANs. VLANs limit the broadcast domain, improve security, performance and are ideal for separating industrial automation systems from information technology systems.

3.11.4 Need Of VLAN

You need to consider using VLANs in any of the following situations :
- You have more than 200 devices on your LAN.

- You have a lot of broadcast traffic on your LAN.
- Groups of users need more security or are being slowed down by too many broadcasts.
- Groups of users need to be on the same broadcast domain because they are running the same applications. An example would be a company that has VoIP phones. The users using the phone could be on a different VLAN, not with the regular users.
- Or, just to make a single switch into multiple virtual switches.

3.11.5 Uses Of VLAN

- VLANs are created to provide the segmentation services traditionally provided by routers in LAN configurations. VLANs address issues such as scalability, security and network management. Routers in VLAN topologies provide broadcast filtering, security, address summarization, and traffic flow management. By definition, switches may not bridge IP traffic between VLANs as it would violate the integrity of the VLAN broadcast domain.
- This is also useful if someone wants to create multiple layer-3 networks on the same layer-2 switch. For example, if a DHCP (Dynamic Host Configuration Protocol) server (which will broadcast its presence) was plugged into a switch it will serve any host on that switch that was configured to use the server. By using VLANs you can easily split the network so that some hosts won't use that server and will obtain Link-local addresses.
- Virtual LANs are essentially layer-2 constructs, compared with IP subnets which are layer-3 constructs. In an environment employing VLANs, a one-to-one relationship often exists between VLANs and IP subnets, although it is possible to have multiple subnets on one VLAN or have one subnet spread across multiple VLANs. Virtual LANs and IP subnets provide independent layer-2 and layer-3 constructs that map to one another and this correspondence is useful during the network design process.
- By using VLANs, one can control traffic patterns and react quickly to relocations. VLANs provide the flexibility to adapt to changes in network requirements and allow for simplified administration.

3.12 VSAN AND BENIFITS

A Storage-Area Network (SAN) is a dedicated high-speed network (or subnetwork) that interconnects and presents shared pools of storage devices to multiple servers. A SAN moves storage resources off the common user network and reorganizes them into an independent, high-performance network. This allows each server to access shared storage as if it were a drive directly attached to the server. When a host wants to access a storage device on the SAN, it sends out a block-based access request for the storage device. A Virtual Storage Area Network (VSAN) is a logical partitioning created within a physical storage area network. This implementation model of a storage virtualization technique divides and allocates some or an entire storage area network into one or more logical SANs to be used by internal or external IT services and solutions. The use of VSANs allows the isolation of traffic within specific portions of the network. If a problem occurs in one VSAN, that problem can be handled with a minimum of disruption to the rest of the network. VSANs can also be configured separately and independently. A storage-area network is typically assembled using three principle components: cabling, Host Bus Adapters (HBAs) and switches. Each switch and storage system on the SAN must be interconnected and the physical interconnections must support bandwidth levels that can adequately handle peak data activities. Storage area networks are managed centrally, and Fibre Channel (FC) SANs have the reputation of being expensive, complex and difficult to manage. The emergence of iSCSI has reduced these challenges by encapsulating SCSI commands into IP packets for transmission over an Ethernet connection, rather than an FC connection. Instead of learning, building and managing two networks an Ethernet Local Area Network (LAN) for user communication and an FC SAN for storage an organization can now use its existing knowledge and infrastructure for both LANs and SANs.

3.12.1 SAN vs. NAS

The terms *SAN* and *NAS* are sometimes confused with one another because the acronyms are so similar. NAS consists of a storage appliance that is plugged directly into a network switch. Although there are exceptions, NAS appliances are often used as file servers. A Virtual Storage Area Network (VSAN) is a logical partition in a Storage Area Network (SAN). VSANs allow traffic to be isolated within specific portions of a storage area network. The use of multiple VSANs can make a system easier to conFig. 3.and scale out. Subscribers can be added or relocated without the need for changing the physical layout. If a problem occurs in one VSAN, that problem can be handled with a minimum of disruption to the rest of the network. Because the independence of VSANs minimizes the total system's vulnerability, security is improved. VSANs also offer the possibility of data redundancy, minimizing the risk of catastrophic data loss. The term is most often associated with Cisco Systems and is often mentioned in conjunction with the zoning. Zoning splits a SAN into multiple, isolated subnetworks. The concept behind a VSAN is often compared to that of a Virtual Local Area Network (VLAN). VLANs segregate broadcasts from other networks. A virtual storage area network is primarily implemented in cloud computing and virtualization environments. A VSAN allows end users and organizations to provision a logical storage area network on top of the physical SAN through storage virtualization. The virtualized SAN can be used to build a virtual storage pool for multiple services; however, it is generally provisioned to be integrated with virtual machines and virtual servers.

A VSAN provides similar services and features as a typical SAN, but because it is virtualized, it allows for the addition and relocation of subscribers without having to change the network's physical layout. It also provides flexible storage capacity that can be increased or decreased over time.

3.12.2 Benefits of VSAN

1. Scalability

SAN has many advantages over DAS in your data center. Here are ten reasons to consider making the leap from local storage to a SAN. If you know, or have heard, one thing about a SAN, it's scalable. What does scalable mean? SAN scalability means that you don't have the limit of a handful of disks that you can attach to a system. SANs can grow to hundreds of disks in size, whereas your server has a physical limit of about a dozen.

2. Performance

SAN performance isn't affected by Ethernet traffic or local disk throughput bottlenecks. Data transmitted to and from a SAN is on its own private network partitioned off from user traffic, backup traffic and other SAN traffic.

3. Data Isolation

There's no chance of your data being copied or stolen by anyone sharing the same SAN with you. Not even the SAN admins can see your data. When correctly configured, SAN data is zoned. These zones protect your data from everyone else's on the same SAN. An example of SAN zone separation is how UNIX servers can connect to a SAN and Windows servers connect to the same SAN, but the data that each group of servers accesses is different. In effect, Windows systems can't "see" UNIX data and vice versa.

4. Uptime

There's nothing quite like a SAN to assure 100-percent storage availability. SAN systems require no reboots to add new disks, to replace disks or to conFig. 3.RAID groups. The ability to stream data between SANs for data backup and recovery also increases performance by bypassing server systems completely.

5. Workload Isolation

Zoning also separates your workloads from one another on a SAN. Not only is your data protected by zoning, but it also provides a barrier against other non-related workloads from affecting your application's performance. Sharing a SAN isn't a performance problem for applications when zones are in place.

6. Long Distance Connectivity

SANs have the advantage over all other storage connectivity for distance at 10 km (about 6 miles). Not that you'll necessarily use that distance capability, but it's there if you need it. Having the advantage of distance allows you to consolidate your storage into an isolated location dedicated to storage and separate from the systems it serves.

7. Increased Utilization

Rather than hundreds or thousands of partially utilized local disks wasting power and generating heat in your data center, you could have dozens of SAN disks have no wasted space on them. How so? Thin provisioning on the storage side (i.e., on the SAN) uses space more effectively than local storage does. As a system requires more storage, the SAN allocates it dynamically. Yes, this means that physical systems can enjoy thin provisioning just like your virtual ones do. Better disk utilization is the primary benefit of using SAN storage. When your storage is available in a centralized manner then everything can be managed as a single entity. This gives you an advantage to slice up the different pools of storage resources at a network level and assign the storage in an intellectual manner to the available server applications. If you missed a SAN deployment then you would have been practicing the tradition of purchasing tons of disks and sticking them to an expensive server. In this practice, high cost investment is needed and disk space also gets wasted as most of your enterprise applications may not need the available space at all times.

8. Bootable

Despite the benefit of more fully utilized disks, as highlighted in advantage No. 7, you do not need to use local disks for the server operating system. It's possible to run diskless physical servers and boot directly to the SAN for your operating system, swap space (pagefile), and all applications. That's right, just like virtual machines.

9. Centralized Management

If you have SAN arrays from several different vendors because your data center has grown over the years, stress not, SAN vendors have created software management tools to manage your heterogeneous environment with ease. But, better than multiple vendor management capability, all of your SAN environments can be centrally managed from this single interface. This capability provides efficient and centralized storage management.

10. SAN for Disaster Recovery for Multiple Applications : If your data center/ IT environment has critical servers running on applications which cannot be let down, then there needs to be a data continuity solution in place, which can act as a failover when a disaster strikes. If this indeed is the scenario then SAN based DR solution will be the right choice. Since the volume of downtime is critical in most organizations when disaster strikes, a SAN solution will effectively reduce the **downtime number to a negligible value.**

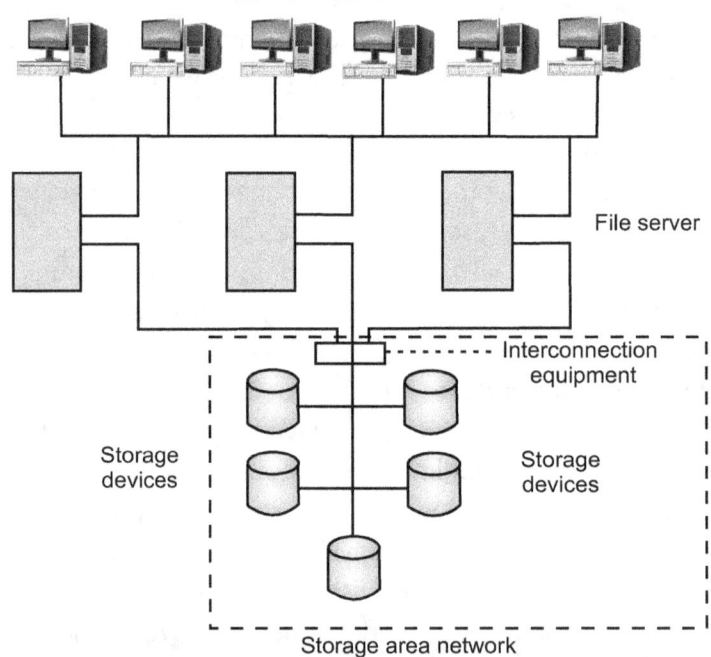

Fig. 3.35 : Storage area network

3.13 NETWORK TRAFFIC MANAGEMENT TECHNIQUES IN VDC

Data centers have been designed for expensive network design. But as the modern data center evolves to a scale-out, dynamic and virtualized shared services platform, network traffic management becomes very important virtual data centers.

Even with the undeniable cost and scalability benefits of virtualization and cloud computing, the elastic and dynamic nature of software-defined cloud computing introduces a whole new set of challenges to IT professionals. While responsiveness to immediate needs has improved, diagnosing problems and analyzing performance has become more complex. With more of the path of application data being shrouded in virtual networks, managing and monitoring network operations with traditional approaches is becoming difficult. IT leaders and stakeholders are constantly struggling with gaining back visibility, maintaining and improving application performance, and enforcing corporate regulatory policies across this new type of network while also leveraging benefits brought by virtualization.

For years, data center networks have been designed according to the same basic concept :

• Single spanning-tree with three layers (top-of-rack/blade, access, and core switches) and significant over subscription at each layer.

• Applications deployed in self-contained racks, with internal Layer 2 switching connected to Layer 3 aggregation switches/routers.

In this design, traffic management is done at the core rather than the edge. Each application crosses rack/edge boundaries, so the only traffic to manage is external. The core switch designs are high-powered and feature-rich, and use a large amount of packet buffering to absorb network spikes and implement traffic shaping. When congestion occurs, packets are dropped to slow down the transmitters.

The delay and jitter created by the buffering does not significantly impact application performance since the main purpose of the core network is external (slow, long haul traffic), and the inter-application traffic (IPC, storage) is confined to the rack.

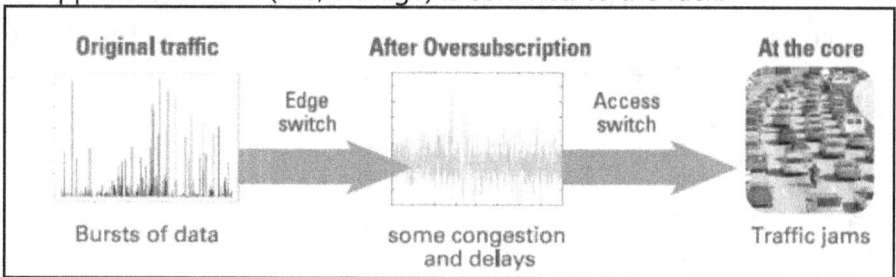

Fig. 3.36 : Network traffic

Now, economical challenges are driving data centers to reach new levels of efficiency. IT departments are now measured against business goals, not just up-time. And so they have adopted a service-oriented approach, consolidating and commoditizing server, storage, and network resources overlaid with virtualization and dynamic workload management. This approach lets IT deliver services faster with less effort and fewer physical resources.

Many of the assumptions that drive the old legacy network design have changed dramatically due to recent technological, organizational, and economical changes:

• Virtualization, cloud, and scale-out applications now drive the need for larger Layer 2 domains that span across multiple switches.

- Delay and jitter-sensitive traffic now goes through the core, requiring lower latency and less oversubscription on core switches.
- Storage and IPC protocols are bursty and sensitive to packet drops, requiring lossless fabric. When they share the same wire with standard protocols, L2 traffic-isolation mechanisms are needed.

Multiple applications and tenants can share the same edge ports and wires. Workloads are virtualized and mobile, requiring end-to-end traffic SLA management across virtual, edge, and core switches and not just in the L3 core.

- Merchant silicon has become denser, cheaper, and loaded with features allowing new vendors to create more innovative and economical solutions.

Heavy network oversubscription is no longer desired since there is now significantly more east-west (rack- to- rack) traffic due to scale-out applications. MapReduce, application and storage clustering, server migration, and fault-tolerance all contribute to this traffic. Adding to the challenge is the inherent oversubscription in the server, with each running multiple virtual machines and acting as a switch with over-subscribed uplinks.

A fresh approach is needed to tackle these new data center challenges. Instead of building a hierarchical and oversubscribed network, the data center should be designed as a flat fabric that is dynamically partitioned to address application services. In the fabric, traffic is managed and buffered close to the source/edge, and the fabric core serves as a fast highway with multiple paths/lanes as well as low end-to-end latency. In a fabric, application workloads can span different locations and even migrate dynamically between physical servers while maintaining security and service levels.

This fabric architecture is built on a large number of simple, fast, low-power switches that are interconnected and orchestrated to deliver overall network services. This results in faster, more scalable, and cost-effective networks.

- **Intra-host Traffic**

Virtualization is creating blind spots, or invisible networks, within the server infrastructure. With a large share of traffic flowing across software-defined cloud infrastructure, being encapsulated across virtual tunnel endpoints, and in many cases not even hitting the physical network at all, VM and network administrators are losing the visibility and control over this communication. This lack of comprehensive visibility is causing reticence among IT professionals seeking to wrap up complex workloads in virtualized infrastructure.

With security and compliance being top of mind in virtualization and cloud deployments, organizations are struggling with how to reconcile competing priorities to virtualize their environments, while still satisfying the existing requirements for visibility. It should therefore come as no surprise to see traffic visibility, compliance, and data security consistently listed among the top inhibitors to cloud adoption.

- **vMotion**

vMotion is Developed by VMware, vSphere vMotion technology enables the live migration of running virtual machines from one physical server to another. vMotion allows the creation of a dynamic, automated, and self-optimizing data center with continuous and automatic optimization of virtual machines. This technology, which includes fault tolerance, high availability, and DRS, is the first step towards keeping downtime to a minimum. However, with this enhanced agility come changes to the server infrastructure as a completely new layer of complexity is added.

To monitor these environments effectively, administrators need to ensure monitoring can seamlessly and automatically be updated to reflect these changes. Further, monitoring solutions need the capability to retain monitoring continuity and history, so administrators can better track and assess these issues over time and set better policies. Without the capability to track and monitor these vMotion events as VMs get reallocated, the resulting configurations can potentially go askew impacting the availability and performance of application and services.

- **vSwitch**

The most common way to provide Virtual Machine (VM) switching connectivity is a Virtual Ethernet Bridge (VEB), commonly referred to as a vSwitch. A vSwitch is a software component associated with a hypervisor that functions like a Layer 2 hardware switch providing inbound/outbound and inter-VM communication. By default, every VM can communicate directly with every other VM on the same host through the simple virtual switch, without any inter-VM traffic monitoring or policy-based inspection and filtering.

Intra-host VM traffic, handled internally by the vSwitch, does not transit the physical network. This communication is not visible to many network-based security and monitoring appliances residing outside a virtual server.

As a result, consolidating multiple physical servers into a single virtual server platform significantly impacts all of the network and application monitoring, firewall, intrusion detection, and other compliance tools that were in place prior to the physical to virtual migration. Simply put, traditional network monitoring and security measures may be unable to effectively manage the growing volume of inter-VM traffic, leaving VMs highly vulnerable to attack. This lack of visibility complicates fault isolation and resolution, potentially erasing cost savings associated with the physical to virtual migration.

Ethernet standards have been enhanced recently to support fabric capabilities taken from InfiniBand and Fibre Channel, such as multi-path, class isolation, lossless behavior, dynamic congestion control, virtual end-points, and capability discovery. These capabilities allow new network designs that are more efficient and facilitate fabric convergence. They also fit better within virtualized data center environments.

These new standards are gradually adopted with pre-standard solutions already delivered to the market.

Enterprise core switches usually function as a junction between multiple communication sources such as desktops, servers, and the Internet, as well as multiple users with different access priorities and rights.

They are designed to address the many flows that cross this individual junction and focus on feature richness and throughput (not response time) while providing security, QoS, and monitoring.

Most vendors have created solutions using a similar architecture that consists of line interfaces that accept and classify the traffic. The traffic is then placed in queues for each destination and/or service (Virtual Output Queues), and traffic is piped to the destination port at the desired speed and priority. To improve utilization, packets may be broken into small cells that are load-balanced across the internal fabric. Later on, the packets are reassembled and sent to the destination.

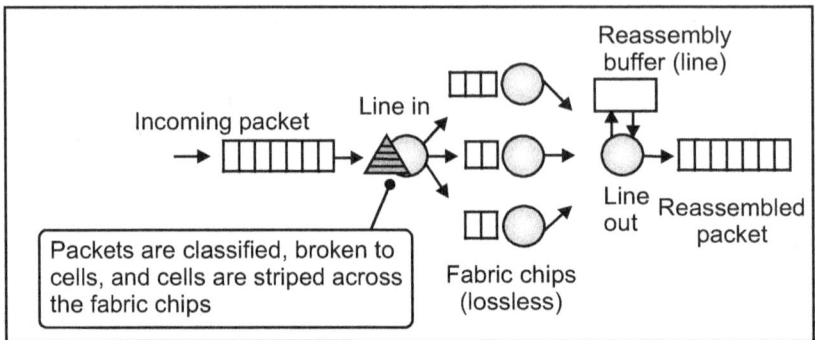

Fig. 3.37 : Network traffic management in VDC

This architecture has a number of key advantages. It is able to manage many flows going through the same junction and improve the switch utilization in oversubscribed environments, and it provides sufficient buffering to overcome unpredictable WAN performance.

However, there are also some drawbacks :

- The improved utilization comes at the expense of high delays/latency due to extensive queuing, packet fragmentation and reassembly, and store-and-forward architecture. With many flows traversing the switch, and as the switch becomes more loaded, the delays increase.

- Traffic management is handled at the congestion point (after the network is already jammed) not at the source.

- More components and a complex architecture lead to expensive, high-powered, and lower MTBF switch designs.

- This solution assumes there is one central junction that all the data flows through. This is not the case in large, scale-out data centers that contain east-west traffic and/or when using multi-path.

- Designing with a proprietary internal fabric limits the product and component options and locks in customers.

In legacy networks, there is only one core/root switch, which can easily become a bottleneck. That's also why there is a lot of emphasis on how to prioritize and schedule traffic in the core since important traffic should not be jammed behind less critical data. However, when building larger configurations that have a first layer of edge switches, the edge switches are typically not synchronized with the core policy or they implement their own load-balancing/trunking which undermines the efficiency of the core.

In new scale-out fabric solutions, there are often multiple cores handling the load. When there are two or more such active-active core switches (rather than an active and a standby core switch as is common in legacy systems), the traffic divides between the cores, which lowers the traffic to less than 50% load per core. This leads to far fewer delays and better throughput than a 100% utilized single core, where any sudden burst causes a delay. The solution cost is often the same or even less due to the simpler design of the fabric core switches. Even if the traffic is not uniformly distributed between all cores due to hash inefficiency, it is still far better than having a saturated core switch.

This fabric design imitates the design of a legacy core switch by scaling it out over multiple boxes. In this scheme, the edge or virtual switches function as line cards that classify and manage the traffic. The core switches function as the fabric cards that focus on low latency and lossless-traffic exchange between line cards. To orchestrate all the fabric switches, there is a fabric manager or operating system, which acts as the scale-out version of a supervisor module in legacy core switches. Fabrics eliminate the need for deep buffers at the core as data traverses the core without stopping and without being dropped. If data needs to be throttled down to eliminate fabric congestion, fabrics use dynamic and fabric-wide congestion control mechanisms that keep traffic out of the center while buffering the traffic at its injection point (such as server-host memory). Just as in legacy core switches, traffic is buffered in the line card and not in the fabric card.

As an analogy, think of a busy road with many traffic lights. The road is fully utilized and prone to traffic jams. Wouldn't it be better to have a highway with two or more such roads or lanes that the traffic can be directed to? Such a highway, by definition, should not be over-utilized since the effectiveness of a highway is measured by how fast cars can travel the length of the highway (delay), and not how many cars can be squeezed onto it (utilization). If the cars on a highway are only few feet apart (i.e. the highway is 80% utilized), it is likely that drivers will experience delays.

The fabric design takes the highway approach :

- Use many simpler switching elements to reduce costs, power, and space.
- Eliminate congestion with fast-forwarding and multiple paths/lanes.
- Manage and buffer the traffic at the entrance (eliminate "traffic lights" inside).
- Minimize packet drops.

Using this method, the fabric cores are not saturated, and delays are not accumulated throughout the fabric. The fabric's bi-sectional bandwidth (overall bandwidth) scales linearly as cores are added, allowing greater scalability and performance at lower costs.

The traditional way to manage congestion is for an oversubscribed network junction to drop packets.

Once the source detects the drop, it retransmits the data and automatically slows down. To reduce drops due to traffic spikes, core switches use deeper buffers. Congestion accumulates, and if the congestion does not subside, packets are dropped after long delays. The traditional TCP protocol implements a slow start mechanism that gradually increases performance to minimize drops. However, when an application wants to send a large burst of data, it takes a much longer time compared to fabrics with hardware flow/congestion control (like FC, InfiniBand, or Converged Ethernet).

More buffers increase the network's ability to absorb over subscription. At the same time, the legacy lossless Ethernet mechanism behaves just like a switch with deep buffers. Packets are not dropped, which eliminates the traffic collapse problem.

With Enhanced Ethernet standards, several new hardware mechanisms were introduced to provide better hardware flow-control and congestion-management to reduce congestion, eliminate collapse, and allow fast bursts without slow starts.

In this scenario, output is oversubscribed with traffic from the four red sources. Green traffic is delayed since it is waiting behind packets leading to the congested output. InfiniBand and Enhanced Ethernet fabrics incorporate congestion-control mechanisms (802.1 Qau/QCN) to address the congestion by throttling the sources of congestion and allowing victim traffic to pass.

This ensures victim traffic is not stuck behind traffic going to an oversubscribed destination. The right diagram demonstrates how enabling the QCN causes victim traffic to jump to its maximum: 6.6 Gb/s, with ~3 Gb/s still flowing to the oversubscribed output.

Maximum performance is achieved when the queue depth is short. This is counter-intuitive as people have been trained to think that deeper buffers lead to better performance. In reality, the best way to improve application performance is to make sure the core is not oversubscribed too much using multi-path architectures. It's also important to control the traffic closer to the edge of the fabric while using host memory as a buffer along with dynamic, hardware-based, congestion-control mechanisms.

3.14 CLOUD FILE SYSTEMS: GFS AND HDFS

3.14.1 GFS

We all know that Google is most popular search engine. This search engine processes a lot of data and it needs an efficient, large, distributed, highly fault tolerant file system. Typical characteristics of Google search engine are :

- More than 15,000 commodity-class PC's.
- Multiple clusters distributed worldwide.
- Thousands of queries served per second.
- One query reads 100's of MB of data.
- One query consumes 10's of billions of CPU cycles.
- Google stores dozens of copies of the entire Web

A GFS cluster consists of a single *master* and multiple *chunk servers* and is accessed by multiple *clients*, as shown in Fig. 3.38.

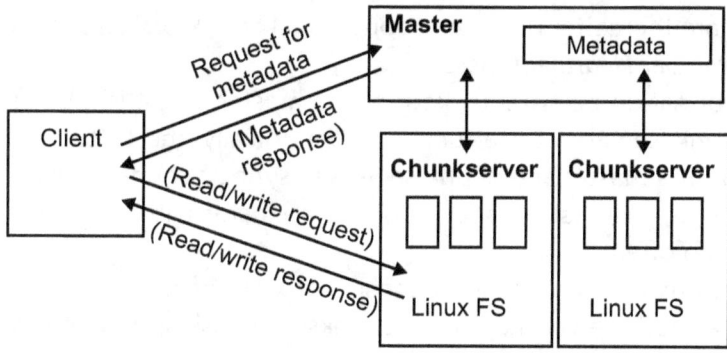

Fig. 3.38 : GFS architecture

Each of these is typically a commodity Linux machine running a user-level server process. It is easy to run both a chunk server and a client on the same machine, as long as machine resources permit and the lower reliability caused by running possibly flaky application code is acceptable. Files are divided into fixed-size *chunks*. Each chunk is identified by an immutable and globally unique 64 bit *chunk handle* assigned by the master at the time of chunk creation. Chunk servers store chunks on local disks as Linux files and read or write chunk data specified by a chunk handle and byte range. For reliability, each chunk is replicated on multiple chunk servers.

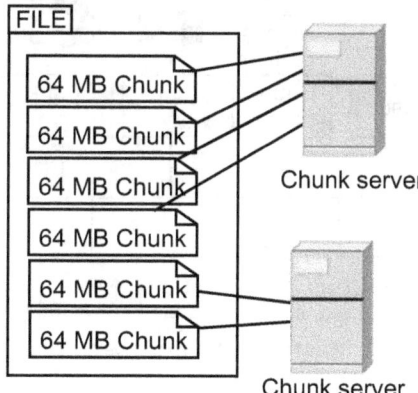

Fig. 3.39 : Chunk server

The master maintains all file system metadata. This includes the namespace, access control information, the mapping from files to chunks, and the current locations of chunks. It also controls system-wide activities such as chunk lease management, garbage collection of orphaned chunks, and chunk migration between chunk servers. The master periodically communicates with each chunk server in Heartbeat messages to give it instructions and collect its state. GFS client code linked into each application implements the file system API and communicates with the master and chunk servers to read or write data on behalf of the application.

Chunk Locations

The master does not keep a persistent record of which chunk servers have a replica of a given chunk. It simply polls chunk servers for that information at startup. The master can keep itself up-to-date thereafter because it controls all chunk placement and monitors chunk server status with regular *Heartbeat* messages.

Chunk location information persistently kept at the master, but it is much simpler to request the data from chunk servers at startup, and periodically thereafter. This eliminated the problem of keeping the master and chunk servers in sync as chunk servers join and leave the cluster, change names, fail, restart, and so on. In a cluster with hundreds of servers, these events happen all too often.

There is no point in trying to maintain a consistent view of this information on the master because errors on a chunk server may cause chunks to vanish spontaneously (e.g., a disk may go bad and be disabled) or an operator may rename a chunk server.

Clients interact with the master for metadata operations, but all data-bearing communication goes directly to the chunk servers. Neither the client nor the chunk server caches file data. Client caches offer little benefit because most applications stream through huge files or have working sets too large to be cached. Not having them simplifies the client and the overall system by eliminating cache coherence issues.

(Clients do cache metadata, however.) Chunk servers need not cache file data because chunks are stored as local files and so Linux's buffer cache already keeps frequently accessed data in memory.

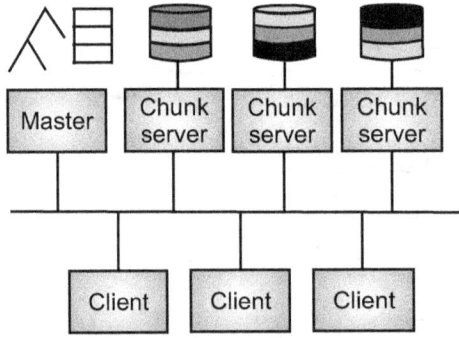

Fig. 3.40 : Master and chunk servers in GFS

Single Master

Having a single master vastly simplifies our design and enables the master to make sophisticated chunk placement and replication decisions using global knowledge. However, we must minimize its involvement in reads and writes so that it does not become a bottleneck. Clients never read and write file data through the master. Instead, a client asks the master which chunk servers it should contact. It caches this information for a limited time and interacts with the chunk servers directly for many subsequent operations. First, using the fixed chunk size, the client translates the file name and byte offset specified by the application into a chunk index within the file. Then, it sends the master a request containing the file name and chunk index. The master replies with the corresponding chunk handle and locations of the replicas. The client caches this information using the file name and chunk index as the key.

The client then sends a request to one of the replicas, most likely the closest one. The request specifies the chunk handle and a byte range within that chunk. Further reads of the same chunk require no more client-master interaction until the cached information expires or the file is reopened.

In fact, the client typically asks for multiple chunks in the same request and the master can also include the information for chunks immediately following those requested. This extra information sidesteps several future client-master interactions at practically no extra cost.

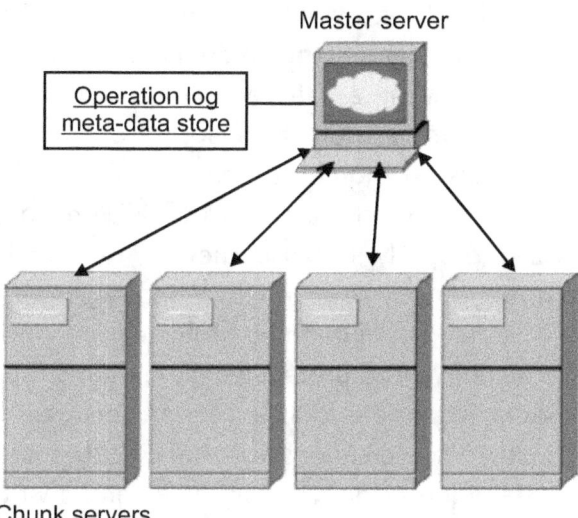

Fig. 3.41 : Master server and Meta-data store

Thus master is a single process running on a separate machine. It stores following information :

- All metadata
- File namespace
- File to chunk mappings
- Chunk location information
- Access control information
- Chunk version numbers

Master Operation

The master executes all namespace operations. In addition, it manages chunk replicas throughout the system : it makes placement decisions, creates new chunks and hence replicas, and coordinates various system-wide activities to keep chunks fully replicated, to balance load across all the chunk servers, and to reclaim unused storage.

Namespace Management and Locking

Many master operations can take a long time: for example, a snapshot operation has to revoke chunk server leases on all chunks covered by the snapshot. We do not want to delay other master operations while they are running. Therefore, we allow multiple operations to be active and use locks over regions of the namespace to ensure proper serialization.

Unlike many traditional file systems, GFS does not have a per-directory data structure that lists all the files in that directory. GFS logically represents its namespace as a lookup table mapping full pathnames to metadata. With prefix compression, this table can be efficiently represented in memory. Each node in the namespace tree (either an absolute file name or an absolute directory name) has an associated read-write lock.

Each master operation acquires a set of locks before it runs. Typically, if it involves /d1/d2/.../dn/leaf, it will acquire read-locks on the directory names /d1,/d1/d2, ..., /d1/d2/.../dn, and either a read lock or a write lock on the full pathname /d1/d2/.../dn/leaf. Note that leaf may be a file or directory depending on the operation.

This locking mechanism can prevent a file /home/user/foo from being created while /home/user is being snapshot to /save/user. The snapshot operation acquires read lock son /home and /save, and write locks on /home/user and /save/user. The file creation acquires read locks on /home and /home/user, and a write lockon /home/user/foo. The two operations will be serialized properly because they try to obtain conflicting locks on /home/user. File creation does not require a write lock on the parent directory because there is no "directory", or *inode*-like, data structure to be protected from modification.

The read locko n the name is sufficient to protect the parent directory from deletion.

One advantage of this locking scheme is that it allows concurrent mutations in the same directory. For example, multiple file creations can be executed concurrently in the same directory: each acquires a read lockon the directory name and a write lockon the file name. The read lockon the directory name suffices to prevent the directory from being deleted, renamed, or snapshot. The write locks on file names serialize attempts to create a file with the same name twice.

Since the namespace can have many nodes, read-write lock objects are allocated lazily and deleted once they are not in use. Also, locks are acquired in a consistent total order to prevent deadlock: they are first ordered by level in the namespace tree and lexicographically within the same level.

Replica Placement

A GFS cluster is highly distributed at more levels than one. It typically has hundreds of chunk servers spread across many machine racks. These chunk servers in turn may be accessed from hundreds of clients from the same or different racks. Communication between two machines on different racks may cross one or more network switch. Additionally, bandwidth into or out of a rack may be less than the aggregate bandwidth of all the machines within the rack.

Multi-level distribution presents a unique challenge to distribute data for scalability, reliability, and availability.

The chunk replica placement policy serves two purposes : maximize data reliability and availability, and maximize network and width utilization. For both, it is not enough to spread replicas across machines, which only guards against disk or machine failures and fully utilizes each machine's network bandwidth.

This ensures that some replicas of a chunk will survive and remain available even if an entire rack is damaged or offline (for example, due to failure of a shared resource like a network switch or power circuit). It also means that traffic, especially reads, for a chunk can exploit the aggregate bandwidth of multiple racks.

Creation, Re-replication, Rebalancing

Chunk replicas are created for three reasons: chunk creation, re-replication, and rebalancing.

When the master *creates* a chunk, it chooses where to place the initially empty replicas. It considers several factors.

(1) Place new replicas on chunk servers with below-average disk space utilization. Over time this will equalize disk utilization across chunk servers.

(2) Limit the number of "recent" creations on each chunk server.

Although creation itself is cheap, it reliably predicts imminent heavy write traffic because chunks are created when demanded by writes, and in our append-once-read-many workload they typically become practically read-only once they have been completely written.

(3) Spread replicas of a chunk across racks.

The master *re-replicates* a chunk as soon as the number of available replicas falls below a user-specified goal. This could happen for various reasons: a chunk server becomes unavailable, it reports that its replica may be corrupted, one of its disks is disabled because of errors, or the replication goal is increased. Each chunk that needs to be re-replicated is prioritized based on several factors. One is how far it is from its replication goal.

Finally, to minimize the impact of failures on running applications, priority of any chunk that is blocking client progress is boosted.

The master picks the highest priority chunk and "clones" by instructing some chunk server to copy the chunk data directly from an existing valid replica. The new replica is placed with goals similar to those for creation: equalizing disk space utilization, limiting active clone operations on any single chunk server, and spreading replicas across racks.

To keep cloning traffic from overwhelming client traffic, the master limits the numbers of active clone operations both for the cluster and for each chunk server. Additionally, each chunk server limits the amount of bandwidth it spends on each clone operation by throttling its read requests to the source chunk server.

Finally, the master *rebalances* replicas periodically: it examines the current replica distribution and moves replicas for better disks pace and load balancing. Also through this process, the master gradually fills up a new chunk server rather than instantly swamps it with new chunks and the heavy write traffic that comes with them. In addition, the master must also choose which existing replica to remove. In general, it prefers to remove those on chunk servers with below-average free space so as to equalize disk space usage.

Garbage Collection

After a file is deleted, GFS does not immediately reclaim the available physical storage. It does so only lazily during regular garbage collection at both the file and chunk levels.

This approach makes the system much simpler and more reliable.

When a file is deleted by the application, the master logs the deletion immediately just like other changes. However instead of reclaiming resources immediately, the file is just renamed to a hidden name that includes the deletion timestamp. During the master's regular scan of the file system namespace, it removes any such hidden files if they have existed for more than three days (the interval is configurable).

Until then, the file can still be read under the new, special name and can be undeleted by renaming it back to normal.

When the hidden file is removed from the namespace, its memory metadata is erased. This effectively severs its links to all its chunks.

In a similar regular scan of the chunk name space, the master identifies orphaned chunks (i.e., those not reachable from any file) and erases the metadata for those chunks. In a *Heartbeat* message regularly exchanged with the master, each chunk server reports a subset of the chunks it has, and the master replies with the identity of all chunks that are no longer present in the master's metadata. The chunk server is free to delete its replicas of such chunks.

Old Replica Detection

Chunk replicas may become old if a chunk server fails and misses mutations to the chunk while it is down. For each chunk, the master maintains a *chunk version number* to distinguish between up-to-date and old replicas. Whenever the master grants a new lease on a chunk, it increases the chunk version number and informs the up-to date replicas. The master and these replicas all record the new version number in their persistent state. This occurs before any client is notified and therefore before it can start writing to the chunk. If another replica is currently unavailable, its chunk version number will not be advanced. The master will detect that this chunk server has a old replica when the chunk server restarts and reports its set of chunks and their associated version numbers. If the master sees a version number greater than the one in its records, the master assumes that it failed when granting the lease and so takes the higher version to be up-to-date.

The master removes old replicas in its regular garbage collection. Before that, it effectively considers a old replica not to exist at all when it replies to client requests for chunk information. As another safeguard, the master includes the chunk version number when it informs clients which chunk server holds a lease on a chunk or when it instructs a chunk server to read the chunk from another chunk server in a cloning operation. The client or the chunk server verifies the version number when it performs the operation so that it is always accessing up-to-date data.

Fault Tolerance And Diagnosis : One of our greatest challenges in designing the system is dealing with frequent component failures.

High Availability : Among hundreds of servers in a GFS cluster, some are bound to be unavailable at any given time. High availability is ensured using following strategies : fast recovery and replication.

Fast Recovery : Both the master and the chunk server are designed to restore their state and start in seconds no matter how they terminated. In fact, there is no distinguish between normal and abnormal termination; servers are routinely shut down just by killing the process. Clients and other servers experience a minor delay as they time out on their outstanding requests, reconnect to the restarted server, and retry.

Chunk Replication

Each chunk is replicated on multiple chunk servers on different racks. Users can specify different replication levels for different parts of the file namespace.

The default is three. The master clones existing replicas as needed to keep each chunk fully replicated as chunk servers go offline or detect corrupted replicas through checksum verification. Although replication has served us well, we are exploring other forms of cross-server redundancy such as parity or erasure codes for our increasing read only storage requirements.

Master Replication

The master state is replicated for reliability. Its operation log and checkpoints are replicated on multiple machines. A mutation to the state is considered committed only after its log record has been flushed to disk locally and on all master replicas. For simplicity, one master process remains in charge of all mutations as well as background activities such as garbage collection that change the system internally.

When it fails, it can restart almost instantly. If its machine or disk fails, monitoring infrastructure outside GFS starts a new master process elsewhere with the replicated operation log. Clients use only the canonical name of the master (e.g. gfs-test), which is a DNS alias that can be changed if the master is relocated to another machine. Moreover, "shadow" masters provide read-only access to the file system even when the primary master is down. They are shadows, not mirrors, in that they may lag the primary slightly, typically fractions of a second. They enhance read availability for files that are not being actively mutated or applications that do not mind getting slightly old results.

In fact, since file content is read from chunk servers, applications do not observe old file content. What could be file names serialize attempts to create a file with the same name twice.

Since the namespace can have many nodes, read-write lock objects are allocated lazily and deleted once they are not in use. Also, locks are acquired in a consistent total order to prevent deadlock: they are first ordered by level in the namespace tree and lexicographically within the same level.

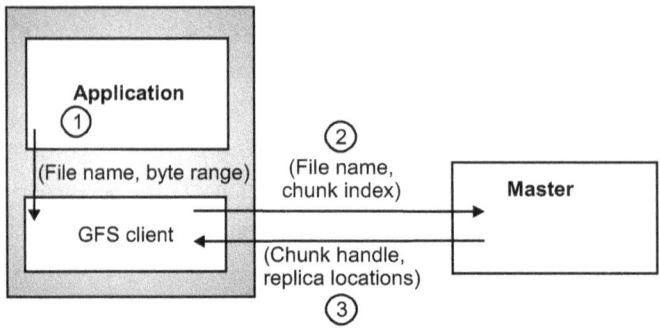

Fig. 3.42 (a) : Read operation

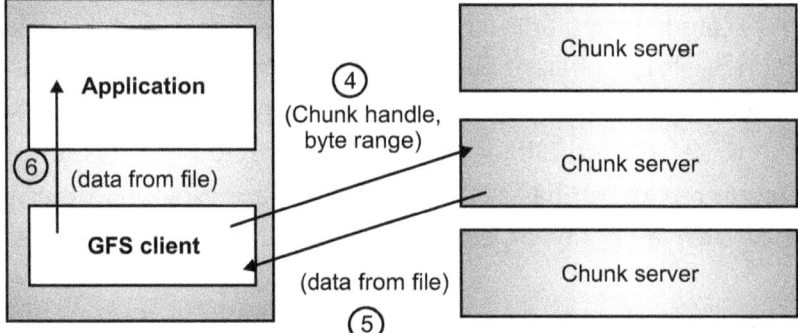

Fig. 3.42 (b) : Read operation

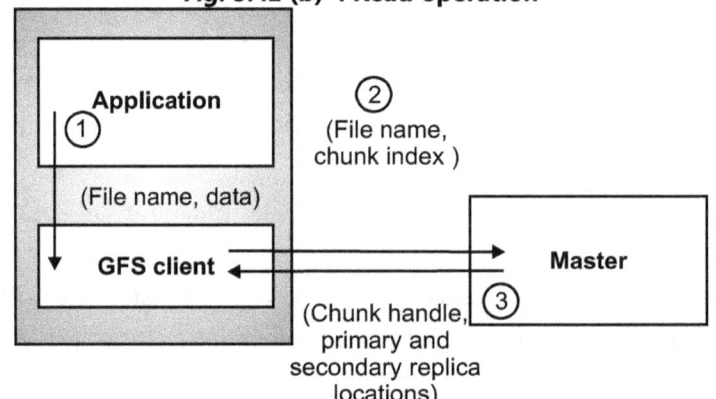

Fig. 3.43 (a) : Write operation

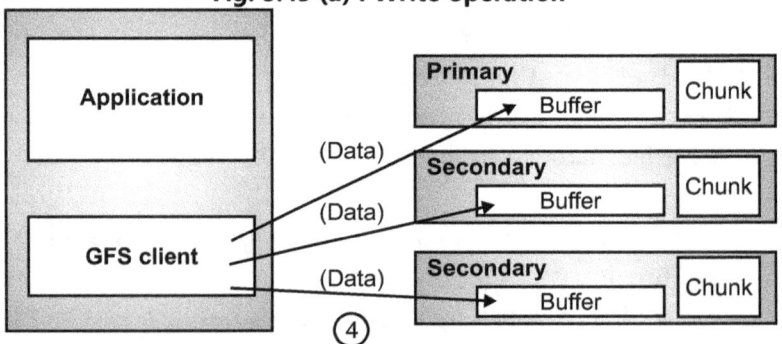

Fig. 3.43 (b) : Write operation

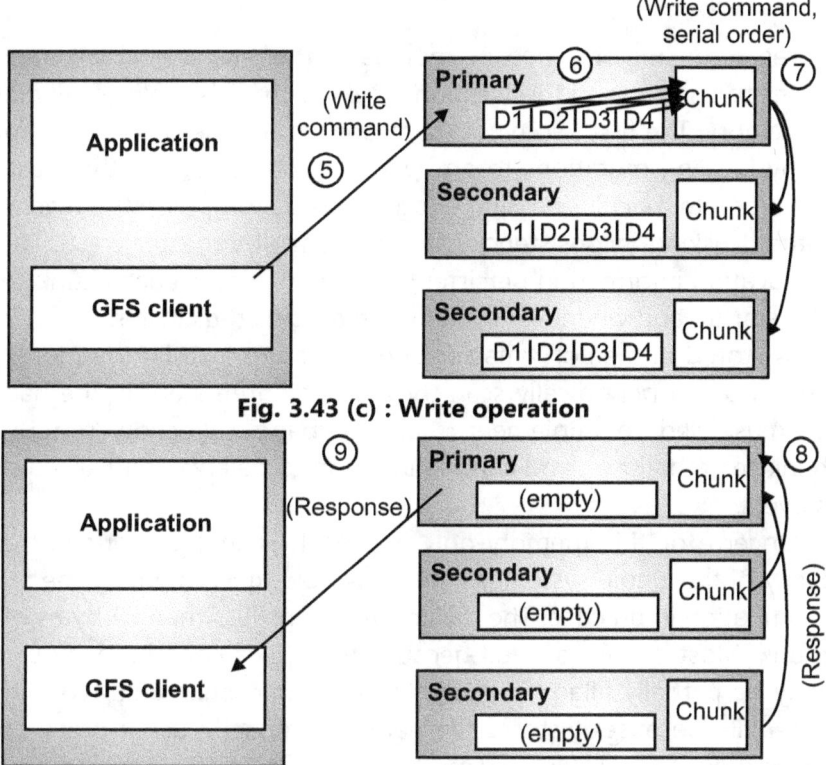

Fig. 3.43 (c) : Write operation

Fig. 3.43 (d) : Write operation

Chunk Size

Chunk size is one of the key design parameters in GFS architecture. Chunk size 64 MB, which is much larger than typical file system block sizes. Each chunk replica is stored as a plain Linux file on a chunk server and is extended only as needed. Lazy space allocation avoids wasting space due to internal fragmentation, perhaps the greatest objection against such a large chunk size. A large chunk size offers several important advantages. First, it reduces clients' need to interact with the master because reads and writes on the same chunk require only one initial request to the master for chunk location information.

The reduction is especially significant for workloads because applications mostly read and write large files sequentially. Even for small random reads, the client can comfortably cache all the chunk location information for a multi-TB working set. Second, since on a large chunk, a client is more likely to perform many operations on a given chunk, it can reduce network overhead by keeping a persistent TCP connection to the chunk server over an extended period of time. Third, it reduces the size of the metadata stored on the master. This allows us to keep the metadata in memory. On the other hand, a large chunk size, even with lazy space allocation, has its disadvantages. A small file consists of a small number of chunks, perhaps just one. The chunk servers storing those chunks may become hot spots if many clients are accessing the same file. In practice, hot spots have not been a major issue because our applications mostly read large multi-chunk files sequentially.

Metadata

The master stores three major types of metadata: the file and chunk namespaces, the mapping from files to chunks, and the locations of each chunk's replicas. All metadata is kept in the master's memory. The first two types (namespaces and file-to-chunk mapping) are also kept persistent by logging mutations to an *operation log* stored on the master's local disk and replicated on remote machines. Using a log allows us to update the master state simply, reliably, and without risking inconsistencies in the event of a master crash. The master does not store chunk location information persistently. Instead, it asks each chunk server about its chunks at master startup and whenever a chunk server joins the cluster.

Since metadata is stored in memory, master operations are fast. Furthermore, it is easy and efficient for the master to periodically scan through its entire state in the background. This periodic scanning is used to implement chunk garbage collection, re-replication in the presence of chunk server failures, and chunk migration to balance load and disk space usage across chunk servers.

One potential concern for this memory-only approach is that the number of chunks and hence the capacity of the whole system is limited by how much memory the master has. This is not a serious limitation in practice. The master maintains less than 64 bytes of metadata for each 64 MB chunk. Most chunks are full because most files contain many chunks, only the last of which may be partially filled. Similarly, the file namespace data typically requires less than 64 bytes per file because it stores file names compactly using prefix compression. If necessary to support even larger file systems, the cost of adding extra memory to the master is a small price to pay for the simplicity, reliability, performance, and flexibility we gain by storing the metadata in memory.

Consistency Model of GFS

GFS has a relaxed consistency model that supports our highly distributed applications well but remains relatively simple and efficient to implement.

File namespace mutations (e.g., file creation) are atomic. They are handled exclusively by the master. Namespace locking guarantees atomicity and correctness. The state of a file region after a data mutation depends on the type of mutation, whether it succeeds or fails, and whether there are concurrent mutations.

A file region is *consistent* if all clients will always see the same data, regardless of which replicas they read from. A region is *defined* after a file data mutation if it is consistent and clients will see what the mutation writes in its entirety. When a mutation succeeds without interference from concurrent writers, the affected region is defined (and by implication consistent): all clients will always see what the mutation has written. Concurrent successful mutations leave the region undefined but consistent: all clients see the same data, but it may not reflect what any one mutation has written. Typically, it consists of mingled fragments from multiple mutations. A failed mutation makes the region inconsistent (hence also undefined): different clients may see different data at different times.

Data mutations may be *writes* or *record appends*. A write causes data to be written at an application-specified file offset. A record appends cause data (the "record") to be appended *atomically at least once* even in the presence of concurrent mutations, but at an offset of GFS's choosing.

The offset is returned to the client and marks the beginning of a defined region that contains the record.

In addition, GFS may insert padding or record duplicates in between. They occupy regions considered to be inconsistent and are typically dwarfed by the amount of user data.

After a sequence of successful mutations, the mutated file region is guaranteed to be defined and contain the data written by the last mutation. GFS achieves this by (a) Applying mutations to a chunk in the same order on all its replicas (b) using chunk version numbers to detect any replica that has become old because it has missed mutations while its chunk server was down. Old replicas will never be involved in a mutation or given to clients asking the master for chunk locations. They are garbage collected at the earliest opportunity. Since clients cache chunk locations, they may read from a old replica before that information is refreshed. This window is limited by the cache entry's timeout and the next open of the file, which purges from the cache all chunk information for that file. Moreover, as most of our files are append-only, a old replica usually returns a premature end of chunk rather than outdated data. When a reader retries and contacts the master, it will immediately get current chunk locations.

Long after a successful mutation, component failures can of course still corrupt or destroy data. GFS identifies failed chunk servers by regular handshakes between master and all chunk servers and detects data corruption by check summing. Once a problem surfaces, the data is restored from valid replicas as soon as possible. A chunk is lost irreversibly only if all its replicas are lost before GFS can react, typically within minutes. Even in this case, it becomes unavailable, not corrupted: applications receive clear errors rather than corrupt data.

GFS Application and Consistency Model

GFS applications can accommodate the relaxed consistency model with a few simple techniques already needed for other purposes: relying on appends rather than overwrites, check pointing, and writing self-validating, self-identifying records.

In one typical use, a writer generates a file from beginning to end. It atomically renames the file to a permanent name after writing all the data, or periodically checkpoints how much has been successfully written.

Checkpoints may also include application-level checksums.

Readers verify and process only the file region up to the last checkpoint, which is known to be in the defined state. Regardless of consistency and concurrency issues, this approach has served us well. Appending is far more efficient and more resilient to application failures than random writes. Check pointing allows writers to restart incrementally and keeps readers from processing successfully written file data that is still incomplete from the application's perspective.

In the other typical use, many writers concurrently append to a file for merged results or as a producer-consumer queue. Record append's append-at-least-once semantics preserves each writer's output. Readers deal with the occasional padding and duplicates as follows. Each record prepared by the writer contains extra information like checksums so that its validity can be verified. A reader can identify and discard extra padding and record fragments using the checksums. If it cannot tolerate the occasional duplicates (e.g., if they would trigger non-idempotent operations), it can filter them out using unique identifiers in the records, which are often needed anyway to name corresponding application entities such as web documents. These functionalities for record I/O (except duplicate removal) are in library code shared by our applications and applicable to other file interface implementations at Google. With that, the same sequence of records, plus rare duplicates, is always delivered to the record reader.

Mutation Operation

A mutation is an operation that changes the contents or metadata of a chunk such as a write or an append operation.

Each mutation is performed at all the chunk's replicas.

The master grants a chunk lease to one of the replicas, which we call the *primary*. The primary picks a serial order for all mutations to the chunk. All replicas follow this order when applying mutations. Thus, the global mutation order is defined first by the lease grant order chosen by the master, and within a lease by the serial numbers assigned by the primary.

The lease mechanism is designed to minimize management overhead at the master. A lease has an initial timeout of 60 seconds. However, as long as the chunk is being mutated, the primary can request and typically receive extensions from the master indefinitely. These extension requests and grants are piggybacked on the *Heartbeat* messages regularly exchanged between the master and all chunk servers.

The master may sometimes try to revoke a lease before it expires (e.g., when the master wants to disable mutations on a file that is being renamed). Even if the master loses communication with a primary, it can safely grant a new lease to another replica after the old lease expires.

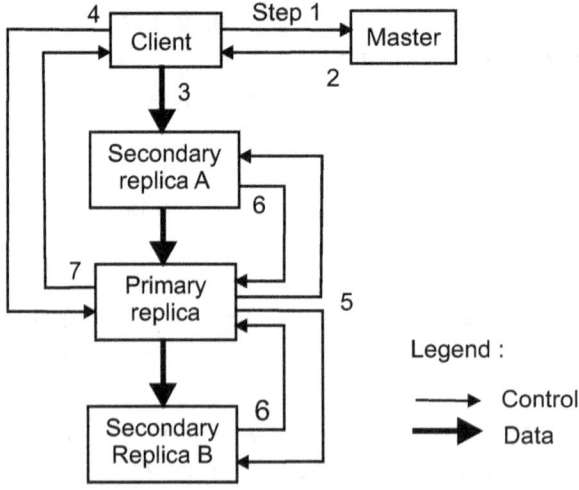

Fig. 3.44 : Mutation operation

The overall process is given as follows :

1. The client asks the master which chunk server holds the current lease for the chunk and the locations of the other replicas. If no one has a lease, the master grants one to a replica it chooses (not shown).

2. The master replies with the identity of the primary and the locations of the other (*secondary*) replicas. The client caches this data for future mutations. It needs to contact the master again only when the primary becomes unreachable or replies that it no longer holds a lease.

3. The client pushes the data to all the replicas. A client can do so in any order. Each chunk server will store the data in an internal LRU buffer cache until the data is used or aged out. By decoupling the data flow from the control flow, we can improve performance by scheduling the expensive data flow based on the network topology regardless of which chunk server is the primary.

4. Once all the replicas have acknowledged receiving the data, the client sends a write request to the primary. The request identifies the data pushed earlier to all of the replicas. The primary assigns consecutive serial numbers to all the mutations it receives, possibly from multiple clients, which provides the necessary serialization. It applies the mutation to its own local state in serial number order.

5. The primary forwards the write request to all secondary replicas. Each secondary replica applies mutations in the same serial number order assigned by the primary.

6. The secondary all reply to the primary indicating that they have completed the operation.

7. The primary replies to the client. Any errors encountered at any of the replicas are reported to the client. In case of errors, the write may have succeeded at the primary and an arbitrary subset of the secondary replicas.

If a write by the application is large or crosses a chunk boundary, GFS client code breaks it down into multiple write operations. They all follow the control flow described above but may be interleaved with and overwritten by concurrent operations from other clients. Therefore, the shared file region may end up containing fragments from different clients, although the replicas will be identical because the individual operations are completed successfully in the same order on all replicas.

Atomic Record Appends

GFS provides an atomic append operation called *record append*. In a traditional write, the client specifies the offset at which data is to be written. Concurrent writes to the same region are not serializable: the region may end up containing data fragments from multiple clients. In a record append, however, the client specifies only the data. GFS appends it to the file at least once atomically (i.e., as one continuous sequence of bytes) at an offset of GFS's choosing and returns that offset to the client. This is similar to writing to a file opened in O APPEND mode in Unix without the race conditions when multiple writers do so concurrently.

Record append is heavily used by our distributed applications in which many clients on different machines append to the same file concurrently. Clients would need additional complicated and expensive synchronization, for example through a distributed lock manager, if they do so with traditional writes. In our workloads, such files often serve as multiple-producer/single-consumer queues or contain merged results from many different clients.

The client pushes the data to all replicas of the last chunk of the file Then, it sends its request to the primary.

The primary checks to see if appending the record to the current chunk would cause the chunk to exceed the maximum size (64 MB). If so, it pads the chunk to the maximum size, tells secondary to do the same, and replies to the client indicating that the operation should be retried on the next chunk. (Record append is restricted to be at most one-fourth of the maximum chunk size to keep worst case fragmentation at an acceptable level.) If the record fits within the maximum size, which is the common case, the primary appends the data to its replica, tells the secondary to write the data at the exact offset where it has, and finally replies success to the client.

If records append fails at any replica, the client retries the operation. As a result, replicas of the same chunk may contain different data possibly including duplicates of the same record in whole or in part. GFS does not guarantee that all replicas are byte wise identical. It only guarantees that the data is written at least once as an atomic unit. This property follows readily from the simple observation that for the operation to report success, the data must have been written at the same offset on all replicas of some chunk. Furthermore, after this, all replicas are at least as long as the end of record and therefore any future record will be assigned a higher offset or a different chunkev en if a different replica later becomes the primary. In terms of our consistency guarantees, the regions in which successful record append operations have written their data are defined (hence consistent), whereas intervening regions are inconsistent (hence undefined).

Snapshot

The snapshot operation makes a copy of a file or a directory tree (the "source") almost instantaneously, while minimizing any interruptions of ongoing mutations. Users use it to quickly create branch copies of huge data sets (and often copies of those copies, recursively), or to checkpoint the current state before experimenting with changes that can later be committed or rolled back easily .

When the master receives a snapshot request, it first revokes any outstanding leases on the chunks in the files it is about to snapshot. This ensures that any subsequent writes to these chunks will require an interaction with the master to find the lease holder. This will give the master an opportunity to create a new copy of the chunk first.

After the leases have been revoked or have expired, the master logs the operation to disk. It then applies this log record to its in-memory state by duplicating the metadata for the source file or directory tree. The newly created snapshot files point to the same chunks as the source files.

The first time a client wants to write to a chunk C after the snapshot operation, it sends a request to the master to find the current lease holder. The master notices that the reference count for chunk C is greater than one. It defers replying to the client request and instead picks a new chunk handle C'. It then asks each chunk server that has a current replica of C to create a new chunk called C'. By creating the new chunk on the same chunk servers as the original. From this point, request handling is no different from that for any chunk: the master grants one of the replicas a lease on the new chunk C' and replies to the client, which can write the chunk normally, not knowing that it has just been created from an existing chunk.

Ensuring Data Integrity

Each chunk server uses check summing to detect corruption of stored data. Given that a GFS cluster often has thousands of disks on hundreds of machines, it regularly experiences disk failures that cause data corruption or loss on both the read and write paths. It is possible to recover from corruption using other chunk replicas, but it would be impractical to detect corruption by comparing replicas across chunk servers. Moreover, divergent replicas may be legal: the semantics of GFS mutations, in particular atomic record append as discussed earlier, does not guarantee identical replicas. Therefore, each chunk server must independently verify the integrity of its own copy by maintaining checksums.

A chunk is broken up into 64 KB blocks. Each has a corresponding 32 bit checksum. Like other metadata, checksums are kept in memory and stored persistently with logging, separate from user data.

For reads, the chunk server verifies the checksum of data blocks that overlap the read range before returning any data to the requester, whether a client or another chunk server.

Therefore chunk servers will not propagate corruptions to other machines. If a block does not match the recorded checksum, the chunk server returns an error to the request or and reports the mismatch to the master. In response, the requestor will read from other replicas, while the master will clone the chunk from another replica. After a valid new replica is in place, the master instructs the chunk server that reported the mismatch to delete its replica. Check summing has little effect on read performance for several reasons. Since most of our reads span at least a few blocks, we need to read and checksum only a relatively small amount of extra data for verification. GFS client code further reduces this overhead by trying to align reads at checksum block boundaries. Moreover, checksum lookups and comparison on the chunk server are done without any I/O, and checksum calculation can often be overlapped with I/Os. Checksum computation is heavily optimized for writes that append to the end of a chunk (as opposed to writes that overwrite existing data). Checksum is updated by incrementing it for the last partial checksum block, and compute new checksums for any brand new checksum blocks filled by the append. Even if the last partial checksum block is already corrupted and we fail to detect it now, the new checksum value will not match the stored data, and the corruption will be detected as usual when the block is next read.

In contrast, if a write overwrites an existing range of the chunk, we must read and verify the first and last blocks of the range being overwritten, then perform the write, and finally compute and record the new checksums. If we do not verify the first and last blocks before overwriting them partially, the new checksums may hide corruption that exists in the regions not being overwritten.

During idle periods, chunk servers can scan and verify the contents of inactive chunks. This allows us to detect corruption in chunks that are rarely read. Once the corruption is detected, the master can create a new uncorrupted replica and delete the corrupted replica. This prevents an inactive but corrupted chunk replica from fooling the master into thinking that it has enough valid replicas of a chunk.

3.14.2 HDFS

The Hadoop File System (HDFS) is as a distributed file system running on commodity hardware. It has many similarities with existing distributed file systems. However, the differences from other distributed file systems are significant. HDFS is highly fault-tolerant and can be deployed on low-cost hardware. HDFS provides high throughput access to application data and is suitable for applications that have large datasets. HDFS relaxes a few POSIX requirements to enable streaming access to file system data.

Similarly to Google File System, Hadoop Distributed File System (HDFS) is a fault tolerant distributed file system designed to run on large commodity clusters, where the storage is attached to the compute nodes. HDFS employs a master-slave architecture where the master (or the Namenode) manages the file system namespace and access permissions. Additionally, there are a large number of slaves (or the Datanodes) which manage the storage attached to the physical nodes on which they run. Each file in HDFS is split into a number of blocks which are replicated and stored on a set of Datanodes. The Namenode manages the file system namespace as well as the metadata about file and block(s) associations as shown in Fig. 3.45. Each data block is identified by a Block ID which specifies its position in the file and a unique, monotonically increasing Generation Timestamp. Since these are assigned by the Namenode, no two HDFS blocks can ever have the same Generation Timestamp. Another distinctive aspect of HDFS is that it relaxes a few POSIX requirements (disabling writes/locks anywhere other than the tail of the file) to enable high speed data streaming access. Being designed for batch processing applications as opposed to interactive usage, it chooses high throughput access to application data over low latency.

HDFS Architecture and Operations

Namenode and Datanode

HDFS has a master/slave architecture. An HDFS cluster consists of a single Namenode, a master server that manages the filesystem namespace and regulates access to files by clients. In addition, there are a number of Datanodes, one per node in the cluster, which manage storage attached to the nodes that they run on. HDFS exposes a file system namespace and allows user data to be stored in files. Internally, a file is split into one or more blocks and these blocks are stored in a set of Datanodes. The Namenode makes filesystem namespace operations like opening, closing, renaming etc. of files and directories. It also determines the mapping of blocks to Datanodes. The Datanodes are responsible for serving read and write requests from filesystem clients. The Datanodes also perform block creation, deletion, and replication upon instruction from the Namenode.

The Namenode and Datanode are pieces of software that run on commodity machines. These machines are typically commodity Linux machines. HDFS is built using the Java language; any machine that support Java can run the Namenode or the Datanode. Usage of the highly portable Java language means that HDFS can be deployed on a wide range of machines. A typical deployment could have a dedicated machine that runs only the Namenode software.

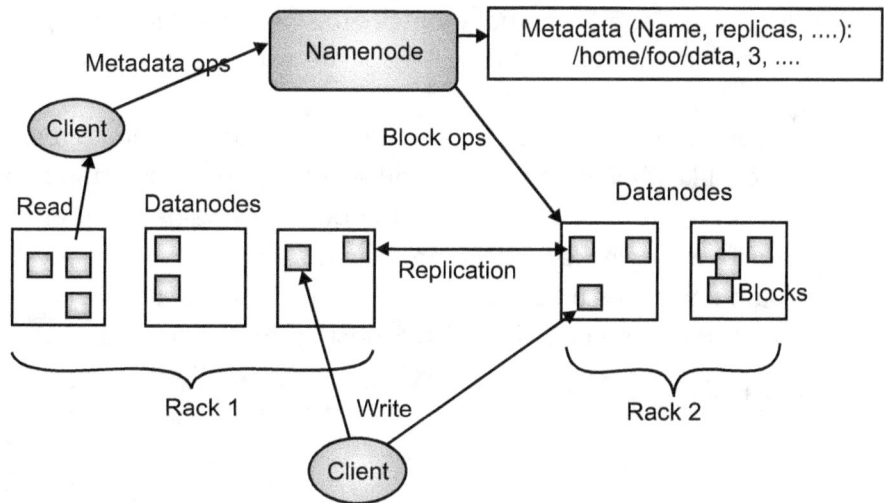

Fig. 3.45 : HDFS architecture

Each of the other machines in the cluster runs one instance of the Datanode software. The architecture does not preclude running multiple Datanodes on the same machine but in a real-deployment that is never the case. The existence of a single Namenode in a cluster greatly simplifies the architecture of the system. The Namenode is the arbitrator and repository for all HDFS metadata. The system is designed in such a way that user data never flows through the Namenode.

MapReduce

Built on top of GFS, Google's MapReduce framework is the heart of the computational model for their approach to cloud computing . The basic idea behind Google's computational model is that a software developer writes a program containing two simple functions *map* and *reduce* to process a collection of data. Google's underlying runtime system then divides the program into many small tasks, which are then run on hundreds or thousands of hosts in the cloud. The runtime system also ensures that the correct subset of data is delivered to each task.

The developer-written *map* function takes as its input a sequence of *<keyin, valuein>* tuples, performs some computation on these tuples, and produces as its output a sequence of *<keyout, valueout>* tuples.

There does not necessarily need to be a one-to-one correspondence between input and output key/value tuples. Also, *keyin* does not necessarily equal *keyout* for a given key/value tuple.

The developer-written *reduce* function takes as its input a key and a set of values corresponding to that key. Thus, for all <key', valuei> tuples produced by the map function that have the same key key', the reduce function will be invoked once with key' and the set of all values valuei. It's important to note that if the tuple <key', valuei> is generated multiple times by the map function, valuei will appear the same number of times in the set of values provided to the *reduce* function, i.e., duplicate values are *not* removed. Once invoked, the *reduce* function will perform some computation on the set of values and produce some output value that the runtime infrastructure will associate with the key that was supplied as input to *reduce*.

In the MapReduce model, computation is divided into a *map* function and a *reduce* function. The map function takes a key/value pair and produces one or more intermediate key/value pairs. The reduce function then takes these intermediate key/value pairs and merges all values corresponding to a single key. The map function can run independently on each key/value pair, exposing enormous amounts of parallelism. Similarly, the reduce function can run independently on each intermediate key, also exposing significant parallelism.

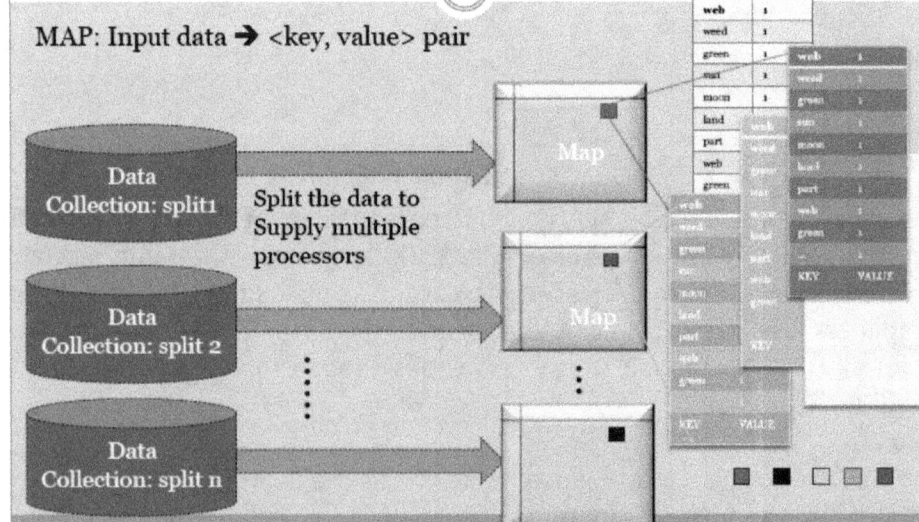

Fig. 3.46 (a) : Map operation

MAP : Input data ➙ <key, value> pair
REDUCE : < key, value> pair ➙ <result>

Fig. 3.46 (b) : Reduce operation

In Hadoop, a centralized *JobTracker* service is responsible for splitting the input data into pieces for processing by independent map and reduce tasks, scheduling each task on a cluster node for execution, and recovering from failures by re-running tasks. On each node, a *TaskTracker* service runs MapReduce tasks and periodically contacts the JobTracker to report task completions and request new tasks. By default, when a new task is received, a new JVM instance will be spawned to execute it.

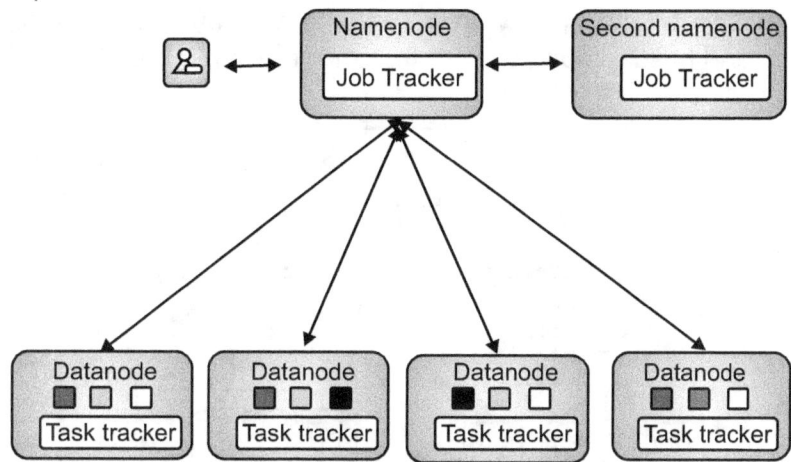

Fig. 3.47 : Namenode and datanodes

The File System Namespace

HDFS supports a traditional hierarchical file organization. A user or an application can create directories and store files inside these directories. The file system namespace hierarchy is similar to most other existing file systems. One can create and remove files, move a file from one directory to another, or rename a file. HDFS does not yet implement user quotas and access permissions. HDFS does not support hard links and soft links. However, the HDFS architecture does not preclude implementing these features at a later time.

The Namenode maintains the file system namespace. Any change to the file system namespace and properties are recorded by the Namenode. An application can specify the number of replicas of a file that should be maintained by HDFS. The number of copies of a file is called the replication factor of that file. This information is stored by the Namenode.

Data Replication

HDFS is designed to reliably store very large files across machines in a large cluster. It stores each file as a sequence of blocks; all blocks in a file except the last block are the same size.

Blocks belonging to a file are replicated for fault tolerance. The block size and replication factor are configurable per file. Files in HDFS are write-once and have strictly one writer at any time. An application can specify the number of replicas of a file. The replication factor can be specified at file creation time and can be changed later.

The Namenode makes all decisions regarding replication of blocks. It periodically receives Heartbeat and a Blockreport from each of the Datanodes in the cluster. A receipt of a heartbeat implies that the Datanode is in good health and is serving data as desired. A Blockreport contains a list of all blocks on that Datanode.

Replica Placement

The selection of placement of replicas is critical to HDFS reliability and performance. This feature distinguishes HDFS from most other distributed file systems. This is a feature that needs lots of tuning and experience. The purpose of a rack-aware replica placement is to improve data reliability, availability, and network bandwidth utilization. The current implementation for the replica placement policy is a first effort in this direction. The short-term goals of implementing this policy are to validate it on production systems, learn more about its behavior and build a foundation to test and research more sophisticated policies in the future.

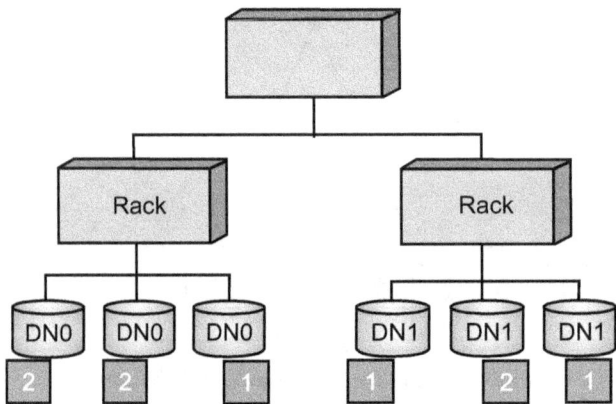

Fig. 3.48 : Replica placement

HDFS runs on a cluster of computers that spread across many racks. Communication between two nodes on different racks has to go through switches. In most cases, network bandwidth between two machines in the same rack is greater than network bandwidth between two machines on different racks.

At startup time, each Datanode determines the rack it belongs to and notifies the Namenode of the rack id upon registration. HDFS provides APIs to facilitate pluggable modules that can be used to determine the rack identity of a machine. A simple but non-optimal policy is to place replicas across racks. This prevents losing data when an entire rack fails and allows use of bandwidth from multiple racks when reading data. This policy evenly distributes replicas in the cluster and thus makes it easy to balance load on component failure. However, this policy increases the cost of writes because a write needs to transfer blocks to multiple racks.

For the most common case when the replica factor is three, HDFS.s placement policy is to place one replica on the local node, place another replica on a different node at the local rack, and place the last replica on different node at a different rack. This policy cuts the inter-rack write traffic and improves write performance. The chance of rack failure is far less than that of node failure; this policy does not impact data reliability and availability guarantees. But it reduces the aggregate network bandwidth when reading data since a block is placed in only two unique racks rather than three. The replicas of a file do not evenly distribute across the racks. One third of replicas are on one node, two thirds of the replicas are on one rack;

the other one third of replicas is evenly distributed across all the remaining racks. This policy improves write performance while not impacting data reliability or read performance.

The implementation of the above policy is work-in-progress.

Replica Selection

HDFS tries to satisfy a read request from a replica that is closest to the reader. If there exists a replica on the same rack as the reader node, then that replica is preferred to satisfy the read request. If a HDFS cluster spans multiple data centers, then a replica that is resident in the local data center is preferred over remote replicas.

Safe Mode of HDFS

On startup, the Namenode enters a special state called Safemode. Replication of data blocks does not occur when the Namenode is in Safemode state. The Namenode receives Heartbeat and Blockreport from the Datanodes. A Blockreport contains the list of data blocks that a Datanode reports to the Namenode. Each block has a specified minimum number of replicas. A block is considered safely-replicated when the minimum number of replicas of that data block has checked in with the Namenode. When a configurable percentage of safely-replicated data blocks checks in with the Namenode (plus an additional 30 seconds), the Namenode exits the Safemode state. It then determines the list of data blocks (if any) that have fewer than the specified number of replicas. The Namenode then replicates these blocks to other Datanodes.

The Persistence of File System Metadata

The HDFS namespace is stored by the Namenode. The Namenode uses a transaction log called the EditLog to persistently record every change that occurs to file system metadata. For example, creating a new file in HDFS causes the Namenode to insert a record into the EditLog indicating this change. Similarly, changing the replication factor of a file causes a new record to be inserted into the EditLog. The Namenode uses a file in its local file system to store the Edit Log. The entire file system namespace, the mapping of blocks to files and filesystem properties are stored in a file called the FsImage. The FsImage is a file in the Namenode.s local file system too.

The Namenode has an image of the entire file system namespace and file Blockmap in memory. This metadata is designed to be compact, so that a 4 GB memory on the Namenode machine is plenty to support a very large number of files and directories. When the Namenode starts up, it reads the FsImage and EditLog from disk, applies all the transactions from the EditLog into the in-memory representation of the FsImage and then flushes out this new metadata into a new FsImage on disk. It can then truncate the old EditLog because its transactions have been applied to the persistent FsImage. This process is called a checkpoint.

In the current implementation, a checkpoint occurs when the Namenode starts up. Work is in progress to support periodic checkpointing in the near future.

The Datanode stores HDFS data into files in its local file system. The Datanode has no knowledge about HDFS files. It stores each block of HDFS data in a separate file in its local file system. The Datanode does not create all files in the same directory. Instead, it uses a heuristic to determine the optimal number of files per directory. It creates subdirectories appropriately. It is not optimal to create all local files in the same directory because the local file system might not be able to efficiently support a huge number of files in a single directory. When a Datanode starts up, it scans through its local file system, generates a list of all HDFS data blocks that correspond to each of these local files and sends this report to the Namenode. This report is called the Blockreport.

The Communication Protocol

All communication protocols are layered on top of the TCP/IP protocol. A client establishes a connection to a well-defined and configurable port on the Namenode machine. It talks the ClientProtocol with the Namenode. The Datanodes talk to the Namenode using the DatanodeProtocol. The details on these protocols will be explained later on. A Remote Procedure Call (RPC) abstraction wraps the ClientProtocol and the DatanodeProtocol. By design, the Namenode never initiates an RPC. It responds to RPC requests issued by a Datanode or a client.

Robustness

The primary objective of HDFS is to store data reliably even in the presence of failures. The three types of common failures are Namenode failures, Datanode failures and network partitions.

Data Disk Failure, Heartbeats and Re-Replication

A Datanode sends a heartbeat message to the Namenode periodically. A network partition can cause a subset of Datanodes to lose connectivity with the Namenode. The Namenode detects this condition be a lack of heartbeat message. The Namenode marks these Datanodes as dead and does not forward any new IO requests to these Datanodes. The data that was residing on those Datanodes are not available to HDFS any more. This may cause the replication factor of some blocks to fall below their specified value. The Namenode determines all the blocks that need to be replicated and starts replicating them to other Datanodes. The necessity for re-replication may arise due to many reasons: a Datanode becoming unavailable, a corrupt replica, a bad disk on the Datanode or an increase of the replication factor of a file.

Cluster Rebalancing

The HDFS architecture is compatible with data rebalancing schemes. It is possible that data may move automatically from one Datanode to another if the free space on a Datanode falls below a certain threshold. Also, a sudden high demand for a particular file can dynamically cause creation of additional replicas and rebalancing of other data in the cluster. These types of rebalancing schemes are not yet implemented.

Data Correctness

It is possible that a block of data fetched from a Datanode is corrupted. This corruption can occur because of faults in the storage device, a bad network or buggy software. The HDFS client implements checksum checking on the contents of a HDFS file. When a client creates a HDFS file, it computes a checksum of each block on the file and stores these checksums in a separate hidden file in the same HDFS namespace. When a client retrieves file contents it verifies that the data it received from a Datanode satisfies the checksum stored in the checksum file. If not, then the client can opt to retrieve that block from another Datanode that has a replica of that block.

Metadata Disk Failure

The FsImage and the EditLog are central data structures of HDFS. A corruption of these files can cause the entire cluster to be non-functional. For this reason, the Namenode can be configured to support multiple copies of the FsImage and EditLog. Any update to either the FsImage or EditLog causes each of the FsImages and EditLogs to get updated synchronously. This synchronous updating of multiple EditLog may degrade the rate of namespace transactions per second that a Namenode can support. But this degradation is acceptable because HDFS applications are very data intensive in nature; they are not metadata intensive. A Namenode, when it restarts, selects the latest consistent FsImage and EditLog to use. The Namenode machine is a single point of failure for the HDFS cluster. If a Namenode machine fails, manual intervention is necessary. Currently, automatic restart and failover of the Namenode software to another machine is not supported.

Snapshots

Snapshots support storing a copy of data at a particular instant of time. One usage of the snapshot-feature may be to roll back a corrupted cluster to a previously known good point in time. HDFS current does not support snapshots but it will be supported it in future release.

Data Organization in HDFS

Data Blocks

HDFS is designed to support large files. Applications that are compatible with HDFS are those that deal with large data sets. These applications write the data only once; they read the data one or more times and require that reads are satisfied at streaming speeds. HDFS supports write-once-read-many semantics on files. A typical block size used by HDFS is 64 MB. Thus, a HDFS file is chopped up into 128 MB chunks, and each chunk could reside in different Datanodes.

Staging

A client-request to create a file does not reach the Namenode immediately. In fact, the HDFS client caches the file data into a temporary local file. An application-write is transparently redirected to this temporary local file.

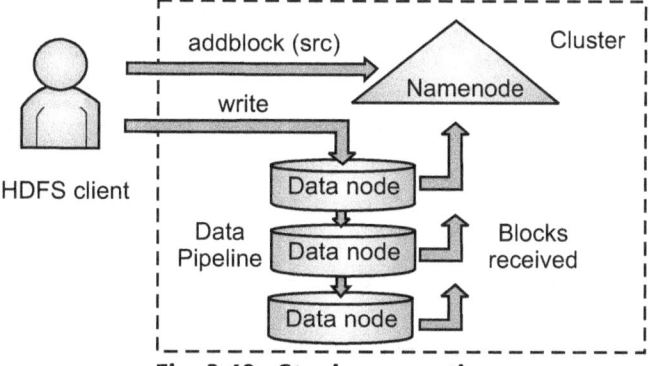

Fig. 3.49 : Staging operation

When the local file accumulates data worth over a HDFS block size, the client contacts the Namenode. The Namenode inserts the file name into the file system hierarchy and allocates a data block for it. The Namenode responds to the client request with the identity of the Datanode(s) and the destination data block. The client flushes the block of data from the local temporary file to the specified Datanode. When a file is closed, the remaining un-flushed data in the temporary local file is transferred to the Datanode. The client then instructs the Namenode that the file is closed. At this point, the Namenode commits the file creation operation into a persistent store. If the Namenode dies before the file is closed, the file is lost. The above approach has been adopted after careful consideration of target applications that run on HDFS. Applications need streaming writes to files. If a client writes to a remote file directly without any client side buffering, the network speed and the congestion in the network impacts throughput considerably. This approach is not without precedence either.

Earlier distributed file system, e.g. AFS have used client side caching to improve performance. A POSIX requirement has been relaxed to achieve higher performance of data uploads.

Pipelining

When a client is writing data to a HDFS file, its data is first written to a local file as explained above. Suppose the HDFS file has a replication factor of three. When the local file accumulates a block of user data, the client retrieves a list of Datanodes from the Namenode. This list represents the Datanodes that will host a replica of that block. The client then flushes the data block to the first Datanode. The first Datanode starts receiving the data in small portions (4 KB), writes each portion to its local repository and transfers that portion to the second Datanode in the list. The second Datanode, in turn, starts receiving each portion of the data block, writes that portion to its repository and then flushes that portion to the third Datanode. The third Datanode writes the data to its local repository. A Datanode could be receiving data from the previous one in the pipeline and at the same time it could be forwarding data to the next one in the pipeline. Thus, the data is pipelined from one Datanode to the next.

Accessibility

HDFS can be accessed by application by many different ways. Natively, HDFS provides a Java API for applications to use. A C language wrapper for this Java API is available. A HTTP browser can also be used to browse the file in HDFS. Work is in progress to expose a HDFS content repository through the WebDAV Protocol.

DFSShell

HDFS allows user data to be organized in the form of files and directories. It provides an interface called DFSShell that lets a user interact with the data in HDFS. The syntax of this command set is similar to other shells (e.g. bash, csh) that users are already familiar with.

Here are some sample commands :

Create a directory named /foodir : hadoop dfs -mkdir /foodir

View a file /foodir/myfile.txt : hadoop dfs -cat /foodir/myfile.txt

Delete a file /foodir/myfile.txt : hadoop dfs -rm /foodir myfile.txt

The command syntax for DFSShell is targeted for applications that need a scripting language to interact with the stored data.

DFSAdmin

The DFSAdmin command set is used for administering a dfs cluster. These are commands that are used only by a HDFS administrator. Here are some sample commands :

Put a cluster in Safe Mode : bin/hadoop dfsadmin -safemode enter

Generate a list of Datanodes : bin/hadoop dfsadmin -report

Decommission a Datanode : bin/hadoop dfsadmin -decommission datanodename

Browser Interface

A typical HDFS install configures a web-server to expose the HDFS namespace through a configurable port. This allows a Web browser to navigate the HDFS namespace and view contents of a HDFS file.

Goals of HDFS

Hardware Failure

Hardware Failure is the norm rather than the exception. The entire HDFS file system may consist of hundreds or thousands of server machines that stores pieces of file system data. The fact that there are a huge number of components and that each component has a non-trivial probability of failure means that some component of HDFS is always non-functional. Therefore, detection of faults and automatically recovering quickly from those faults are core architectural goals of HDFS.

Streaming Data Access

Applications that run on HDFS need streaming access to their data sets. They are not general purpose applications that typically run on a general purpose file system. HDFS is designed more for batch processing rather than interactive use by users. The emphasis is on throughput of data access rather than latency of data access. POSIX imposes many hard requirements that are not needed for applications that are targeted for HDFS. POSIX semantics in a few key areas have been traded off to further enhance data throughput rates.

Large Data Sets

Applications that run on HDFS have large data sets. This means that a typical file in HDFS is gigabytes to terabytes in size. Thus, HDFS is tuned to support large files. It should provide high aggregate data bandwidth and should scale to hundreds of nodes in a single cluster. It should support tens of millions of files in a single cluster.

Simple Coherency Model

Most HDFS applications need write-once-read-many access model for files. A file once created, written and closed need not be changed. This assumption simplifies data coherency issues and enables high throughout data access. A Map-Reduce application or a Web-Crawler application fits perfectly with this model. There is a plan to support appending-writes to a file in future.

Moving Computation is Cheaper than Moving Data

A computation requested by an application is most optimal if the computation can be done near where the data is located. This is especially true when the size of the data set is huge.

This eliminates network congestion and increase overall throughput of the system. The assumption is that it is often better to migrate the computation closer to where the data is located rather than moving the data to where the application is running. HDFS provides interfaces for applications to move themselves closer to where the data is located.

Portability Across Heterogeneous Hardware and Software Platforms

HDFS should be designed in such a way that it is easily portable from one platform to another. This facilitates widespread adoption of HDFS as a platform of choice for a large set of applications.

Space Reclamation

File Deletes and Undelete

When a file is deleted by a user or an application, it is not immediately removed from HDFS. HDFS renames it to a file in the /trash directory. The file can be restored quickly as long as it remains in /trash. A file remains in /trash for a configurable amount of time. After the expiry of its life in /trash, the Namenode deletes the file from the HDFS namespace. The deletion of the file causes the blocks associated with the file to be freed. There could be an appreciable time delay between the time a file is deleted by a user and the time of the corresponding increase in free space in HDFS.

A user can Undelete a file after deleting it as long as it remains in the /trash directory. If a user wants to undelete a file that he/she has deleted, he/she can navigate the /trash directory and retrieve the file. The /trash directory contains only the latest copy of the file that was deleted. The /trash directory is just like any other directory with one special feature: HDFS applies specified policies to automatically delete files from this directory. The current default policy is to delete files that are older than 6 hours. In future, this policy will be configurable through a well defined interface.

Decrease Replication Factor

When the replication factor of a file is reduced, the Namenode selects excess replicas that can be deleted. The next Heartbeat transfers this information to the Datanode. The Datanode then removes the corresponding blocks and the corresponding free space appears in the cluster.

The point to note here is that there might be a time delay between the completion of the setReplication API and the appearance of free space in the cluster.

File Read and Write

An application adds data to HDFS by creating a new file and writing the data to it. After the file is closed, the bytes written cannot be altered or removed except that new data can be added to the file by reopening the file for append. HDFS implements a single-writer, multiple-reader model.

The HDFS client that opens a file for writing is granted a lease for the file; no other client can write to the file. The writing client periodically renews the lease by sending a heartbeat to the NameNode. When the file is closed, the lease is revoked. The lease duration is bound by a soft limit and a hard limit.

Until the soft limit expires, the writer is certain of exclusive access to the file. If the soft limit expires and the client fails to close the file or renew the lease, another client can preempt the lease. If after the hard limit expires (one hour) and the client has failed to renew the lease, HDFS assumes that the client has quit and will automatically close the file on behalf of the writer, and recover the lease. The writer's lease does not prevent other clients from reading the file; a file may have many concurrent readers.

An HDFS file consists of blocks. When there is a need for a new block, the NameNode allocates a block with a unique block ID and determines a list of DataNodes to host replicas of the block. The DataNodes form a pipeline, the order of which minimizes the total network distance from the client to the last DataNode. Bytes are pushed to the pipeline as a sequence of packets. The bytes that an application writes first buffer at the client side. After a packet buffer is filled (typically 64 KB), the data are pushed to the pipeline. The next packet can be pushed to the pipeline before receiving the acknowledgement for the previous packets. The number of outstanding packets is limited by the outstanding packets window size of the client.

After data are written to an HDFS file, HDFS does not provide any guarantee that data are visible to a new reader until the file is closed. If a user application needs the visibility guarantee, it can explicitly call the *hflush* operation. Then the current packet is immediately pushed to the pipeline, and the hflush operation will wait until all DataNodes in the pipeline acknowledge the successful transmission of the packet. All data written before the hflush operation are then certain to be visible to readers.

If no error occurs, block construction goes through three stages as shown in Fig. illustrating a pipeline of three DataNodes (DN) and a block of five packets.

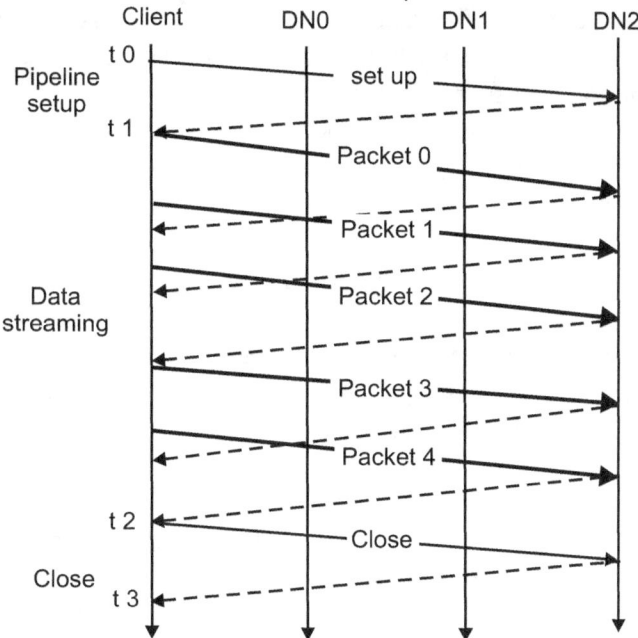

Fig. 3.50 : Pipeline of three datanodes

In the figure, bold lines represent data packets, dashed lines represent acknowledgment messages, and thin lines represent control messages to setup and close the pipeline. Vertical lines represent activity at the client and the three DataNodes where time proceeds from top to bottom. From t0 to t1 is the pipeline setup stage. The interval t1 to t2 is the data streaming stage, where t1 is the time when the first data packet gets sent and t2 is the time that the acknowledgment to the last packet gets received. Here an hflush operation transmits the second packet. The hflush indication travels with the packet data and is not a separate operation. The final interval t2 to t3 is the pipeline close stage for this block. In a cluster of thousands of nodes, failures of a node (most commonly storage faults) are daily occurrences. A replica stored on a DataNode may become corrupted because of faults in memory, disk, or network. HDFS generates and stores checksums for each data block of an HDFS file. Checksums are verified by the HDFS client while reading to help detect any corruption caused either by client, DataNodes, or network.

When a client creates an HDFS file, it computes the checksum sequence for each block and sends it to a DataNode along with the data. A DataNode stores checksums in a metadata file separate from the block's data file. When HDFS reads a file, each block's data and checksums are shipped to the client. The client computes the checksum for the received data and verifies that the newly computed checksums matches the checksums it received. If not, the client notifies the NameNode of the corrupt replica and then fetches a different replica of the block from another DataNode.

When a client opens a file to read, it fetches the list of blocks and the locations of each block replica from the NameNode. The locations of each block are ordered by their distance from the reader. When reading the content of a block, the client tries the closest replica first. If the read attempt fails, the client tries the next replica in sequence. A read may fail if the target DataNode is unavailable, the node no longer hosts a replica of the block, or the replica is found to be corrupt when checksums are tested.

HDFS permits a client to read a file that is open for writing. When reading a file open for writing, the length of the last block still being written is unknown to the NameNode. In this case, the client asks one of the replicas for the latest length before starting to read its content.

The design of HDFS I/O is particularly optimized for batch processing systems, like MapReduce, which require high throughput for sequential reads and writes. However, many efforts have been put to improve its read/write response time in order to support applications like Scribe that provide real-time data streaming to HDFS, or HBase that provides random, realtime access to large tables.

Benefits of HDFS

Built-In Redundancy and Failover

HDFS supplies out-of-the-box redundancy and failover capabilities that require little to no manual intervention (depending on the use case). Having such features built into the storage layer allows system administrators and developers to concentrate on other responsibilities versus having to create monitoring systems and/or programming routines to compensate for another set of storage software that lacks those capabilities.

Moreover, with downtime being a real threat to many modern businesse's bottom line, features that minimize outages and contribute to keeping a batch analytic data store up, operational, and feeding any online system that requires its input are welcomed by both IT and business professionals.

Big Data Capable

The hallmark of HDFS is its ability to tackle big data use cases and most of the characteristics that comprise them (data velocity, variety, and volume). The rate at which HDFS can supply data to the programming layers of Hadoop equates to faster batch processing times and quicker answers to complex analytic questions.

Portability

Any tenured data professional can relay horror stories of having to transfer, migrate, and convert huge data volumes between disparate storage/software vendors. One benefit of HDFS is its portability between various Hadoop distributions, which helps minimize vendor lock-in.

Cost-Effective

As previously stated, HDFS is open source software, which translates into real cost savings for its users. As many companies can attest, high-priced storage solutions can take a significant bite out of IT budgets and are many times completely out of reach for small or startup companies.

3.15 BIG TABLE

Big Table is a compressed, high performance, and proprietary database system built on Google File System (also known as the "GFS"), Chubby Lock Service, SSTable and a few other Google technologies. It is not distributed outside Google, although Google offers access to it as part of its Google App Engine.

Big Table maps two arbitrary string values (row key and column key) and timestamp (hence three dimensional mapping) into an associated arbitrary byte array. It is not a relational database and can be better defined as a sparse, distributed multi-dimensional sorted map. Big Table is designed to scale into the petabyte range across "hundreds or thousands of machines, and to make it easy to add more machines to the system and automatically start taking advantage of those resources without any reconfiguration".

Each table has multiple dimensions (one of which is a field for time, allowing for versioning and garbage collection). Tables are optimized for GFS by being split into multiple tablets - segments of the table as split along a row chosen such that the tablet will be ~200 megabytes in size. When sizes threaten to grow beyond a specified limit, the tablets are compressed using the algorithm BMDiff and the Zippy compression algorithm publicly known and open-sourced as Snappy, which is a less space-optimal variation of LZ77 but more efficient in terms of computing time. The locations in the GFS of tablets are recorded as database entries in multiple special tablets, which are called "META1" tablets. META1 tablets are found by querying the single "META0" tablet, which typically resides on a server of its own since it is often queried by clients as to the location of the "META1" tablet which itself has the answer to the question of where the actual data is located. Like GFS's master server, the META0 server is not generally a bottleneck since the processor time, bandwidth necessary to discover and transmit META1 locations is minimal and clients aggressively cache locations to minimize queries.

Some of the important terms in Big Table are as follows :

Rows :

These rows are like normal rows of a tables, Each row has given a unique id i.e. Key. So every row is identified by unique key. Also, data regarding a particular item is stored a single row only.

Columns :

In No SQL databases, no of columns for a row in a table may or may not be same.

E.g. In table for Employees, each row will represent a single Employee and all the information regarding that Employee will be stored in the same row.

Employee Table			
Employee id- 1	Name – ABC	Address- PQR	Contact No- 12345
Employee Id- 2		Name – ABC	Mobile - 547898875453
Employee Id- 3		Name – XYZ	

As you can see in above shown table, here a specific schema will not be defined for a particular table.

Key :

Each entity in a row has got a unique value associated with it, called as Key.

Value :

Each key has got a value associated with it.

Timestamp :

For each and every entry, a timestamp is maintained in system and is associated with the value entered in db.

Key	Value	Timestamp
2345789457857	ABC	345:4578:57890

This the way a record is maintained in Big Table database.

3.16 HBASE AND DYNAMO

HBase is the Hadoop database. Think of it as a distributed scalable Big Data store.

When Would I Use HBase?

Use HBase when you need random, realtime read/write access to your Big Data. This project's goal is the hosting of very large tables billions of rows X millions of columns atop clusters of commodity hardware. HBase is an open-source, distributed, versioned, column oriented store modeled after Google's Big table: A Distributed Storage System for Structured Data by Chang et al. Just as Bigtable leverages the distributed data storage provided by the Google File System, HBase provides Big table-like capabilities on top of Hadoop and HDFS.

Features

HBase provides :

- Linear and modular scalability.
- Strictly consistent reads and writes.
- Automatic and configurable sharding of tables.
- Automatic failover support between RegionServers.
- Convenient base classes for backing Hadoop MapReduce jobs with HBase tables.
- Easy to use Java API for client access.
- Block cache and Bloom Filters for real-time queries.
- Query predicate push down via server side Filters.
- Thrift gateway and a REST-ful Web service that supports XML, Protobuf, and binary data encoding options.
- Extensible jruby-based (JIRB) shell.
- Support for exporting metrics via the Hadoop metrics subsystem to files or Ganglia; or via JMX.

HBase is a type of "NoSQL" database. "NoSQL" is a general term meaning that the database isn't an RDBMS which supports SQL as it's primary access language, but there are many types of NoSQL databases: BerkeleyDB is an example of a local NoSQL database, whereas HBase is very much a distributed database. Technically speaking, HBase is really more a "Data Store" than "Data Base" because it lacks many of the features you find in an RDBMS, such as typed columns, secondary indexes, triggers, and advanced query languages, etc.

However, HBase has many features which supports both linear and modular scaling. HBase clusters expand by adding RegionServers that are hosted on commodity class servers. If a cluster expands from 10 to 20 RegionServers, for example, it doubles both in terms of storage and as well as processing capacity. RDBMS can scale well, but only up to a point - specifically, the size of a single database server - and for the best performance requires specialized hardware and storage devices. HBase features of note are :

- **Strongly Consistent Reads/Writes :** HBase is not an "eventually consistent" DataStore. This makes it very suitable for tasks such as high-speed counter aggregation.
- **Automatic Sharding :** HBase tables are distributed on the cluster via regions, and regions are automatically split and re-distributed as your data grows.
- Automatic RegionServer failover
- **Hadoop/HDFS Integration :** HBase supports HDFS out of the box as it's distributed file system.
- **MapReduce :** HBase supports massively parallelized processing via MapReduce for using HBase as both source and sink.

- **Java Client API :** HBase supports an easy to use Java API for programmatic access.
- **Thrift/REST API :** HBase also supports Thrift and REST for non-Java front-ends.
- Block Cache and Bloom Filters: HBase supports a Block Cache and Bloom Filters for high volume query optimization.
- **Operational Management :** HBase provides build-in web-pages for operational insight as well as JMX metrics.

Best Case Scenarios for the use of HBase

HBase isn't suitable for every problem.

First, make sure you have enough data. If you have hundreds of millions or billions of rows, then HBase is a good candidate. If you only have a few thousand/million rows, then using a traditional RDBMS might be a better choice due to the fact that all of your data might wind up on a single node (or two) and the rest of the cluster may be sitting idle.

Second, make sure you can live without all the extra features that an RDBMS provides (e.g., typed columns, secondary indexes, transactions, advanced query languages, etc.) An application built against an RDBMS cannot be "ported" to HBase by simply changing a JDBC driver, for example. Consider moving from an RDBMS to HBase as a complete redesign as opposed to a port.

Third, make sure you have enough hardware. Even HDFS doesn't do well with anything less than 5 DataNodes (due to things such as HDFS block replication which has a default of 3), plus a NameNode.

HBase can run quite well stand-alone on a laptop but this should be considered a development configuration only.

What is the Difference Between HBase and Hadoop/HDFS?

HDFS is a distributed file system that is well suited for the storage of large files. It's documentation states that it is not, however, a general purpose file system, and does not provide fast individual record lookups in files. HBase, on the other hand, is built on top of HDFS and provides fast record lookups (and updates) for large tables. This can sometimes be a point of conceptual confusion. HBase internally puts your data in indexed "StoreFiles" that exist on HDFS for high-speed lookups.

DynamoDB

Amazon DynamoDB is a fully managed NoSQL database service that provides fast and predictable performance with seamless scalability. With a few clicks in the AWS Management Console, customers can launch a new Amazon DynamoDB database table, scale up or down their request capacity for the table without downtime or performance degradation, and gain visibility into resource utilization and performance metrics. Amazon DynamoDB enables customers to offload the administrative burdens of operating and scaling distributed databases to AWS, so they don't have to worry about hardware provisioning, setup and configuration, replication, software patching, or cluster scaling.

Amazon DynamoDB is designed to address the core problems of database management, performance, scalability, and reliability. Developers can create a database table that can store and retrieve any amount of data, and serve any level of request traffic. DynamoDB automatically spreads the data and traffic for the table over a sufficient number of servers to handle the request capacity specified by the customer and the amount of data stored, while maintaining consistent, fast performance. All data items are stored on Solid State Drives (SSDs) and are automatically replicated across multiple Availability Zones in a Region to provide built-in high availability and data durability.

Amazon DynamoDB enables customers to offload the administrative burden of operating and scaling a highly available distributed database cluster while only paying a low variable price for the resources they consume.

Amazon DynamoDB Functionality

To Use Amazon DynamoDB you simply :

- Use the AWS Management Console or the Amazon DynamoDB APIs to create a table and specify your required request capacity.
- Use the Amazon DynamoDB APIs to write and retrieve data.
- Monitor the status and performance of your Amazon DynamoDB tables using Amazon CloudWatch in the AWS Management Console.
- Pay for what you use. Your monthly bill is based on the provisioned request capacity of your table and the amount of data stored.

Service Highlights

- **Scalable :** Amazon DynamoDB is designed for seamless throughput and storage scaling.
- **Provisioned Throughput :** When creating a table, simply specify how much request capacity you require. DynamoDB allocates dedicated resources to your table to meet your performance requirements, and automatically partitions data over a sufficient number of servers to meet your request capacity. If your throughput requirements change, simply update your table's request capacity using the AWS Management Console or the Amazon DynamoDB APIs. You are still able to achieve your prior throughput levels while scaling is underway.
- **Automated Storage Scaling :** There is no limit to the amount of data you can store in a DynamoDB table, and the service automatically allocates more storage, as you store more data using the DynamoDB write APIs.
- **Fully Distributed, Shared Nothing Architecture :** Amazon DynamoDB scales horizontally and can seamlessly scale a single table over hundreds of servers.
- **Fast, Predictable Performance :** Average service-side latencies for Amazon DynamoDB are typically single-digit milliseconds. The service runs on solid state drives, and is built to maintain consistent, fast latencies at any scale.
- **Easy Administration :** Amazon DynamoDB is a fully managed service – you simply create a database table and let the service handle the rest. You don't need to worry about hardware or software provisioning, setup and configuration, software patching, operating a reliable, distributed database cluster, or partitioning data over multiple instances as you scale.

- **Built-in Fault Tolerance :** Amazon DynamoDB has built-in fault tolerance, automatically and synchronously replicating your data across multiple Availability Zones in a Region for high availability and to help protect your data against individual machine, or even facility failures.

- **Flexible :** Amazon DynamoDB does not have a fixed schema. Instead, each data item may have a different number of attributes. Multiple data types (strings, numbers, and sets) add richness to the data model.

- **Strong Consistency, Atomic Counters :** Unlike many non-relational databases, Amazon DynamoDB makes development easier by allowing you to use strong consistency on reads to ensure you are always reading the latest values. Amazon DynamoDB supports multiple native data types (numbers, strings, and multi-valued attributes). The service also natively supports Atomic Counters, allowing you to atomically increment or decrement numerical attributes with a single API call.

- **Cost Effective :** Amazon DynamoDB is designed to be extremely cost-efficient for workloads of any scale. You can get started with a free tier that allows more than 40 million database operations per month, and pay low hourly rates only for the resources you consume above that limit. With easy administration and efficient request pricing, DynamoDB, can offer significantly lower Total Cost of Ownership (TCO) for your workload compared to operating a relational or non-relational database on your own.

- **Secure :** Amazon DynamoDB uses proven cryptographic methods to authenticate users and prevent unauthorized data access. It also integrates with AWS Identity and Access Management (IAM) for fine-grained access control for users within your organization.

- **Integrated Monitoring :** Amazon DynamoDB displays key operational metrics for your table in the AWS Management Console. The service also integrates with Amazon CloudWatch so you can see your request throughput and latency for each Amazon DynamoDB table, and easily track your resource consumption.

- **Elastic MapReduce Integration :** Amazon DynamoDB also integrates with Amazon Elastic MapReduce (Amazon EMR). Amazon EMR allows businesses to perform complex analytics of their large datasets using a hosted pay-as-you-go Hadoop framework on AWS. With the launch of Amazon DynamoDB, it is easy for customers to use Amazon EMR to analyze datasets stored in DynamoDB and archive the results in Amazon Simple Storage Service (Amazon S3), while keeping the original dataset in DynamoDB intact. Businesses can also use Amazon EMR to access data in multiple stores (i.e. Amazon DynamoDB, Amazon RDS, and Amazon S3), do complex analysis over this combined dataset, and store the results of this work in Amazon S3.

When Should I Use DynamoDB?

When should I use Amazon DynamoDB vs. a Relational Database Engine?

Today's web-based applications generate and consume massive amounts of data. For example, an online game might start out with only a few thousand users and a light database workload consisting of 10 writes per second and 50 reads per second. However, if the game becomes successful, it may rapidly grow to millions of users and generate tens (or even hundreds) of thousands of writes and reads per second. It may also create terabytes of data per day. Developing your applications against Amazon DynamoDB enables you to start small and simply dial-up your request capacity for a table as your requirements scale, without incurring downtime or having to write or change a single line of code. Amazon DynamoDB provides a fully managed experience at any scale.

While Amazon DynamoDB tackles the core problems of database scalability, management, performance, and reliability, it is not a relational database and does not support complex relational queries (e.g. joins) or complex transactions. If your workload requires this functionality, or you are looking for compatibility with an existing relational engine, try Amazon Relational Database Service (RDS). You can also run your own relational database on Amazon EC2. While relational database engines provide rich features and functionality, workloads with scaling needs may require you to manage the partitioning and re-partitioning of your data over multiple instances. This can be a complex undertaking. As such, if you anticipate significant scaling requirements for your new application and do not need relational features, Amazon DynamoDB will be a better fit for you.

How does Amazon DynamoDB differ from Amazon SimpleDB? Which should I use?

Both services are non-relational databases that remove the work of database administration. Amazon DynamoDB focuses on providing seamless scalability and fast, predictable performance. Amazon DynamoDB automatically manages the spreading of your data and workload over a sufficient number of servers to meet your scaling requirements. There is no limit on the amount of data you can store in an Amazon DynamoDB table and you can grow the request capacity to the level that you need. On the other hand, Amazon SimpleDB is a good fit for lower-scale workloads that require query flexibility. Amazon SimpleDB automatically indexes all item attributes and supports greater query functionality than Amazon DynamoDB. However, a table in Amazon SimpleDB has a size limit of 10 GB and is limited in the request capacity it can achieve. You can manually partition your data over additional SimpleDB tables if you need additional scale.

3.17 FEATURES AND COMPARISONS AMONG GFS AND HDFS

Google File System (GFS)

Google File System is a proprietary distributed file system developed by Google and specially designed to provide efficient, reliable access to data using large clusters of commodity servers. Files are divided into chunks of 64 megabytes, and are usually appended to or read and only extremely rarely overwritten or shrunk.

Compared with traditional file systems, GFS is designed and optimized to run on data centers to provide extremely high data throughputs, low latency and survive individual server failures. Inspired by GFS, the open source Hadoop.

Distributed File System (HDFS) stores large files across multiple machines. It achieves reliability by replicating the data across multiple servers. Similarly to GFS, data is stored on multiple geo-diverse nodes. The file system is built from a cluster of data nodes, each of which serves blocks of data over the network using a block protocol specific to HDFS. In order to perform the certain operations in GFS and HDFS a programming model is required. GFS has its own programming model called Mapreduce. It is an open-source programming model developed by Google Inc. Apache adopted the ideas of Google Mapreduce and developed Hadoop Mapreduce.

Google File System (GFS)

The Google file system is implemented to meet the rapidly growing demands of Google's data processing needs. Google faces the requirements to manage large amounts of data including but not being limited to the crawled web content to be processed by the indexing system. Relying on large numbers of comparable small servers, GFS is designed as a distributed file system to be run on clusters up to thousands of machines. In order ease the development of applications based on GFS, the file system provides a programming interface aimed at abstracting from these distribution and management aspects. Running on commodity hardware, GFS is not only challenged by managing distribution, it also has to cope with the increased danger of hardware faults. Consequently, one of the assumptions made in the design of GFS is to consider disk faults, machine faults as well as network faults as being the norm rather than the exception. Ensuring safety of data as well as being able to scale up to thousands of computers while managing multiple terabytes of data can thus be considered the key challenges faced by GFS. Having distilled the aims and non-aims of a prospective file system in detail, Google has opted not to use an existing distributed file system. Instead it decided to develop a new file system. GFS has been fully customized to suite Google's needs. This specialization allows the design of the file system to withdraw from many compromises made by other file systems. As an example, a file system targeting general applicability is expected to be able to efficiently manage files with sizes ranging from very small (i.e. few bytes) to large (i.e. gigabyte to multi-terabyte). GFS, however, being targeted at a particular set of usage scenarios, is optimized for usage of large files only with space efficiency being of minor importance. Moreover, GFS files are commonly modified by appending data, whereas modifications at arbitrary file offsets are rare. The majority of files can thus, in sharp contrast to other file immutable (write once, read many). Coming along with being optimized for large files and acting as the basis for large-volume data processing systems, the design of GFS has been optimized for large streaming reads and generally favors throughput over latency. GFS implements a proprietary interface applications can use.

Architecture Of GFS

A GFS cluster consists of a single *master* and multiple *chunk servers* and is accessed by multiple *clients*, as shown in Figure. Each of these is typically a commodity Linux machine running a user-level server process. It is easy to run both a chunk server and a client on the same machine, as long as machine resources permit and the lower reliability caused by running possibly crumbling application code is acceptable. Files are divided into fixed-size *chunks*. Each chunk is identified by an immutable and globally unique 64 bit *chunk handle* assigned by the master at the time of chunk creation. Chunk servers store on local disks as Linux files and read or write chunk data specified by a chunk handle and byte range. For reliability, each chunk is replicated on multiple servers. By default, we store three replicas, though users can designate different replication levels for different regions of the file namespace. The master maintains all file system metadata. This includes the namespace, access control information, the mapping from files to chunks, and the current locations of chunks. It also controls system-wide activities such as chunk lease management, garbage collection of orphaned chunks, and chunk migration between chunk servers. The master periodically communicates with each chunk server in Heart Beat messages to give it instructions and collect its state. GFS client code linked into each application implements the file system API and communicates with the master and chunk servers to read or write data on behalf of the application. Clients interact with the master for metadata operations, but all data-bearing communication goes directly to the chunk servers. POSIX API are not provided and therefore need not hook into the Linux vnode layer. Neither the client nor the chunk server caches file data. Client caches offer little benefit because most applications stream through huge files or have working sets too large to be cached. Not having them simplifies the client and the overall system by eliminating cache coherence issues. (Clients do cache metadata, however.) Chunk servers need not cache file data because chunks are stored as local files and so Linux's buffer cache already keeps frequently accessed data in memory.

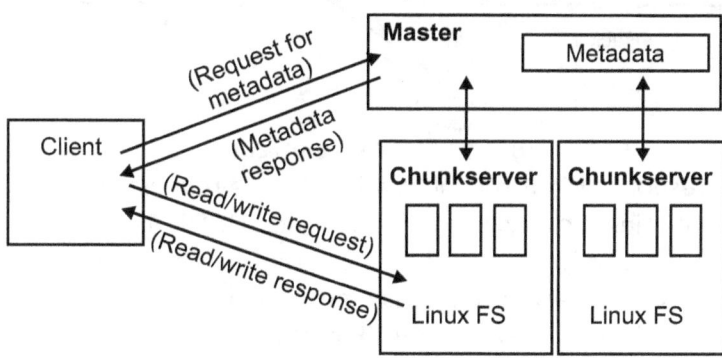

Fig. 3.51 : GFS architecture

Hadoop Distributed File System (Hdfs)

HDFS is the file system which is used in Hadoop based distributed file system. The Hadoop is an open-source distributed computing framework and provided by Apache. Many network stations use it to create systems such as Amazon, Facebook. The Hadoop cores are Mapreduce and HDFS. The mapreduce can make the decomposition of tasks and integration of results. The HDFS is a distributed file system and provide the base support for the storage of file in the storage node. The mapreduce provides job trackers and task trackers.

Mapreduce is a programming model Google has used successfully in processing big data sets. A map function extracts some intelligence from raw data and a reduce function aggregates according to some guides the data output by map. Mapreduce needs a distributed file system and an engine that can distribute, coordinate, monitor and gather the results. The HDFS is a master and slaver framework and which contains nodes and name node. The namenode is a center server and manage the namespace in the file system. The data node manages the data stored in it.

Architecture Of HDFS

HDFS stores data on the compute nodes, providing very high aggregate bandwidth across the cluster. A HDFS installation consists of single name node as the master node and a number of data nodes as the slave nodes. The name node manages the file system namespace and regulates access to files by clients. The data nodes are distributed, one data node per machine in the cluster, which manage data blocks attached to the machines where they run. The namenode executes the operations on file system namespace and maps data blocks to data nodes.

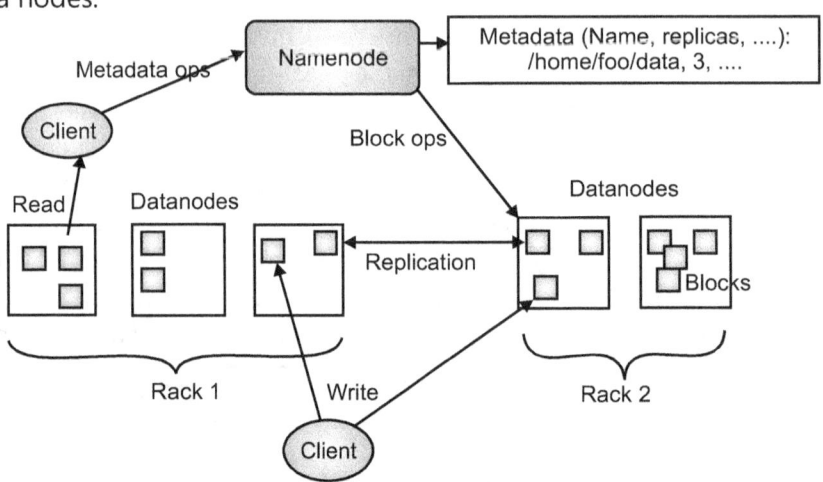

Fig. 3.52 : HDFS architecutre

The data nodes are responsible for serving read and write requests from clients and perform block operations upon instructions from namenode. HDFS distributes data chunks and replicas across the server for higher performance, load-balancing and resiliency. With data distributed across all servers, any server may be participating in the reading, writing, or computation of a data-block at any time. HDFS replicates file blocks for fault tolerance. An application can specify the number of replicas of a file at the time it is created, and this number can be changed any time after that. The name node makes all decisions concerning block replication. For a large cluster, it may not be practical to connect all nodes in a flat topology. The common practice is to spread the nodes across multiple racks. Nodes of a rack share a switch, and rack switches are connected by one or more core switches. Communication between two nodes in different racks has to go through multiple switches. In most cases, network bandwidth between nodes in the same rack is greater than network bandwidth between nodes in different racks.

Mapreduce

The primary role of Mapreduce is to provide an infrastructure that allows development and execution of large-scale data processing jobs. As such, Mapreduce aims at efficiently exploiting the processing capacity provided by computing clusters while at the same time offering a programming model that simplifies the development of such distributed applications. Moreover and similar to the requirements of GFS, Mapreduce is designed to be resilient to failures such as machine crashes. Google uses mapreduce to process data sets upto multiple terabytes in size for purposes such as indexing web content. To achieve the goals mentioned, Mapreduce has been inspired by the idea of higher order functions, in particular the functions map (also referred to as fold) and reduce. These functions are an integral part of functional programming languages such as Lisp. The primary benefit the functional programming paradigm and these functions in particular promise is to allow the creation of a system that incorporates automatic parallelization of tasks. One of the assumptions made by mapreduce is that all data to be processed can be expressed in the form of key/value pairs and lists of such pairs. Both keys and values are encoded as strings. Based on these assumptions, the key idea of Msapreduce is to implement the application exclusively by writing appropriate map and reduce functions. Provided these functions, the infrastructure not only transparently provides for all necessary communication between cluster nodes, it also automatically distributes and load-balances the processing among the machines. Map is a function written by the user that takes a key/value pair as input and yields a list of key/value pairs as result. A canonical use case for map is thus to digest raw data and generate (potentially very large quantities of) unaggregated intermediate results. Reduce is the second function implemented by the user. It takes a key and a list of values as input and generates a list of values as result. The primary role of reduce is thus to aggregate data.

Properties	GFS	HDFS
Design Goals	The main goal of GFS is to support large files • Built based on the assumption that terabyte data sets will be distributed across thousands of disks attached to commodity compute nodes. Used for data intensive computing . • Store data reliably, even when failures occur within chunk servers, master, or network partitions. • GFS is designed more for batch processing rather than interactive use by users.	One of the main goals of HDFS is to support large files. • Built based on the assumption that terabyte data sets will be distributed across thousands of disks attached to commodity compute nodes. • Used for data intensive computing . • Store data reliably, even when failures occur within name nodes, data nodes, or network partitions. • HDFS is designed more for batch processing rather than interactive use by users.
Processes	Master and chunk server	Name node and Data node
File Management	Files are organized hierarchically in directories and identified by path names. • GFS is exclusively for Google only.	HDFS supports a traditional hierarchical file organization • HDFS also supports third-party file systems such as CloudStore and Amazon Simple Storage Service

...Conti

Scalability	Cluster based architecture	Cluster based architecture
	• The file system consists of hundreds or even thousands of storage machines built from inexpensive commodity parts. • The largest cluster have over 1000 storage nodes, over 300 TB of disk storage, and are heavily accessed by hundreds of clients on distinct machines on a continuous basis.	• Hadoop currently runs on clusters with thousands of nodes. • E.g. Face book has two major clusters : - A 1100-machine cluster with 8800 cores and about 12PB raw storage. - A 300-machine cluster with 2400 cores and about 3PB raw storage. - Each (commodity) node has 8 cores and 12 TB of storage. • EBay uses 532 nodes cluster (8*532 cores, 5.3 PB) • Yahoo uses more than 100,000 CPUs in > 40,000 computers running Hadoop - biggest cluster: 4500 nodes(2*4 cpu boxes w 4*1 TB disk and 16 GB RAM)
	Google have their own file system called GFS. With GFS, files are split up and stored in multiple pieces on multiple machines. Filenames are random (they do not match content type or owner). There are hundreds of thousands of files on a single disk, and all the data is obfuscated so that it is not human readable. The algorithms uses for obfuscation changes all the time.	The HDFS implements a permission model for files and directories that shares much of the POSIX model. • File or directory has separate permissions for the user that is the owner, for other users that are members of the group, and for all other users.

...Conti.

Security	Google has dozens of datacenters for redundancy. These datacenters are in undisclosed locations and most are unmarked for protection. • Access is allowed to authorized employees and vendors only. Some of the protections in place include: 24/7 guard coverage, Electronic key access, Access logs, Closed circuit televisions, Alarms linked to guard stations, Internal and external patrols, Dual utility power feeds and Backup power UPS and generators.	HDFS security is based on the POSIX model of users and groups. • Currently is security is limited to simple file permissions. • The identity of a client process is just whatever the host operating system says it is. • Network authentication protocols like Kerberos for user authentication and encryption of data transfers are yet not supported.
Database Files	Bigtable is the database used by GFS. Bigtable is a proprietary distributed database of Google Inc.	HBase provides Bigtable (Google) -like capabilities on top of Hadoop Core.
File Serving	A file in GFS is comprised of fixed sized chunks. The size of chunk is 64 MB. Parts of a file can be stored on different nodes in a cluster satisfying the concepts load balancing and storage management.	HDFS is divided into large blocks for storage and access, typically 64MB in size. Portions of the file can be stored on different cluster nodes, balancing storage resources and demand
Cache Management	Clients do cache metadata. • Neither the sever nor the client caches the file data. • Chunks are stored as local files in a Linux system. So, Linux buffer cache already keeps frequently accessed data in memory. Therefore chunk servers need not cache file data.	HDFS uses distributed cache • It is a facility provided by Mapreduce framework to cache application-specific, large, read-only files (text, archives, jars and so on) • Private (belonging to one user) and Public (belonging to all the user of the same node) Distributed Cache Files
Cache Consistency	Append-once-read-many model is adapted by Google. It avoids the locking mechanism of files for writing in distributed environment is avoided.	HDFS's write-once-read-many model that relaxes concurrency control requirements, simplifies data coherency, and enables high throughput access.

	• Client can append the data to the existing file.	• Client can only append to existing files (yet not supported).
Communication	TCP connections are used for communication. Pipelining is used for data transfer over TCP connections.	RPC based protocol on top of TCP/IP
Replication Strategy	Chunk replicas are spread across the racks. Master automatically replicates the chunks. • A user can specify the number of replicas to be maintained. • The master re-replicates a chunk replica as soon as the number of available replicas falls below a user-specified number.	Automatic replication system. • Rack based system. By default two copies of each block are stored by different Data Nodes in the same rack and a third copy is stored on a Data Node in a different rack (for greater reliability) An application can specify the number of replicas of a file that should be maintained by HDFS . • Replication pipelining in case of write operations.
Available Implementation	GFS is a proprietary distributed file system developed by Google for its own use.	Yahoo, Facebook, IBM etc. are based on HDFS.

QUESTIONS

1. Write short note on storage system architecture. Draw a neat diagram of three layer storage system architecture.
2. Explain the various terms and terminologies associated with big data.
3. Explain the concept of Virtualize Data Center (VDC) architecture and environment with suitable diagram.
4. Explain the techniques for application and desktop virtualization. Also mention the advantages and disadvantages of these techniques.
5. Explain various techniques for converting physical machine to virtual machine which technique is better and why?
6. Explain various types of storage virtualization.
7. What is virtual provisioning ? Explain in detail with suitable diagram.
8. Write short note on automated storage tiering mention few advantages of it.
9. Write short note on (Diagram is expected) : (a) VLAN (b) VSAN
10. Explain following cloud file systems in short (a) GIS (b) HDFC (c) Big table (d) Hbase (e) Dynamo
11. Differentiate between GFS and HDFS.

CLOUD COMPUTING PLATFORMS

4.1 INTRODUCTION

In cloud, everything from storage to computation is provided as a service. Depending in the nature of service, it is divided into following services:

- Software as a service (SaaS)
- Platform as a Service (PaaS)
- Infrastructure as a Service (IaaS)

4.1.1 Software as a Service (SaaS)

Software as service is cloud deployment model in which a software is built centrally by provider and is given for use to the end users on-demand via a thin client like web browser. Here instead of buying a software, user pays per use.

SaaS is model,

- of Software Deployment where an application is hosted as service provided to customers across internet.
- where Applications (word processor, CRM etc) or Application Services (mail, schedule, calendar) execute in the **cloud** using the interconnectivity of the internet to propagate data. SaaS has become a common delivery model for most business applications, including accounting, collaboration, customer relationship management (CRM), enterprise resource planning (ERP), invoicing, human resource management (HRM), content management (CM) and service desk management. SaaS has been incorporated into the strategy of all leading enterprise software companies.

Benefits of SaaS

- Faster Time to Market of Business Apps
- Means the time, application is ready for use, can be made available to end user. Suppose, a SaaS provider develops an application, he does not have to market it, no need to the licensing, what all he has to do is just make that available on centralized server.
- Any Time any Where Access
- Means if I purchase a software service, I can use it anywhere and on any device as I don't have to actually install it on my PC, I just have to access the service through a web browser. So a software service purchased can be accessible on my desktop, laptop or any other media device.
- Elimination of Licensing Risk

- As we have all seen, piracy is a big issue at the moment in software industry, but if make all softwares as service, piracy can be controlled on larger extent. Also, to the licensing of software is a big overhead, that can be avoided by the use of SaaS.
- Elimination of Version Compatibility
- Here, we are maintaining the software centrally. So any changes or updates to the software can be made available to all users in just one commit to the central server. So, compatibility and version controlling is a very easy task for the software provider.
- Reduced Hardware Foot Print
- As we can access any software services on just a click of a web browser, there is no need to buy the expensive hardware to install the software. Any commodity hardware can be used to access the services.
- Lower Operating and Maintenance Cost
- Software is service is developed and maintained on centralized server, so there is an efficient use of space and energy, which ultimately results in low cost of operating. Also, if there is any need of up-gradation, can be achieved through minimum resources, which reduces the maintenance cost when compared to traditional computing
- Consumption Based Expenditure
- As it's a pay per use model, we can access the services only when required and pay for only that usage, which makes it costand energy effective.

Challenges of SaaS

- Extension of the On-premises Security Model to the SaaS Provider (data privacy and ownership)
  Here, from computation to storage, we don't have direct control on data. So, our data will always be with SaaS provider and we have to be dependent on its availability.
- Governance and Billing Management
  Pay per use model has to be customized depending on the end user's preference. Some common pay per use models are as follows
- Per user per month
- Per transaction
- Per GB of storage per month
Sometimes its difficult to keep governance on such usage, for that there is need of good metering devices.
- Synchronization of Client and Vendor Migration
  Sometimes if there is a need to change the software service provider, migration from one such provider to other is a difficult thing as every software provider uses its own way of storage and computation. So migration of already existing data from one provider is not possible as of now, as there is no standardization followed in SaaS industry.
- Need of Good Connectivity
  As all service are available on clouds, and nothing is present on local machine, we have to be dependant on internet connectivity. Performance of that service is greatly affectedby

speed and availability of the network. But we live in the edge of 3G and 4G network services, so connectivity is not a big issue at the moment.

Some important SaaS providers are as follows:

- Salesforce.com

4.1.2 Platform as a Service (Paas)

Platform as a service is a cloud model, in which a computation platform is provided as a service to end user. PaaS is mainly used by developers to deploy their code on public cloud. Once the code is deployed, from computation to storage everything happens in cloud, at provider's end.PaaS offerings facilitate the deployment of applications without the cost and complexity of buying and managing the underlying hardware and software and provisioning hosting capabilities, providing all of the facilities required to support the complete life cycle of building and delivering web applications and services entirely available from the Internet.

In PaaS,

- Applications are built on the 'Cloud platform, using variety of technologies. Like Java, Python, .NET, Ruby etc.
- PaaS offers development environments that can be used to develop'cloud-ready' applications.
- Has got inherent dynamic scalling capabilities
- Development environment + runtime = Provides everything a developer needs to build an application
- Developer only needs to deploy his code on platform and rest will be taken care by PaaS provider.

Benefits of PaaS

- Enables Developer to Focus on the Application Code and the Business Logic.
- In PaaS, we only have to deploy the code, irrespective of what is the run time platform, its capacity, database storage. So it makes developer to focus on code building rather than wasting time in buying the server space, buying the hardware, buying the database etc.
- Natural fit for Development, Testing and Production Environments.
- In development environment, it is expected to make the environments available quick and ready to use, so PaaS becomes a natural fit for development. Also, if someone wants to try some web application's success, then he can first try launching that application on PaaS and if successful, can be developed on larger scale.
- Instant Provisioning – Takes Few Minutes.
- Its quick, in most popular PaaS providers like Google App Engine and Cloud Foundry, it takes seconds to get the environment development ready.
- Inherent Dynamic Scalability
- As its in Clouds, applications can scale to any extent without any delay or discontinuity in application presence.
- Eliminates the Complexities of Hardware and Software Dependencies.

- In PaaS, developer is only need to deploy the code in cloud, so that can be achieved through simple desktop with commodity hardware. As the code will be running on provider platform, this eliminates the complexities of hardware and software dependencies.

Challenges of PaaS

- Risk of Vendor Lock-in.
- Vendor lock-in poses a big challenge when the application needs to be migrated to a different PaaS provider/platform, since platform is proprietary of to the vendor and not standardized.
- Interoperabilty and connectivity with existing on-premises applications
- Computation platform changes from vendor to vendor. So its difficult to have an integrate Pass and an application which is running on traditional computation logic as the PaaS application will be running at provider's premise and normal application will be in-premise
- Has to rely on 3rd party performance and scalability SLAs.
- When we deploy an application on PaaS provider's platform, we loose control on it and we have to be dependent on their system's performance. Consider a scenario where there is PaaS provider, developer company and service consuming company, here the Service Level Agreement just cannot be between Service consuming company and developer company, we have consider the PaaS provider for its SLAs.
- Potential security risk and loss of control over the data since it's located out of Premises.
- As we are deploying code on Public Cloud, sometimes it can be a threat to the sensitive data. Also, complete data, though produced by user, is owned by PaaS provider and the end user won't be having any control over it.
- Currently supported to few programming Languages like java, python, .NET, ruby etc.
- Some PaaS Providers,
- Google App Engine,
- Cloud Foundry,
- Hereko,
- Rails Engine.

4.1.3 Infrastructure as a Service(IaaS)

Infrastructure as a service is to take the servers on rent instead of buying them directly and pay for the use.

IaaS is,

- The Computer infrastructure comprising of servers, storage and network is delivered as a service
- Rather than buying and owning the infrastructure, clients can buy this as a fully outsourced service

- Clients pay only for the resources they consume on a **Utility Computing** basis. Similar to public utility services such as electricity, public transport etc.
- IaaS has the ability to provide single server up to entire data centers
- With IaaS the processing, storage, network capacity and other fundamental computing resources are rented out on need basis.

Benefits of IaaS

- Effective infrastructure utilization.
- Its been found that, on an average a server just uses 30%-40% of its capacity in a year when it comes to computation and storage. In Iaas, resources are used on shared basis as in 2-3 applications are deployed on a single server. By using shared pool of resources we are actually saving the energy and other expenses. If a sudden demand comes, cloud applications can be scaled up in no time.
- Highly automated resulting in faster provisioning of resources.
- To get a server for development is just a matter of few clicks. Most of IaaS providers gives template for servers required. Also, to use the server space, neither you actually need to buy the floor space for server nor you have to buy the expensive hardware.
- Cab quickly and easily meet the changing dynamic demand for consumption.
- There is one device called Load balancer so when a Load balancer comes to know that server has met the threshold capacity (70% or more) it triggers an event to add a new server to the service. So when needed service is available.
- Reduced cost due to :
- Less hardware resources.
- Less real estate space for on-premise.
- Less power consumption.
- Less manual work and hence lesser administration.

Challenges in IaaS

- Integration outside the enterprise firewall across the cloud boundry for consuming resources from the public cloud IaaS.

   Use of Public cloud to store the sensitive data is threat. In public cloud, as control over data is lost, we have to be dependent on IaaS provider's availability. Its difficult to make a gateway when we are trying to integrate in-premise, firewall protected application with application hosted on public cloud.

- Migration of applications in terms of assessing the fitment from dimensions such as Technology, Security etc.

   As we have seen in case of PaaS and SaaS, its difficult to migrate an application, hosted on traditional devices to an IaaS cloud as there is no stardardized process followed.

- Vendor reliability and potential security risk when the service are consumed from public cloud IaaS providers.

   As there is no control over data, we have to be dependent on vendor for the availability of the application.

- Need of good connectivity in termsof network bandwidth and internet availability IaaS Providers :
    - Amazon Web services
    - Rackspace Cloud Hosting

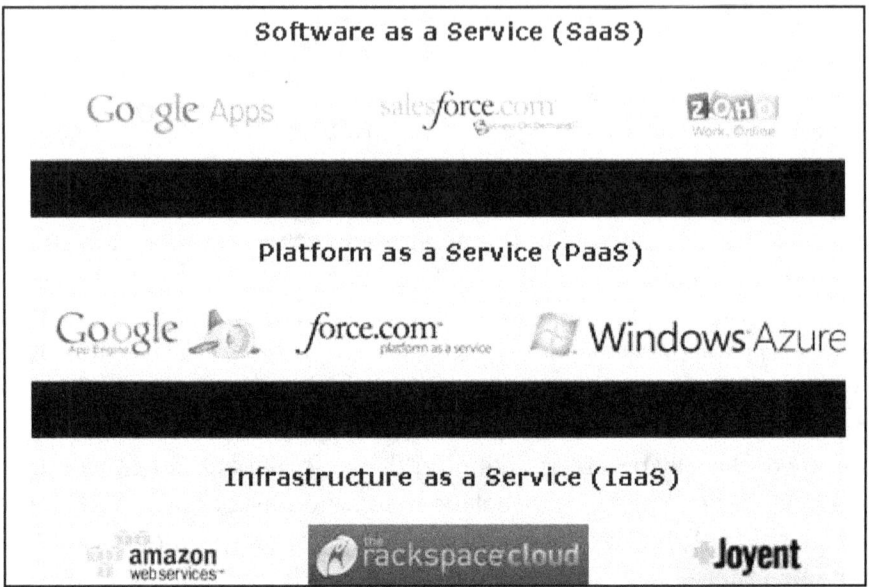

Fig. 4.1 : Software as a Service (SaaS)

4.2 BEST-OF BREED CLOUD INFRASTRUCTURE COMPONENTS

Successful implementation of cloud computing requires proper implementation of certain components. Without any of these components, cloud computing will not be possible. These components can't be easily implemented by one person alone.

Cloud computing will require persons with different expertise, experiences and backgrounds. As it will require more people in the industry, it's no wonder why cloud computing is a very expensive venture. But even with the expenses that the company would often have to spend, the advantages provided by cloud computing is far more than the initial spending.

Some would resort to a cloud computing vendor because of the lack of resources while others have the resources to build their cloud computing applications, platforms and hardware. But either way, components have to be implemented with the expectation of optimal performance.

4.2.1 The Client – The End User

Everything ends with the client. The hardware components, the application and everything else developed for cloud computing will be used in the client. Without the client, nothing, will be possible.

The client could come in two forms: the hardware component or the combination of software and hardware components. Although it's a common conception that cloud computing solely relies on the cloud (internet), there are certain systems that requires pre-installed applications to ensure smooth transition. The hardware on the other hand will be the platform where everything has to be launched.

Optimization is based on two fronts : the local hardware capacity and the software security. Through optimized hardware with security, the application will launch seamlessly.

4.2.2 The Service – the Functions in Cloud Computing

Cloud computing always has a purpose. One of the main reasons cloud computing become popular is due to the adoption of businesses as the easier way to implement business processes. Cloud computing is all about processes and the services launched through cloud computing always has to deal with processes with an expected output.

The optimization on services is based on two things: the proper development of the application and the end user. Sometimes, the service could be used by the user wherein their experience is greatly affected by their gadget.

4.2.3 The Application – Backbone of Service

The service is often though as the application. Although it's partly correct given the fact that it provides the functions, the application is entirely different because it is through the application that the service is realized. This is where software developers have to focus in terms of ensuring the application will work as expected.

Optimization of the application is based the actual coding of developers. Through extensive testing on load handling, security and functionality, the application could work as expected.

4.2.4 The Platform – "Soft Infrastructure" for the Application

In regular websites or applications that don't deal with cloud computing, the application is directly connected to the server. In cloud computing, the application is still launched to another application called the platform. The platform usually comes as the programming language such as Ajax (Asynchronous JavaScript and XML) or Ruby on Rails.

At this point, those who opted to seek cloud computing providers will have to follow the set programming languages that could be run in the platform. Although most programming languages could be launched in different platform, a powerful application with real time updating capability is a must for cloud computing.

4.2.5 The Storage – The Warehouse of Cloud Computing

Everything that the application knows and the functions that could be provided by service are possible through storage. The storage holds pertinent data and information on function on how they will be implemented.

Optimization on storage is based on how the storage facility protected from different attacks and availability of back-up. Cloud computing is always about consistency and availability of service which will naturally require the storage to be available all the time.

4.2.6 The Infrastructure – The Backbone of Cloud Computing

Every function, service and the ability of storage to provide the needed data is only possible through optimized infrastructure. This could be considered as the platform behind the storage as the infrastructure helps the storage deal with load problems.

The infrastructure is a platform wherein it weights the ability of the storage against the number of requests. The infrastructure has the ability to make some changes by load balancing and even management.

These are the components for cloud computing. Each of these components have to be optimized for a secured and well functioning application for cloud computing.

Cloud computing architecture refers to the components and subcomponents required for cloud computing. These components typically consist of a front end platform (fat client, thin client, mobile device), back end platforms (servers, storage), a cloud based delivery, and a network (Internet, Intranet, Intercloud). Combined, these components make up cloud computing architecture.

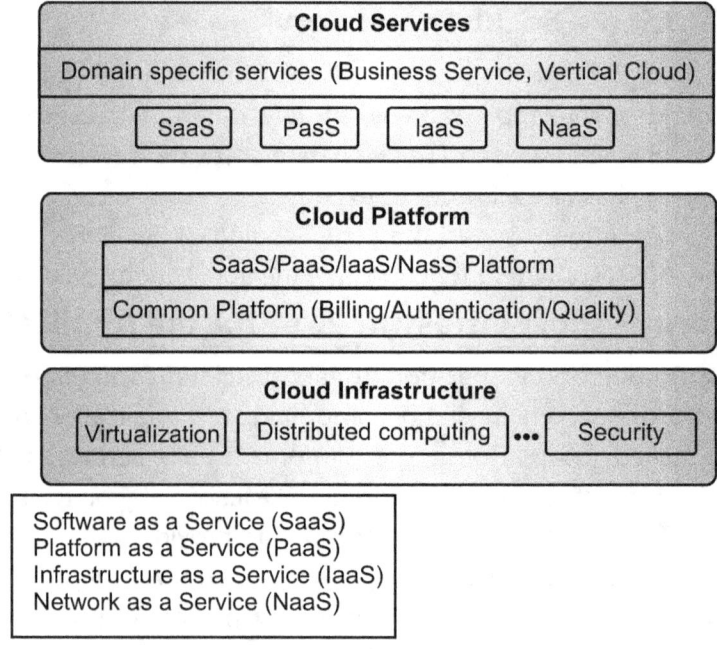

Fig. 4.2 : Components of cloud compouting

- **Cloud Client Platforms**

Cloud computing architectures consist of front-end platforms called clients or cloud clients. These clients comprise servers, fat (or thick) clients, thin clients, zero clients, tablets and mobile devices. These client platforms interact with the cloud data storage via an application (middleware), via a web browser, or through a virtual session.

- **The Zero Client**

The zero or ultra-thin client initializes the network to gather required configuration files that then tell it where its OS binaries are stored. The entire zero client device runs via the network.

This creates a single point of failure, in that, if the network goes down, the device is rendered useless.

- **Cloud Storage**

An online network storage where data is stored and accessible to multiple clients. Cloud storage is generally deployed in the following configurations: public cloud, private cloud, community cloud, or some combination of the three also known as hybrid cloud.

In order to be effective, the cloud storage needs to be agile, flexible, scalable, multi-tenancy, and secure.

Cloud Based Delivery

- **Software as a Service (SaaS)**

The software-as-a-service (SaaS) service-model involves the cloud provider installing and maintaining software in the cloud and users running the software from their cloud clients over the Internet (or Intranet). The user's client machines require no installation of any application-specific software cloud applications run on the server (in the cloud). SaaS is scalable, and system administration may load the applications on several servers. In the past, each customer would purchase and load their own copy of the application to each of their own servers, but with the SaaS the customer can access the application without installing the software locally. SaaS typically involves a monthly or annual fee.

Software as a service provides the equivalent of installed applications in the traditional (non-cloud computing) delivery of applications.

Software as a service has four common approaches :

1. Single instance,
2. Multi instance,
3. Multi-tenant,
4. Flex tenancy.

- **Development as a Service (DaaS)**

Development as a service is web based, community shared development tools. This is the equivalent to locally installed development tools in the traditional (non-cloud computing) delivery of development tools.

- **Platform as a service (PaaS)**

Platform as a service is cloud computing service which provides the users with application platforms and databases as a service. This is equivalent to middleware in the traditional (non-cloud computing) delivery of application platforms and databases.

- **Infrastructure as a Service (IaaS)**

Infrastructure as a service is taking the physical hardware and going completely virtual (e.g. all servers, networks, storage, and system management all existing in the cloud). This is the equivalent to infrastructure and hardware in the traditional (non-cloud computing) method running in the cloud. In other words, businesses pay a fee (monthly or annually) to run virtual servers, networks, storage from the cloud. This will mitigate the need for a data center, heating, cooling, and maintaining hardware at the local level.

Cloud Networking

Generally, the cloud network layer should offer :

- High bandwidth (low latency).
- Allowing users to have uninterrupted access to their data and applications.
- Agile network.
- On-demand access to resources requires the ability to move quickly and efficiently between servers and possibly even clouds.
- Network security.
- Security is always important, but when you are dealing with multi-tenancy, it becomes much more important because you're dealing with segregating multiple customers.

4.3 CLOUD READY CONVERGED INFRASTRUCTURE

Converged infrastructure operates by grouping multiple Information Technology (IT) components into a single, optimized computing package. Components of a converged infrastructure may include servers, data storage devices, networking equipment and software for IT infrastructure management, automation and orchestration.

IT organizations use converged infrastructure to centralize the management of IT resources, to consolidate systems, to increase resource-utilization rates, and to lower costs. Converged infrastructures foster these objectives by implementing pools of computers, storage and networking resources that can be shared by multiple applications and managed in a collective manner using policy-driven processes.

IT vendors and IT industry analysts use various terms to describe the concept of a converged infrastructure. These include "converged system", "unified computing", "fabric-based computing", and "dynamic infrastructure".

Data Centers

Historically, to keep pace with the growth of business applications and the terabytes of data they generate, IT resources were deployed in a silo-like fashion. One set of resources has been devoted to one particular computing technology, business application or line of business. These resources support a single set of assumptions and cannot be optimized or reconfigured to support varying usage loads.

The proliferation of IT sprawl in data centers has contributed to rising operations costs, reducing productivity, and stifling agility and flexibility. Maintenance and operations can consume two-thirds of an organization's technology budget, according to a 2009 Information Week survey of executives in 500 companies with annual revenue over $250 million. That leaves just a third of the budget for new IT initiatives. This ratio prevents IT from supporting new business initiatives or responding to real application demands.

A converged infrastructure addresses the problem of storage tower architectures and IT sprawl by pooling and sharing IT resources. Rather than dedicating a set of resources to a particular computing technology, application or line of business, converged infrastructure creates a pool of virtualized servers, storage and networking capacity that is shared by multiple applications and lines of business.

4.3.1 Converged Infrastructure and Cloud Computing

Converged infrastructure can serve as an enabling platform for private and public cloud computing services, including Infrastructure as a Service (IaaS), Platform as a Service (PaaS), and Software as a Service (SaaS) offerings.

Several characteristics make converged infrastructure well suited to cloud deployments. These include the ability to pool IT resources, to automate resource provisioning and to scale up and down capacity quickly to meet the needs of dynamic computing workloads.

IT has once again found itself engaging in the age-old practice of "white boxing." This time, however, we're not piecing together our servers; virtualization has instead driven us to white box our entire data center infrastructure.

The end result of white boxing servers often ended up being a data center full of inconsistencies, with additional administrative overhead and an increased chance of failure following every configuration change. This is why converged infrastructure has quickly become our industry's hottest topic, as white boxes are now being assembled to create virtual environments.

Solving this problem and beating back our industry's second generation of white boxing is what converged infrastructure intends to achieve.

At the end , virtual infrastructure or private cloud runs on monitoring data. That data explains how much capacity is on-hand, broken down into major categories: Compute, memory, networking and storage.

It also knows how many of those resources your virtual Machines (VMs) require. This second number represents demand. With supply and demand now abstracted into some set of numerical values, you have now generated an easy-to-understand "economics of resources" that represents the state of your data center.

In a converged infrastructure, this provides a recognizable warning as to when more resources are needed. Trending the use of resources means knowing that more networking, storage or compute power will be required at a specific time. Supplied and consumed resources are now quantified and used, rather than organizations relying on best guesses. Trending also makes purchases substantially easier to plan and budget.

To achieve its goals, converged infrastructure hardware is completely modularized. Each module connects with minimal effort into the greater whole that is your data center, much as an additional hard drive is snapped into a server or SAN today. The modules also contribute a known quantity of resources, increasing your economic supply. You can add to your total storage, computing power or memory in the same way.

More importantly, each module is something you'll purchase by popping over to a manufacturer's website and clicking "buy." You've done this for years with servers; why couldn't you do it with your entire data center? What will arrive are ready-to-insert components with minimal cabling and trivial installation. Wrapping around this entire system is a management toolset that recognizes new hardware and seamlessly adds it to your pool of resources.

And this isn't all in the future. For some manufacturers, the hardware is already here. For others, it's on the roadmap. Some of the components blades, modularized storage, dense networking and so on are being advertised by the major manufacturers, even if they haven't yet explained how this new approach works. And the management toolsets are also well on their way.

With names like BladeSystem Matrix and Advanced Infrastructure Manager, these prepackaged virtual computing environments manifest the resource economics at the hardware layer while your hypervisor management tools deal with individual VM actions. The combination of these two pieces is the source of what we now think of as private cloud computing. Converged infrastructure is just the enabler.

Converged infrastructure is both a fancy name and an actual technology. Not there to eliminate hypervisor management but to augment it. Converged infrastructure's hardware and management tools provide a way to end, for the second time, our nasty practice of white boxing.

Converged infrastructures assemble components from multiple IT domains into one integrated system by combining virtualization, storage, networking and compute. A management framework is also included that allows orchestration of the entire infrastructure so that each constituent technology doesn't have to be managed separately. But from that set of basic parameters, the individual flavors vary significantly, and those different flavors are well worth a closer look.

The idea of converged infrastructure is rooted at the intersection of a number of different trends. It used to be that, given the available technology, IT was forced onto a path of sprawl and inefficiency. We routinely reacted by buying more gear and adding to the sprawl. But in the past three years, a bevy of new technologies have become available that should allow us to reverse this trend :

- Solid-state has all but solved the storage performance bottleneck, making it possible to squeeze out performance efficiencies from storage systems.
- Virtualization has simplified the networks and pipes in our data centers.
- The cloud allows us to store enterprise data with better and more ubiquitous access, while pushing much of the low-priority data that contributed to sprawl into a flatter, more scalable and often outsourced infrastructure.
- WAN optimization, deduplication, data transmission, dispersal and caching enhancements have all helped these other technologies work a bit better.

Meanwhile, all of these innovations have come together just when IT had seemingly reached its limit, with many shops running up against hard limits on inflexible things such as available data center power or capital dollars.

4.3.2 Benefits of Converged Infrastructure

Converged infrastructure provides both technical and business efficiencies, according to industry researchers and observers. These gains stem in part from the pre-integration of technology components, the pooling of IT resources and the automation of IT processes. Converged infrastructure further contributes to efficient data centers by enhancing the ability of cloud computing systems to handle enormous data sets, using only a single integrated IT management system. Converged infrastructures, combining server, storage, and networks into a single framework, help to transform the economics of running the datacenter thus accelerating the transition to IP storage to help build infrastructures that are "cloud-ready". The combination of storage and compute into a single entity is known as converged storage. Decreased complexity, through the use of pre-integrated hardware with virtualization and automation management tools, is another important value proposition for converged infrastructure.

Two long-term advantages of a unified data center infrastructure :

1. Lower costs as the result of both :
    *   lower capital expenses resulting from higher utilization, less cabling, and fewer network connections.
    *   lower operating costs resulting from reduced labor via automated data center management and a consolidating storage and network management infrastructure teams.
2. Increased IT agility by :
    *   Virtualizing IP and Fibre Channel storage networking.
    *   Allowing for single console management.

Data centers around the world are reaching limits in power, cooling and space. At the same time, capital constraints are requiring organizations to rethink data center strategy. Converged infrastructure offers a solution to these challenges.

The reality, though, is that the old ways of doing things had already crossed the line of practicality. We've been suffering through escalating complexity for a number of years, so these new technologies have created a significant shift in IT expectations. With the new choices and their ability to solve serious data center problems, technology practitioners have decided that it's time to forgo temporary fixes and patches. We need to apply new technologies to lifecycle problems, from deployment to decommissioning. What was once a never-ending exercise of trying to fit pieces of disparate technologies together, is giving way to the host of integrated technology offerings now available.

Converged infrastructure delivers on promises, such as providing a right-sized, completely packaged solution that could be ordered as one item. When that pre-integrated and largely pre-configured item arrives in the data center, it can effectively put an end to complex deployments and configuration exercises. And once deployed, that converged infrastructure operates as a unit, giving users a single point of management for all the underlying components, as well as application-layer elements that may also be packaged in the solution. But perhaps more importantly, converged infrastructure solutions promise easy repeatability as well. When additional infrastructure is needed, users can simply order another unit. In building block fashion, that additional unit could then be deployed alongside the existing system, with both managed under the same umbrella.

Convergence is also developing into a source of innovation. One of the shortcomings of this first generation of converged infrastructure products was that units didn't elegantly add to the whole without introducing new boundaries. These converged infrastructures still build on limited storage pools and complex network infrastructures that force users into more complicated workload partitioning and storage movement, with significant management complexity across components. All that added up to costs in the form of time and effort, troubleshooting and potential outages.

4.3.3 Case Study

HP Converged Infrastructure

Through years of focused engineering, R&D investments, and decades of data center experience, HP Converged Infrastructure solutions have been designed to make the data center simpler, more flexible, more efficient and less expensive to operate. HP Converged Infrastructure is achieved through a systematic approach that brings together.

- All server, storage, and networking resources together into pools of resources.
- Management tools, policies, and processes so resources and applications are managed in a holistic, integrated manner.
- Security management to provide protection from today's sophisticated security threats.
- Power and cooling management capabilities so systems and facilities work together.

One of the big differences with HP Converged Infrastructure solutions is that it's not a one size fits all approach. Our broad portfolio has been engineered to help you gain the value of convergence based upon your unique requirements. And this portfolio includes a broad range of "best-in-class" solution partners who have validated their applications in the HP Converged Infrastructure environment. Our alliance partner's efforts demonstrate their expertise in delivering solutions that are Converged Infrastructure compliant, making it easy for you to deploy their solutions with confidence.

4.4 VIRTUAL MACHINE PROVISIONING AND MIGRATION SERVICES

Computing-as-a-service is a vision of cloud-based solutions and virtualization is a key concept in triggering this vision. Virtual machine related features such as flexible resource provisioning, and isolation and migration of machine state have improved efficiency of resource usage and dynamic resource provisioning capabilities. Live virtual machine migration transfers "state" of a virtual machine from one physical machine to another, and can mitigate overload conditions and enables uninterrupted maintenance activities.

Virtual machine provisioning can simplify server provisioning and the management of resource allocation. Know the challenges that come with the benefits and how to overcome them.

Virtual machine provisioning, or virtual server provisioning, is a systems management process that creates a new Virtual Machine (VM) on a physical host server and allocates computing resources to support the VM. These computing resources typically include CPU cycles (or entire cores) and memory space, but can also involve I/O cycles and storage.

Although virtual machine provisioning can be accomplished manually, administrators generally prefer to automate server provisioning by creating a generic VM, called a VM template. This generic VM is loaded from storage (usually the corporate SAN) to the desired host server.

A corporation may maintain an extensive library of various VM templates each with a unique suite of computing resources that it can deploy in response to varied needs. For example, a Windows Server 2003 VM template may allocate 384 MB of memory and 10 GB of disk space, while a Windows Server 2008 VM template may allocate 512 MB of memory and 30 GB of disk space.

The more recent trend toward rapid virtual machine provisioning shifts the focus to the SAN, where a generic VM can be replicated and presented to a host server without the time and bandwidth needed to copy a blank VM to the host over the network. Administrators can also add or subtract desired elements of the new VM without having to create a larger number of complete VM templates.

Virtual server provisioning should be approached carefully. An application with inadequate computing resources can suffer from poor performance, poor availability or crash entirely, so it's vital for administrators to allocate sufficient resources. Testing prior to rolling out the virtual application can help ensure these resources are adequate.

Server resources are finite, so a given server can only support a limited number of virtual machines. The exact number really depends on the age and sophistication of the physical server itself. Most administrators prefer to load a physical server at 50% to 80% of its total resource capacity. This includes a VM for the server's host operating system. The unused computing resources can be pooled and reallocated dynamically as workload demands change, or left in reserve to support additional VMs that are migrated to the server.

Virtual machines generally do not use all of the resources that are allocated to them, so virtual machine provisioning may also involve some amount of over-provisioning allocating more resources than the server has available. For example, "thin provisioning," a common practice in storage, is appearing in virtual platform features like memory overcommit. When implemented properly, over-provisioning makes it possible for a server to host more VMs than might otherwise be feasible.

Finally, administrators face a challenge of process control in virtual server provisioning. VMs are so simple to create that servers can easily be overwhelmed by an uncontrolled proliferation of virtual machines (a phenomenon called VM sprawl). To control VM sprawl, organizations should be able to justify the creation of new VMs, limit the actual creation rights to a few knowledgeable administrators and employ lifecycle management tools.

4.4.1 Analogy for Virtual Machine Provisioning

- Historically, when there is a need to install a new server for a certain workload to provide a particular service for a client, lots of effort was exerted by the IT administrator, and much time was spent to install and provision a new server.

1. Check the inventory for a new machine
2. get one
3. format, install OS required
4. and install services; a server is needed along with lots of security batches and appliances.

- Now, with the emergence of virtualization technology and the cloud computing IaaS model :

- It is just a matter of minutes to achieve the same task. All you need is to provision a virtual server through a self-service interface with small steps to get what you desire with the required specifications. (1) Provisioning this machine in a public cloud like Amazon Elastic Compute Cloud (EC2), or (2) Using a virtualization management software package or a private cloud management solution installed at your data center in order to provision the virtual machine inside the organization and within the private cloud setup.

4.4.2 Analogy for Migration Services

- Previously, whenever there was a need for performing a server's upgrade or performing maintenance tasks, you would exert a lot of time and effort, because it is an expensive operation to maintain or upgrade a main server that has lots of applications and users.
- Now, with the advance of the revolutionized virtualization technology and migration services associated with hypervisor's capabilities, these tasks (maintenance, upgrades, patches, etc.) are very easy and need no time to accomplish.
- Provisioning a new virtual machine is a matter of minutes, saving lots of time and effort, Migrations of a virtual machine is a matter of milliseconds :

1. Saving time
2. Effort
3. Making the service alive for customers
4. Achieving the SLA/SLO agreements and Quality-of-Service (QoS) specifications required.

The virtualization layer partitions the physical resource of the underlying physical server into multiple virtual machines with different workloads. Refer Fig. 4.3 The virtualization layer :

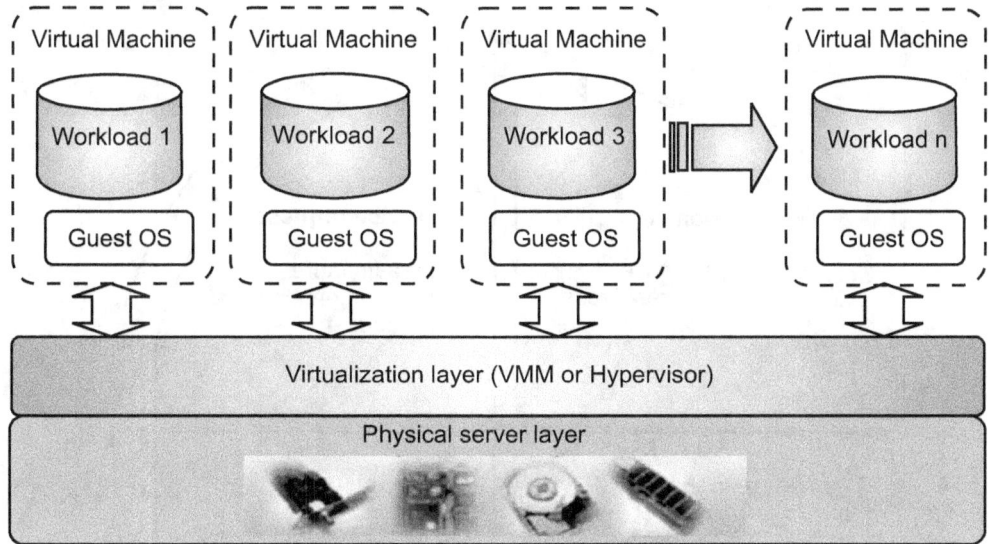

Fig. 4.3 : Layered architecture of virtualization

1. Schedules resources,
2. Allocates physical resources,
3. Makes each virtual machine think that it totally owns the whole underlying hardware's physical resource (Preprocessor, disks, etc.)
4. Makes it flexible and easy to manage resources.
5. Improve the utilization of resources by multiplexing many virtual machines on one physical host.
6. The machines can be scale up and down on demand with a high level of resource's abstraction.
7. Enables High, Reliable, and agile deployment mechanism.
8. Provides On-demand cloning and live migration.
9. Having efficient management suite for managing virtual machines.

Virtual Machine Life Cycle

- The cycle starts by a request delivered to the IT department, stating the requirement for creating a new server for a particular service.
- This request is being processed by the IT administration to start seeing the server's resource pool, matching these resources with requirements.
- Starting the provision of the needed virtual machine.
- Once it provisioned and started, it is ready to provide the required service according to an SLA.
- Virtual is being released; and free resources.

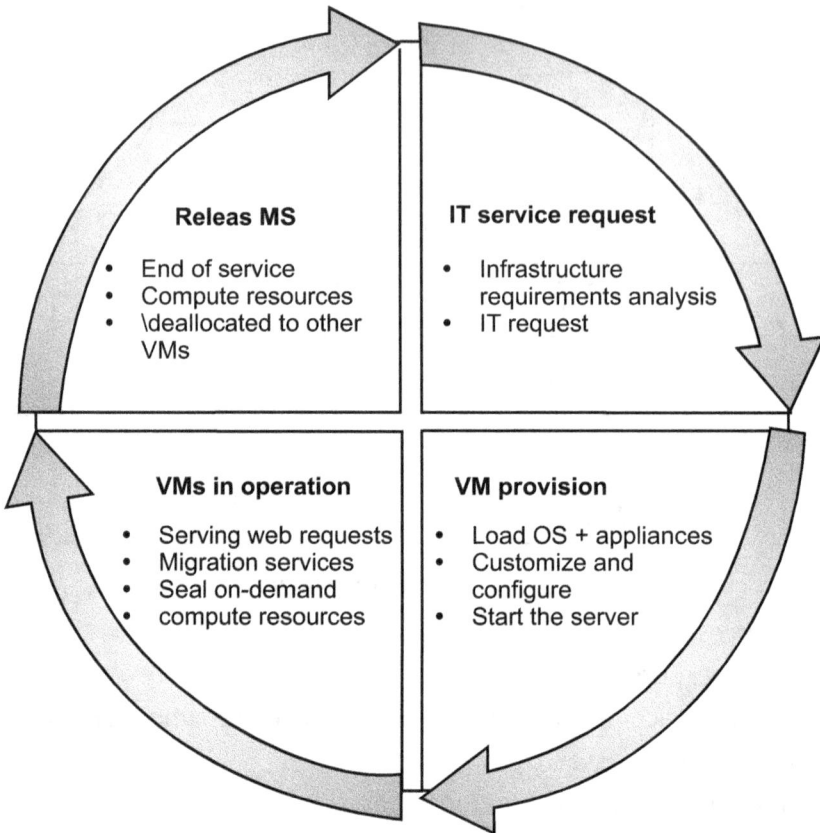

Fig. 4.4 : Virtual machine life cycle

4.4.3 VM Provisioning Process

- The common and normal steps of provisioning a virtual server are as follows :
- Firstly, you need to select a server from a pool of available servers (physical servers with enough capacity) along with the appropriate OS template you need to provision the virtual machine.
- Secondly, you need to load the appropriate software (operating System you selected in the previous step, device drivers, middleware, and the needed applications for the service required).
- Thirdly, you need to customize and configure the machine (e.g., IP address, Gateway) to configure an associated network and storage resources.
- Finally, the virtual server is ready to start with its newly loaded software.

To summarize, server provisioning is defining server's configuration based on the organization requirements, a hardware, and software component (processor, RAM, storage, networking, operating system, applications, etc.).

Normally, virtual machines can be provisioned by manually installing an operating system, by using a preconfigured VM template, by cloning an existing VM, or by importing a physical server or a virtual server from another hosting platform. Physical servers can also be virtualized and provisioned using P2V (Physical to Virtual) tools and techniques (e.g., virt-p2v).

After creating a virtual machine by virtualizing a physical server, or by building a new virtual server in the virtual environment, a template can be created out of it.

Most virtualization management vendors (VMware, XenServer, etc.) provide the data center's administration with the ability to do such tasks in an easy way.

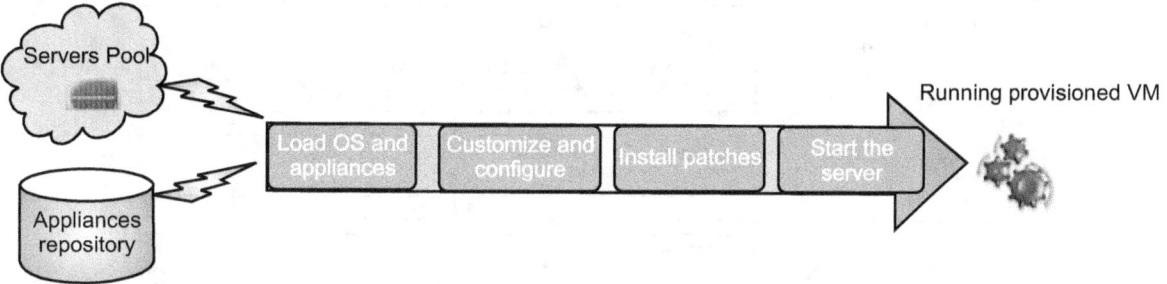

Fig. 4.5 : VM provisioning

- Provisioning from a template is an invaluable feature, because it reduces the time required to create a new virtual machine.

- Administrators can create different templates for different purposes. For example, you can create a Windows 2003 Server template for the finance department, or a Red Hat Linux template for the engineering department. This enables the administrator to quickly provision a correctly configured virtual server on demand.

4.4.4 Virtual Machine Migration Services

Live Migration and High Availability

Live migration (which is also called **hot or real-time migration**) can be defined as the movement of a virtual machine from one physical host to another while being powered on.

When it is properly carried out, this process takes place without any noticeable effect from the end user's point of view **(a matter of milliseconds)**.

One of the most significant advantages of live migration is the fact that **it facilitates proactive maintenance in case of failure**, because the potential problem can be resolved before the disruption of service occurs.

Live migration can also be used for **load balancing** in which work is shared among computers in order to optimize the utilization of available CPU resources.

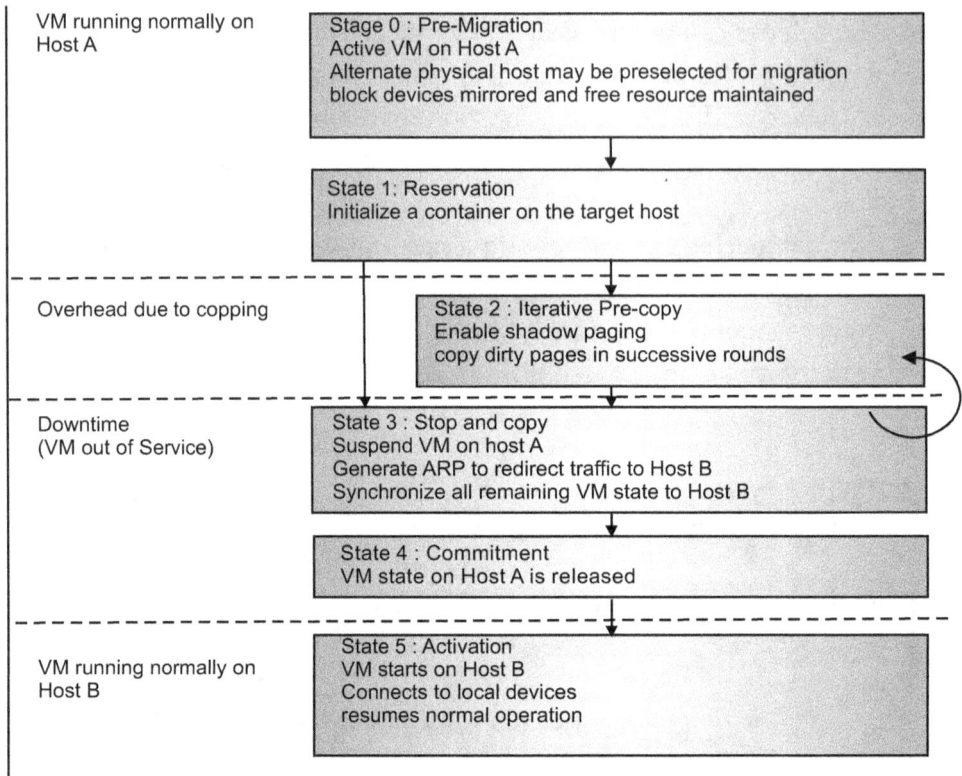

Fig. 4.6 : Timeline of live migration

4.4.5 Live Migration Stages

Stage-0 : Pre-Migration : An active virtual machine exists on the physical host A.

Stage-1 : Reservation : A request is issued to migrate an OS from host A to host B (a precondition is that the necessary resources exist on B and a VM container of that size)

Stage-3 : Stop-and-Copy : Running OS instance at A is suspended, and its network traffic is redirected to **B**. As described in reference 21, CPU state and remaining inconsistent memory pages are then transferred. At the end of this stage, there is a consistent suspended copy of the VM at both A and B. The copy at A is considered primary and is resumed in case of failure.

Stage-4 : Commitment : Host B indicates to A that is has successfully received a consistent OS image. Host A acknowledges this message as a commitment of migration transaction.

Stage-5 : Activation : The migrated VM on B is now activated. Post-migration code runs to reattach the device's drivers to the new machine and advertise moved IP addresses.

This approach to failure management ensures that at least on host has a consistent VM image at all times during migration :

1. Original host remains stable until migration commits and that the VM may be suspended and resumed on that host with no risk of failure.

2. A migration request essentially attempts to move the VM to a new host and on any sort of failure, execution is resumed locally, aborting the migration.

4.4.6 Regular/Cold Migration

Cold migration is the migration of a powered-off virtual machine. With cold migration:

* You have options of moving the associated disks from one data store to another.
* The virtual machines are not required to be on a shared storage. (1) Live migrations needs to a shared storage for virtual machines in the server's pool, but cold migration does not. (2) In live migration for a virtual machine between two hosts, there should be certain CPU compatibility checks, but in cold migration this checks do not apply.
* Cold migration (VMware product) is easy to implement and is summarized as follows:
* The configuration files, including NVRAM file (BIOS Setting), log files, and the disks of the virtual machines, are moved from the source host to the destination host's associated storage area.
* The virtual machine is registered with the new host.
* After the migration is completed, the old version of the virtual machine is deleted from the source host.

4.4.7 Live Storage Migration of Virtual Machines

* This kind of migration constitutes moving the virtual disks or configuration file of a running virtual machine to a new data store without any interruption in the availability of the virtual machine's service.
* As mentioned earlier, migration is the process of transferring the state (all memory pages) of a VM from one physical machine to another. Different techniques for live migration exist *suspend and copy*, *pre-copy* and *post-copy*. Suspend and copy, suspends a VM, copies all its pages and then resumes the VM on the target machine. The pre-copy approach transfers pages iteratively to the target machine without suspending the VM (and hence is live). Once "sufficient" pages are transferred, the VM is suspended at the source and remaining state transferred to the target machine.

While suspend-and-copy minimizes migration time, the downtime is proportional to the "size" of the VMs and network resources available for state transfer. Live migration techniques, aim to minimize downtime, by either copying pages (pre-copy) before a VM is suspended for final state transfer or copying minimal state (post copy) to start the VM and using demand-paging over the network to fetch the remaining state. While both pre-copy and post-copy techniques differ in overheads and migration time tradeoffs, they provide *live migration* semantics, so the VMs have minimal downtime and execute during the migration process.

4.4.8 Dynamic Provisioning Using Virtual Machine Migration

Virtual machine migration is a key enabler for dynamic resource management in cloud-based systems. Figure depicts the important components of resource management from a cloud provider's perspective.

The first step toward deploying a VM, is to determine the expected resources required on deployment.

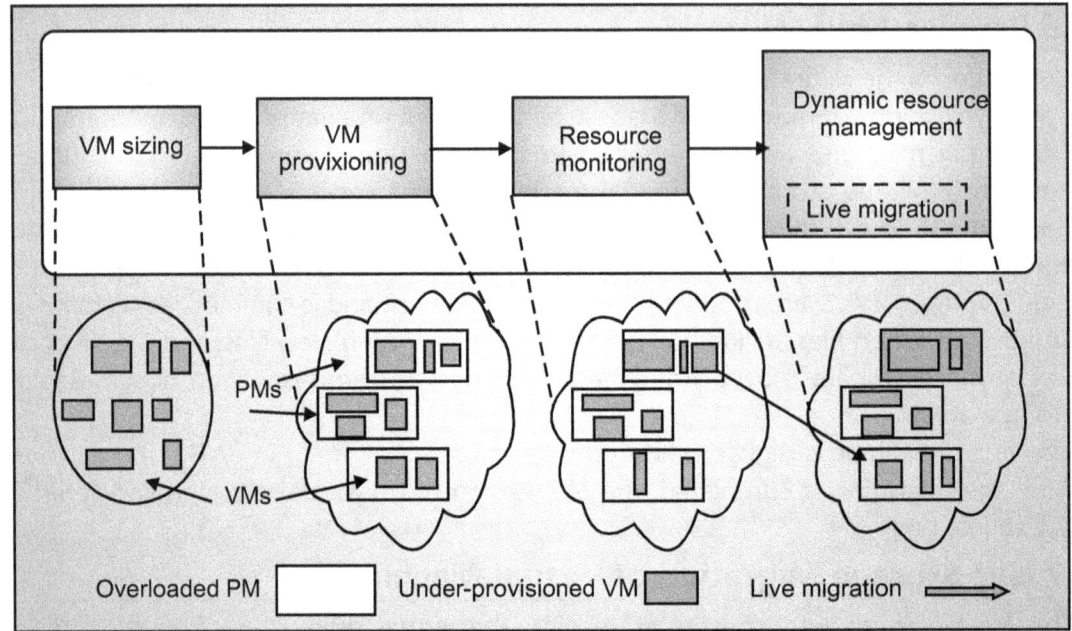

Fig. 4.7 : Dynamic provisioning using virtual machine migration

Once these levels are determined, a provisioning step determines where to "place" the VM and instantiate it. Once a VM is instantiated, a resource monitoring engine tracks the resource usage and performance indicators related to the (applications of the) VM. Under dynamic workload conditions, VMs can experience "hot spots" (inadequate resources to meet performance demands) and "cold spots" (over provisioned resources with low utilization). Moving VMs in order to allocate more resources (to alleviate hot spots) or consolidate VMs on fewer PMs to tackle cold spots is enabled through migration. From a cloud provider's perspective, alleviating hot spots is essential to meet SLAs with clients and tackling cold spots to use resources (including power consumption) efficiently.

Here we must consider two important cases: load balancing and consolidation of VMs based on migration.

In the first case, either the goal is to distribute "load" evenly across PMs, or a VM needs more resources and hence is migrated to another PM. With consolidation, machines are migrated to fewer PMs to reduce *server collapse.*

A cloud provider's resource management actions toward simultaneously minimizing resource usage and maximizing SLA adherence can be classified as follows:

- **Server Consolidation**

The goal of consolidation is to avoid server collapse many PMs host low-resource-usage VMs. As shown in Fig. 4.7 VMs on lightly loaded hosts can be "packed" onto fewer machines to meet resource requirements. The freed-up PMs can either be switched off (to save power) or represent higher resource availability for new VMs.

- **Load Balancing**

The goal of load balancing is to avoid a situation where there is a large discrepancy in resource utilization levels of the PMs. A desired scenario could be to have equal residual resource capacity across PMs (to help increase local resource allocations during increase demands). Virtual machine migrations can be employed to achieve this balance.

- **Hotspot Mitigation**

Active resource and application-level monitoring of VMs is required to identify hot spot conditions in which a VM has inadequate resources to meet its SLA requirements. Under such conditions, additional resources can be allocated either locally (on the same PM) or within the set of PMs available for provisioning. When local resources are not sufficient to remove the hot spot, VMs can be migrated to another host to make the resources required available to mitigate the hot spot.

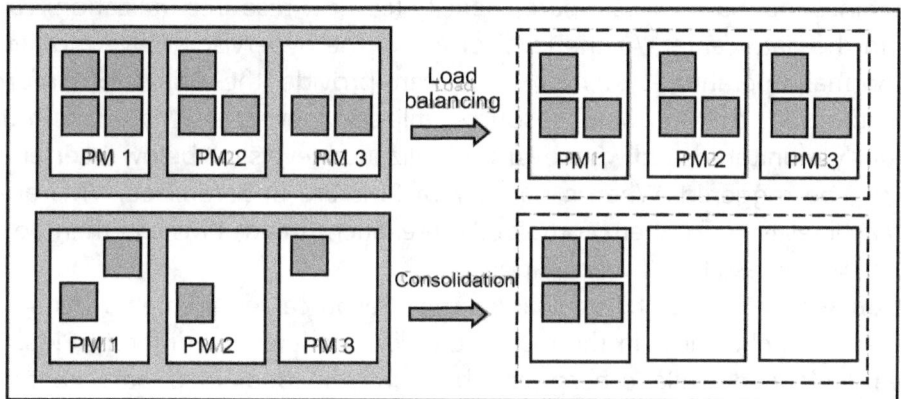

Fig. 4.8 : Physical machine : Load balancing and consolidation

- **Resource Management Using Migration**

For each of the three goals : Consolidation, hotspot mitigation and load balancing, following issues need to be addresses :

- When to migrate
- Which VMs to migrate
- The set of destination host machines for migration

When to Migrate?

There are many situations when migration of VMs becomes necessary to maintain the overall efficiency of the data center.

Periodic : The migrations in a data center can be triggered periodically. For example, data centers in one part of world may be heavily used in daytime, whereas they may be underloaded during the night. Such "time of day" based migration of VMs ensures that VMs are "near" clients, and the communication delays and overheads are minimized. Migrations can also be done periodically to consolidate the reduced loads.

Due to Hot Spot : A hot spot is the overloaded condition of a PM. It can also be defined as the state when performance of a system falls below the minimum acceptance level. Detection of a hot spot can be done both proactively and reactively. Proactive hot spot detection techniques predict the occurrence of a hot spot by analyzing the trends in resource utilizations of the VM. If the resource utilization shows an increase for some time window, it is likely that it may result in a hot spot in the future. Such time series analysis-based techniques help avoid hot spots even before they occur. Increase in request arrivals suggests that the VM will require more resources to fulfill them, thus causing a potential hot spot. Reactive hot spot detection techniques use more direct techniques like observing the page thrashing rate, CPU and memory utilization levels, and so on. Hot spots can be locally mitigated if enough capacity is available at the host PM. Extra resources can be allocated to the VM showing signs of overload.

When extra capacity is not available locally, migration is the only option available.

Excess Spare Capacity : Low utilization of PMs results in resource wastage. An optimum level of utilization is required to be maintained for the efficient working of a data center. Physical machines that have excess spare capacity (i.e., low resource utilization) cause overall inefficiency in the data center. At the level of a PM, the hypervisors have monitoring tools, similar to normal operating systems, which can provide the utilization information of different resources for that machine. Resource utilization levels of PMs across a data center are continuously monitored, and whenever the utilization levels fall below a certain threshold, migrations can be triggered. When a number of PMs are underutilized, VMs are migrated from such machines to make them completely free. Such "freed" PMs can then be shut down to save power, which results in consolidation.

Load Imbalance : Virtual machines change their resource requirements dynamically. This dynamism leads to imbalances in the resource utilization levels of different PMs. Some PMs can get heavily loaded while others may be lightly loaded. In a data center, resource utilization levels of PMs are monitored continuously. If there is large discrepancy in the utilization levels of different.

PMs, load balancing is triggered. Load balancing involves migration of VMs from highly loaded PMs to low loaded ones. An overloaded PM is undesirable as it causes delays in service of user requests. Similarly, the PMs that are lightly loaded cause inefficient resource utilization.

Addition/Removal of Virtual Machines and Physical Machines : Virtual machines and PMs can be added and removed in a virtualization- based data center. Addition/removal of VMs and PMs affects the availability of the resources and may require a change in the placement plan of VMs. A new PM can be used to offset the load of an overloaded PM by migrating VMs from the latter to the former. Similarly, hosting new VMs may result in future overloads of some PMs, which again require migrations to be triggered.

Which Virtual Machine To Migrate

Selecting one or more VMs for migration is a crucial decision of the resource management team. The migration process not only makes the VM unavailable for a certain amount of time but also consumes resources like network and CPU on source and destination PMs. Performance of other VMs that are hosted on source and destination PMs are also affected due to increased resource requirements during migration.

Some VM selection approaches are straightforward and only consider the VM that is resource constrained (e.g., in a hot spot); other approaches employ a more holistic approach where all the VMs on a PM are considered before selecting the candidate VM. Generally, the aim of VM selection is to minimize the migration effort.

Resource Constrained Virtual Machine

This is the easiest way to select the candidate VM for migration. The VM whose resource requirements cannot be locally fulfilled is selected for migration. During hot spots, it is easy to find the most loaded VMs; hence, this simple selection can work. However, in operations like consolidation and load balancing, where the cause is not a single VM, the choice is not straightforward.

Load Optimization Approach : During hot spots, it may not always be efficient to select the overloaded VM for migration. Consider a case where the VM facing a resource crunch is utilizing a large amount of memory. In such a case the time and effort required for migration will be high.

Instead, if a comparatively smaller memory VM is selected for migration, the time required will be less (assuming that the freed memory is sufficient to mitigate the hot spot). Also, the memory freed by the smaller VM can then be allocated to the larger VM. Such an approach of VM selection requires a holistic view of all the VMs and PMs present in the system in terms of their resource needs and availability, respectively. The VMs can be arranged in order of their resource utilizations, and a suitable sized VM can then be selected for migration. The decision also depends on the availability of a destination PM that has enough resources available. Such a holistic approach requires quantification of resource requirement of VMs and PMs in order to compare them. In other words, they need to differentiate between two VMs or (PMs) on the basis of utilizations on multiple resource dimensions. As there are multiple resource types.

(e.g., CPU, MEM, I/O), it becomes difficult to directly compare the resource requirements of different machines. Generally, a function of different resource types is used for comparison.

Affinity Based : These heuristics also incorporate other objectives instead of considering the resource requirement only. For example, some *affinity-aware* migration techniques consider communication costs among VMs while performing migration. For instance, if two VMs are communicating with each other, it is better to host them on the same PM. This will reduce the overall communication cost among the VMs by reducing network usage. Similarly, memory sharing between VMs can also affect the VM selection for migration. Migrating a VM to a PM where it can share memory with other hosted VMs can result in effective memory usage. Virtual machines, which share memory, can be migrated together with less effort as similar-content memory pages are required to be transferred only once. Such a scheme is known as *gang scheduling* of VMs. The approach is to proactively track the identical contents of collocated VMs and transfer those contents only once while migrating all those VMs simultaneously to another PM. This method optimizes both memory and network overhead of migration. Such mechanisms can be fruitful when an entire rack of servers have to be evacuated and all the collocated.

VMs running on them have to be shifted to a different location.

Where To Migrate

During migration, the destination PM should have enough resources so that it can support the incoming migrating VM. Here we discuss factors for selecting a PM as a destination for a migrating VM.

Depending on Available Resource Capacity

Only considering the availability of resources at the destination is not enough. Some other factors also need to be taken into consideration, such as whether the destination is a *best fit* (leaving minimum remaining resources) for the migrating VM, how will the performance of VMs that are already hosted on destination PM get affected. The destination selection to minimize waste of resources is a field of research in itself.

Virtual machines and PMs are sorted in some order based on their resource requirements, and then the First Fit or Best Fit scheme is applied to select the most suitable PM.

Depending on Affinity of Virtual Machines

Apart from selecting PMs solely on the basis of resource availability, some schemes try to leverage the relations (or affinity) between the VMs to identify a suitable host PM. For example, a scheme mentioned in tries to achieve consolidation by collocating VMs that have high memory sharing potential. Periodically, based on memory fingerprints of VMs, best matches of hosts for VMs can be found and migrations can be triggered. This scheme is called memory aware migration. The VM can be re-migrated if some other VM on some other PM becomes a better memory sharing partner. The overhead of migration is taken into consideration. The rationale behind this method is that VMs that can share part of their memory will require less overall memory than VMs that do not share memory. Similarly, if two VMs, hosted on different PMs, communicate heavily, one of the VMs can be migrated to the PM where its communicating partner is hosted.

4.5 ANATOMY OF CLOUD INFRASTRUCTURE

Cloud storage (or data storage as a service) is the abstraction of storage behind an interface where the storage can be administered on demand. Further, the interface abstracts the location of the storage such that it is irrelevant whether the storage is local or remote (or hybrid). Cloud storage infrastructures introduce new architectures that support varying levels of service over a potentially large set of users and geographically distributed storage capacity. Learn about the key architectural attributes of cloud storage architectures from data protection and integrity to security and storage optimization.

At the rate data is growing today, it's not surprising that cloud storage is also growing in popularity. The fastest-growing data is archive data, which is ideal for cloud storage given a number of factors, including cost, frequency of access, protection, and availability. But not all cloud storage is the same. One provider may focus primarily on cost, while another focuses on availability or performance. No one architecture has a singular focus, but the degrees to which an architecture implements a given characteristic defines its market and appropriate use models.

Frequently used acronyms

- API : Application programming interface
- FTP : File transfer protocol
- HTTP : Hypertext transfer protocol
- HTTPS : HTTP over secure sockets layer
- JFS : Journaling file system
- NFS : Network file system
- NIC : Network interface card
- RAID : Redundant array of independent disks
- REST : Representational state transfer
- SAN : Storage area network
- SCSI : Small computer system interface
- SLA : Service level agreement
- TCP : Transmission control protocol
- UDP : User datagram protocol
- WAN : Wide area network

It's difficult to talk about architectures without the perspective of utility. Here the word architecture carries meaning from a variety of characteristics, including cost, performance, remote access, and so on. Therefore a set of criteria are given by which cloud storage models are measured, and then explore some of the interesting implementations within cloud storage architectures.

First, let's discuss a general cloud storage architecture to set the context for the later exploration of unique architectural features.

4.5.1 General Architecture

Cloud storage architectures are primarily about delivery of storage on demand in a highly scalable and multi-tenant way. Generically (see figure), cloud storage architectures consist of a front end that exports an API to access the storage. In traditional storage systems, this API is the SCSI protocol; but in the cloud, these protocols are evolving. There, you can find Web service front ends, file-based front ends, and even more traditional front ends (such as Internet SCSI, or iSCSI). Behind the front end is a layer of middleware called as *storage logic*. This layer implements a variety of features, such as replication and data reduction, over the traditional data-placement algorithms (with consideration for geographic placement). Finally, the back end implements the physical storage for data. This may be an internal protocol that implements specific features or a traditional back end to the physical disks.

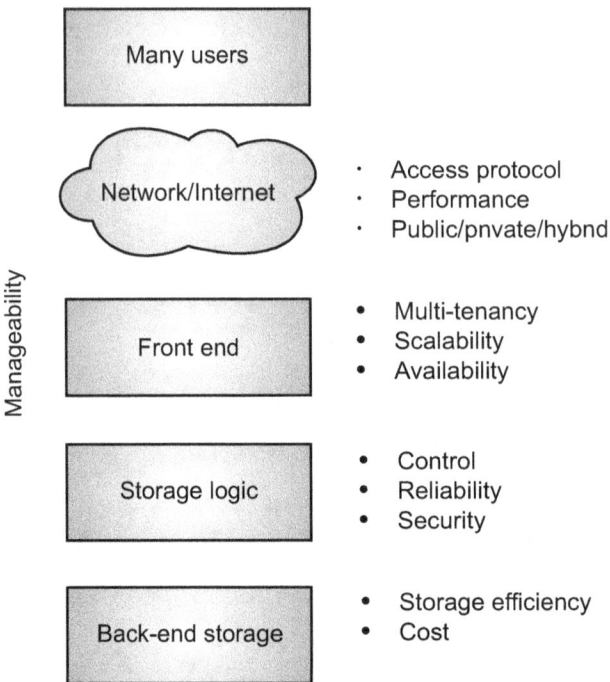

Fig. 4.9 : Generic cloud storage architecture

From Fig. 4.9 , you can see some of the characteristics for current cloud storage architectures. Note that no characteristics are exclusive in the particular layer but serve as a guide for specific topics that this article addresses. These characteristics are defined in table 4.1.

Table 4.1 : Cloud storage characteristics

Characteristic	Description
Manageability	The ability to manage a system with minimal resources
Access method	Protocol through which cloud storage is exposed
Performance	Performance as measured by bandwidth and latency
Multi-tenancy	Support for multiple users (or tenants)
Scalability	Ability to scale to meet higher demands or load in a graceful manner
Data availability	Measure of a system's uptime
Control	Ability to control a system in particular, to configure for cost, performance, or other characteristics
Storage efficiency	Measure of how efficiently the raw storage is used
Cost	Measure of the cost of the storage (commonly in dollars per gigabyte)

- **Manageability**

One key focus of cloud storage is cost. If a client can buy and manage storage locally compared to leasing it in the cloud, the cloud storage market disappears. But cost can be divided into two high-level categories: the cost of the physical storage ecosystem itself and the cost of managing it. The management cost is hidden but represents a long-term component of the overall cost. For this reason, cloud storage must be self-managing to a large extent. The ability to introduce new storage where the system automatically self-configures to accommodate it and the ability to find and self-heal in the presence of errors are critical. Concepts such as autonomic computing will have a key role in cloud storage architectures in the future.

- **Access Method**

One of the most striking differences between cloud storage and traditional storage is the means by which it's accessed (see Fig. 4.10). Most providers implement multiple access methods, but Web service APIs are common. Many of the APIs are implemented based on REST principles, which imply an object-based scheme developed on top of HTTP (using HTTP as a transport). REST APIs are stateless and therefore simple and efficient to provide. Many cloud storage providers implement REST APIs, including Amazon Simple Storage Service (Amazon S3), Windows Azure™, and Mezeo Cloud Storage Platform.

One problem with Web service APIs is that they require integration with an application to take advantage of the cloud storage. Therefore, common access methods are also used with cloud storage to provide immediate integration. For example, file-based protocols such as NFS/Common Internet File System (CIFS) or FTP are used, as are block-based protocols such as iSCSI. Cloud storage providers such as Six Degrees, Zetta, and Cleversafe provide these access methods.

Although the protocols mentioned above are the most common, other protocols are suitable for cloud storage. One of the most interesting is Web-based Distributed Authoring and Versioning (WebDAV). WebDAV is also based on HTTP and enables the Web as a readable and writable resource. Providers of WebDAV include Zetta and Cleversafe in addition to others. Fig. 4.10 Cloud storage access methods.

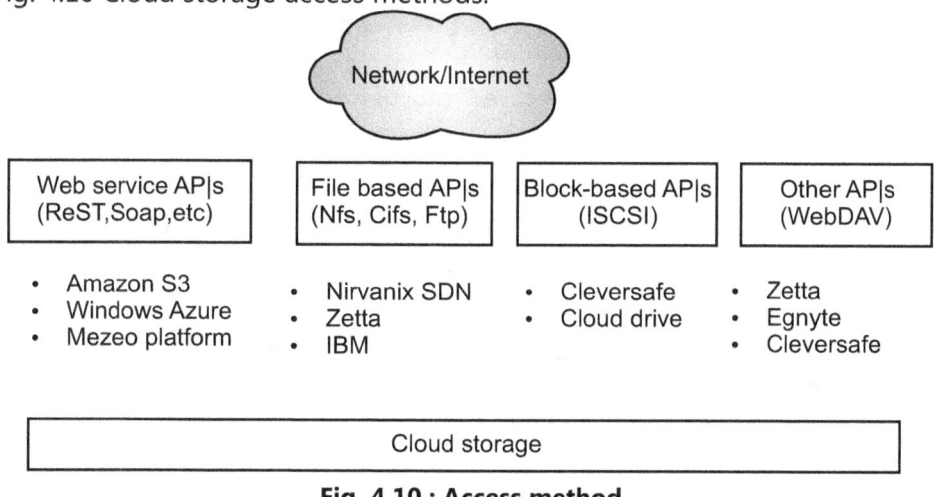

Fig. 4.10 : Access method

You can also find solutions that support multi-protocol access. For example, IBM Smart Business Storage Cloud enables both file-based (NFS and CIFS) and SAN-based protocols from the same storage-virtualization infrastructure.

- **Performance**

There are many aspects to performance, but the ability to move data between a user and a remote cloud storage provider represents the largest challenge to cloud storage. The problem, which is also the workhorse of the Internet, is TCP. TCP controls the flow of data based on packet acknowledgements from the peer endpoint. Packet loss, or late arrival, enables congestion control, which further limits performance to avoid more global networking issues. TCP is ideal for moving small amounts of data through the global Internet but is less suitable for larger data movement, with increasing Round-Trip Time (RTT).

Amazon, through Aspera Software, solves this problem by removing TCP from the equation. A new protocol called the Fast and Secure Protocol (FASP) was developed to accelerate bulk data movement in the face of large RTT and severe packet loss. The key is the use of the UDP, which is the parter transport protocol to TCP. UDP permits the host to manage congestion, pushing this aspect into the application layer protocol of FASP (see Fig. 4.11).

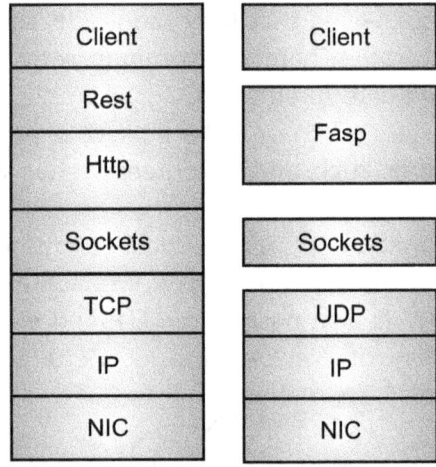

Fig. 4.11 : The Fast and Secure Protocol from Aspera Software

Using standard (non-accelerated) NICs, FASP efficiently uses the bandwidth available to the application and removes the fundamental bottlenecks of conventional bulk data-transfer schemes. The Resources section provides some interesting statistics on FASP performance over traditional WAN, intercontinental transfers, and lossy satellite links.

- **Multi-tenancy**

One key characteristic of cloud storage architectures is called multi-tenancy. This simply means that the storage is used by many users (or multiple "tenants"). Multi-tenancy applies to many layers of the cloud storage stack, from the application layer, where the storage namespace is segregated among users, to the storage layer, where physical storage can be segregated for particular users or classes of users. Multi-tenancy even applies to the networking infrastructure that connects users to storage to permit quality of service and carving bandwidth to a particular user.

- **Scalability**

You can look at scalability in a number of ways, but it is the on-demand view of cloud storage that makes it most appealing. The ability to scale storage needs (both up and down) means improved cost for the user and increased complexity for the cloud storage provider.

Scalability must be provided not only for the storage itself (functionality scaling) but also the bandwidth to the storage (load scaling). Another key feature of cloud storage is geographic distribution of data (geographic scalability), allowing the data to be nearest the users over a set of cloud storage data centers (via migration). For read-only data, replication and distribution are also possible (as is done using content delivery networks). This is shown in Fig. 4.12.

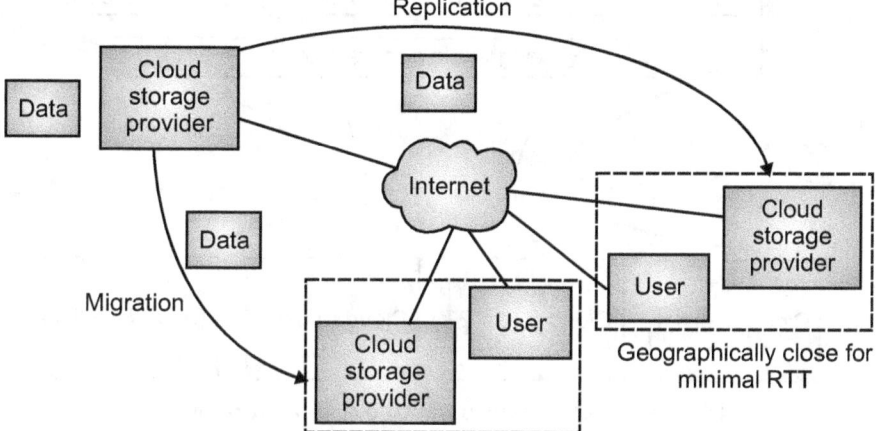

Fig. 4.12 : Scalability of cloud storage

Internally, a cloud storage infrastructure must be able to scale. Servers and storage must be capable of resizing without impact to users. As discussed in the Manageability section, autonomic computing is a requirement for cloud storage architectures.

- **Availability**

Once a cloud storage provider has a user's data, it must be able to provide that data back to the user upon request. Given network outages, user errors, and other circumstances, this can be difficult to provide in a reliable and deterministic way. Any web application needs to be available to legitimate visitors from all over the world. A true cloud creates spans the entire globe, defeating the speed of light on behalf of its customers with a server point of presence in multiple simultaneous locations. The cloud provider needs to effectively receive and route incoming requests to the appropriate virtualized application instance on behalf of its customers.

Google and Microsoft replicate each application instance to multiple physical locations. AT&T Synaptic Hosting spans multiple locations for its enterprise customers.

There are some interesting and novel schemes to address availability, such as information dispersal. Cleversafe, a company that provides private cloud storage uses the Information Dispersal Algorithm (IDA) to enable greater availability of data in the face of physical failures and network outages. IDA, which was first created for telecommunication systems by Michael

Rabin, is an algorithm that allows data to be sliced with Reed-Solomon codes for purposes of data reconstruction in the face of missing data. Further, IDA allows you to configure the number of data slices, such that a given data object could be carved into four slices with one tolerated failure or 20 slices with eight tolerated failures. Similar to RAID, IDA permits the reconstruction of data from a subset of the original data, with some amount of overhead for error codes (dependent on the number of tolerated failures). This is shown in Fig. 4.13 .

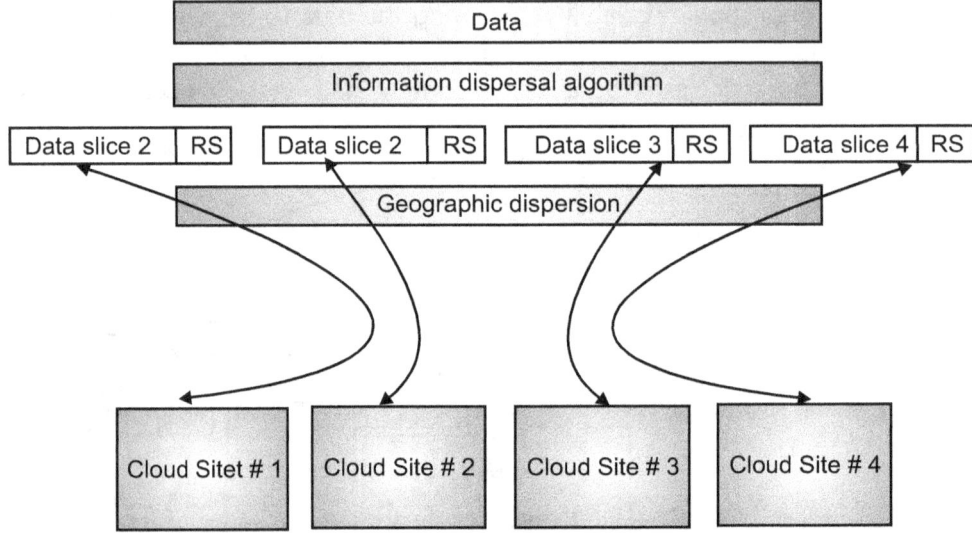

Fig. 4.13 : Cleversafe's approach to extreme data availability

With the ability to slice data along with cauchy Reed-Solomon correction codes, the slices can then be distributed to geographically disparate sites for storage. For a number of slices (p) and a number of tolerated failures (m), the resulting overhead is p/(p-m). So, in the case of Figure , the overhead to the storage system for p = 4 and m = 1 is 33%.

The downside of IDA is that it is processing intensive without hardware acceleration. Replication is another useful technique and is implemented by a variety of cloud storage providers. Although replication introduces a large amount of overhead (100%), it's simple and efficient to provide.

- **Security**

Web applications should be protected from intrusion and abuse at the network layer. In a cloud computing world application security is a lot like click fraud in advertising: every bad action carries a marginal cost. Cloud providers need to guard customers against potential external abuse and intrusion.

Google, Microsoft, and Amazon have their eyes on many incoming requests each day. Google serves App Engine requests off the same hardware handling Google Front End, keeping bad requests away from search, ads, and your apps.

- **Stable, efficient OS**

Web applications rely on a stable, efficient operating system to interface with hardware, manage filesystems, and allocate resources. The cloud server operating system is a stripped down version of standard installations without a need for direct hard drive interfaces or other peripherals.

- **Control**

A customer's ability to control and manage how his or her data is stored and the costs associated with it is important. Numerous cloud storage providers implement controls that give users greater control over their costs.

Amazon implements Reduced Redundancy Storage (RRS) to provide users with a means of minimizing overall storage costs. Data is replicated within the Amazon S3 infrastructure, but with RRS, the data is replicated fewer times with the possibility for data loss. This is ideal for data that can be recreated or that has copies that exist elsewhere.

- **Efficiency**

Storage efficiency is an important characteristic of cloud storage infrastructures, particularly with their focus on overall cost. The next section speaks to cost specifically, but this characteristic speaks more to the efficient use of the available resources over their cost.

To make a storage system more efficient, more data must be stored. A common solution is data reduction, whereby the source data is reduced to require less physical space. Two means to achieve this include compression the reduction of data through encoding the data using a different representation and de-duplication the removal of any identical copies of data that may exist. Although both methods are useful, compression involves processing (re-encoding the data into and out of the infrastructure), where de-duplication involves calculating signatures of data to search for duplicates.

- **Cost**

One of the most notable characteristics of cloud storage is the ability to reduce cost through its use. This includes the cost of purchasing storage, the cost of powering it, the cost of repairing it (when drives fail), as well as the cost of managing the storage. When viewing cloud storage from this perspective (including SLAs and increasing storage efficiency), cloud storage can be beneficial in certain use models.

An interesting peak inside a cloud storage solution is provided by a company called Backblaze (see Resources for details). Backblaze set out to build inexpensive storage for a cloud storage offering. A Backblaze POD (shelf of storage) packs 67 TB in a 4U enclosure for under US$8,000. This package consists of a 4U enclosure, a motherboard, 4GB of DRAM, four SATA controllers, 45 1.5TB SATA hard disks, and two power supplies. On the motherboard, Backblaze runs Linux (with JFS as the file system) and GbE NICs as the front end using HTTPS and Apache Tomcat. Backblaze's software includes de-duplication, encryption, and RAID6 for data protection. Backblaze's description of their POD (which shows you in detail how to build your own) shows you the extent to which companies can cut the cost of storage, making cloud storage a viable and cost-efficient option.

- **Cloud Storage Models**

Models for cloud storage allow users to maintain control over their data. Cloud storage has evolved into three categories, one of which permits the merging of two categories for a cost-efficient and secure option. Private clouds use the concepts of public cloud storage but in a form that can be securely embedded within a user's firewall. Finally, hybrid cloud storage permits the two models to merge, allowing policies to define which data must be maintained privately and which can be secured within public clouds (see Fig. 4.14).

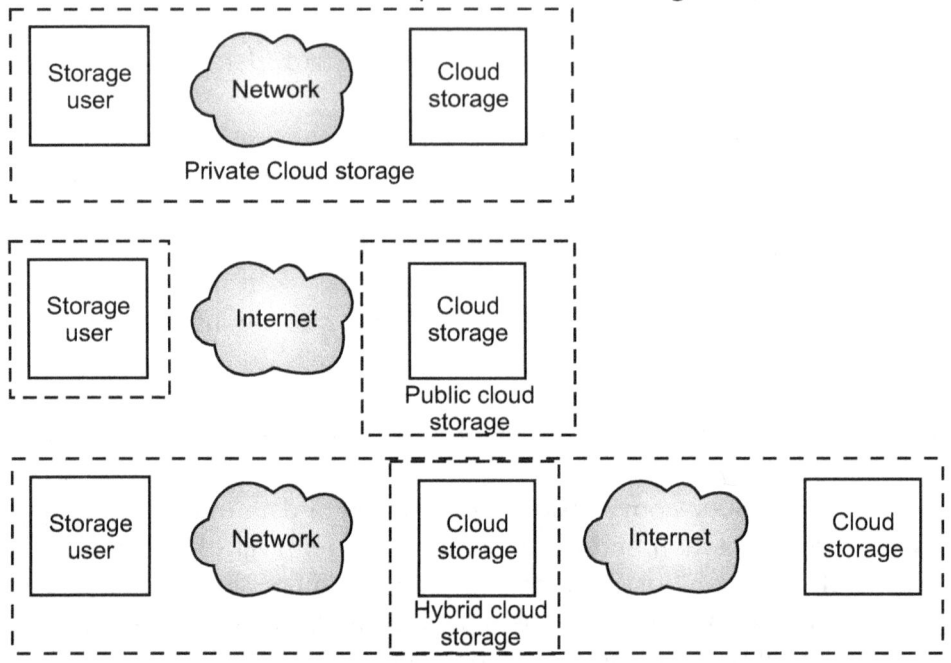

Fig. 4.14 : Cloud storage models

The cloud models are shown graphically in Figure. Examples of public cloud storage providers include Amazon (which offer storage as a service). Examples of private cloud storage providers include IBM, Parascale, and Cleversafe (which build software and/or hardware for internal clouds). Finally, hybrid cloud providers include Egnyte, among others.

Hardware and data operations are again consolidating towards major players. These specialist providers are building at a scale and specialization most web businesses can't match. On-demand infrastructure of the cloud makes it cheaper and more efficient to outsource needed operational function to teams of experts already keeping some of the largest web companies in the world running every day.

• The Platforms

Microsoft and Google are the newest entrants into the cloud computing arena, focusing their efforts their respective programming languages of expertise. Microsoft's Windows Azure services platform will likely be the best platform for C# and ASP.Net development as it is tuned by the creators of .Net, IIS, and SQL Server. Google has similarly applied its expertise in the Python language and distributed web nodes to its Google App Engine product. App Engine utilizes custom Google software, Google Front End and Megastore, for web serving and storage. Cloud developers on either platform are using a similar set of hardware and software as the proven web-scale platforms of Live.com and Google. Language specialists are building managed stacks on top of generic cloud platforms such as Amazon Web Service's

EC2. Engine Yard sells a custom, managed AMI optimized for the Ruby language and its Rails framework.

Amazon's EC2 is the most well-known cloud computing provider and, as previously mentioned, the baseline service for other companies building value-added solutions. The AMI, a machine image formatted deployment in the Amazon cloud, is the basic building block of EC2 virtualization and the primary interaction point of Amazon's customers. Amazon resells premium operating system and application packages on behalf of companies such as Microsoft, IBM, and Oracle but it's possible such specializations will instead be absorbed by the software publishers themselves as they roll out their own hosted clouds (such as Azure or IBM Blue Cloud).

The cloud computing software stack is trending towards an integrated, managed experience maintained by some of the top contributors to each programming language and related components. More generic cloud platforms will need to stay up-to-date with managed technologies on their platform and/or establish a strong reseller relationship to more specialized cloud managers.

The Managed Cloud Stack

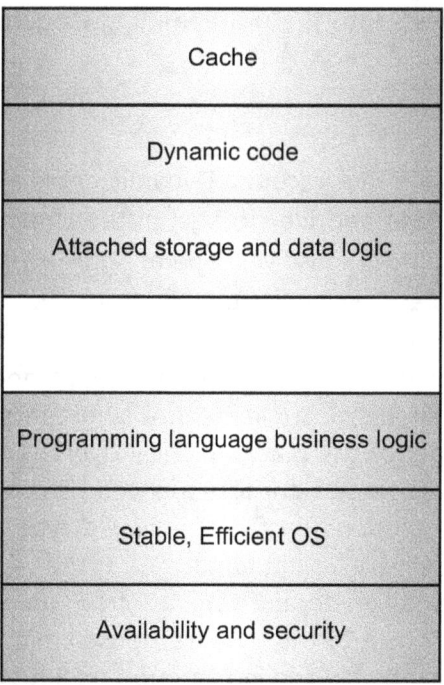

Fig. 4.15 : The managed cloud stack

Managed cloud providers handle an entire stack of infrastructure needed to deliver web applications at scale. A solid cloud computing environment abstracts the basics of a computing environment away from the implementers and lets them focus on adding value with each new application. Managed cloud hosting providers need to offer the following basic layers to stay relevant in a web developer's world.

Amazon EC2 highlights the operating system behind every machine image. Older versions of Fedora and Windows Server are the default "quick start" options available to each new account. Google and Microsoft clouds run on custom operating systems tailored for web use. Windows Azure is a stripped-down version of the latest Windows Server. Google runs a Linux-based OS tuned by its infrastructure team.

- **Programming Language Business Logic**

Every managed cloud platform includes a dynamic language virtual machine and an appropriate web services gateway. Language functions too closely associated with the parent operating system and its libraries are stripped away, leaving only a pure operating environment for a machine interpreter. External dependencies such as GNU tools and custom compilers will not function within the cloud language abstraction layer. Cloud services bundle a dynamic language runtime into an easily spawned instance for standard and efficient interpretation across many application instances.

Google App Engine supports most functions of the Python language with additional support for the Django framework, WebOb, and PyYAML. Developers may replace these built-in libraries with newer or customized versions at an additional performance and usage cost. App Engine passes web requests into the programming language environment through the Web Server Gateway Interface.

The cloud client layer

- **Attached Storage**

Cloud applications don't operate in a vacuum. Dynamic applications persist their application state and logic through database and file storage. In the cloud world the database and the file server are cloud services unto themselves, operating in an isolated and specialized layer. This isolation makes the storage layer swappable from the rest of the cloud stack and presents new opportunities for competition.

Static files fall into two major categories based on their planned consumption. Files under 1 MB in size can be consumed by most clients in a single request, matching the expected simple request/response model of the platform. Files over 1 MB in size need to be broken into more manageable parts, or ranges, for a sequenced download. Static cloud storage can be broken up into differing solutions by file size or file type, providing the best possible solution for the storage and delivery task at hand.

Google App Engine offers static file storage separate from its dynamic runtime. App Engine supports up to 1,000 files and has a 10 MB HTTP response limit.

Amazon Web Services offers static file serving through its Simple Storage Service (S3) origin server and CloudFront CDN services. Amazon allows private and public file storage and can even charge individual users of third-party services for their use through DevPay.

Attached storage is by far the most diverse service offering for companies evaluating a specialized solution. I prefer storage providers with widely supported file management APIs, smart settings for MIME types and caching HTTP headers, and a primary functionality of serving files to the worldwide web.

- **Database Storage**

Databases are the preferred way of persisting structured data powering web applications. Cloud service providers have tuned and rewritten database functionality for the cloud, opening up new opportunities for scalable data services across multiple dynamic application instances. Cloud databases are distributed, replicated, and largely transactional. Cloud databases can be separated from the rest of the cloud stack through RESTful APIs between different vendors but there is a definite latency advantage to coupling of data and its interpreter.

Microsoft offers SQL Server as a web service as part of the Azure services stack. Google App Engine offers Megastore, an abstraction layer on top of BigTable, as a service API within an App Engine instance or as a separate remote API. Amazon's SimpleDB brings together EC2 processing with S3 data storage. Greenplum offers PostgreSQL as a stand-alone cloud offering.

Cloud databases are typically more limited in functionality than their local counterparts. App Engine returns up to 1000 results. SimpleDB times out within 5 seconds. Joining records from two tables in a single query breaks databases optimized for scale. App Engine offers specialized storage and query types such as geographical coordinates.

The database layer of a cloud instance can be abstracted as a separate best-of-breed layer within a cloud stack but developers are most likely to use the local solution for both its speed and simplicity.

- **Cloud Consumers**

The target market of a cloud computing platform will affect its stack completeness, feature sets, and future support. Cloud terminology seems to be thrown around as a magical buzzword but there are major usage cases emerging.

- **Web Application Developers**

New web applications start small and may sometimes experience exponential growth on a worldwide basis. Web developers evaluating the cloud stack are likely starting from scratch without the concerns of switching from a legacy system or alternate implementation.

Cloud computing abstracts tiered architecture, operations planning, and other nuances from companies specializing in bring new ideas to market quickly. Web developers prefer a cloud stack tuned for fast web performance. Geographically distributed dynamic instances are important at least as an upgrade option to protect a new business from a rewrite at varying levels of scale.

- **Back Office Tasks**

Enterprise applications are moving out of the local server closet and into the cloud. Medium-to large-sized companies are replacing in-house maintenance of machines and applications with software and infrastructure as a service. Project management, employee tracking, payroll, and many other common functions have made their way into the software-as-a-service realm. More customized applications will migrate to cloud hosting and take their place alongside the anchor tenants of the groupware and collaboration suites.

Windows Azure, Salesforce's Force.com, and Google App Engine show strong promise as integrated back office add-ons. Microsoft and Google already have a solid footing in enterprise groupware services through Exchange Online and Google Apps respectively. Force.com can be closely tied to the popular Salesforce CRM application for sales and marketing teams.

More generic back office functions can operate on any cloud hosting provider with a properly maintained disk image. A new class of hosting provider operates as an abstraction layer between multiple clouds by maintaining the appropriate images and deployment scripts for any given task. Companies such as Aptana, CohesiveFT, RightScale, and many others span multiple cloud hosting providers with a single management interface. Cloud management companies can monitor multiple providers and create spot pricing market for computing resources.

Back office solutions represent the largest possible growth area for cloud hosting providers. Platforms with strong existing anchor tenants can add on new services combining software-as-a-service and infrastructure-as-a-service. Generic cloud hosting providers will likely be tapped for general tasks directly or through a cloud management layer.

Microsoft is promoting its cloud hosting solutions through its partner channels. Microsoft partners receive a 12% commission on the first year of revenues and 6% commission on all future revenues. Google offers a 20% discount to Google Apps Authorized Resellers over the life of the account.

- **Excess Capacity**

Hosting solutions need to scale up to meet peak demand. Peak demand could occur for an hour each day, one day a year (Black Monday in the retail sector), or one month out of twelve (college basketball playoffs). Cloud computing lets businesses pay only for what they use when they use it. Servers are not sitting around in your datacenter depreciating in value and consuming resources while you wait for peak load to occur.

Excess capacity needs may be predictable and cyclical, allowing a business to integrate cloud computing into their computing workflow with ease. Generic cloud computing platforms offer the best migration costs as businesses clone their own local machine images for execution in a cloud computing environment.

Disaster Recovery

Business operations need to stay online when catastrophe strikes. An earthquake in California, a hurricane in Florida or Texas, or a power outage anywhere in the world could knock your business offline instantly. A hot backup in the cloud spins up when your primary site is down. An on-demand backup facility is a lot cheaper than physical investments as companies invest in contingency planning.

Amazon Web Services recently introduced reserved machine instances for companies who must be absolutely sure they will be able to operate in an environment of strained cloud capacity. Reserved instances receive priority allocation of cloud resources in exchange for an upgrade fee and lower monthly usage charges. Reserved instances are the VIP treatments of the cloud hosting world.

Demand response programs are common in utility sectors such as electricity. Businesses can opt to be the last ones kicked off the grid in a low-capacity environment in exchange for higher consumption costs.

4.6 DISTRIBUTED MANAGEMENT OF VIRTUAL INFRASTRUCTURE

Virtualized IT resource management is often supported by virtualization infrastructure management (VIM) tools that collectively manage virtual IT resources and rely on a centralized management module, otherwise known as a controller, that runs on a dedicated computer. VIMs are commonly encompassed by the resource management system.

The VIM coordinates the server hardware so that virtual server instances can be created from the most expedient underlying physical server. It can be used to manage a range of virtual IT resources across multiple physical servers, and provides for centralized administration of virtualized resources including creating, storing, backing up, patching and monitoring.

As an example, a VIM can create and manage multiple instances of a hypervisor across different physical servers, and can move a virtual server from one physical server to another.

Complex challenges of virtual infrastructure management are mandatory control of physical and virtual resources availability, usage and access; deployment of disaster recovery solutions; provisioning of new virtual machines and other tasks; and monitoring and reporting of data center usage.

Adopting virtualization in the enterprise is always a multi-step process. The first step is to identify servers to virtualize, and that's followed by a careful evaluation of Return-On-Investment (ROI) and capacity planning. That work has to be done before you get to the actual physical-to-virtual migration. Then, after the migration, you always face challenges in virtual infrastructure management.

These responsibilities can be quite time-consuming even on small environments, but they become even more complex in virtual infrastructures. In virtual infrastructures, IT managers have to worry about a new class of problems, like efficient and controlled deployment of virtual machines, rational physical resources assignment and accountability.

The ease with which you can create new virtual machines and their independence from underlying hardware leads to the idea of liquid computing; it can be hard to understand what is where in your computing environment.

The paradigm of liquid computing increases the risk of so-called "virtual machine sprawl." To avoid sprawl, virtualization management tools provide a reliable security system, wherein permissions can limit unauthorized creation of new machines. The tools also offer a strong monitoring system that reports on allocated but unused resources.

As of today, most virtualization platforms can leverage virtual infrastructure access with LDAP centralized accounting systems, but administrators are still in big troubles when they need to compute the efficiency of virtual data centers.

Going further, when a new virtual machine has been created, the virtual infrastructure manager faces the problem of deciding where it has to be hosted. As we already saw during the capacity planning phase, virtual workloads should be deployed carefully, considering along the way which existing workloads could be complementary in order to avoid overloading resources.

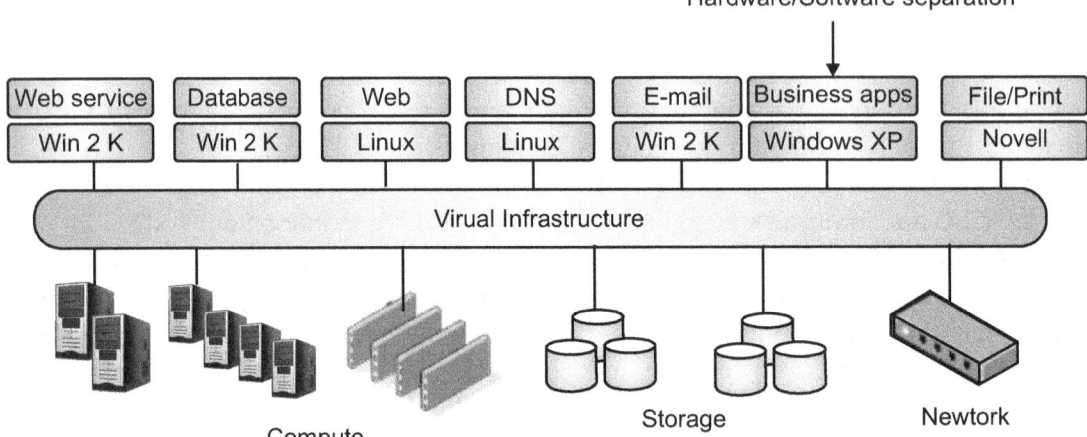

Fig. 4.16 : Virtual infrastructure

The upcoming Virtual Machine Manager from Microsoft, for example, will offer a rating system for physical machines, assigning one or more stars to each, helping administrators to immediately identify where a new virtual machine would best fit. This scoring system will adapt to the evolving infrastructure.

But even with such a system, in some environments, virtual machine creation may be not easy enough. For example, a big ISP remodeling its offerings with virtualization might need smart tools to deploy hundreds or even thousands of virtual machines on demand, in seconds.

At the moment, few third-party products can fill all virtualization management holes, and many companies opt to develop in-house solutions rather than spending money for available tools that have little flexibility. In such complex scenarios, virtualization management solutions have to offer Software Development Kits (SDK) that allow wide customizations and different degrees of automation.

A wide, open programmable interface and strong support are key selling points; so far, VMware has done a pretty good job compared to its competitors.

Last, but not least, today's IT managers face a new problem: accountability. In a medium complexity corporation, several departments may work with virtual machines and share the same physical servers, using them in different percentages during a fiscal year.

When each of these departments has a cost center of its own, it can be difficult to track who should be responsibility for paying the costs of the underlying hardware. And even when costs are handled by a single entity inside the company, managers are challenged to enforce controls on who may use physical resources and how much can be requested of them.

- **Multiple platforms, multiple issues**

The above-mentioned needs increase further when a big company has to handle more than one virtualization platform.

In a large corporation, each department often has autonomy in choosing its preferred solutions, even if only one product will be used for a production environment. IT managers may need to concurrently manage VMware ESX server and Xen at the same time, hoping to leverage control with a single, centralized tool.

The market offering for such tools is multiplexing as the demand for them rises. Solutions from IBM, Cassatt, BMC Software, Enomaly and Scalent are the most popular, but new contenders like Opsware are coming.

Support for multiple virtual infrastructures often means IT managers do not have to worry about what technology has been used for creating a virtual machine; these tools are able to maintain control. Where possible, tools can perform application migration from one virtual hardware set to another -- something that is otherwise possible only with dedicated P2V tools.

When choosing one of these super-consoles, it's critical to verity that the console can leverage the existing management tools provided by virtualization vendors. Otherwise, return on investment may never come.

4.7 SCHEDULING TECHNIQUES

Scheduling is the one of the most prominent activities that executes in the cloud computing environment. To increase the efficiency of the work load of cloud computing, scheduling is one of the tasks performed to get maximum profit.

The main objective of the scheduling algorithms in cloud environment is to utilize the resources properly while managing the load between the resources so that to get the minimum execution time.

4.7.1 Why Scheduling

Cloud computing has recently received considerable attention, as a promising approach for delivering Information and Communication Technologies (ICT) services as a utility. In the mechanism of providing these services it is necessary to improve the utilization of datacenter resources which are operating in most dynamic workload environments. Datacenters are the essential parts of cloud computing. In a single datacenter generally hundreds and thousands of virtual servers run at any instance of time, hosting many tasks and at the same time the cloud system keeps receiving the batches of task requests. During this context, one has to notice few target servers out many powered on servers, which can fulfill a batch of incoming tasks. So Task scheduling is an valuable issue which is greatly influences the performance of cloud service provider. Traditional approach that are used in optimization are deterministic, fast, and give perfect answers but often tends to get stuck on local optima.

Complexity of the task scheduling problem belongs to Non Polynomial -complete involving extremely large search space with correspondingly large number of potential solutions and takes much longer time to find the optimal answer. There is no readymade and well outlined methodology to solve the problems under such circumstances. However in cloud, it is tolerable to find near best solution, preferably in a short period of time.

4.7.2 Cloud Service Scheduling

Cloud service scheduling is categorized at user level and system level. At user level scheduling deals with problems raised by service provision between providers and customers. The system level scheduling handles resource management within datacenter.

Datacenter consists of many physical machines. Millions of tasks from users are received; assignment of these tasks to physical machine is done at datacenter. This assignment or scheduling significantly impacts the performance of datacenter. In addition to system utilization, other requirements like QoS, SLA, resource sharing, fault tolerance, reliability, real time satisfaction etc should be taken into consideration.

4.7.3 Scheduling Algorithms

Batch Mode Heuristic Scheduling Algorithms (BMHA) .

In BMHA, Jobs are queued and collected into a set gone they arrive in the system. The scheduling algorithm will begin after a good idea time of era. The main examples of BMHA based algorithms are; First Come First Served scheduling algorithm (FCFS), Round Robin scheduling algorithm (RR), Min-Min algorithm, Max-Min algorithm and Most-fit algorithm.

- In the First Come First Serve job scheduling the jobs are queued in the order of which arrive first.
- In Round Robin job scheduling jobs are dispatched in FCFS logic and the period slice of the process examines the part.
- In the Min-Min scheduling algorithm little jobs are executed first, where large jobs are waiting for more time.
- The Max-Min job scheduling algorithm they choose the largest job to be executed first, well along the little jobs are executed and takes long period.
- In the Most-fit task scheduling algorithm pick the best fit job executed first, failure to pick opt job.

On-Line Mode Heuristic Scheduling Algorithm

Jobs are scheduled behind they come in the system. Since the cloud setting is a heterogeneous system and the speed of each processor varies speedily, the upon-stock mode heuristic scheduling algorithms are more seize for a cloud atmosphere. Most fit task scheduling algorithm (MFTF) is pleasing enough example of On-stock mode heuristic scheduling algorithm.

A QoS Guided Task Scheduling Model

This model is composed of some scheduling strategies and a QoS guided scheduling Sufferage-min heuristic algorithm. This model includes the QoS level of both resources and tasks. The strategy of this model is based upon partitioning. The tasks and resources are not speaking into charity of two levels, first is high QoS level and second is low QoS level. This model has substitute scheduling door for both the levels. This model reduces the make-span value and balances the workload. This model is familiar with the sufferage-min algorithm.

An Efficient Multi Queue Job Scheduling

A Multi Queue Scheduling [MQS] algorithm reduces the cost of both reservation and going concerning for demand plans using global scheduler. The proposed methodology is based upon the concept of clustering the tasks according to their burst their burst times. Starvation and Fragmentation hardship is found in usual methods bearing in mind FCFS, SJF. To overcome these problems Multi Queue Scheduling is introduced. To combine the court prosecution of scheduling algorithm MQS utilize the set wandering unused appearance. In this algorithm job selection is done dynamically to achieve the optimum scheduling encumbrance and therefore it solves the fragmentation millstone.

Priority Based job Scheduling Algorithm

In this algorithm priority is assigned to each job that is introduced in the system. The priority is based considering reference to the theory of Analytical process. Multi-criteria Decision Making Model [MCDM] and a Multi-attribute Decision Making Model [MADM] are the base models to set the priority to the jobs. The Task comparison is over and curtains in the midst of by comparison matrix technique. Since lot of comparisons is done along as well as tasks the profundity of algorithm is high. The priority is based harshly speaking the three levels , First is Objective level, Second is Attribute level and third level is Alternative level.

Scheduling Algorithm Based on Berger Model

Job scheduling is over and ended along in the midst of considering the characteristics of communication and virtualization. Two constraints are applied in this algorithm. The First constraint is user job classification by QoS preferences, and establishes the general expectation take steps. This classification enhances fairness in the resource selection process. The second constraint is to portray resource fairness justice perform for the judgment of resource allocation fairness. Thus On the basis of Berger model scheduling is done coarsely the system justice and task justice fairness constraints. The experimental result of this algorithm has shown the Better fairness.

4.8 SLA COMMITMENT

A Service Level Agreement (SLA) is a contract document or a formal negotiated agreement based upon the purpose and objectives that exists between the Cloud Service Providers and the cloud users. It includes the brief terms and conditions upon which the services being provided by the service providers. SLAs gives a transparent view to the cloud users for understanding about the cloud environment, which includes the advantages and disadvantages of the cloud, cloud services, cloud deployment and security issues, responsibilities, guarantees and warranties of the services.

4.8.1 Needs Of Using SLA

(a) It gives a clear idea about the cloud service providers.

(b) It describes the list of services (SaaS, PaaS and IaaS) the providers will provide along with complete description of each service.

(c) The purpose and objectives about the business level policies i.e Service Level Agreement (SLA) in transparent manner, which includes the roles of the cloud service providers and the cloud users.

(d) It is used to know about the key security and privacy management policies for cloud environment.

(e) It monitors the service quality, performance, priorities, and responsibilities from service point of view.

(f) It gives a transparent view to Know about the service management requirements in case of cloud service failure.

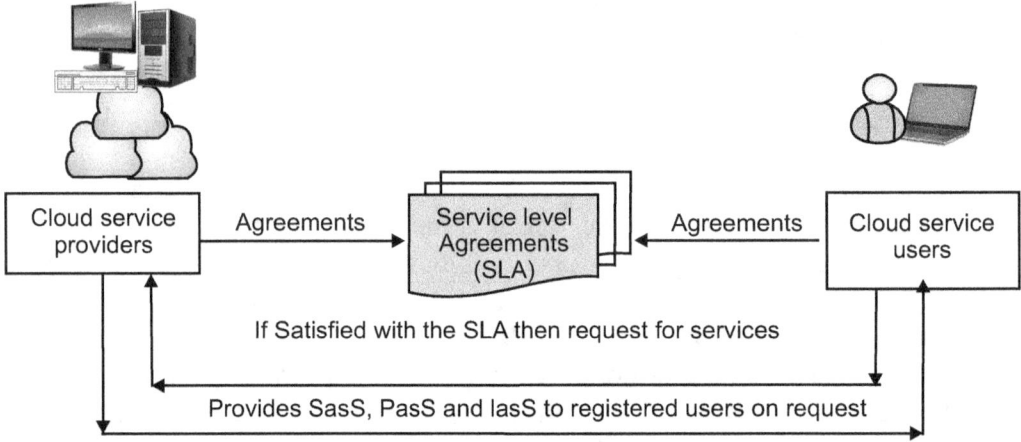

Fig. 4.17 : SLA commitment

4.8.2 Types Of SLA

Service Level Agreement (SLA) is important for using the cloud services, as it is a contract for business arrangements of all types, that understood by both service providers and the users. So based on the types of users and the services, SLAs are classified into 5 types

(a) Customer-based SLA : It is the agreement with entity personal group which covers all services use by the users.

(b) Service-based SLA : It is a contract or agreement between the cloud service provider and all registered users using the service.

(c) Multilevel SLA : Such SLA consist of different levels, each level shows the situations of different customers for same service.

(d) Customer Level SLA : It contains all SLA (Service Level Management) issues relevant to group of particular users.

(e) Service Level SLA : It contains all SLA (Service Level Management) issues relevant to specific service, in relation with user group.

4.8.3 Components Of SLA

An SLA defines the delivery ability of a provider, the performance target of the user's requirement, the scope of guaranteed availability of the services. A list of SLA component descriptions is given below

(A) Business Level Objectives

An organization must define *why* it will use the cloud services before it can define exactly what services it will use. This part is more organizational politics than technical issues: Some groups may get funding cuts or lose control of their infrastructure.

(B) Responsibilities of Both Parties

It is important to define the balance of responsibilities between the Cloud service provider and the cloud user.

For example, the provider will be responsible for the Software-as-a-Service aspects, but the users may be software and works with sensitive data.

(C) Cloud Security

This includes organizational and technical issues related to keeping cloud services at an acceptable level of security by ensuring the computing resources available and usable by its authentic users. Security threats to cloud infrastructure would affect multiple users even if only one site is attacked. These risks can be overcome by using encrypted file systems, security applications, data loss software and buying security hardware.

(D) Privacy in Cloud

Privacy is the process of making sure that the user's data remains private, confidential and restricted from unauthorized users. Due to data virtualization the users data may be stored in various virtual data centers rather than in the local computers. So the unauthorized users may access the private information of the authorized users. Data authentication is one of the most popular options of security before putting the sensitive data into cloud.

(E) Data Integrity and Reliability

Using cloud computing anyone from any location can access the data. Cloud does not differentiate between common data and sensitive data. So an important aspect of cloud services is availability of user's data with reliability. It is necessary for the cloud service provider to ensure the integrity by making their system capable to check over the cloud data from any unauthorized access.

(F) Performance and Bandwidth Cost

The major issues that can affect performance in cloud based environment is due to the unethical transaction oriented and data access applications. So the users who are at a long distance from cloud providers may experience high latency and delay, this is due to the availability bandwidth in the network. Bandwidth cost may be low for smaller Internet-based applications, which are not data intensive, but could significantly, grow for data-intensive applications. The service providers instead of saving money on hardware, they should spend more for the bandwidth. This can deliver intensive and complex application over the network.

(G) Business Continuity/Disaster Recovery

The users should ensure, the provider maintains adequate disaster protection. Two examples come to mind: Storing valuable data on the cloud as backup and cloud bursting (switchover when in-house data centers are unable to handle processing loads).

(H) Redundancy

Consider how redundant your provider's systems are. That helps for data replications and data migration in case of database failure.

(I) Maintenance

One of the nicest aspects of using a cloud is that the provider handles the maintenance. But users should know, when providers will do maintenance tasks:

a. Will services be unavailable during that time?

b. Will services be available, but with much lower throughput?

c. Will the consumer have a chance to test their applications against the updated service?

(J) Data Location

There are regulations that certain types of data can only be stored in certain physical locations. Providers can respond to those requirements with a guarantee that a user's data will be stored in certain locations only and the ability to audit that situation.

(K) Data Seizure

If law enforcement seizes a provider's equipment to capture the data and applications belonging to particular registered users, that seizure is likely to affect other users that use the same provider. Consider a third party to provide additional backup.

(L) Provider Failure

Make contingency plans that take into account the financial health of the provider.

(M) Jurisdiction

Again, understand the local laws that apply to your provider as well as you do the laws that apply to you.

(N) Brokers and Resellers

If your provider is a broker or reseller of cloud services, you need to understand the policies of your provider and the actual provider. The figure shown below gives a clear idea regarding the trust based SLA model for cloud environment

QUESTIONS

1. Explain the term cloud computing in the context of Infrastructure as a service.
2. Explain various components of Cloud Infrastructure. Draw a suitable diagram.
3. Write short note on cloud ready converged infrastructure. What components are involved in cloud ready converged infrastructure ?
4. Explain various terms and terminologies involved in cloud infrastructure.
5. Write short note on distributed management of virtual infrastructure.
6. Explain various scheduling techniques in the context of cloud computing.
7. Write short note on Service Level Agreement (SLA) commitment. Draw suitable diagram.

Unit - V

CLOUD MONITORING AND MANAGEMENT

5.1 AN ARCHITECTURE FOR FEDERATED CLOUD COMPUTING

- Utility computing, a concept envisioned back in the 1960s, is finally becoming a reality. Just as we can power a variety of devices, ranging from a simple light bulb to complex machinery, by plugging them into the wall, today we can satisfy, by connecting to the Internet, many of our computing needs, ranging from full pledge productivity applications to raw compute power in the form of virtual machines.
- Cloud computing, in all its different forms, is rapidly gaining momentum as an alternative to traditional IT, and the reasons for this are clear: In principle, it allows individuals and companies to fulfill all their IT needs with minimal investment and controlled expenses (both capital and operational).
- Cloud computing enables companies and individuals to lease resources on-demand from a virtually unlimited pool. The "pay as you go" billing model applies charges for the actually used resources per unit time.
- This way, a business can optimize its IT investment and improve availability and scalability.
- While cloud computing holds a lot of promise for enterprise computing, there are a number of inherent deficiencies in current offerings such as:

Inherently Limited Scalability of Single-Provider Clouds

- Although most infrastructure cloud providers today claim infinite scalability, in reality it is reasonable to assume that even the largest players may start facing scalability problems as cloud computing usage rate increases.
- In the long term, scalability problems may be expected to worsen as cloud providers serve an increasing number of on-line services, each accessed by massive amounts of global users at all times.

Lack of Interoperability Among Cloud Providers

- Contemporary cloud technologies have not been designed with interoperability in mind. This results in an inability to scale through business partnerships across clouds providers.
- In addition, it prevents small and medium cloud infrastructure providers from entering the cloud provisioning market. Overall, this stifles competition and locks consumers to a single vendor.

No Built-In Business Service Management Support

- Business Service Management (BSM) is a management strategy that allows businesses to align their IT management with their high-level business goals.

- The key aspect of BSM is Service-Level Agreement (SLA) management.
- Current cloud computing solutions are not designed to support the BSM practices that are well established in the daily management of the enterprise IT departments. As a result, enterprises looking at transforming their IT operations to cloud-based technologies face a non-incremental and potentially disruptive step.

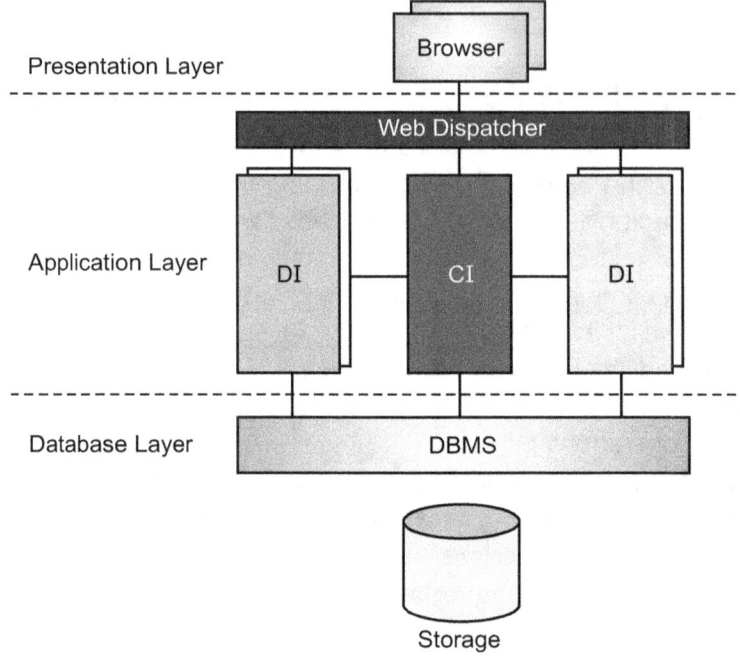

Fig. 5.1 : An Architecture for Federated Cloud Computing

The components can be arranged in a variety of configurations, from a minimal configuration where all components run on a single machine, to larger ones where there are several DI, each running on a separate machine, and a separate machine with the CI and the DBMS.

5.1.1 Federation

- All cloud computing providers, regardless of how big they are, have a finite capacity. To grow beyond this capacity, cloud computing providers should be able to form federations of providers such that they can collaborate and share their resources.
- The need for federation-capable cloud computing offerings is also derived from the industry trend of adopting the cloud computing paradigm internally within companies to create private clouds and then being able to extend these clouds with resources leased on-demand from public clouds.
- Any federation of cloud computing providers should allow virtual application to be deployed across federated sites. Furthermore, virtual applications need to be completely location free and allowed to migrate in part or as a whole between sites.
- At the same time, the security privacy and independence of the federation members must be maintained to allow competing providers to federate.

5.1.2 Independence

- Just as in other utilities, where we get service without knowing the internals of the utility provider and with standard equipment not specific to any provider (e.g., telephones), for cloud computing services to really fulfill the computing as a utility vision, we need to offer cloud computing users full independence.
- Users should be able to use the services of the cloud without relying on any provider specific tool, and cloud computing providers should be able to manage their infrastructure without exposing internal details to their customers or partners.
- As a consequence of the independence principle, all cloud services need to be encapsulated and generalized such that users will be able to acquire equivalent virtual resources at different providers.

5.1.3 Isolation

- Cloud computing services are, by definition, hosted by a provider that will simultaneously host applications from many different users. For these users to move their computing into the cloud, they need warranties from the cloud computing provider that their stuff is completely isolated from others.
- Users must be ensured that their resources cannot be accessed by others sharing the same cloud and that adequate performance isolation is in place to ensure that no other user may possess the power to directly affect the service granted to their application.

5.1.4 Elasticity

- One of the main advantages of cloud computing is the capability to provide, or release, resources on-demand. These "elasticity" capabilities should be enacted automatically by cloud computing providers to meet demand variations, just as electrical companies are able (under normal operational circumstances) to automatically deal with variances in electricity consumption levels. Clearly the behavior and limits of automatic growth and shrinking should be driven by contracts and rules agreed on between cloud computing providers and consumers.
- The ability of users to grow their applications when facing an increase of real-life demand needs to be complemented by the ability to scale.
- Cloud computing services as offered by a federation of infrastructure providers is expected to offer any user application of any size the ability to quickly scale up its application by unrestricted magnitude and approach Internet scale.
- At the same time, user applications should be allowed to scale down facing decreasing demand. Such scalability although depended on the internals of the user application is prime driver for cloud computing because it helps users to better match expenses with gain.

5.1.5 Trust

- Probably the most critical issue to address before cloud computing can become the preferred computing paradigm is that of establishing trust. Mechanisms to build and maintain trust between cloud computing consumers and cloud computing providers, as well as between cloud computing providers among themselves, are essential for the success of any cloud computing offering.

5.2 A MODEL FOR FEDERATED CLOUD COMPUTING

- In our model for federated cloud computing we identify two major types of actors :
- Service Providers (SPs) are the entities that need computational resources to offer some service.
- However, SPs do not own these resources; instead, they lease them from Infrastructure Providers (IPs), which provide them with a seemingly infinite pool of computational, network, and storage resources.
- A Service Application is a set of software components that work collectively to achieve a common goal. Each component of such service applications executes in a dedicated VEE. SPs deploy service applications in the cloud by providing to an IP, known as the primary site, with a Service Manifest that is, a document that defines the structure of the application as well as the contract and SLA between the SP and the IP.
- To create the illusion of an infinite pool of resources, IPs shared their unused capacity with each other to create a federation cloud. A Framework Agreement is document that defines the contract between two IPs that is, it states the terms and conditions under which one IP can use resources from another IP.
- Within each IP, optimal resource utilization is achieved by partitioning physical resources, through a virtualization layer, into Virtual Execution Environments (VEEs) fully isolated runtime environments that abstract away the physical characteristics of the resource and enable sharing.
- We refer to the virtualized computational resources, alongside the virtualization layer and all the management enablement components, as the Virtual Execution Environment Host (VEEH).
- With these concepts in mind, we can proceed to define a reference architecture for federated cloud computing. The design and implementation of such architecture are the main goals of the reservoir European research project. The reservoir architecture, shown in Fig. 5.2, identifies the major functional components needed within an IP to fully support the cloud computing paradigm. The rationale behind this particular layering is to keep a clear separation of concerns and responsibilities and to hide low-level infrastructure details and decisions from high-level management and service providers.

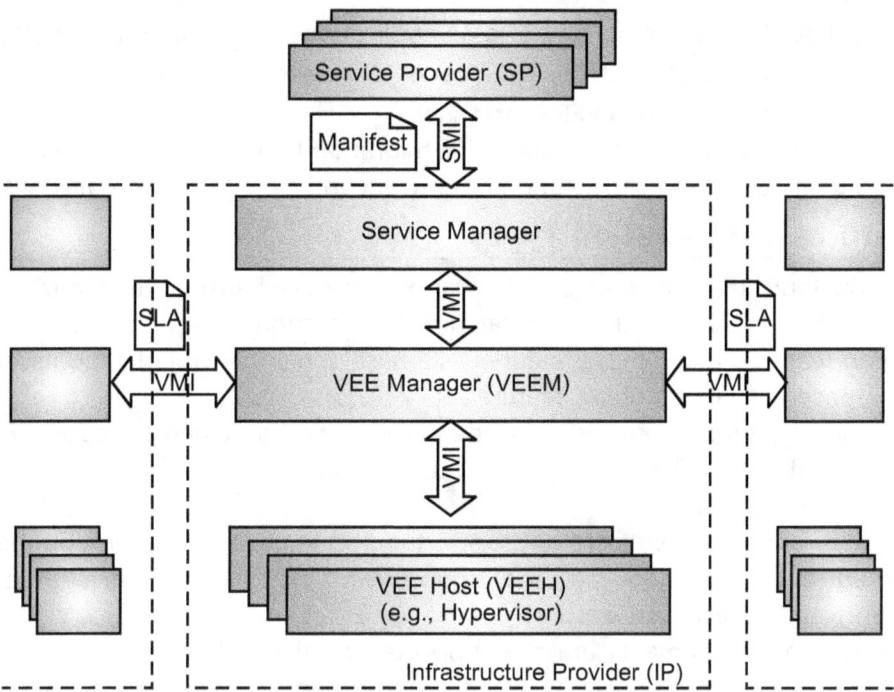

Fig. 5.2 : A model for Federated Cloud Computing

- The Service Manager is the only component within an IP that interacts with SPs. It receives Service Manifests, negotiates pricing, and handles billing. Its two most complex tasks are

   (1)   Deploying and provisioning VEEs based on the Service Manifest and

   (2)   Monitoring and enforcing SLA compliance by throttling a service application's capacity.

- The Virtual Execution Environment Manager (VEEM) is responsible for the optimal placement of VEEs into VEE Hosts subject to constraints determined by the Service Manager.

- The continuous optimization process is driven by a site-specific programmable utility function.

- The VEEM is free to place and move VEEs anywhere, even on the remote sites (subject to overall cross-site agreements), as long as the placement satisfies the constraints. Thus, in addition to serving local requests (from the local Service Manager), VEEM is responsible for the federation of remote sites.

- The Virtual Execution Environment Host (VEEH) is responsible for the basic control and monitoring of VEEs and their resources (e.g., creating a VEE, allocating additional resources to a VEE, monitoring a VEE, migrating a VEE, creating a virtual network and storage pool, etc.).

- Given that VEEs belonging to the same application may be placed on multiple VEEHs and even extend beyond the boundaries of a site, VEEHs must support isolated virtual networks that span VEEHs and sites.

Moreover, VEEHs must support transparent VEE migration to any compatible VEEH within the federated cloud, regardless of site location or network and storage configurations.

5.2.1 Features of Federation Types

Federations of clouds may be constructed in various ways, with disparate feature sets offered by the underlying implementation architecture. This section is devoted to present these differentiating features. Using these features as a base, a number of federation scenarios are defined, comprised of subsets of this feature set.

- The first feature to consider is the framework agreement support: Framework agreements, as defined in the previous section, may either be supported by the architecture or not.
- If framework agreements are not supported, this implies that federation may only be carried out in a more ad hoc opportunistic manner. Another feature is the opportunistic placement support.
- If framework agreements are not supported by the architecture, or if there is not enough spare capacity even including the framework agreements, a site may choose to perform opportunistic placement.
- It is a process where remote sites are queried on-demand as the need for additional resources arises, and the local site requests a certain SLA-governed capacity for a given cost from the remote sites.
- One interesting feature to take into account is the advance resource reservation support. This feature may be used both when there is an existing framework agreement and when opportunistic placement has been performed. Both types of advance reservations are only valid for a certain time, since they impact the utilization of resources at a site. Because of this impact, they should be billed as actual usage during the active time interval.
- The ability to migrate machines across sites defines the federated migration support. There are two types of migration: cold and hot (or live). In cold migration, the VEE is suspended and experiences a certain amount of downtime while it is being transferred. Most modern operating systems have support for being suspended, which includes saving all RAM contents to disk and later restoring the runtime state to its prior state. Hot or live migration does not allow for system downtime, and it works by transferring the runtime state while the VEE is still running.
- Focusing on networks, there can be cross-site virtual network support: VEEs belonging to a service are potentially connected to virtual networks, should this be requested by the SP. Ideally, these virtual networks will span across sites. However, this requires substantial effort and advanced features of the underlying architecture. In the same line, the federation can offer public IP addresses retention post cross-site

migration. With fully virtualized networks, this may be a directly supported feature; but even if virtualized networks are not available, it may still be possible to maintain public IP addresses by manipulating routing information. Information disclosure within the federation has also to be taken into account. The sites in the federation may provide information to different degrees (for instance, the information exchange between sites may be larger within the same administrative domain than outside it). Information regarding deployed VEEs will be primarily via the monitoring system, whereas some information may also potentially be exposed via the VMI as response to a VEE deployment request.

The last identified feature useful to define scenario is the VMI operation support: Depending on the requirements of the federation scenario, only a subset of the VMI operations may be made available. Which operations are required may be related to the amount of information that is exposed by the remote sites; access to more information may also increase the possibility and need to manipulate the deployed VEEs.

5.3 PERFORMANCE PREDICTION FOR HPC ON CLOUD

- High-performance computing (HPC) is one of the contexts in which the adoption of the cloud computing paradigm is debated. Traditionally, HPC users are accustomed to managing directly very complex parallel systems and performing a very fine-tuning of their applications on the target hardware. The matter is to ascertain if it may be convenient to deploy such applications on a cloud, where users "voluntarily" lose almost all control on the execution environment, leaving the management of datacenters to the cloud owner.

- In order to understand fully the implications of this issue, it is probably necessary to take a step back and to clarify how the cloud paradigm can be applied to HPC. Cloud computing may be exploited at three different levels: IaaS (Infrastructure as a Service), PaaS (Platform as a Service), and AaaS (Application as a Service). In one way or another, all of them can be useful for HPC. However, now days the most common solution is the adoption of the IaaS paradigm.

- IaaS lets users run applications on fast pay-per-use machines they don't want to buy, to manage, or to maintain. Furthermore, the total computational power can be easily increased (by additional charge). For the sporadic HPC user, this solution is undoubtedly attractive: no investment in rapidly-obsolescing machines, no power and cooling nightmares, and no system software updates.

- An IaaS cloud environment hinges on a virtualization engine. Basically, this engine provides by means of a hypervisor the illusion of multiple independent replicas of every physical machine in the cloud. Each replica has its own address space, devices, and network connections and is capable of running any software (O.S. included) that could be run on a stand-alone machine. Currently, a number of different Virtual Machine (VM) environments are readily available and can be used to provide server virtualization (VMware [1], Xen [2], and Virtual Box [3]).

- The virtual engines differ in the approach used to run the host operating systems [unmodified (fully virtualized approach) or aware of the presence of the hypervisor-or (paravirtualized approach)] on the exploitation of hardware CPU virtualization technologies (like Intel VT and AMD-V) and on the type of licensing (open- source or closed-source).
- On the top of such virtualization engines, which physically manage the hardware, cloud environments offer a service-oriented interface for managing the virtual machines (create, destroy, suspend, migrate from a physical system to another, change the amount of available memory or the number of virtual CPUs assigned), as well as a large set of ancillary services for managing the secure access to resources and for auditing (and billing).

5.3.1 Background

- As outlined in the introduction, the main question related to the adoption of the cloud paradigm in HPC is related to the evaluation (and, possibly, to the reduction) of possible performance losses compared to physical HPC hardware.
- In clouds, performance penalties may appear at two different levels:
- Virtual Engine (VE). These are related to the performance loss introduced by the virtualization mechanism. They are strictly related to the VE technology adopted
- Cloud Environment (CE). These are the losses introduced at a higher level by the cloud environment, and they are mainly due to overheads and to the sharing of computing and communication resources.
- The actual hardware used in the cloud, along with the losses at the VE and CE levels, will determine the actual performance of applications running in the cloud. As will be discussed later, for HPC users the final perceived performance will be not so much affected by VE and CE levels as by the class of the physical hardware (computing and interconnect) making up the cloud. Even if the computing nodes adopted in cloud are not too different from those making up (economical) HPC clusters, it is a fact that these usually adopt suitable network switches, like Myrinet or Infiniband, which provide high bandwidth and low latency. These networks typically are not available, at the state of the art, in commercial cloud environments. In practice, their relatively slow interconnects can easily dwarf the effect of VE and CE overheads. However, we will not consider here this hardware factor, because it is not under the cloud user's control.

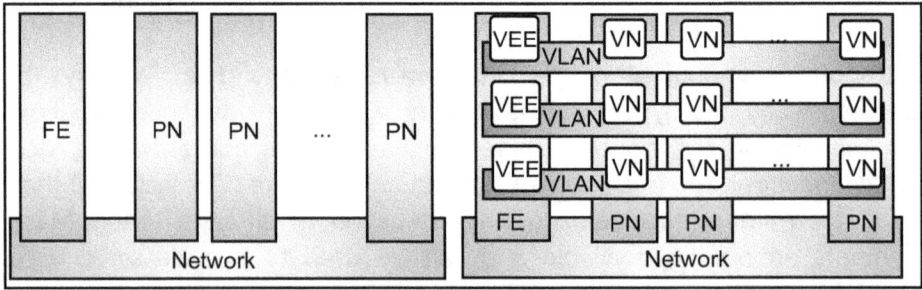

Fig. 5.3 : Physical and virtual cluster

- The configuration and performance analysis of virtual clusters poses problems that are considerably more complex than those involved in the use of physical clusters. The objective of this section is to present the main problems and to introduce a clear and sound terminology, which is still lacking in the literature.

- A traditional cluster that is, a physical cluster can be schematized as in Fig. 5.3. It is essentially made up of a front-end (typically used only for administration purposes, often the only node with a public IP address) and a number of (physical) processing nodes. These are, turn, provided with a single CPU or with multiple CPUs sharing a common memory and I/O resources. The multiple CPUs may be multiple cores on a single processor chip, a traditional single-core CPUs working in SMP mode, a "fictitious" CPU obtained by hyper threading, or a mixture of all the above.

- A physical cluster can execute multiple jobs in parallel, by assigning to every job a subset of the total number of CPUs. Usually the choice is to use non- overlapping subsets of CPUs, in order to avoid processor sharing among multiple jobs. But, even doing so, the interconnection network (and the front- end) are inevitably shared.

- This may, or may not, introduce significant overheads, depending on the type of computations and their communication requirements and, above all, on the characteristics of the interconnect. Anyway, very often this overhead is tolerable.

- A parallel application running in a physical cluster is composed of processes. To exploit all the available computing resources, the application should use at least a number of processes equal to the number of available CPUs (or, in the case of concurrent jobs, equal to the number of CPU exclusively reserved for the job). Redundant application decompositions (i.e., applications made up of a number of processes higher than the number of CPUs) are possible and, in some cases, they may even be more efficient.

- The main problem with physical clusters is that all jobs running on the cluster, whether concurrent or non-concurrent, have to share the same Operating System (OS), the system and application libraries, and the operating environment (system applications and tools). The frequently recurring requirements for mutually exclusive or incompatible libraries and support software make physical cluster management a nightmare for system administrators.

5.3.2 Grid and Cloud

- "Grid vs Cloud" is the title of an incredible number of recent Web blogs and articles in on-line forums and magazines, where many HPC users express their own opinion on the relationship between the two paradigms . Cloud is simply presented, by its supporters, as an evolution of the grid. Some consider grids and clouds as alternative options to do the same thing in a different way. However, there are very few clouds on which one can build, test, or run compute-intensive applications. In fact it still necessary to deal with some open issues. One is when, in term of performance, a cloud is better than a grid to run a specific application. Another problem to be addressed concerns the effort to port a grid application to a cloud. In the following it will be discussed how these and other arguments suggest that we investigate the integration of grids and clouds to improve the exploitation of computing resources in HPC.

- The frequently recurring requirements for mutually exclusive or incompatible libraries and support software make physical cluster management a nightmare for system administrators. Basically, a virtual cluster is made up of a virtual front-end and a number of virtual nodes (see Fig. 5.3).

- Virtual front-ends are obtained by virtualization of a physical front-end machine, and virtual nodes are obtained by virtualization of physical processing nodes. Even if, strictly speaking, in a virtual cluster the front-end could be virtualized as compute nodes, a simpler and less resource-demanding solution is to use a physical front-end. Both with physical or virtual front-ends, virtual cluster may have an execution environment of its own (OS, libraries, tools, etc.) that is loaded and initialized when the cluster is created. The advantages of cluster virtualization are clear: Every application can set up a proper execution environment, which does not interfere with all other applications and virtual clusters running on the hardware. Moreover, the network traffic of every virtual cluster is encapsulated in a separate VLAN. However, most likely all VLANs will share the physical network resources.

- Fig. 5.3, every virtual processing node can host one or several Virtual Machines (VMs), each running a private OS instance. These may belong to the same or to different virtual clusters. At least in theory, the number of VMs is limited only by resource consumption (typically, physical memory). In turn, each VM is provided with several virtual CPUs (VCPUs). A virtual machine manager running in every node makes it possible to share the physical CPUs among the VCPUs defined on the node (which may belong to a single virtual cluster or to several virtual clusters). Typically, it is possible to define VCPU affinity and to force every VCPU to run on a subset of the physical CPUs available.

- It is worth noting that, given a physical node provided with n CPUs, there are two possibilities to exploit all the computing resources available:
  - Using n VMs (each running its OS instance) with one, or even several, VCPUs;
  - Using a single VM with at least n VCPUs.

On the other hand, the use in a node of v VCPUs, with v, n, whether in a single or in multiple VMs, leads to a fictitious multiplication of computing resources. In nodes where CPU resources are multiplied, the virtual clusters not only share memory, communication hardware, and the virtual machine manager, but also share CPU cycles, with a more direct effect on overall computing performance.

5.3.3 Grid and Cloud as Alternatives

Both grid and cloud are technologies that have been conceived to provide users with handy computing resources according to their specific   requirements.

- Grid was designed with a bottom-up approach. Its goal is to share hardware or software among different organizations by means of common protocols and policies. The idea is to deploy interoperable services in order to allow the access to physical resources (CPU, memory, mass storage, etc.) and to available software utilities. Users get access to a real machine. Grid resources are administrated by their owners. Authorized users can invoke grid services on remote machines without paying and without service level guarantees. A grid middleware provides a set of API (actually services) to program a heterogeneous, geographically distributed system.

- On the other hand, cloud technology was designed using a top-down approach. It aims at providing its users with a specific high-level functionality: storage, a computing platform, a specialized service. They get virtual resources from the cloud. The underlying hardware/software infrastructure is not exposed. The only information the user needs to know is the Quality of Service (QoS) of the services he is paying for. Bandwidth, computing power, and storage represent parameters that are used for specifying the QoS and for billing. Cloud users ask for a high-level functionality (service, platform, and infrastructure), pay for it, and become owners of a virtual machine. From a technological point of view, virtualization is exploited to build an insulated environment, which is configured to meet users' requirements and is exploited for easy reconfiguration and backup. A single enterprise is the owner of the cloud platform (software and underlying hardware), whereas customers be- come owners of the virtual resources they pay for.

5.3.4 Grid and Cloud Integration

- To understand why grids and clouds should be integrated, we have to start by considering what the users want and what these two technologies can provide. Then we can try to understand how cloud and grid can complement each other and why their integration is the goal of intensive research activities. We know that a supercomputer runs faster than a virtualized resource. For example, a LU benchmark on EC2 (the cloud platform provided by Amazon) runs slower, and some overhead is added to start VMs.

- On the other hand, the probability to execute an application in fixed time on a grid resource depends on many parameters and cannot be guaranteed. As experimented in Foster, if 400 msec is the time that an EC2 requires to execute an LU benchmark, then the probability of obtaining a grid resource in less than 400 msec is very low (34%), even if the same benchmark can take less than 100 msec to complete.

- If you want to get your results as soon as possible, you are adopting the cloud end-user perspective. If you want to look for the optimum resources that solve the problem, overcoming the boundaries of a single enterprise, you are using the grid perspective that aims at optimizing resources sharing and system utilization.

- The integration of cloud and grid, or at least their integrated utilization, has been proposed since there is a trade-off between application turnaround and system utilization, and sometimes it is useful to choose the right compromise between them.

- Some issues to be investigated have been pointed out :
  1. Integration of virtualization into existing e-infrastructures.
  2. Deployment of grid services on top of virtual infrastructures.
  3. Integration of cloud-base services in e-infrastructures.

4. Promotion of open-source components to build clouds.

5. Grid technology for cloud federation.

- In light of the above, the integration of the two environments is a debated issue, At the state of the art, two main approaches have been proposed.

- **Grid on Cloud :** A cloud IaaS (Infrastructure as a Service) approach is adopted to build up and to manage a flexible grid system .Doing so, the grid middleware runs on a virtual machine. Hence the main drawback of this approach is performance. Virtualization inevitably entails performance losses as compared to the direct use of physical resources.

- **Cloud on Grid :** The stable grid infrastructure is exploited to build up a cloud environment. This solution is usually preferred because the cloud approach mitigates the inherent complexity of the grid. In this case, a set of grid services is offered to manage (create, migrate, etc.) virtual machines. The use of Globus workspaces .along with a set of grid services for the Globus Toolkit 4 is the prominent solution, as in the Nimbus project.

- The integration could simplify the task of the HPC user to select, to configure, and to manage resources according to the application requirements. It adds flexibility to exploit available resources, but both of the above-presented approaches have serious problems for overall system management, due to the complexity of the resulting architectures. Performance prediction, application tuning, and benchmarking are some of the relevant activities that become critical and that cannot be performed in the absence of performance evaluation of clouds.

5.3.5 HPC in the Cloud : Performance-Related Issues

This section will discuss the issues linked to the adoption of the cloud paradigm in the HPC context. In particular, we will focus on three different issues :

1. The difference between typical HPC paradigms and those of current cloud environments, especially in terms of performance evaluation.

2. A comparison of the two approaches in order to point out their advantages and drawbacks, as far as performance is concerned.

3. New performance evaluation techniques and tools to support HPC in cloud systems.

5.4 SERVICE LEVEL AGREEMENT

5.4.1 Service-Level Agreement (SLA) Definition

A Service-Level Agreement (SLA) is a contract between a service provider and its internal or external customers that documents what services the provider will furnish.

Learn the best strategies IT solution providers can leverage for starting up and securing a cloud practice, successful approaches to selling and marketing cloud, and why it is urgent partners to transition now.

SLAs measure the service provider's performance and quality in a number of ways. Some metrics that SLAs may specify include :

- Availability and uptime the percentage of the time services will be available.
- The number of concurrent users that can be served.
- Specific performance benchmarks to which actual performance will be periodically compared.
- Application response time.
- The schedule for notification in advance of network changes that may affect users.
- Help desk response time for various classes of problems.
- Usage statistics that will be provided.

In addition to establishing performance metrics, an SLA may include a plan for addressing downtime and documentation for how the service provider will compensate customers in the event of a contract breach. SLAs, once established, should be periodically reviewed and updated to reflect changes in technology and the impact of any new regulatory directives (changes to the PCI DSS standard, for instance).

5.4.2 Types of SLA

- Service-level agreement provides a framework within which both seller and buyer of a service can pursue a profitable service business relationship. It outlines the broad understanding between the service provider and the service consumer for conducting business and forms the basis for maintaining a mutually beneficial relationship. From a legal perspective, the necessary terms and conditions that bind the service provider to provide services continually to the service consumer are formally defined in SLA.
- SLA can be modelled using Web Service Level Agreement (WSLA) language specification. Although WSLA is intended for web-service-based applications, it is equally applicable for hosting of applications. Service-level parameter, metric, function, measurement directive, service-level objective, and penalty are some of the important components of WSLA.
- There are two types of SLAs from the perspective of application hosting. These are described in detail here.

Infrastructure SLA. The infrastructure provider manages and offers guarantees on availability of the infrastructure, namely, server machine, power, network connectivity, and so on. Enterprises manage themselves, their applications that are deployed on these server machines. The machines are leased to the customers and are isolated from machines of other customers.

Application SLA. In the application co-location hosting model, the server capacity is available to the applications based solely on their resource demands. Hence, the service providers are flexible in allocating and de-allocating computing resources among the co-located applications. Therefore, the service providers are also responsible for ensuring to meet their customer's application SLOs.

It is also possible for a customer and the service provider to mutually agree upon a set of SLAs with different performance and cost structure rather than a single SLA. The customer has the flexibility to choose any of the agreed SLAs from the available offerings. At runtime, the customer can switch between the different SLAs.

However, from the SLA perspective there are multiple challenges for provisioning the infrastructure on demand. These challenges are as follows :

(a) The application is a black box to the MSP and the MSP has virtually no knowledge about the application runtime characteristics. Therefore, the MSP needs to determine the right amount of computing resources required for different components of an application at various workloads

(b) The MSP needs to understand the performance bottlenecks and the scalability of the application.

(c) The MSP analyzes the application before it goes on-live. However, subsequent operations/enhancements by the customer's to their applications or auto updates beside others can impact the performance of the applications, thereby making the application SLA at   risk.

(d) The risk of capacity planning is with the service provider instead of the customer. If every customer decides to select the highest grade of SLA simultaneously, there may not be a sufficient number of servers for provisioning and meeting the SLA obligations of all the customers.

- SLO – Service Level Objective. That is, the objective to be achieved.
- KPI – Key Performance Indicators.
- **Service Level Objective:** Objective of service quality that has to be achieved.
- Set of measurable KPIs with thresholds to decide if the objective is fulfilled or not.
- Automated SLA protection is based on a set of policy rules.
- Each policy rule is formed by one or more conditions (KPI's value matching pattern) and one or more actions.
- KPIs are periodically evaluated according to defined policies.
- If one or more conditions are met, then appropriate actions are triggered.
- Service Level Agreement (SLA) describes agreement on non-functional requirements between provider and customer.
- SLA consists of Service Level Objectives (SLOs) that are evaluated according to measurable Key Performance Indicators (KPIs)
- Automatic SLA protection enables further increase of the system utilization and system profit.
- In currently available systems only some basic SLAs like "uptime over a time period guarantee" are available.
- SLAs originated with network service providers, but are now widely used by telecommunication service providers and cloud computing service providers. Corporate IT organizations, particularly those that have embraced IT Service Management (ITSM), enter SLAs with their in-house customers (users in other departments within the enterprise). An IT department creates an SLA so that its services can be measured, justified and perhaps compared with those of outsourcing vendors

5.4.3 Why is Service Level Agreement Important in Cloud Computing?

Many cloud providers are vague on the specifics of the underlying hardware and software stack they use to deliver a virtual server to the end customer, which allows for over commitment. Techniques for overcommitting hardware include :

- Specify memory allocation and leave CPU allocation unspecified, allowing total hardware memory to dictate the number of customers the hardware can support
- Quote shared resource maximums instead of private allocations
- Offer a range of performance for a particular instance, such as a range of GHz
- Over allocate resources on a physical server, or thin provisioning. Commercial virtualization management software such as VMware or Virtuozzo offers the ability to over allocate resources on the underlying hardware, resulting in reduced performance during peak loads.
- Variable Performance : People can see advertisements for cloud computing breaking through the previous price floor for a virtual server instance. It makes one wonder how cloud providers can do this and stay in business.
- They overcommit their computing resources and cut corners on infrastructure. The result is variable and unpredictable performance of the virtual infrastructure. SLA ensures the customer gets the quality of service expects.

SLA has to point the volume of service rendered for the cloud services. Contract KPIs :

- The volume of service
- The quality of service
- Peak and average loads of work
- The volume of demand at different times of day

5.4.4 SLA Requirements

The penalty for the cloud provider in case the provider fails to meet these service requirements.

- A signed agreement with each customer.
- Transactions by hour and jobs by day for each application.
- A method of reporting SLA results.
- Priority of services in case of insufficient availability.
- Agreed methods of penalty in case customer exceeds his limits.
- Agreed methods of penalty in case cloud provider fails to meet contract specifications.
- Schedule of virtual or actual meeting between the customer and the cloud provider if necessary.

5.4.5 Life Cycle of SLA

Each SLA goes through a sequence of steps starting from identification of terms and conditions, activation and monitoring of the stated terms and conditions, and eventual termination of contract once the hosting relationship ceases to exist. Such a sequence of steps is called SLA life cycle and consists of the following five phases :

1. Contract definition
2. Publishing and discovery
3. Negotiation
4. Operationalization
5. De-commissioning

Here, we explain in detail each of these phases of SLA life cycle.

- **Contract Definition :** Generally, service providers define a set of service offerings and corresponding SLAs using standard templates. These service offerings form a catalog. Individual SLAs for enterprises can be derived by customizing these base SLA templates.

- **Publication and Discovery :** Service provider advertises these base service offerings through standard publication media, and the customers should be able to locate the service provider by searching the catalog. The customers can search different competitive offerings and shortlist a few that fulfill their requirements for further negotiation.

- **Negotiation :** Once the customer has discovered a service provider who can meet their application hosting need, the SLA terms and conditions needs to be mutually agreed upon before signing the agreement for hosting the application. For a standard packaged application which is offered as service, this phase could be automated. For customized applications that are hosted on cloud platforms, this phase is manual. The service provider needs to analyze the application's behavior with respect to scalability and performance before agreeing on the specification of SLA. At the end of this phase, the SLA is mutually agreed by both customer and provider and is eventually signed off. SLA negotiation can utilize the WS-negotiation specification.

- **Operationalization :** SLA operation consists of SLA monitoring, SLA accounting, and SLA enforcement. SLA monitoring involves measuring parameter values and calculating the metrics defined as a part of SLA and determining the deviations. On identifying the deviations, the concerned parties are notified. SLA accounting involves capturing and archiving the SLA adherence for compliance. As part of accounting, the application's actual performance. Guaranteed as a part of SLA is reported. Apart from the frequency and the duration of the SLA breach, it should also provide the penalties paid for each SLA violation. SLA enforcement involves taking appropriate action when the runtime monitoring detects a SLA violation. Such actions could be notifying the concerned parties, charging the penalties besides other things. The different policies can be expressed using a subset of the Common Information Model (CIM).The CIM model is an open standard that allows expressing managed elements of data center via relationships and common objects.

- **De-commissioning :** SLA decommissioning involves termination of all activities performed under a particular SLA when the hosting relationship between the service provider and the service consumer has ended. SLA specifies the terms and conditions of contract termination and specifies situations under which the relationship between a service provider and a service consumer can be considered to be legally ended.

5.4.6 Guide for Evaluating Cloud Service Level Agreements

Before evaluating any cloud SLA, consumers must first develop a strong business case and strategy for their cloud computing environment. This includes identifying specific services that will be deployed in the cloud along with a clear understanding of the criticalness of these services to the business. A check on the exit clauses of current hosted services contracts is also important. Only after this strategic analysis has been completed can the consumer effectively evaluate and compare SLAs from different providers.

With the cloud business case and strategy as a prerequisite, this section provides a prescriptive series of steps that should be taken by cloud consumers to evaluate cloud SLAs with the goal of comparing cloud service providers or negotiating terms with a provider. The following steps are discussed in detail :

1. Understand roles and responsibilities
2. Evaluate business level policies
3. Understand service and deployment model differences
4. Identify critical performance objectives
5. Evaluate security and privacy requirements
6. Identify service management requirements
7. Prepare for service failure management
8. Understand the disaster recovery plan
9. Define an effective management process
10. Understand the exit process

Requirements and best practices are highlighted for each step. In addition, each step takes into account the realities of today's cloud computing landscape and postulates how this space is likely to evolve in the future, including the important role that standards will play to improve interoperability and comparability across providers.

Step 1 : Understand Roles and Responsibilities

In order for consumers to understand specific roles and responsibilities explicitly or implicitly stated in a cloud SLA, it is important that they are aware of the various actors that can potentially participate in a cloud computing environment. The National Institute of Standards and Technology (NIST) Reference Architecture[1] identifies 5 unique cloud actors:

- **Cloud Consumer :** The person or organization that maintains a business relationship with, and uses service from, cloud providers.
- **Cloud Provider :** The person, organization or entity responsible for making a service available to cloud consumers.
- **Cloud Carrier :** The intermediary that provides connectivity and transport of cloud services from cloud providers to cloud consumers.
- **Cloud Broker :** An organization that manages the use, performance and delivery of cloud services, and negotiates relationships between cloud providers and cloud consumers.

Cloud Auditor : A party that can conduct independent assessments of cloud services, information system operations, performance and security of the cloud implementation.

The use of the term "broker" varies significantly and should be clarified with the various stakeholders, especially in context of a cloud SLA. An entity may provide broker services and functionality, but as a legal organizational entity not be recognized as a cloud broker. For example, an entity may perform research and negotiate on behalf of a consumer, but the actual SLA and contract terms are between the cloud consumer and cloud provider. The distinction of acting "broker like" vs. being an actual "broker" will evolve as the cloud computing industry matures and terminologies become more consistent. Due to these complexities this paper does not address all the SLA considerations for cloud brokering.

Consumers need to recognize the activities and responsibilities of each cloud actor that is engaged in delivering their cloud environment, and precisely define requirements and desired service levels for each actor. This paper focuses primarily on the cloud consumer/cloud provider SLA, although other SLAs may be addressed in a particular context. In some cases, the consumer/provider relationship will indirectly include additional actors. Fig. 5.4 below illustrates an environment where a cloud provider has established a SLA with two cloud carriers to establish service levels for communication and transport. In addition to cloud provider expectations, the consumer/provider SLA in this example may also include specific carrier and transport expectations. In this case, the cloud provider is also acting as a "broker" for the other two cloud carriers.

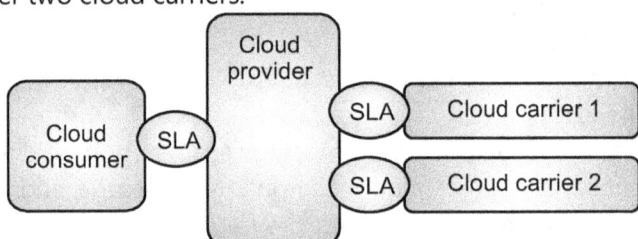

Fig. 5.4 : Indirect relationships

Each cloud SLA will be unique based upon the consumers' requirements and the cloud ecosystem under consideration. SLAs can contain various expectations between the actors and are not limited to quantitative measures, but can include other qualitative aspects such as alignment with standards and data protection. It is strongly recommended that cloud consumers gain a solid understanding of the spectrum of SLAs that currently exist for cloud providers (and other actors as appropriate) in order to compare providers and assess tradeoffs between cost and service levels 2.

The following sections, which cover the cloud SLA evaluation steps in detail, will each elaborate on the expected responsibilities between consumer and provider for both business level and service level objectives. In order to make sound business decisions, it is important that consumers understand what to expect from their cloud provider. This, in turn, will help them define their own responsibilities and help them assess the true cost of moving to the cloud.

Step 2 : Evaluate Business Level Policies

Consumers must consider key policy issues when reviewing a cloud SLA since there are interdependencies between the policies expressed in the SLA and the business strategy and policies developed in other aspects of the business. The data policies of the cloud provider, as expressed in the SLA, are perhaps the most critical business level policies that should be carefully evaluated.

The duty of care a cloud provider has to its clients and their data is partly governed by the data protection legislation applicable in the user's local jurisdiction and also in those jurisdictions in which its data may reside or made available. Consumers should carefully consider these legal requirements and how the SLA their provider(s) offers deals with issues such as movement of data to offer multisite redundancy across several jurisdictions.

Step 3 : Understand Service and Deployment Model Differences

Services offered by cloud providers typically fall into one of the three major groups of service models: Infrastructure as a Service (IaaS), Platform as a Service (PaaS), and Software as a Service (SaaS). For each category, there are significant differences in the levels of cloud resource abstraction, service level objectives, and key performance indicators that will potentially be included in a cloud SLA. In addition, the level of clarity varies significantly for each service model. In general, PaaS and SaaS objectives are less precise than IaaS objectives since the variety of solutions and applications offered by providers is much broader for these service models.

Step 4 : Identify Critical Performance Objectives

Performance goals within the context of cloud computing are directly related to efficiency and accuracy of service delivery. Performance considerations often include: availability, response time, transaction rate, processing speed, but can include many other performance and system quality perspectives. Consumers must decide which measures are most critical to their specific cloud environments and ensure these measures are included in their SLA.

Performance statements that are important to the cloud consumer should be measureable and auditable, and documented in the SLA providing a comfort level to both parties. Performance considerations are dependent on the supported service model (IaaS, PaaS and SaaS) and the type of services provided within that model, for example, network, storage and computing services for IaaS.

Step 5 : Evaluate Security and Privacy Requirements

Security controls in cloud computing are, for the most part, no different than security controls in any IT environment. However, because of the cloud service models employed, the operational models, and the technologies used to enable cloud services, cloud computing may present different risks to an organization than traditional IT solutions. At a basic level, assets supported by the cloud fall into two general categories :

- Data
- Applications/Functions/Processes

Information is either being moved into the cloud or applications are being executed in the cloud (from partial functions all the way up to full applications).

A critical initial step for ensuring sufficient cloud security is establishing a classification scheme that applies throughout the enterprise, based on the criticality and sensitivity of enterprise data. This scheme should include details about data ownership, definition of appropriate security levels and protection controls, and a brief description of data retention and destruction requirements. The classification scheme should be used as the basis for applying controls such as access controls, archiving or encryption.

Step 6 : Identify Service Management Requirements

The fundamental goals of any cloud computing environment are to reduce cost, improve flexibility and increase reliability of the delivery of a service. Critical to meeting these goals is a uniform, straightforward, transparent and extensible system for managing and monitoring cloud services.

In this section we will outline some key considerations in service management when entering into a service level agreement with a cloud computing provider.

Every computing system requires internal controls, management, automation and self-healing in order to operate in today's interconnected world, and the cloud is no different. Although the standards for SLA language for service management are evolving, it is of upmost importance to include provisions for the considerations outlined below in your agreements.

Step 7 : Prepare for Service Failure Management

Service failure management outlines what happens when the expected delivery of a service does not occur. Service capabilities and performance expectations should be explicitly documented in the cloud SLA. If not, the likelihood of misunderstandings between consumer and provider increases significantly. For example, a web service performing poorly in terms of response time may not be considered a service failure to the provider unless it is clearly called out in the SLA

The level of service failure management will vary greatly dependent upon provider, and the ability to negotiate a greater level will vary upon size of the consumer. As a result, it is important for consumers to incorporate their own service failure management capabilities to ensure they are made aware of any issues in a timely fashion.

Remedies

The primary remedy for service failure is service credits. These are based upon a percentage of the fees paid by the consumer during the billing cycle. The actual percentage will vary depending on the provider. However, it is common that these service credits will not exceed 100% of the paid fees. This often results in service credits not being in proportion to business cost or risk.

It is also important to note that common service level agreements put the responsibility of reporting a service interruption on the consumer. The consumer will need to contact the provider and be prepared to show that their service has been impacted by a service interruption.

Limitations

Within each cloud provider's agreement there are likely liability limitations for certain types of service interruptions. While these may vary dependent upon the provider, a sampling of several major providers shared the following exclusions :

- Scheduled or emergency outages.

- Acts of force measure.
- Suspension of service due to legal reasons.
- Internet access issues outside the control of the provider.

In addition to common, shared limitations, there are providers who may also cite unscheduled downtime as being excluded from the SLA metrics. Consumers are strongly encouraged to fully understand all facets of their cloud SLA.

Given these limitations, it is important that consumers plan for unavailability. This may include keeping a separate, on-premise backup copy of the cloud data. While this may be more feasible for a large company, a small company may need to either ensure the provider is backing up data or contract a second provider to complete these backups. The frequency of the backups would be dependent upon the criticality of the data and the data's rate of change.

Roles / Responsibilities

The roles of cloud computing service failure management are similar to the Information Technology Infrastructure Library (ITIL) incident management roles. The consumer incident manager would have responsibility to drive the incident and crisis management process. Assuming the failure is impactful to service delivery, the consumer incident manager should be plugged into the provider's incident management process as well. This collaboration should be negotiated into the agreed upon SLA. This may also be more easily negotiated for large organizations. Smaller organizations may need to proactively reach out to the provider when an incident occurs and engage in a more manual fashion.

Step 8 : Understand the Disaster Recovery Plan

Disaster recovery is a subset of business continuity and focuses on processes and technology for resumption of applications, data, hardware, communications (such as networking), and other IT infrastructure in case of a disaster. By the term disaster we mean either natural disaster or man-made events that have an impact of availability of IT infrastructure or software systems.

It is common to see a false sense of security among cloud consumers regarding disaster recovery planning. Just because businesses are outsourcing the infrastructure (IaaS), applications (SaaS), or platforms (PaaS) to the cloud does not absolve them of the need for serious disaster planning. Every company is unique in the importance it assigns to specific infrastructure/ applications, thus, a cloud disaster recovery plan is specific to each organization, and business objectives should play an important role in determining the specificity of disaster recovery planning.

The process of devising a disaster recovery plan starts with identifying and prioritizing applications, services and data, and determining for each one the amount of downtime that's acceptable before there is a significant business impact. Service priority, required Recovery Time Objectives (RTOs), and Recovery Point Objectives (RPO's) will determine the overall disaster recovery approach. For example, in some applications maintaining uptime may be more important than having the data precisely replicated as of the last time of failure.

Further, while 99%+ uptime SLAs are common in cloud computing (approximately 4 days of down time a year), it may not be adequate for specific application and business needs.

In general, current cloud SLAs provide inadequate guarantees in case of a service outage due to a disaster. Most cloud SLAs provide cursory treatment of disaster recovery issues, procedures and processes. That being said, it is rare for SMBs the primary customer of clouds today, to internally develop the extensive disaster recovery infrastructure of large and established cloud providers.

Despite the limitations in cloud SLAs, cloud adopters should address key disaster recovery questions/issues with their service providers early in the process of cloud adoption. The key areas to address with cloud providers are :

- How is service outage defined?
- What level of redundancy is in place to minimize outages including co-location of services in different geographical regions?
- Will there be a need for a scheduled down time?
- Who has the burden of proof to report outages? This can be difficult to prove in case of conflicts with the cloud providers.
- What is the process that will be followed to resolve unplanned incidents?
- How will unplanned incidents be prevented or reduced?
- When does the time clock start on lack of service availability in order to measure service credits?
- How will incidents be documented or logged?

What actions will be taken in the event of a prolonged disruption or a disruption with a serious business impact?

Step 9 : Develop an Effective Management Process

In the evolving world of cloud computing, there is a need for an effective management process for any problems that may arise. Today's reality is that cloud SLAs contain very limited information on consumer-provider management processes except possibly for large enterprises that are capable of negotiating unique terms. Implementing an effective management process is an important step to ensuring internal and external user satisfaction with cloud based service(s).

Step 10 : Understand the Exit Process

An exit clause should be part of every cloud SLA and describes the details of the exit process including the responsibilities of the cloud provider and consumer in case the relationship terminates prematurely or otherwise there are numerous potential scenarios that could cause the termination of service between consumer and producer which would result in the execution of the exit process. For example, a provider may be unable to deliver the required levels of performance and availability specified in the SLA, or it may be the case that the provider is going out of the business. Regardless of the reason, a clearly defined exit process that ensures secure and speedy transfer of consumer data and applications is essential.

A consumer exit plan should always be prepared at the outset of the SLA and is an integral contractual annex. This plan should ensure minimal business disruption for the customer and ensure a smooth transition. The exit process should include detailed procedures for ensuring business continuity and it should specify measurable metrics to ensure the cloud producer is effectively implementing these procedures.

By far, the most important aspect of any exit plan is the transmission and preservation of consumer data which is critical to achieving business continuity. In addition, consumers must ensure that their data is completely removed from the provider's environment once the exit process is complete. Consumers should look out for and beware of the following details when they evaluate the exit clause included in a cloud SLA.

- The level of provider assistance in the exit process and associated fees should be clear in the SLA. In most cases, there should be no additional cost associated with the exit process.
- Providers should be responsible for extracting consumer data from their IT environments, or at least aid the consumer in extracting their data by providing clear and concise documentation.
- The format of the data transmitted from the provider to the consumer should be specified in the cloud SLA and should leverage standard data formats whenever possible to ease and enhance portability.

5.5 SLA MANAGEMENT IN CLOUD COMPUTING

SLA management of applications hosted on cloud platforms involves five phases.
1. Feasibility
2. On-boarding
3. Pre-production
4. Production
5. Termination

Different activities performed under each of these phases. These activities are explained in detail in the following subsections.

1. Feasibility Analysis

MSP conducts the feasibility study of hosting an application on their cloud platforms. This study involves three kinds of feasibility :
1. Technical feasibility,
2. Infrastructure feasibility,
3. Financial feasibility.

The technical feasibility of an application implies determining the following:
- Ability of an application to scale out.
- Compatibility of the application with the cloud platform being used within the MSP's data centre.

- The need and availability of a specific hardware and software required for hosting and running of the application.
- Preliminary information about the application performance and whether they can be met by the MSP.
- Performing the infrastructure feasibility involves determining the availability of infrastructural resources in sufficient quantity so that the projected demands of the application can be met.

The financial feasibility study involves determining the approximate cost to be incurred by the MSP and the price the MSP charges the customer so that the hosting activity is profitable to both of them. A feasibility report consists of the results of the above three feasibility studies. The report forms the basis for further communication with the customer. Once the provider and customer agree upon the findings of the report, the outsourcing of the application hosting activity proceeds to the next phase, called "on- boarding" of application. Only the basic feasibility of hosting an application has been carried in this phase. However, the detailed runtime characteristics of the application are studied as part of the on-boarding activity.

2. On-Boarding

Once the customer and the MSP agree in principle to host the application based on the findings of the feasibility study, the application is moved from the customer servers to the hosting platform. Moving an application to the MSP's hosting platform is called on-boarding. As part of the on-boarding activity, the MSP understands the application runtime characteristics using runtime profilers. This helps the MSP to identify the possible SLAs that can be offered to the customer for that application. This also helps in creation of the necessary policies (also called rule sets) required to guarantee the SLOs mentioned in the application SLA. The application is accessible to its end users only after the on- boarding activity is completed.

3. On-boarding Activity Consists of the Following Steps :

- Packing of the application for deploying on physical or virtual environments. Application packaging is the process of creating deployable components on the hosting platform (could be physical or virtual). Open Virtualization Format (OVF) standard is used for packaging the application for cloud platform.
- The packaged application is executed directly on the physical servers to capture and analyze the application performance characteristics. It allows the functional validation of customer's application. Besides, it provides a baseline performance value for the application in non virtual environment. This can be used as one of the data points for customer's performance expectation and for application SLA. Additionally, it helps to identify the nature of application that is, whether it is CPU-intensive or I/O- intensive or network-intensive and the potential performance bottlenecks.
- The application is executed on a virtualized platform and the application performance characteristics are noted again. Important performance characteristics like the

application's ability to scale (out and up) and performance bounds (minimum and maximum performance) are noted.

4. Preproduction

Once the determination of policies is completed as discussed in previous phase, the application is hosted in a simulated production environment. It facilitates the customer to verify and validate the MSP's findings on application's runtime characteristics and agree on the defined SLA. Once both parties agree on the cost and the terms and conditions of the SLA, the customer sign-off is obtained. On successful completion of this phase the MSP allows the application to go on-live.

5. Production

In this phase, the application is made accessible to its end users under the agreed SLA. However, there could be situations when the managed application tends to behave differently in a production environment com- pared to the preproduction environment. This in turn may cause sustained breach of the terms and conditions mentioned in the SLA. Additionally, customer may request the MSP for inclusion of new terms and conditions in the SLA. If the application SLA is breached frequently or if the customer requests for a new non-agreed SLA, the on-boarding process is performed again. In the case of the former, on-boarding activity is repeated to analyze the application and its policies with respect to SLA fulfillment. In case of the latter, a new set of policies are formulated to meet the fresh terms and conditions of the SLA.

6. Termination

When the customer wishes to withdraw the hosted application and does not wish to continue to avail the services of the MSP for managing the hosting of its application, the termination activity is initiated. On initiation of termination, all data related to the application are transferred to the customer and only the essential information is retained for legal compliance. This ends the hosting relationship between the two parties for that application, and the customer sign-off is obtained.

- Cloud computing is essentially changing the way services are built, provided and consumed. As a paradigm building on a set of combined technologies, it enables service provision through the commoditization of IT assets and on-demand usage patterns. Now a days, cloud computing refers to a computing paradigm whose foundation is the delivery of services and ICT assets, often denoted as XaaS (Everything as a Service).
- The term refers to an increased number of cloud-based resources and services provided over the Internet, with the most common examples, following the SPI model, Software (SaaS), Platform (PaaS) and Infrastructure (IaaS) as a service.
- As the aforementioned cloud service model matures and becomes ubiquitous, it raises the possibility of improving the way services are provisioned and managed, thus allowing providers to address the (diverse) needs of consumers.
- In this context, Service Level Agreements (SLAs) emerge as a key aspect, since they serve as the foundation for the expected quality level of the service between the consumer and

the provider. Nevertheless, the diversity of the proposed SLAs by providers (with marginal overlaps), has led to multiple different definitions of cloud SLAs.

- Furthermore, misconceptions exist on what is (if there is) the difference between SLAs and contract, what is the borderline, what are the terms included in each one of these documents and if and how are these linked. We provide the following definitions according to ITIL.

- A Service Level Agreement (SLA) is a formal, negotiated document that defines (or attempts to define) in quantitative (and perhaps qualitative) terms the service being offered to a Customer. Any metrics included in a SLA should be capable of being measured on a regular basis and the SLA should record by whom.

- A Contract is a legally binding agreement between two or more parties. Contracts are subject to specific legal interpretations. An alternative definition going a bit away from the pure process oriented ITIL one has been provided by the TM Forum: "A Service Level Agreement (SLA) is a formal negotiated agreement between two parties.

- It is a contract that exists between the Service Provider (SP) and the Customer.

- It is designed to create a common understanding about Quality of Service (QoS), priorities, responsibilities, etc. SLAs can cover many aspects of the relationship between the Customer and the SP, such as performance of services, customer care, billing, service provisioning, etc.

- However, although a SLA can cover such aspects, agreement on the level of service is the primary purpose of a SLA".

5.5.1 Scope and Purpose

- The purpose of this document is to serve as a starting point for the exploitation of research results stemming from European and National projects. To this end, the report identifies and delivers short descriptions of the main SLA-related contribution of each project. What is more, a set of recommendations is provided to address the requirements of different entities in the cloud ecosystem.

- The recommendations aim at facilitating wider adoption of cloud solutions and enable providers to offer a wider set of services through approaches that enable the provision of QoS guarantees (as required, for example : in future internet and mission critical applications) and facilitate efficient collaborations amongst providers. The content regarding the research outcomes has been compiled following a working group meeting that was organized and hosted by the EC in Brussels, 27 May 2013.

- As consumers move towards adopting such a Service-Oriented Architecture, the quality and reliability of the services become important aspects. However the demands of the service consumers vary significantly.

- It is not possible to fulfill all consumer expectations from the service provider perspective and hence a balance needs to be made via a negotiation process.

- At the end of the negotiation process, provider and consumer commit to an agreement. In SOA terms, this agreement is referred to as a SLA.

- This SLA serves as the foundation for the expected level of service between the consumer and the provider.
- The QoS attributes that are generally part of an SLA (such as response time and throughput) however change constantly and to enforce the agreement, these parameters need to be closely monitored.

Due to the complex nature of consumer demands, a simple"measure and trigger" process may not work for SLA enforcement.

- Four different types of monitoring demands made by consumers are mentioned. One scenario is a consumer demands the data exposed by a service provider without further refinement such as transaction count, which is a raw metric. Second scenario is consumer requests that collected data should put into meaningful context.
- This scenario creates the requirement for a process which collects data from different sources and applies suitable algorithms for calculating meaningful results. Such metrics

Include statistical measures such as average or standard deviation that need to be computed from a raw set of numbers.

- The third scenario is the consumer requests certain customized data to be collected. In the fourth scenario the consumer even specifies the way how data should be collected. Both the latter mentioned scenarios imply an advanced consumer who would have a knowledge of the inner workings of a provider and somewhat rare in practice. Other issues such as trust also need to be considered during SLA enforcement. For example: consumers may not completely trust the certain measurements provided solely by a service provider and regularly employ third party mediators.
- These mediators are responsible for measuring the critical service parameters and reporting violations of the agreement from either party.
- We believe the upcoming trend of cloud computing is an extension of the SOA paradigm and the above mentioned issue of striking a balance applies to the cloud as well. The process of managing the provider-consumer agreements in computing clouds closely resemble the generic provider-consumer agreement process we mentioned above. Hence we propose architecture for managing cloud consumer and provider SLAs, based on the WSLA specification. We highlight two reasons to justify the importance of this research.

1. The most prominent cloud provider, Amazon EC2, puts the burden of proving SLA violations on the consumer. i.e. the consumer should take steps to enforce the SLA . Having a formalized SLA enables the setup of the enforcement process to be automated and hence relieves consumers from that burden.

2. We believe the work that significantly intersects with ours is where WSLA has been used as a base for grid service monitoring. However computing grids are very different from computing clouds in terms of
   - Business model,
   - Architecture,
   - Resource management,

- Programming model,
- Application model and
- Security model.

• Hence we believe applying WSLA to the cloud context would be a significantly different effort from the previous work. Some of the important aspects we discovered are detailed. To the best of our knowledge this is the first use of WSLA in the context of cloud computing.

5.5.2 SLA Lifecycle Metamodel

This section introduces a metamodel that captures the main phases, structures, processes and entities interactions in the SLA lifecycle. The goal of each phase, the participating actors and their role, the potential dependencies as well as the outcomes of each phase are described as follows.

- **Service Use**

Service use reflects the usage of the cloud service by a service customer. As already described the service customer may not be the end user. However, the aim of this phase is to obtain the service and thus an SLA may be signed between the customer and the service provider. The SLA includes high-level attributes related to the service / application.

- **Service Modeling**

The service modeling process aims at providing additional information with respect to the service that will be deployed in a cloud infrastructure. As the only actor having the required knowledge for the service, the developer is using a set of frameworks in order to design, model and analyze the service.

Service design may be extended to include potential dependencies between service components of an application (in the case of a composite service), elasticity rules for the application or / and performance and behavior hints that are required to guarantee the offered level of quality (e.g. increasing number of users by a factor of 1000 in a multi-tier web application requires the usage of Three times the deployed application servers and two replicas of the deployed database). The outcome of the process is captured in an artifact / document (usually in a structured XML format), which includes all the parameters affecting the service execution, usage and delivery. This artifact is named in some cases Blueprint or Manifest.

- **SLA Template Definition**

The SLA template definition process aims at generating and refining the SLA templates. All providers (i.e. service, platform and infrastructure) analyze their business objectives through a business modeling process (that may use business and pricing models simulation frameworks) in order to optimize their offerings. Furthermore, the service provider uses as a basis the blueprint / manifest of the service and refines the SLA templates (in terms of attributes values) following business modeling outcomes, while the service provider may also include additional attributes in the SLA templates reflecting for example the use of licenses. Thus, an SLA template may include the outcomes of one or more service blueprints / manifests. The outcome of this phase is an SLA template that will be published by the providers in order to be negotiated and signed by the participating entities.

- **SLA Instantiation and Management**

The goal of this phase is to instantiate an SLA (i.e. electronically signed agreement). The main process refers to the SLA negotiation, which may be extended with mechanisms for dynamic negotiation between different entities as well as with mechanisms for automatic renegotiation during runtime. Moreover, discovery is used to identify providers for specific services (based on the service parameters captured in the service blueprint / manifest). Mapping / translation refers to a process of analysing the high-level application-related attributes and mapping them to low-level resource parameters (e.g. transmission of 24 frames per second maps to network links of 13MB/s). Besides such functional parameters, nonfunctional parameters (e.g. redundancy, security, etc) may also be mapped / translated. The outcome of this phase is a signed SLA between the participating entities that includes low-level (resource-related) attributes.

- **SLA Enforcement**

The SLA enforcement phase aims at ensuring that the quality parameters (agreed in signed SLAs) are retained. All providers exploit monitoring mechanisms to obtain both infrastructure and application monitoring data, while adaptable approaches focus on adjusting the monitoring time intervals or the monitoring metrics based on the collected information during runtime. Evaluation tools are exploited to analyze the monitoring data and trigger corrective actions using SLA violation detection mechanisms, some of which enable proactive violation detection.

5.6 SOAP AND REST

- SOAP/WSDL web services evolved from the need to programmatically inter- connect web-based applications. As a result SOAP/WSDL web services are essentially a form of remote procedure calls over HTTP, while also including support for nested structures (objects) in a manner similar to earlier extensions of RPC, such as CORBA;.
- The specifications of the service, including the service URL and other parameters, are made available by the service provider (in this case Google) as another XML file, in WSDL1 format, as illustrated in the rest of the figure.
- The WSDL file specifies the service endpoint, i.e. the URL that responds to SOAP requests to this web service, as shown in the bottom right of the figure. Above this are a number of port types, within which are listed the operations (functions, methods) that are included in this service, along with their input and output parameter types; for example the operation do Google Search has input and output messages doGoogleSearch and do Google Search Response respectively.
- The types of these messages are also specified in detail in the WSDL file, as XML schemas. For example in the case of a doGoogleSearch operation, the input messages are composed of simple types (i.e. strings, etc.), whereas the output, i.e. search result, is a complex type comprising of an array of results whose schema is also specified in the WSDL. Finally, the WSDL binding links these abstract set of operations with concrete transport protocols and serialization formats.

- SOAP documents, i.e. the XML messages exchanged over HTTP, comprise of a body as well as an optional header that is an extensible container where message layer information can be encoded for a variety of purposes such as security, quality of service, transactions, etc. A number of WS-* specifications have been developed to incorporate additional features into SOAP web services that extend and utilize the header container: For example, WS-Security for user authentication, WS-Transactions to handle atomic transactions spanning multiple service requests across multiple service providers, WS-Resource Framework enabling access to resource state behind a web service (even though each web service is inherently stateless) and WS-Addressing to allow service endpoints to be additionally addressed at the messaging level so that service requests can be routed on non-HTTP connections (such as message queues) behind an HTTP service facade, or even for purely internal application integration.

- The origin of the rather complex structure used by the SOAP/WSDL approach can be traced back to the RPC (remote procedure call) standard and its later object oriented variants, such as CORBA. In the original RPC protocol (also called SUN RPC), the client-server interface would be specified by a <..>.x file, from which client and server stubs in C would be generated, along with libraries to handle complex data structures and data serialization across machine boundaries. In CORBA, the .x files became IDL descriptions using a similar overall structure; Java RMI (remote method invocation) also had a similar structure using a common Java interface class to link client and server code. SOAP/WSDL takes the same approach for enabling RPC over HTTP, with WSDL playing the role of .x files, IDLs or interface classes.

5.6.1 REST Web Services

- Representational State Transfer (REST) was originally introduced as an architectural style for large-scale systems based on distributed resources, one of whose embodiments is the hypertext driven HTML-based web itself. The use of REST as a paradigm for service-based interaction between application pro- grams began gaining popularity at about the same time as, and probably in reaction to, the SOAP/WSDL methodology that was being actively propagated by many industry players at the time, such as IBM and Microsoft.

- REST web services are merely HTTP requests to URIs, using exactly the four methods GET, POST, PUT and DELETE allowed by the HTTP protocol. Each URI identifies a resource, such as a record in a database. As an example, consider accessing a customer record with the REST ser- vice http://x.y.com/customer/11998, which returns the record in XML format. In case the record contains links (foreign keys) to related records, such as the customer's accounts or address, links to these are embedded in the returned XML, such as http://x.y.com/account/334433. Alternatively, these links might be directly accessed via a REST service http://x.y.com /customer/11998/accounts. The client application merely accesses the URIs for the resources being managed in this 'RESTful' manner using simple HTTP requests to retrieve data. Further, the same mechanism can allow manipulation of these resources as well; so a customer record may be retrieved using a GET method, modified by the client pro- gram, and sent back using a PUT or a POST request to be updated on the server.

- REST web services with the above example as well as two real-life examples using Yahoo! and Google, both of whom also provide a REST web service interface to their core search engine. Notice that the URLs of these search service s include parameters (appid and query for Yahoo!, ver and q for Google); strictly speaking these service definitions deviate from the 'strong' REST paradigm, where resources are defined by pure URIs alone. In principle, such purity could have easily been maintained: Note that version is part of the URI in the Yahoo! service while it is a parameter in the case of Google, which need not have been the case; the input URL would simply need to have been processed differently. In practice however, the use of parameters in REST services has now become widespread.

5.6.2 Soap Versus Rest

- Many discussions of SOAP versus REST focus on the point that encoding services as SOAP/WSDL makes it difficult to expose the semantics of a web service in order for it to be easily and widely understood, so that many different providers can potentially offer the same service. Search is a perfect example. It is abundantly clear that the SOAP/WSDL dentition of Google search does not in any way define an 'obvious' standard, and it is just as acceptable for an alternative API to be provided by other search engines. However, in the case of REST, there is the potential for such standardization:

- If for example, the REST standard for search were http://<provider-URL>/<query-string>, multiple providers could make this available; the response documents in XML could be self-describing by referring to provider specific name spaces where needed but adhering to a publicly specified top-level schema. We do not take a view on this aspect of the SOAP vs. REST debate, since standardization and reuse are difficult goals. As is apparent from the two very different REST APIs for web search, it is not SOAP or REST that drives standardization. Nevertheless, the relative simplicity of creating and using REST-based services as compared to the more complex SOAP/WSDL approach is immediately apparent from our examples. Further, REST can avoid expensive XML parsing by using alternatives such as JSON. So our view is that the case for using SOAP/WSDL needs to be explicitly made depending on the context, with REST being the option of choice from the perspective of simplicity as well as efficiency.

- To examine when SOAP services may in fact be warranted, we now compare the SOAP and REST paradigms in the context of programmatic communication between applications deployed on different cloud providers, or between cloud applications and those deployed in-house.

- we compare these along six dimensions: The location where servers providing the service can reside; how secure the interaction is; whether transactions can be sup- ported; how dependent the protocol is on HTTP technology; the extent of development tools and support required; the efficiency of the resulting implementations; and finially the software development productivity to be expected using each. We conclude from this analysis that for most requirements SOAP is an overkill; REST interfaces are simpler, more efficient and cheaper to develop and maintain. The shift from SOAP to REST especially in the cloud setting is apparent: The Google SOAP service is now deprecated, and essentially replaced by the REST API using JSON. While Amazon web services publish both SOAP as well as REST APIs, the SOAP APIs are hardly used (15 percent is a number quoted on the web). In our opinion REST web ser- vices will gradually overtake SOAP/WSDL, and it is likely that mechanisms to address more complex functionality, such as transactions, will also be developed for REST in the near future.

5.7 SYSTEM INTEGRATION AND WORK FLOW MODELING

5.7.1 Architectural Overview

- Workflow Management System (WfMS) utilizes cloud resources to drive the execution of a scientific workflow application.
- The workflow system comprises the workflow engine, a resource broker and plug-ins for communicating with various technological platforms, such as Aneka and Amazon EC2. A detailed architecture describing the components of a WfMS is given
- User applications could only use cloud services or use cloud together with existing grid/cluster-based solutions. The Aneka platform is used in its entirety to complete the workflow, and the other where Amazon EC2 is used to supplement a local cluster when there are insufficient resources to meet the QoS requirements of the application.
- A PaaS cloud and can be run on a corporate network or a dedicated cluster or can be hosted entirely on an IaaS cloud. Given limited resources in local networks, Aneka is capable of transparently provisioning additional resources by acquiring new resources in third-party cloud services such as Amazon EC2 to meet application demands. This relieves the WfMS from the responsibility of managing and allocating resources directly, to simply negotiating the required resources with Aneka.
- Aneka also provides a set of Web services for service negotiation, job submission, and job monitoring. The WfMS would orchestrate the workflow execution by scheduling jobs in the right sequence to the Aneka Web Services. The typical flow of events when executing an application workflow on Aneka would begin with the WfMS staging in all required data for each job onto a remote storage resource, such as Amazon S3 or an FTP server. In this case, the data would take the form of a set of files, including the application binaries. These data can be uploaded by the user prior to execution, and they can be stored in storage facilities offered by cloud services for future use.

The WfMS then forwards workflow tasks to Aneka's scheduler via the Web service interface. These tasks are subsequently examined for required files,

storage service is instructed to stage them in from the remote storage server, so that they are accessible by the internal network of execution nodes. The execution begins by scheduling tasks to available execution nodes (also known as worker nodes).

- The workers download any required files for each task they execute from the storage server, execute the application, and upload all output files as a result of the execution back to the storage server. These files are then staged out to the remote storage server so that they are accessible by other tasks in the workflow managed by the WfMS. This process continues until the workflow application is complete.

- The second scenario describes a situation in which the WfMS has greater control over the compute resources and provisioning policies for executing workflow applications. Based on user-specified QoS requirements, the WfMS schedules workflow tasks to resources that are located at the local cluster and in the cloud. Typical parameters that drive the scheduling decisions in   such a scenario include deadline (time) and budget (cost) For instance, a policy for scheduling an application workflow at minimum execution cost would utilize local resources and then augment them with cheaper cloud resources, if needed, rather than using high-end but more expensive cloud resource. On the contrary, a policy that scheduled workflows to achieve minimum execution time would always use high-end cluster and cloud resources, irrespective of costs. The resource provisioning policy determines the extent of additional resources to be provisioned on the public clouds. In this second scenario, the WfMS interacts directly with the resources provisioned. When using Aneka, however, all interaction takes place via the Web service interface.

- The following sections focuses on the integration of workflow management systems and clouds and describes in detail practical issues involved in using clouds for scientific workflow applications.

5.7.2 Architecture of Workflow Management Systems

- Scientific applications are typically modeled as workflows, consisting of tasks, data elements, control sequences and data dependencies. Workflow management systems are responsible for managing and executing these workflows.

- Scientific workflow management systems are engaged and applied to the following aspects of scientific computations : (1) Describing complex scientific procedures (using GUI tools, workflow specific languages), (2) Automating data derivation processes (data transfer components), (3) High-Performance Computing (HPC) to improve throughput and performance (distributed resources and their coordination), and (4) provenance management and query (persistence components). The Cloudbus Workflow Management System consists of components that are responsible for handling tasks, data and resources taking into account users' QoS requirements. Its architecture is depicted in Fig. 5.6.

- The architecture consists of three major parts : (a) The user interface, (b) The core, and (c) Plug-ins. The user interface allows end users to work with workflow composition, workflow execution planning, submission, and monitoring. These features are delivered through a Web portal or through a stand-alone application that is installed at the user's end. Workflow composition is done using an XML-based Workflow Language (xWFL). Users define task properties and link them based on their data dependencies. Multiple tasks can be constructed using copy-paste functions present in most GUIs.

- The components within the core are responsible for managing the execution of workflows. They facilitate in the translation of high-level workflow descriptions (defined at the user interface using XML) to task and data objects. These objects are then used by the execution subsystem. The scheduling component applies user-selected scheduling policies and plans to the workflows at various stages in their execution. The tasks and data dispatchers interact with the resource interface plug-ins to continuously submit and monitor tasks in the workflow. These components form the core part of the workflow engine.

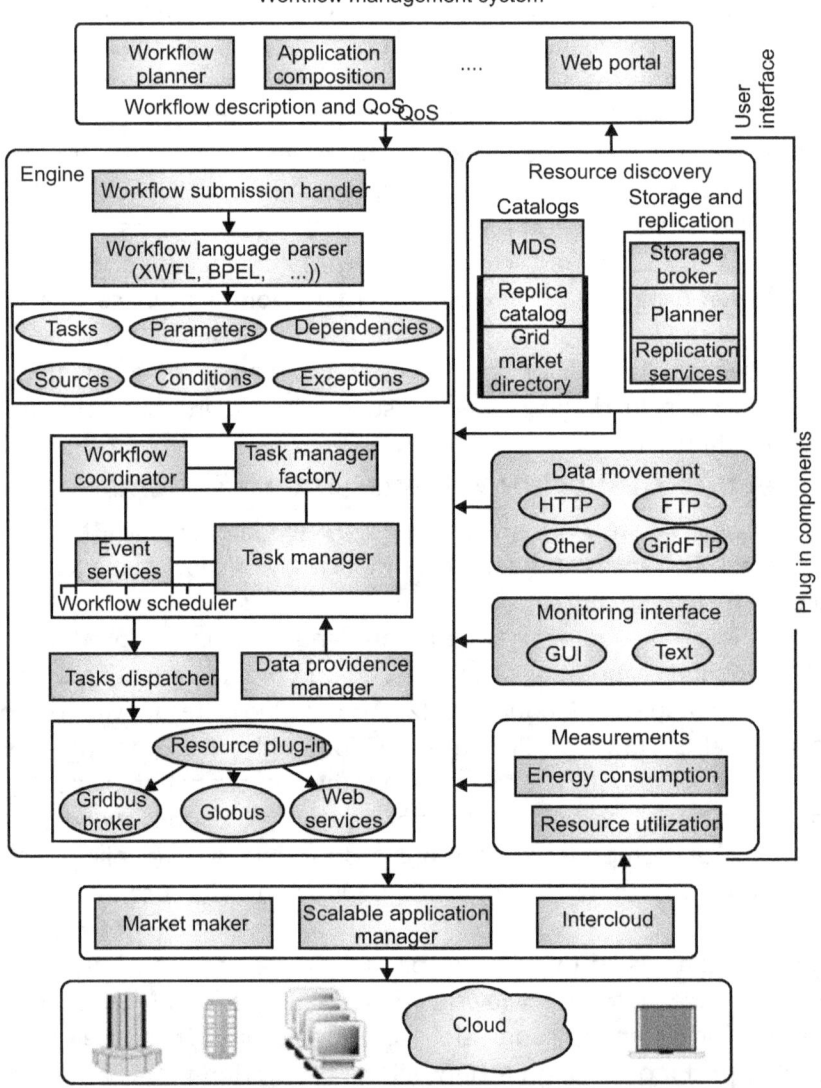

Fig. 5.6 : Architecture of Workflow Management System

- The plug-ins support workflow executions on different environments and platforms. Our system has plug-ins for querying task and data characteristics (e.g., querying metadata services, reading from trace files), transferring data to and from resources (e.g., transfer protocol implementations, and storage and replication services), monitoring the execution status of tasks and applications (e.g., real-time monitoring GUIs, logs of execution, and the scheduled retrieval of task status), and measuring energy consumption.

• The resources are at the bottom layer of the architecture and include clusters, global grids, and clouds. The WfMS has plug-in components for interacting with various resource management systems present at the front end of distributed resources. Currently, the Cloudbus WfMS supports Aneka, Pbs, Globus, and fork-based middleware. The resource managers may communicate with the market maker, scalable application manager, and InterCloud services for global resource management

5.7.3 Utilizing Clouds For Workflow Execution

Taking the leap to utilizing cloud services for scientific workflow applications requires an understanding of the types of clouds services available, the required component changes in workflow systems for interacting with cloud services, the set of tools available to support development and deployment efforts, the steps involved in deploying workflow systems and services on the cloud, and an appreciation of the key benefits and challenges involved. In the sections to follow, we take a closer look at some of these issues. We begin by introducing the reader to the Aneka Enterprise Cloud service. We do this for two reasons. First, Aneka serves as a useful tool for utilizing clouds, including platform abstraction and dynamic provisioning. Second, we describe later in the chapter a case study detailing the use of Aneka to execute a scientific workflow application on clouds.

5.8 CLOUD SERVICE LIFE CYCLE

The input to the production of a cloud services are all the resources and assets that will compose the cloud service (i.e., in the form of hardware, software, man power required from developer to the management level and cost). The outcome of the cloud services production is an acceptable and marketable cloud service, which will provide a measurable value to the business objectives and outcomes. The sets of inputs are transformed to derive the outcome by using the cloud service life cycle. The cloud service life cycle consists of five phases as shown in Fig. 5.7 and Table 5.1 summarizes each of the phase in cloud service life-cycle.

At the core of the cloud service life cycle is service strategy, which is the fundamental phase in defining the service principles. The main core of the cloud

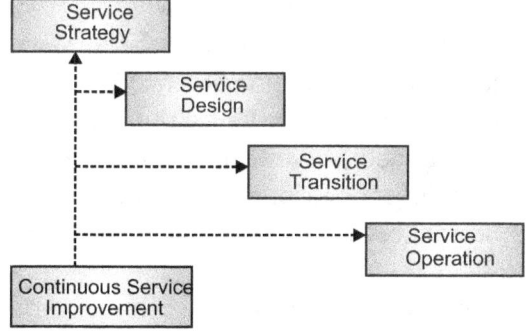

Fig. 5.7 : Cloud service lifecycle

Table 5.1 : Cloud Service Life Cycle

Service Phase	Service Strategy	Service Design	Service Transition	Service Operation	Continuous Service Improvement
Description	Defines the business strategies, policies, objectives	Design of the cloud services, processes, and capabilities	Develop the cloud services for the transition of services to production	Production of cloud services and service operational support	Maintain and Improve value of cloud service to consumer
Objectives	Determines the business decision	Design the new/ improved cloud service to meet business requirements	Development, deployment and validation to ensure that the cloud service has correct capabilities	Ensure the cloud service value to consumer	Continuously maintain and improve the value of cloud service to meet business needs
Outcome	Business requirements and cloud service descriptions	Cloud service blue- print or Service Design Package (SDP)	Production of the cloud services that is ready to go live	Monitoring report, cloud service feedback	Cloud services improvement

Service life cycle is the key principle that all services must provide measurable value to business objectives and outcomes, which is reinforced in ITIL service management as its primary focus. Service design, transition, and operation are the revolving life-cycle stages and are anchored by continual service improvement. This life cycle revolves through the continuous service improvement process to provide performance measurement at each individual phase and a feedback for improvement. This has become crucial as IT organizations are increasingly forced to operate as businesses in order to demonstrate a clear return on investment and equate service performance with business value to the IT's internal customers. The necessity of specialization and coordination in the life-cycle approach has been made available via feedback and control between the functions and processes across the life-cycle phases.

The cloud service life-cycle approach mimics reality of most organizations where effective management requires uses of multiple control perspectives.

1. Service Strategy

Service strategy is the core of the service life cycle. It signifies the birth of the service. This is the phase where the business defines the strategies, policies, and objectives and establishes an understanding of the constraints, requirements, and business values. Fig. 5.8 illustrates the inputs and outcomes of the service strategy phase.

In the service strategy phase, the cloud service provider would be under- taking strategic planning on various value creation activities, including what services are to be designed, what resources are required to build this cloud services, and what capabilities of the cloud service are to be developed. Typically, the planning includes the detailed description of the cloud services (value to be created), defining the market, service portfolio, project timeline, resources required (number of man-power, budget), risks, and other key factors influencing the cloud service production.

The service strategy phase involves a business decision to determine if the cloud service provider has sufficient resources to develop this type of service

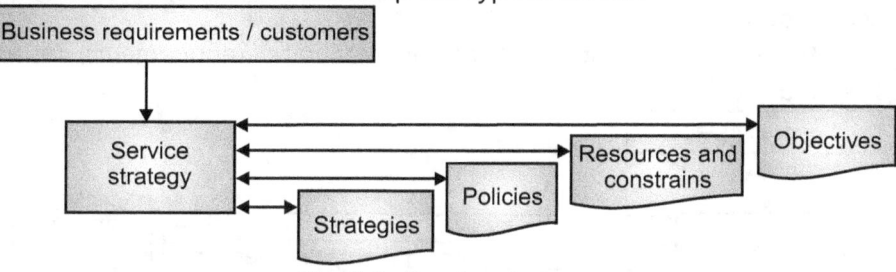

Fig. 5.8 : Service strategy

and also to determine if production of a cloud service has a business value. The service strategy is comprised of the following key concepts :

- Value creation,
- Service provider types,
- Defining the service market,
- Demand management,
- Financial management,
- Return of investment,
- Service assets, assessment, and portfolios,
- Service capabilities and resources,
- Service structures and developing service offerings,

The outcome of the service strategy phase is service strategy documentation, which includes the following components :

- Business requirements target consumer market and   stakeholders,
- Risks involved,
- Resources required (man-power and budget),
- Functional service requirements,
- Service descriptions,
- New/improved service timeline,

2. Service Design

The second phase in the cloud service life cycle is service design. The main purpose of the service design stage of the life cycle is the design of new or improved service for introduction into the live environment. Fig. 5.9 shows the input and the outcome of the service design phase. In this phase, the service requirements and specification are translated into a detailed cloud service design including the detailed desired outcome. The main objectives of service design are :

- Aspects of service design
- Service catalogue management
- Service requirements
- Service design models
- Capacity, availability, and service-level management

The key concepts of service design revolve around the five design aspects, the design of services, service processes and service capabilities to meet business demand. The five key aspects of service design are:

The design of the services, including all of the functional requirements, resources, and capabilities needed and agreed.

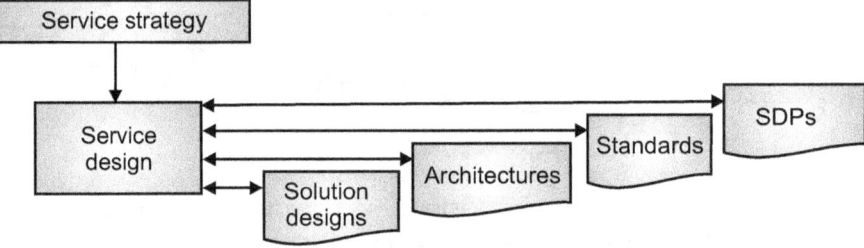

Fig. 5.9 : Service design

- The design of service management systems and tools, for the control and management of sustainable services through the life cycle.
- The design of the technology architectures, hardware and software, required to form the underlying technical aspects to provide the services.
- The design of the policies and processes needed to design, transition, operate, and improve the services, the architectures and the processes.
- The design of key measurement methods, performance metrics for the service, cloud service architectures, and their constituent components and the processes.

The key output of the service design phase is a blueprint of the Service Solution, Architectures, and standards. This output is what ITIL would term the Service Design Package (SDP). The SDP defines the following with respect to the service:

- Service-level requirements
- Service design and topology
- Service and operational management requirements
- Organizational readiness assessment plan
- Service program

- Service transition plan
- Service operational acceptance plan
- Service acceptance criteria

3. Service Transition

The service transition phase intends to implement and deploy what has been designed and planned. As shown in Fig. 5.10, the service transition phase takes knowledge formulated out of the service design phase, and uses it to plan for the validation, release and deployment of the service to production. Key disciplines in service transition are :

- Service development or service change is service built according to service design package.
- Service release and deployment ensures the correct release in live environment.
- Service validation and test ensures that the service has validated correct capabilities and functionalities.
- Service knowledge management is to share information within the organization to avoid rediscovering of cloud service capabilities.

Service transition provides a consistent and rigorous framework for evaluating the service capability and risk profile before a new or a changed service is released or deployed. The key output of the service transition is production of the services that is ready to go live, which includes:

- Approved service release package and associated deployment packages.
- Updated service package or bundle that defines end-to-end service(s) offered to customers.
- Updated service portfolio and service catalogue.
- Updated contract portfolio.
- Documentation for a transferred service.

4. Service Operation

Service operation is the stage in the cloud service life cycle to provide the production of the cloud service and the service operational support. Service operation spans the execution and business performance of processes to continually strike the balance between cost optimization and quality of services. It is responsible for effective functioning of components that support services.

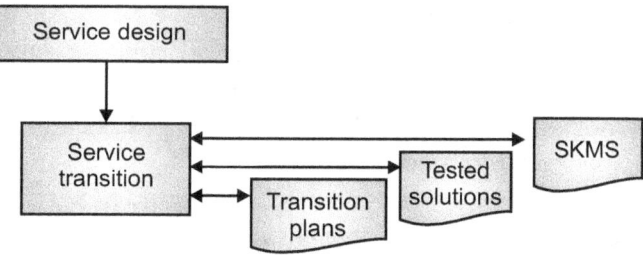

Fig. 5.10 : Service transition

Effective service operation relies on the ability to know the status of the infrastructure and to detect any deviation from normal or expected operation. This is provided by good monitoring and control systems, which are based on two types of tools:

- Active monitoring tools that poll key Configuration Items (CIs) to deter- mine their status and availability. Any exceptions will generate an alert that needs to be communicated to the appropriate tool or team for   action.
- Passive monitoring tools that detect and correlate operational alerts or communications generated by CIs.

5.9 SOFTWARE DEFINED APPROACH AND MANAGING IT RESOURCE

Cloud computing has become ubiquitous for the federal IT workforce, as many if not most agencies have begun to move functions like email or data storage into the cloud. But approaching cloud as a software-defined environment is still a relatively new concept in government. A software-defined approach holistically automates network, computing and storage capabilities and opens the lines of communication between them.

Essentially, software-defined environments break down the silos between network, storage and computing capabilities. And in times of tight budgets, agencies are beginning to adopt the software-defined approach to delivering IT services in order to automate and improve on the infrastructure they already have in place.

In traditional IT environments, there is a separate way of managing compute, network and storage capabilities, and most operations are done manually a human being is reconfiguring storage and the area network.

Software-defined environments also offer a more secure universe for servers and services to operate in. By centralizing the infrastructure to one location, organizations are less vulnerable to attacks on multiple locations.

If you have an existing IT project, by leveraging a software-defined approach agencies can deliver more services on the same amount of hardware. "Delivering services more quickly and improving security posture is actionable and measurable, and possible through a software-defined approach.

Rather than having distributed infrastructure in several locations, like multiple data canters housing servers, in a software-defined environment it is all in the cloud. By leveraging a software-defined approach, you can deliver an enhanced security posture by protecting data in the organization and across cloud services providers,

In the traditional approach to networking, most network functionality is implemented in a dedicated appliance; i.e., switch, router, application delivery controller. In addition, within the dedicated appliance, most of the functionality is implemented in dedicated hardware such as an ASIC (Application Specific Integrated Circuit

Some of the key characteristics of this approach to developing network appliances are

The ASICs that provide the network functionality evolve slowly;

The evolution of ASIC functionality is under the control of the provider of the appliance;

The appliances are proprietary

Each appliance is configured individually

Tasks such as provisioning, change management provisioning are very time consuming and error prone.

Networking organizations are under increasing pressure to be more efficient and agile than is possible with the traditional approach to networking. One source of that pressure results from the widespread adoption of server virtualization. As part of server virtualization, virtual machines (VMs) are dynamically moved between servers in a matter of seconds or minutes. However, if the movement of a VM crosses a Layer 3 boundary, it can take days or weeks to reconfigure the network to support the VM in its new location. It can sometimes be difficult to define exactly what it means for a network to be agile. That said, if it takes weeks to reconfigure the network to support the movement of a VM, that network isn't agile. The bottom line is that a traditional network evolves slowly; is limited in functionality by what is provided by the vendors of the ASICs and the vendors of the network appliances; has a relatively high level of OPEX and is relatively static in nature. SDN holds the promise of overcoming those limitations.

The Shift to Software

As noted, the traditional data network has been largely hardware-centric. However, over the last few years the adoption of virtualized network appliances and the burgeoning interest in software defined data centers (SDDCs) have lead a movement towards an increased reliance on software- based network functionality. For example, in the mid to late 2000s, network appliances such as WAN Optimization Controllers (WOCs) and Application Delivery Controllers (ADCs) were purpose- built, hardware appliances. That means that functions such as encryption/decryption and the processing of TCP flows were performed in hardware that was designed specifically for those functions. Driven largely by the need for increased agility, it is now common to have WOC or ADC functionality provided by software running on a general purpose server or on a VM.

A SDDC can be looked at as the complete opposite of the traditional data center network that was previously described. For example, one of the key characteristics of a software-defined data center is that the entire data center infrastructure is virtualized and delivered as a service. Another key characteristic is that the automated control of data center applications and services is provided by a policy-based management system.

Possible Opportunities

One of the characteristics that is often associated with any fundamentally new approach to technology is that there is confusion about the opportunities that can be addressed by that new approach. In order to successfully evaluate and adopt a new approach to technology such as SDN, IT organizations need to identify which opportunity or opportunities that are important to the organization are best addressed by that new approach

After all of the SDN-related discussions that have occurred over the last couple of years, the following have emerged as the most likely set of opportunities that SDN can address Support the dynamic movement, replication and allocation of virtual resources;

1. Ease the administrative burden of the configuration and provisioning of functionality;
2. such as QoS and security;
3. More easily deploy and scale network functionality;
4. Perform traffic engineering with an end-to-end view of the network;
5. Better utilize network resources;
6. Reduce OPEX;
7. Have network functionality evolve more rapidly based on a software development lifecycle;
8. Enable applications to dynamically request services from the   network;
9. Implement more effective security functionality;
10. Reduce complexity

Software Defined Networking

The Open Networking Foundation (ONF) is the group that is most associated with the development and standardization of SDN. According to the ONF, "Software-Defined Networking (SDN) is an emerging architecture that is dynamic, manageable, cost-effective, and adaptable, making it ideal for the high-bandwidth, dynamic nature of today's applications. This architecture decouples the network control and forwarding functions enabling the network control to become directly programmable and the underlying infrastructure to be abstracted for applications and network services. The OpenFlow™ protocol is a foundational element for building SDN solutions."

According to the ONF, the SDN architecture is :

- Directly programmable: Network control is directly programmable because it is decoupled from forwarding functions.
- Agile: Abstracting control from forwarding lets administrators dynamically adjust network-wide traffic flow to meet changing   needs.
- Centrally managed: Network intelligence is (logically) centralized in software-based SDN controllers that maintain a global view of the network, which appears to applications and policy engines as a single, logical switch.
- Programmatically configured: SDN lets network managers configure, manage, secure, and optimize network resources very quickly via dynamic, automated SDN programs, which they can write themselves because the programs do not depend on proprietary   software.
- Open standards-based and vendor-neutral: When implemented through open standards, SDN simplifies network design and operation because instructions are provided by SDN controllers instead of multiple, vendor-specific devices and protocols.

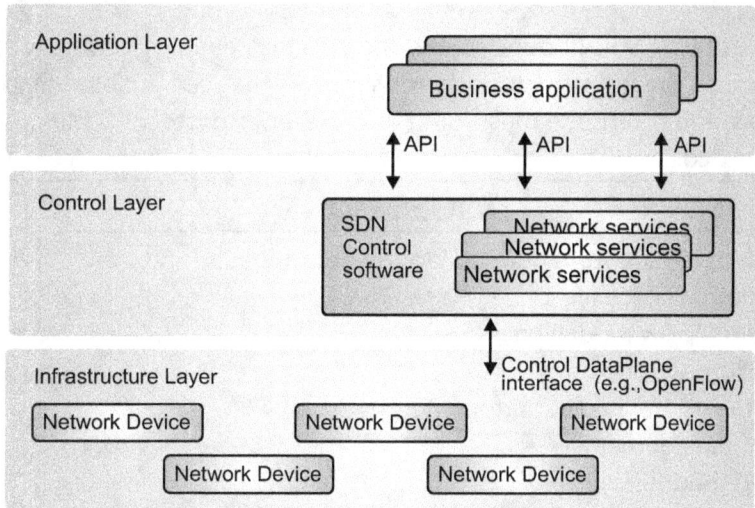

Fig. 5.11 : The SDN system Architecture

Below is a description of some of the key concepts that are part of the SDN system architecture that is shown in Fig. 5.11.

Business Applications

This refers to applications that are directly consumable by end users. Possibilities include video conferencing, supply chain management and customer relationship management.

Network and Security Services

This refers to functionality that enables business applications to perform efficiently and securely. Possibilities include a wide range of L4 – L7 functionality including ADCs, WOCs and security capabilities such as firewalls, IDS/IPS and DDoS protection.

Pure SDN Switch

In a pure SDN switch, all of the control functions of a traditional switch (i.e., routing protocols that are used to build forwarding information bases) are run in the central controller. The functionality in the switch is restricted entirely to the data plane.

Hybrid Switch

In a hybrid switch, SDN technologies and traditional switching protocols run simultaneously. A network manager can configure the SDN controller to discover and control certain traffic flows while traditional, distributed networking protocols continue to direct the rest of the traffic on the network.

Hybrid Network

A hybrid network is a network in which traditional switches and SDN switches, whether they are pure SDN switches or hybrid switches, operate in the same   environment.

Northbound API

Relative to Fig. 5.11, the northbound API is the API that enables communications between the control layer and the business application layer. There is currently not a standards-based northbound API

Southbound API

Relative to Fig. 5.11, the southbound API is the API that enables communications between the control layer and the infrastructure layer. Protocols that can enable this communications include OpenFlow, the extensible messaging and presence protocol (XMPP) and the network configuration protocol.

QUESTIONS

1. Explain architecture for federated cloud computing.
2. Explain cloud service life-cycle phases
3. Explain work-flow modelling.
4. Write short note on :
   (a) Performance prediction for HPC on Cloud
   (b) SLA management
   (c) SOAP and REST
   (d) Software defined approach and techniques for managing IT resources

SECURITY IN CLOUD COMPUTING

6.1 INTRODUCTION

- Cloud evolution can be considered synonymous to banking system evolution. Earlier people used to keep all their money, movable assets (precious metals, stones etc.) in their personal possessions and even in underground lockers as they thought that depositing their hard earned money with bank can be disastrous.
- Banking system evolved over the period of time. Legal and security process compliances protected by Law played a big role in making banking and financial systems trustworthy.
- Now, people hardly keep any cash with them
- Most of us carry plastic money and transact digitally, cloud computing is also evolving the same way.
- Robust cloud architecture with strong security implementation at all layers in the stack powered with legal compliances and government protection is the key to cloud security.
- As Banks didn't vanish despite frauds, thefts and malpractices, cloud security is going to get evolved but as much faster rate. Digital world has zero tolerance for waiting. Evolution is natural and is bound to happen.
- So what are the steps typically a cloud service provider should follow in order to secure its cloud?
- Cloud is complex and hence security measures are not simple too. Cloud needs to be secured at all layers in its stack. Let's briefly look into major areas.

6.1.1 At Platform Level

Security model at this level relies more on the provider to maintain data integrity and availability. Platform must take care of following security aspects :
- Integrity.
- Confidentiality.
- Authentication.
- Defence against intrusion and DDoS attack.
- SLA.

6.1.2 At Application Level

The following key security elements should be carefully considered as an integral part of the SaaS application development and deployment process :

SaaS Deployment Model

- Data security.
- Network security.
- Regulatory compliance.
- Data segregation.
- Availability.
- Backup/Recovery procedure.
- Identity management and sign-on process.

Most of the above are provided by PaaS and hence optimal utilization of PaaS in modeling SaaS is very important.

Some of the steps which can be taken to make SaaS secured are :

- Secure product engineering.
- Secure deployment.
- Governance and regulatory compliance audits.
- Third-Party SaaS Security Assessment.

6.1.3 At Infrastructure Level

A system administrator of the cloud provider can attack the systems since he/she has got all the admin rights. With root privileges at each machine, the system administrator can install or execute all sorts of software to perform an attack. Furthermore, with physical access to the machine, a system administrator can perform more sophisticated attacks like cold boot attacks and even tamper with the hardware.

Protection Measures

- No single person should accumulate all these privileges.
- Provider should deploy stringent security devices, restricted access control policies, and surveillance mechanisms to protect the physical integrity of the hardware.
- Thus, we assume that, by enforcing a security processes, the provider itself can prevent attacks that require physical access to the machines.
- The only way a sysadmin would be able to gain physical access to a node running a costumer's VM is by diverting this VM to a machine under his/her control, located outside the IaaS's security perimeter. Therefore, the cloud computing platform must be able to confine the VM execution inside the perimeter, and guarantee that at any point a sysadmin with root privileges remotely logged to a machine hosting a VM cannot access its memory.
- TCG (Trusted Computing Group), a consortium of industry leader to identify and implement security measures at infrastructure level proposes a set of hardware and software technologies to enable the construction of trusted platforms suggests use of "remote attestation" (a mechanism to detect changes to the user's computers by authorized parties).

6.2 GLOBAL RISK COMPLIANCE ASPECTS

6.2.1 Global, Risk, and Compliance (GRC)

CSPs are typically challenged to meet the requirements of a diverse client base. To build a sustainable model, it is essential that the CSP establish a strong foundation of controls that can be applied to all of its clients. In that regard, the CSP can use the concept of GRC that has been adopted by a number of leading traditional outsourced service providers and CSPs. GRC recognizes that compliance is not a point-in-time activity, but rather is an ongoing process that requires a formal compliance program. Figure 6.1 depicts such a programmatic approach to compliance.

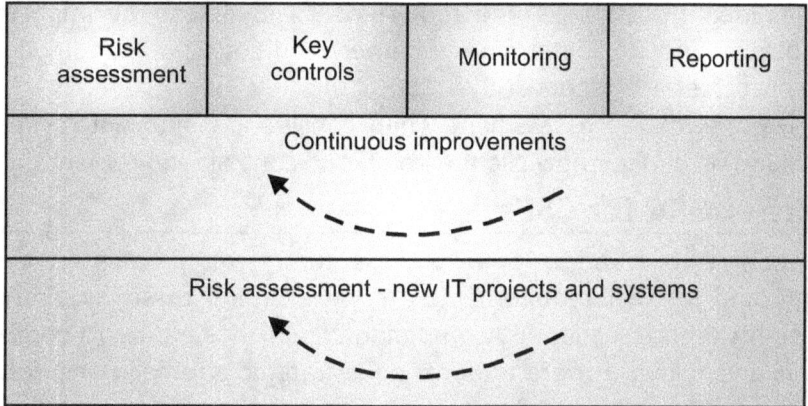

Fig. 6.1 : A programmatic approach to compliance

Key components of this approach include :

1. **Risk Assessment**

   This approach begins with an assessment of the risks that face the CSP and identification of the specific compliance regimes/requirements that are applicable to the CSP's services. The CSP should address risks associated with key areas such as appropriate user authentication mechanisms for accessing the cloud, encryption of sensitive data and associated key management controls, logical separation of customer's data, and CSP administrative access.

2. **Key Controls**

   Key controls are then identified and documented to address the identified risks and compliance requirements. These key controls are captured in a unified control set that is designed to meet the requirements of the CSP's customers and other external requirements. The CSP drives compliance activities based on its key controls rather than disparate sets of externally generated compliance requirements.

3. **Monitoring**

   Monitoring and testing processes are defined and executed on an ongoing basis for key controls. Gaps requiring remediation are identified with remediation progress tracked.

   The results of ongoing monitoring activities may also be used to support any required external audits.

4. **Reporting**

   Metrics and Key Performance Indicators (KPIs) are defined and reported on an ongoing basis. Reports of control effectiveness and trending are made available to CSP management and external customers as appropriate.

5. **Continuous Improvement**

   Management improves its controls over time acting swiftly to address any significant gaps identified during the course of monitoring and taking advantage of opportunities to improve processes and controls.

6. **Risk Assessment New IT Projects and Systems**

   The CSP performs a risk assessment as new IT projects, systems, and services are developed to identify new risks and requirements, to assess the impact on the CSP's current controls, and to determine whether additional or modified controls and monitoring processes are needed.

   The CSP also performs an assessment when considering entry into a new industry or market or taking on a major new client with unique control requirements.

6.2.2 Benefits of GRC for CSPs

- CSPs must adhere to a variety of IT process control requirements including external requirements and internal requirements. As we examine these requirements, we find numerous points of intersection. By combining compliance efforts to address all of these requirements and taking a more uniform and strategic approach, increased efficiencies and compliance can be attained. Instead of performing control review and testing cycles separately, control language and testing can be structured to address the needs of multiple sets of requirements. Therefore, control review and testing need to be completed only once to meet the demands of multiple sets of requirements.

- This strategic approach results in a decreased level of effort to meet control requirements and increased compliance due to the control language being defined in a more efficient manner to support many compliance needs. CSPs often struggle to meet the many demands of compliance requirements. These efforts are often in silos, unstructured, and reactive in nature. Repeatedly non-compliant controls are discovered during the course of an audit or as a result of a security incident. By implementing a structured compliance program and organization, significant benefits can be deriving.

- Achieving periodic silos of compliance mostly as a result of third-party reviews will be replaced by an ongoing focus on compliance to increase overall IT process compliance in a more efficient manner.

- The use of KPIs and compliance based risk assessments will provide valuable insight into areas of IT control weaknesses. Improved visibility into IT control weaknesses can greatly enhance decision making for new investments, placing precious resources where there is the greatest need. Continuous controls monitoring will be performed to shift from a detective approach discovering compliance failures to a more preventive approach of regularly reviewing control effectiveness and thereby avoiding compliance failures before they can occur. With proactive compliance management performed by control and compliance subject matter professionals, control changes required through the introduction of new regulations, threats, and IT systems can be more smoothly managed and integrated into the control environment.

Compliance benefits can be further extended by more effectively using automation to improve control compliance.

A GRC approach helps a CSP to :

- Reduce risks through a structured risk management approach.
- Improve monitoring of IT compliance.
- Improve security.
- Rationalize compliance requirements and control assessment processes.
- Reduce the burden of compliance monitoring and testing.

6.2.3 Auditing the Cloud for Compliance

- When it comes to auditing cloud computing against the compliance requirements discussed earlier, there are two perspectives that must be dealt with. First is what your organization's internal audit department's expectations are for meeting requirements, as well as, of course, the expectations that your external auditors have with regard to meeting requirements.

- The "Right to Audit" (RTA) clause is often used in outsourcing contracts to ensure that clients can conduct audits for various assurance reasons. In the case of a CSP, the RTA can be applied. Customers need to define the scope of the RTA. For example, customers should validate service level performances, the security of data-at-rest, and the physical security of the data center. However, due to multitenancy and shared logical environment, it becomes difficult to conduct an audit without the CSP breaching the confidentiality of other tenants sharing the infrastructure. In such cases, the CSP should adopt a compliance program based on standards such as ISO 27001 and provide assurance via SysTrust or ISO certification to its customers.

6.2.4 Internal Audit Perspective

- A programmatic approach to compliance is particularly important in a cloud computing environment as the impact of a control failure could be quite severe. The CSP cannot afford to wait until the annual external audit to determine whether controls have operated effectively during the past year, because of the increased potential for control failures impacting multiple customers.

- Key controls must be identified early on and proactively monitored so that any potential issues can be investigated and addressed in a timely manner. For example, a failure to detect errors in the automated system configuration and activity logging processes on a near-real-time basis could lead to system downtime, breached security, or data loss. Although controls should be designed to prevent the occurrence of such issues, near-real-time detection and rapid correction of any such issues will go a long way toward demonstrating the CSP's commitment to security and continuous improvement.

- Combined with an emphasis on automated preventive controls, proactive monitoring of key controls will help the CSP to make risk-based IT investment decisions, meet its customer commitments, and at least keep pace with emerging developments. Whether control monitoring activities are performed by the internal audit department, the information security function, the IT organization, or a combination thereof, it is important that a disciplined approach be implemented.

6.2.5 External Audit Perspective

- An external audit of the CSP will likely be required for customers to gain comfort in the effectiveness of the CSP's controls. Historically, a variety of audit frameworks have been used to assess the controls of outsourced service providers, including CSPs. Although some CSPs have been completing such external audits for five or more years, an increasing number of CSPs are now initiating external audits for the first time in response to increasing market pressure. Audit of controls based on control objectives and control activities (defined by the service provider). Auditor opinion on the design, operational status, and operating effectiveness of controls. Intended to cover services that are relevant for purposes of customer's financial statement audits.

- **SysTrust**

Audit of controls based on defined principles and criteria for security, availability, confidentiality, and processing integrity. Intended to apply to the reliability of any system.

- **WebTrust**

Audit of controls based on defined principles and criteria for security, availability, confidentiality, processing integrity, and privacy. Intended to apply to online/e-commerce systems.

- **ISO 27001**

Audit of an organization's Information Security Management System (ISMS), as defined in documented ISMS.

6.2.6 Defining Security in the Cloud

- If we wish to enable cloud-driven growth and innovation through security, we must have a clear framing on what is meant by security.
- Security has been notoriously hard to define in the general case. The canonical goals of information security are Confidentiality, Integrity, and Availability.
- We borrow from NIST to include Accountability and Assurance, and then add a sixth category of Resilience.
- We define these terms below and map them to the cloud context, with a few examples of how they can be supported by both technical and non-technical mechanisms.
- **Confidentiality** refers to keeping data private. Privacy is of amount importance as data leaves the borders of the organization. Not only must internal secrets and sensitive personal data be safeguarded, but metadata and transactional data can also leak important details about firms or individuals. Confidentiality is supported by, among other things, technical tools such as encryption and access control, as well as legal protections.

- **Integrity** is a degree confidence that the data in the cloud is what is supposed to be there, and is protected against accidental or intentional alteration without authorization. It also extends to the hurdles of synchronizing multiple databases. Integrity is supported by well audited code, well-designed distributed systems, and robust access control mechanisms.

- **Availability** means being able to use the system as anticipated. Cloud technologies can increase availability through widespread internet-enabled access, but the client is dependent on the timely and robust provision of resources. Availability is supported by capacity building and good architecture by the provider, as well as well-defined contracts and terms of agreement.

- **Accountability** maps actions in the system to responsible parties. Inside the cloud, actions must be traced uniquely back to an entity, allowing for integration into organizational processes, conflict resolution and deterrence of bad behaviour. Accountability is supported by robust identity, authentication and access control, as well as the ability to log transactions and then, critically, audit these logs.

- **Assurance** refers to the need for a system to behave as expected. In the cloud context, it is important that the cloud provider provides what the client has specified. This is not simply a matter of the software and hardware behaving as the client expects but that the needs of the organization are understood, and that these needs are accurately translated into information architecture requirements, which are then faithfully implemented in the cloud system. Assurance is supported by a trusted computing architecture in the cloud, and a by careful processes mapping from business case to technical details to legal agreements.

- **Resilience** in a system allows it to cope with security threats, rather than failing critically. Cloud technology can increase resilience, with a broader base, backup data and systems, and the potential identify threats and dynamically counteract. However, by shifting critical systems and functions to an outside party, organizations can aggravate resilience by introducing a single point of failure. Resilience is supported by redundancy, diversification and real-time forensic capacity.

6.2.7 Security Issues Associated with the Cloud

- There is number of security issues/concerns associated with cloud computing but these issues fall into two broad categories : Security issues faced by cloud providers (organizations providing Software, Platform, or Infrastructure-as-a-Service via the cloud) and security issues faced by their customers.

- In most cases, the provider must ensure that their infrastructure is secure and that their clients data and applications are protected while the customer must ensure that the provider has taken the proper security measures to protect their information.

- The extensive use of virtualization in implementing cloud infrastructure brings unique security concerns for customers or tenants of a public cloud service. Virtualization alters the relationship between the OS and underlying hardware - be it computing, storage or even networking.

- This introduces an additional layer virtualization that itself must be properly configured, managed and secured. Specific concerns include the potential to compromise the virtualization software, or "hypervisor". While these concerns are largely theoretical, they do exist.

6.2.8 Dimensions of Cloud Security

Correct security controls should be implemented according to asset, threat, and vulnerability risk assessment matrices. While cloud security concerns can be grouped into any number of dimensions these dimensions have been aggregated into three general areas :

- Security and Privacy.
- Compliance.
- Legal or Contractual Issues.

6.2.9 Security and Privacy

In order to ensure that data is secure (that it cannot be accessed by unauthorized users or simply lost) and that data privacy is maintained, cloud providers attend to the following areas

- **Data Protection**

  To be considered protected, data from one customer must be properly segregated from that of another, it must be stored securely when "at rest" and it must be able to move securely from one location to another. Cloud providers have systems in place to prevent data leaks or access by third parties. Proper separation of duties should ensure that auditing or monitoring cannot be defeated, even by privileged users at the cloud provider.

- **Physical Control**

  Physical control of the private cloud equipment is more secure than having the equipment off site and under someone else's control. Having the ability to visually inspect the data links and access ports is required in order to ensure data links are not compromised.

- **Identity Management**

  Every enterprise will have its own identity management system to control access to information and computing resources. Cloud providers either integrate the customer's identity management system into their own infrastructure, using federation or SSO technology, or provide an identity management solution of their own.

- **Physical and Personnel Security**

  Providers ensure that physical machines are adequately secure and that access to these machines as well as all relevant customer data is not only restricted but that access is documented.

- **Availability**

  Cloud providers assure customers that they will have regular and predictable access to their data and applications.

- **Application Security**

  Cloud providers ensure that applications available as a service via the cloud are secure by implementing testing and acceptance procedures for outsourced or packaged application code. It also requires application security measures (application-level firewalls) be in place in the production environment.

- **Privacy**

  Finally, providers ensure that all critical data (credit card numbers, for example) are masked and that only authorized users have access to data in its entirety. Moreover, digital identities and credentials must be protected as should any data that the provider collects or produces about customer activity in the cloud.

- **Legal Issues**

  In addition, providers and customers must consider legal issues, such as Contracts and E-Discovery, and the related laws, which may vary by country.

6.2.10 Compliance

Numerous regulations pertain to the storage and use of data, including Payment Card Industry Data Security Standard (PCI DSS), the Health Insurance Portability and Accountability Act (HIPAA), the Sarbanes-Oxley Act, among others. Many of these regulations require regular reporting and audit trails. Cloud providers must enable their customers to comply appropriately with these regulations.

- **Business Continuity and Data Recovery**

  Cloud providers have business continuity and data recovery plans in place to ensure that service can be maintained in case of a disaster or an emergency and that any data loss will be recovered. These plans are shared with and reviewed by their customers.

- **Logs and Audit Trails**

  In addition to producing logs and audit trails, cloud providers work with their customers to ensure that these logs and audit trails are properly secured, maintained for as long as the customer requires, and are accessible for the purposes of forensic investigation (e.g., discovery).

- **Unique Compliance Requirements**

  In addition to the requirements to which customers are subject, the data canters maintained by cloud providers may also be subject to compliance requirements. Using a Cloud Service Provider (CSP) can lead to additional security concerns around data jurisdiction since customer or tenant data may not remain on the same system, or in the same data center or even within the same provider's cloud.

6.2.11 Legal and Contractual Issues

Aside from the security and compliance issues enumerated above, cloud providers and their customers will negotiate terms around liability (stipulating how incidents involving data loss or compromise will be resolved, for example), intellectual property, and end-of-service (when data and applications are ultimately returned to the customer.

6.2.12 Cloud Security Guidance

As consumers transition their applications and data to use cloud computing, it is critically important that the level of security provided in the cloud environment be equal to or better than the security provided by their traditional IT environment. Failure to ensure appropriate security protection could ultimately result in higher costs and potential loss of business thus eliminating any of the potential benefits of cloud computing.

This section provides a prescriptive series of steps that should be taken by cloud consumers to evaluate and manage the security of their cloud environment with the goal of mitigating risk and delivering an appropriate level of support. The following steps are discussed in detail :

1. Ensure effective governance, risk and compliance processes exist.
2. Audit operational and business processes.
3. Manage people, roles and identities.
4. Ensure proper protection of data and information.
5. Enforce privacy policies.
6. Assess the security provisions for cloud applications.
7. Ensure cloud networks and connections are secure.
8. Evaluate security controls on physical infrastructure and facilities.
9. Manage security terms in the cloud SLA.
10. Understand the security requirements of the exit process.

6.2.13 Cloud Security Assessment

The critical questions that cloud consumers should ask themselves and their cloud providers during each step of the security assessment are highlighted in Table 6.1.

Table 6.1 : Steps of the security assessment

Security Steps	Assessment Questions
1. **Ensure effective governance, risk and compliance processes exist**	Does the consumer have governance and compliance processes in place for the use of cloud services?
	Does the provider have appropriate governance and notification processes for their services, as required by the consumer?
	Is it clear what legal and regulatory controls apply to the provider's services?

...Conti

2.	**Audit and ensure proper reporting of operational and business processes**	Is audit information available for the provider services? Does the audit information conform to one of the accepted standards for security audit such as ISO 27001?
		Does the provider have mechanisms in place to provide reporting for both normal or exception behavior relating to their services?
		Is it clear that the provider's management interfaces (for use by consumers) have adequate security controls in place?
		Is there an Incident Reporting and Incident Handling process that meets the needs of the consumer?
3.	**Manage people, roles and identities**	Do the provider services offer fine grained access control?
		Is single sign-on possible with the provider's services?
		Can the provider give reports for monitoring user access?
		Is it possible to integrate consumer identity management with the provider's services ?
4.	**Ensure proper protection of data and information**	Is there a data asset catalog for all data which will be used or stored in the cloud environment?
		Is there a description of responsible parties and roles?
		Has the handling of all forms of data been considered, in particular unstructured data such as images?
		For structured data held in databases within the cloud provider's environment, is there proper separation of data belonging to different consumers in a multi-tenant environment?
		Has appropriate confidentiality, integrity and availability been applied to data used or stored in the cloud environment?

...Conti

5.	Enforce privacy policies	Is PII going to be stored/processed by the cloud services?
		Do the provider's services have appropriate controls in place for handling PII?
		Are responsibilities for handling PII stated in the SLA?
		If there is a security breach, are responsibilities for reporting and resolving the breach clear, including priorities and timescales?
6.	Assess the security provisions for cloud applications	Is it clear whether responsibility for applications running on cloud infrastructure lies with the consumer or with the provider?
		Where the responsibility lies with the consumer, does the consumer have governance and policies in place that ensure the appropriate security provisions are applied to each application?
		Where the responsibility lies with the provider, does the SLA make the provider's responsibilities clear and require specific security provisions to be applied to each application and all data?
7.	Ensure cloud networks and connections are secure	Is network traffic screened?
		Does the provider's network have intrusion detection and prevention in place?
		Does the network provide the consumer with logging and notification?
		Is there separation of network traffic in a shared multi-tenant provider environment?
		Is consumer network access separated from provider network access?
8.	Evaluate security controls on physical infrastructure and facilities	Can the cloud service provider demonstrate appropriate security controls applied to their physical infrastructure and facilities?
		Does the service provider have facilities in place to ensure continuity of service in the face of environmental threats or equipment failures?
		Does the cloud service provider have necessary security controls on their human resources?

...Conti

9. **Manage security terms in the cloud SLA**	Does the cloud SLA specify security responsibilities of the provider and of the consumer?
	Does the SLA require that all security terms must also pass down to any peer cloud service providers used by the provider?
	Does the SLA have metrics for measuring performance and effectiveness of security management?
	Does the SLA explicitly document procedures for notification and handing of security incidents?
10. **Understand the security requirements of the exit process**	Is there a documented exit process as part of the contract/SLA?
	Is it clear that all consumer data is deleted from the provider's

6.2.14 Traditional Security Challenges

Although the security concerns in traditional communication systems also apply to the cloud, the use of cloud computing introduces new attack vectors that will make attacks either possible or simply easier to carry out. Some of the traditional security issues which also affect the SaaS model have been described below :

1. Authentication and Authorization

The authentication and authorization applications for enterprise environments may need to be changed, to work with a safe cloud environment. Forensics tasks may become much more difficult since the investigators may not be able to access system hardware physically. The design proposed allows user to use a single set of credentials. They have proposed a solution with de-facto standards of open authorization in which there is a trust party auditor which maintains all the credentials and cloud provider can uniquely distinguish one user from other. The model verifies user authenticity using two-step verification, which is based on password, smartcard and out of band (i.e. strong two factors) authentication. In addition, the scheme also provides mutual authentication, identity management, session key establishment, user privacy and security against many popular attacks, however the formal security proofing hasn't yet been formalized.

2. Availability

- The availability ensures the reliable and timely access to cloud data or cloud computing resources by the appropriate personnel. The availability of cloud service providers is also a big concern, since if the cloud service is disrupted, it affects more customers than in the traditional model. For instance, the recent disruption of the Amazon cloud service in the year 2011, took down a number of websites including Reddit, Foursquare, and Quora.

The SaaS application providers are required to ensure that the systems are running properly when needed and enterprises are provided with services around the clock.

- This involves making architectural changes at the application and infrastructural levels to add scalability and high availability. Resiliency to hardware/software failures, as well as to denial of service attacks, needs to be built from the ground up within the application. At the same time, an appropriate action plan for business continuity and Disaster Recovery (DR) needs to be considered for any exigencies. This is essential to ensure the safety of the enterprise data while maintaining minimal downtime for the enterprises.

- With Amazon for instance, the Amazon Web Services (AWS) API end points are hosted on the same Internet-scale, world-class infrastructure that supports the Amazon retail site. Standard Distributed Denial of Service (DDoS) mitigation techniques such as synchronous cookies and connection limiting are used. To further mitigate the effect to potential DDoS attacks, Amazon maintains internal bandwidth that exceeds its provider supplied Internet bandwidth.

3. Data Confidentiality

- Confidentiality refers to the prevention of intentional or unintentional unauthorized disclosure of information. Confidentiality in cloud system is related to the areas of intellectual property rights, covert channels, traffic analysis, encryption, and inference. Cloud computing involves the sharing or storage of information on remote servers owned or operated by others, while accessing through the Internet or any other connections.

- Cloud computing services exist in many variations, including data storage sites, video sites, tax preparation sites, personal health record websites and many more. The entire contents of a user's storage device may be stored with a single cloud provider or with multiple cloud providers. Whenever an individual, a business, a government agency, or any other entity shares information in the cloud, privacy or confidentiality questions arise.

4. Virtual Machine Security

- Although the global adoption of virtualization is a relatively a recent phenomenon, threats to the virtualized infrastructure are evolving just as quickly. The hypervisor and virtual machines used in cloud providers may also have vulnerabilities. Such vulnerabilities represent an even more serious problem in multi-tenant environments, where compromise of even a single virtual machine can affect all users on the same physical server.

- Virtualization is one of the main components of a cloud. But this poses major security risks. Ensuring that different instances running on the same physical machine are isolated from each other is a major task of virtualization which is not met completely in today's scenario. The other issue is the control of administrator on host and guest operating systems. Current Virtual Machine Monitor (VMMs) do not offer perfect isolation. Many bugs have been found in all popular VMMs that allow escaping from VM.

Virtual machine monitor should be 'root secure', meaning that no privilege within the virtualized guest environment permits interference with the host system. Some vulnerability has been found in all virtualization software which can be exploited by malicious, local users to bypass certain security restrictions or gain privileges. For example, the vulnerability of Microsoft Virtual PC and Microsoft Virtual Server could allow a guest operating system user to run code on the host or another guest operating system. Vulnerability in Virtual PC and Virtual Server could allow elevation of privilege. Cloud providers, therefore, might need to reconsider traditional security concerns from different angles. Fig 6.2 shows that security issues in SAAS.

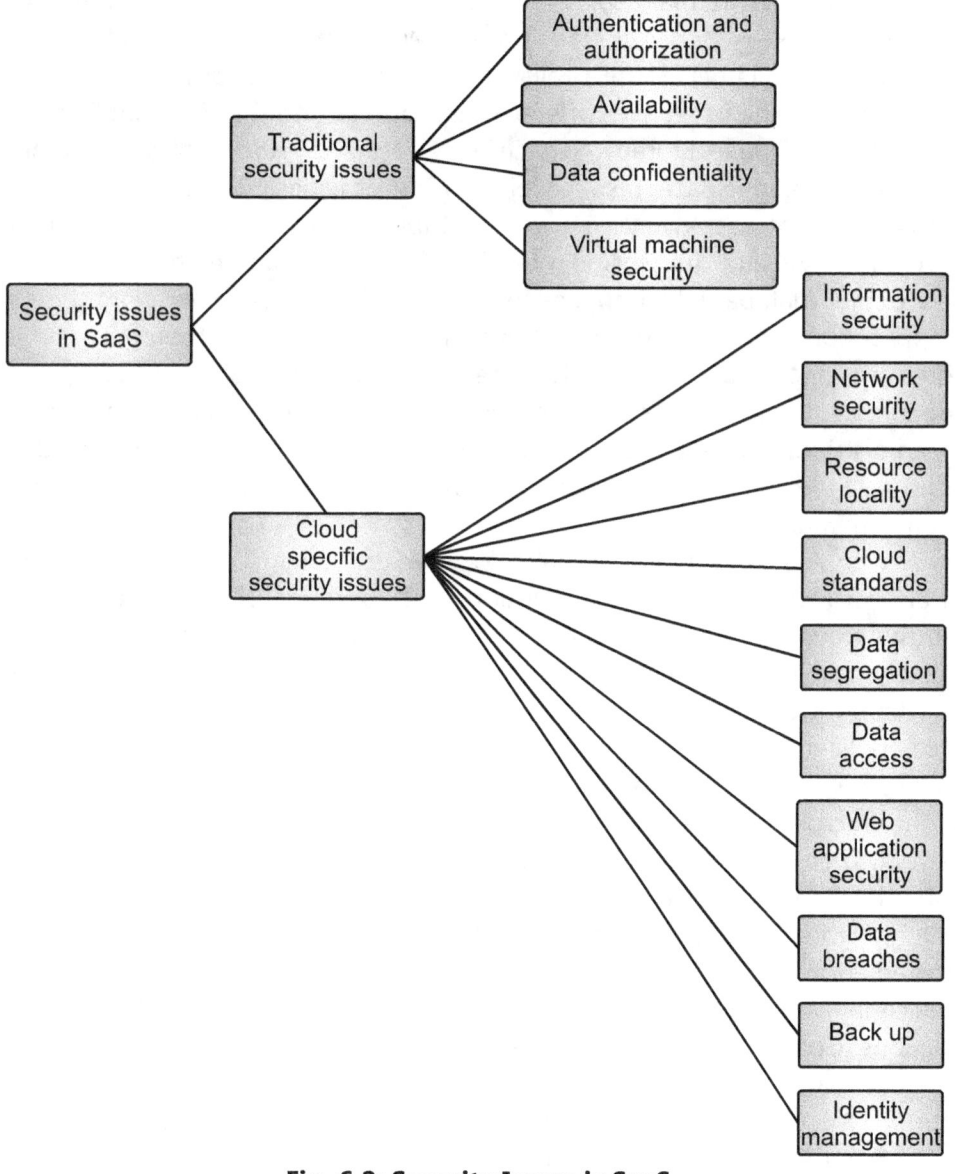

Fig. 6.2: Security Issues in SaaS

6.3 TECHNOLOGY FOR DATA SECURITY

- Cloud computing covers the entire computing stack from hardware infra-structure to end-user software applications. Hence, there are heterogeneous offerings addressing different niches of the market. In this section we will concentrate mostly on the Infrastructure as a Service (IaaS) and Platform as a Service (PaaS) implementations of the cloud computing model by first presenting a subset of the most representative commercial solutions and then discussing the few research projects and platforms, which attracted considerable attention.

- Amazon is probably the major player for what concerns the Infrastructure as a Service solutions in the case of public clouds. Amazon Web Services deliver a set of services that, when composed together, form a reliable, scalable, and economically accessible cloud. Within the wide range of services offered, it is worth noting that Amazon Elastic Compute Cloud (EC2) and Simple Storage Service allow users to quickly obtain virtual compute resources and storage space, respectively. GoGrid provides customer with a similar offer: it allows users to deploy their own distributed system on top of their virtual infrastructure. By using the GoGrid Web interface users can create their custom virtual images, deploy database and application servers, and mount new storage volumes for their applications. Both GoGrid and Amazon EC2 charge their customers on a pay-as-you-go basis, and resources are priced per hours of usage. 3Tera AppLogic lays at the foundation of many public clouds, it provides a grid operating system that includes workload distribution, metering, and management of applications. These are described in a platform- independent manner, and AppLogic takes care of deploying and scaling them on demand.

- Together with AppLogic, which can also be used to manage and deploy private clouds, 3Tera also provides cloud hosting solutions and, because of its grid operating system, makes the transition from the private to the public virtual infrastructure simple and completely transparent. Solutions that are completely based on a PaaS approach for public clouds are Microsoft Azure and Google AppEngine. Azure allows developing scalable applications for the cloud. It is a cloud services operating system that serves as the development, Runtime, and control environment for the Azure Services Platform. By using the Microsoft Azure SDK, developers can create services that leverage the .NET framework. These services are then uploaded to the Microsoft Azure portal and executed on top of Windows Azure. Additional services such as workflow management and execution, web services orchestration, and SQL data storage are provided to empower the hosted applications. Azure customers are billed on a pay-per-use basis and by taking into account the different services: compute, storage, bandwidth, and storage transactions. Google AppEngine is a development platform and a runtime environment focusing primarily on web applications that will be run on top of Google's server infrastructure. It provides a set of APIs and an application model   that allow developers to take advantage of additional services provided by Google such as Mail, Datastore,

Memcache, and others. Developers can create applications in Java, Python, and JRuby. These applications will be run within a sandbox, and AppEngine will take care of automatically scaling when needed. Google provides a free limited service and utilizes daily and per minute quotas to meter and price applications requiring professional service.

We select to illustrate the unique requirements for cloud computing data security from a few different perspectives :

- **Database Outsourcing and Query Integrity Assurance :** Researchers have pointed out that storing data into and fetching data from devices and machines behind a cloud are essentially a novel form of database outsourcing. The technologies of Database Out- sourcing and Query Integrity Assurance on the clouding computing platform.

- **Data Integrity in Untrustworthy Storage :** One of the main challenges that prevent end users from adopting cloud storage services is the fear of losing data or data corruption. It is critical to relieve the user's fear by providing technologies that enable users to check the integrity of their data. It presents two approaches that allow users to detect whether the data has been touched by unauthorized people.

- **Web-Application-Based Security :** Once the dataset is stored remotely, a Web browser is one of the most convenient approaches that end users can use to access their data on remote services. In the era of cloud computing, Web security plays a more important role than ever. The most important concerns in Web security and analyzes a couple of widely used attacks.

- **Multimedia Data Security :** With the development of high-speed network technologies and large bandwidth connections, more and more multi-media data are being stored and shared in cyber space. The security requirements for video, audio, pictures, or images are different from other applications.

6.3.1 Authentications and Identity

- Maintaining confidentiality, integrity, and availability for data security is a function of the correct application and configuration of familiar network, system, and application security mechanisms at various levels in the cloud infrastructure.
- Authentication of users takes several forms, but all are based on a combination of authentication factors: something an individual knows (such as a password), something they possess (such as a security token), or some measurable quality that is intrinsic to them (such as a fingerprint).

6.3.2 Applications of Encryption for Data in Motion

- Encryption is used to assure that if there was a breach of communication integrity between the two parties that the data remains confidential.
- Authentication is used to assure that the parties communicating data are who they say they are.
- Common means of authentication themselves employ cryptography in various ways.

6.3.3 Data Masking

- Data masking is a technique that is intended to remove all identifiable and distinguishing characteristics from data in order to render it anonymous and yet still be operable.
- This technique is aimed at reducing the risk of exposing sensitive information.
- Data masking has also been known by such names as data obfuscation, de-identification, or depersonalization

6.3.4 Advantages

- Reduces the exposure of sensitive data.
- Simplifies security auditing and testing.
- Enables automated security management.
- Improves redundancy and disaster recovery.
- Access to highly qualified IT security personnel.
- Prevent or curtail viruses and malware infection.
- Secure sensitive or confidential information in motion.
- Achieve compliance with leading self-regulatory frameworks.
- Conduct training and awareness for all system users.
- In contrast, cloud providers are least confident about the following security requirements.
- Identify and authenticate users before granting access.
- Secure vendor relationships before sharing information assets.
- Prevent or curtail external attacks.
- Encrypt sensitive or confidential information assets whenever feasible.
- Determine the root cause of cyber attacks.

6.3.5 Platforms

- Amazon's Elastic Compute Cloud, or EC2, is probably the most generalized and best known of the cloud computing service offerings.
- IBM Computing on Demand or Blue Cloud is a highly enterprise focused cloud computing offering that, because it is related to and built with the same technology sold to enterprises, can cross over between public and private cloud applications.
- Microsoft's Azure cloud computing, based on Microsoft Vista and .NET technology, includes both cloud computing and cloud-hosted extension.

6.3.6 Cloud Security Architecture

- Cloud application developers and develops have been successfully developing applications for IaaS (Amazon AWS, Rackspace, etc) and PaaS (Azure, Google App Engine, Cloud Foundry) platforms.
- These platforms provide basic security features including support for authentication, DoS attack mitigation, firewall policy management, logging, basic user and profile management but security concerns continue to be the number one barrier for enterprise cloud adoption.

- Cloud security concerns range from securely configuring virtual machines deployed on an IaaS platform to managing user privileges in a PaaS cloud.

- Given that the cloud services can be delivered in many flavors i.e. in any combination of service delivery models, SaaS, PaaS and IaaS (SPI), and operational models, public, private and hybrid, the cloud security concerns and solutions are context (pattern) dependent.

- Hence, the solution architecture should match these concerns and build security safeguards (controls) into the cloud application architecture.

- So what are the architectural frameworks and tools that cloud application architects and develops have at their disposal when developing applications for IaaS and PaaS platforms.

Cloud Security – Shared Responsibility

- First, let's talk about the cloud security operational model. By definition, cloud security responsibilities in a public cloud are shared between the cloud customer (your enterprise) and the cloud service provider where as in a private cloud, the customer is managing all aspects of the cloud platform.

- Cloud service providers are responsible for securing the shared infrastructure including routers, switches, load balancers, firewalls, hypervisors, storage networks, management consoles, DNS, directory services and cloud API.

- The Fig. 6.3 highlights the layers, within a cloud service, that are secured by the provider versus the customer.

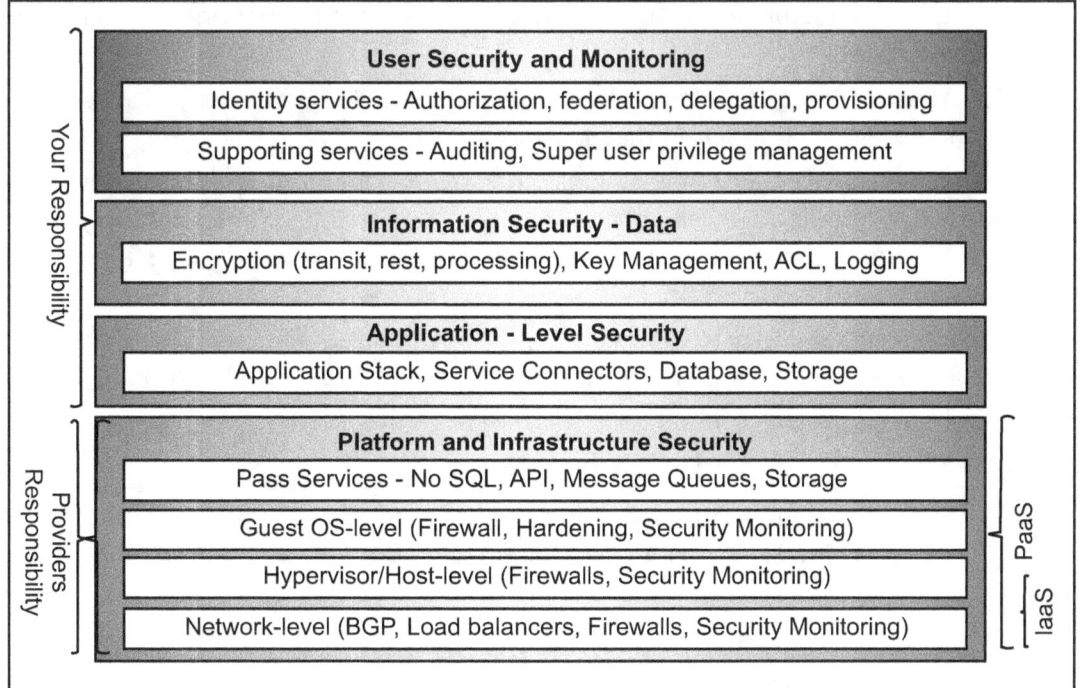

Fig. 6.3 : Cloud security architecture

- Prior to signing up with a provider, it is important to perform a gap analysis on the cloud service capabilities.

- This exercise should benchmark the cloud platform's maturity, transparency, compliance with enterprise security standards (e.g. ISO 27001) and regulatory standards such as PCI DSS, HIPAA and SOX.

- Cloud security maturity models can help accelerate the migration strategy of applications to the cloud. The following are a set of principles you can apply when evaluating a cloud service provider's security maturity :

- **Disclosure of Security Policies, Compliance and Practices:** The cloud service provider should demonstrate compliance with industry standard frameworks such as ISO 27001, SS 16 and CSA Cloud controls matrix. Controls certified by the provider should match control expectations from your enterprise data protection standard standpoint. When cloud services are certified for ISO 27001 or SSAE 16, the scope of controls should be disclosed. Clouds that host regulated data must meet compliance requirements such as PCI DSS, Sarbanes-Oxley and HIPAA.

- **Disclosure when Mandated :** The cloud service provider should disclose relevant data when disclosure is imperative due to legal or regulatory needs.

- **Security Architecture :** The cloud service provider should disclose security architectural details that either help or hinder security management as per the enterprise standard. For example, the architecture of virtualization that guarantees isolation between tenants should be disclosed.

- **Security Automation :** The cloud service provider should support security automation by publishing API(s) (HTTP/SOAP) that support :

  Export and import of security event logs, change management logs, user entitlements (privileges), user profiles, firewall policies, access logs in a XML or enterprise log standard format. Continuous security monitoring including support for emerging standards such as Cloud Audit.

- **Governance and Security Responsibility :** Governance and security management responsibilities of the customer versus those of the cloud provider should be clearly articulated.

6.3.7 Cloud Security Architecture – Plan

As a first step, architects need to understand what security capabilities are offered by cloud platforms (PaaS, IaaS). The Fig. 6.4 illustrates the architecture for building security into cloud services.

- Security offerings and capabilities continue to evolve and vary between cloud providers. Hence you will often discover that security mechanisms such as key management and data encryption will not be available.

- For example : the need for a AES 128 bit encryption service for encrypting security artifacts and keys escrowed to a key management service. For such critical services, one will continue to rely on internal security services.

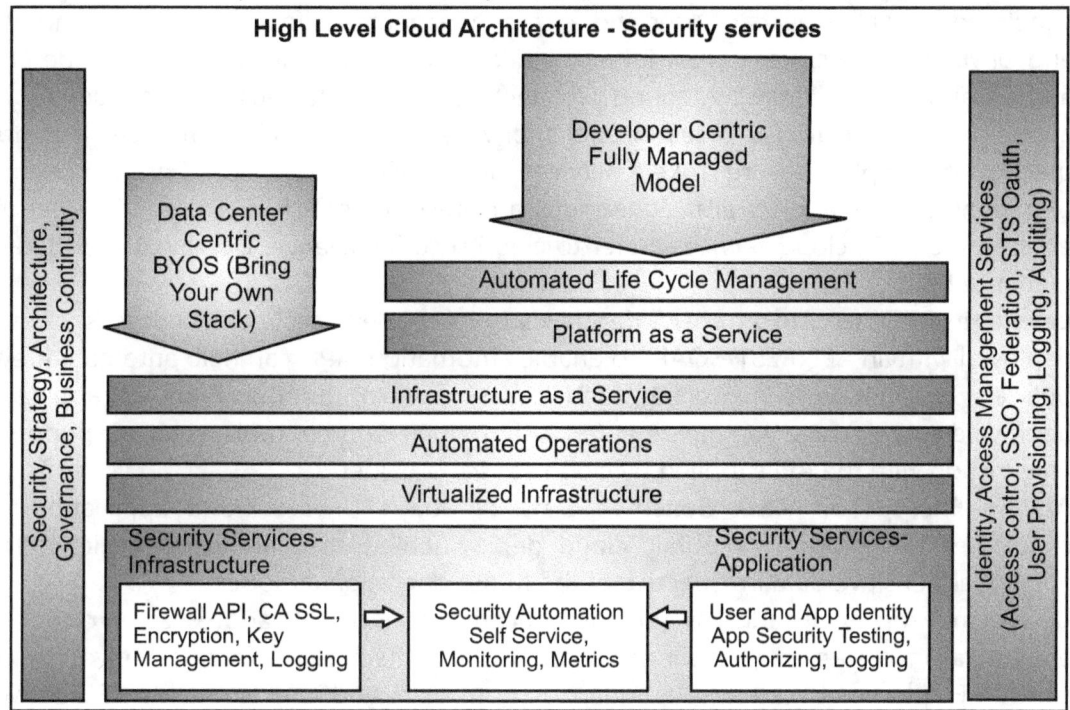

Fig. 6.4 : Cloud security architecture - plan

- A "Hybrid cloud" deployment architecture pattern may be the only viable option for such applications that dependent on internal services. Another common use case is Single Sign-On (SSO).

- SSO implemented within an enterprise may not be extensible to the cloud application unless it is a federation architecture using SAML 1.1 or 2.0 supported by the cloud service provider.

The following are cloud security best practices to mitigate risks to cloud services :

- **Architect for Security-as-a-Service :** Application deployments in the cloud involve orchestration of multiple services including automation of DNS, load balancer, network QoS, etc. Security automation falls in the same category which includes automation of firewall policies between cloud security zones, provisioning of certificates (for SSL), virtual machine system configuration, privileged accounts and log configuration. Application deployment processes that depend on security processes such as firewall policy creation, certificate provisioning, key distribution and application pen testing should be migrated to a self-service model. This approach will eliminate human touch points and will enable a security as a service scenario. Ultimately this will mitigate threats due to human errors, improve operational efficiency and embed security controls into the cloud applications.

- **Implement Sound Identity, Access Management Architecture and Practice :** Scalable cloud bursting and elastic architecture will rely less on network based access controls and warrant strong user access management architecture. Cloud access control architecture should address all aspects of user and access management lifecycles for both end users and privileged users, user provisioning and deprovisioning, authentication, federation, authorization and auditing. A sound architecture will enable reusability of identity and access services for all use cases in public, private and hybrid cloud models. It is good practice to employ secure token services along with proper user and entitlement provisioning with audit trails. Federation architecture is the first step to extending enterprise SSO to cloud services. Refer to cloud security alliance, Domain 12 for detailed guidance here.

- **Leverage APIs to Automate Safeguards :** Any new security services should be deployed with an API (REST/SOAP) to enable automation. APIs can help automate firewall policies, configuration hardening, and access control at the time of application deployment. This can be implemented using open source tools such as puppet in conjunction with the API supplied by cloud service provider.

- **Always Encrypt or Mask Sensitive Data :** Today's private cloud applications are candidates for tomorrow's public cloud deployment. Hence architect applications to encrypt all sensitive data irrespective of the future operational model.

  Do not rely on an IP address for authentication services, IP addresses in clouds are ephemeral in nature so you cannot solely rely on them for enforcing network access control. Employ certificates (self-signed or from a trusted CA) to enable SSL between services deployed on cloud.

- **Log :** Applications should centrally log all security events that will help create an end-to-end transaction view with non-repudiation characteristics. In the event of a security incident, logs and audit trails are the only reliable data leveraged by forensic engineers to investigate and understand how an application was exploited. Clouds are elastic and logs are ephemeral hence it is critical to periodically migrate log files to a different cloud or to the enterprise data center.

- **Continuously Monitor Cloud Services :** Monitoring is an important function given that prevention controls may not meet all the enterprise standards. Security monitoring should leverage logs produced by cloud services, APIs and hosted cloud applications to perform security event correlation. Cloud audit (cloudaudit.org) from CSA can be leveraged towards this mission.

6.4 DATA SECURITY RISK

In today's world of (network-, host-, and application-level) infrastructure Security, data security becomes more important when using cloud computing at all "levels": infrastructure-as-a-service (IaaS), platform-as-a-service (PaaS), and software-as-a-service (SaaS). This chapter describes several aspects of data security, including :

- Data-in-transit
- Data-at-rest

- Processing of data, including multitenancy
- Data lineage
- Data provenance
- Data remanence

The objective of this chapter is to help users evaluate their data security scenarios and make informed judgments regarding risk for their organizations. As with other aspects of cloud computing and security, not all of these data security facets are of equal importance in all topologies (e.g., the use of a public cloud versus a private cloud, or non-sensitive data versus sensitive data).

6.4.1 Aspects of Data Security

- With regard to data-in-transit, the primary risk is in not using a vetted encryption algorithm. Although this is obvious to information security professionals, it is not common for others to understand this requirement when using a public cloud, regardless of whether it is IaaS, PaaS, or SaaS.

- It is also important to ensure that a protocol provides confidentiality as well as integrity (e.g., FTP over SSL [FTPS], Hypertext Transfer Protocol Secure [HTTPS], and Secure Copy Program [SCP]), particularly if the protocol is used for transferring data across the Internet. Merely encrypting data and using a non-secured protocol (e.g., "vanilla" or "straight" FTP or HTTP) can provide confidentiality, but does not ensure the integrity of the data (e.g., with the use of symmetric streaming ciphers).Although using encryption to protect data-at-rest might seem obvious, the reality is not that simple.

- If you are using an IaaS cloud service (public or private) for simple storage (e.g., Amazon's Simple Storage Service or S3), encrypting data-at-rest is possible and is strongly suggested. However, encrypting data-at-rest that a PaaS or SaaS cloud-based application is using (e.g., Google Apps, Salesforce.com) as a compensating control is not always feasible. Data-at-rest used by a cloud-based application is generally not encrypted, because encryption would prevent indexing or searching of that data. Generally speaking, with data-at-rest, the economics of cloud computing are such that PaaS- based applications and SaaS use a multitenancy architecture.

- In other words, data, when processed by a cloud-based application or stored for use by a cloud-based application, is commingled with other user's data (i.e., it is typically stored in a massive data store, such as Google's Big Table). Although applications are often designed with features such as data tagging to prevent unauthorized access to commingled data, unauthorized access is still possible through some exploit of application vulnerability. Although some cloud providers have their applications reviewed by third parties or verified with third-party application security tools, data is not on a platform dedicated solely to one organization. Although an organization's data-in-transit might be encrypted during transfer to and from a cloud provider, and its data-at-rest might be encrypted if using simple storage (i.e., if it is not associated with a specification application), an organization's data is definitely not encrypted, if it is processed in the cloud (public or private).

6.4.2 Protecting Data from Unauthorized Access by the Vendor's Customers

(a) Customer Segregation : What assurance do I have that the virtualization and multi-tenancy mechanisms guarantee adequate logical and network segregation between multiple tenants, so that a malicious customer using the same physical computer as me cannot access my data? For Infrastructure as a Service, the virtualization software used to share hardware and provide each customer with their own operating system environment was typically not originally designed to provide segregation for security purposes. However, the developers of such virtualization software are increasingly focusing their efforts on making their software more suitable for this purpose. What controls are in place to detect and prevent a tenant exploiting a publicly unknown or unpatched vulnerability in a hypervisor? For Software as a Service, the logical separation between customers is usually less well defined, and in some cases the separation mechanism may be retrofitted to an existing software application such as email server or database software. For example, in December 2010 a major vendor of Software as a Service admitted that a configuration mistake caused a security breach that resulted in the exposure of "offline" email address books belonging to customers, and confirmed there was unauthorized access by the vendor's other customers.

(b) Weakening My Security Posture : How would using the vendor's cloud infrastructure weaken my agency's existing network security posture? Would the vendor advertise me as one of their customers without my explicit consent, thereby assisting an adversary that is specifically targeting me? For example, an adversary could use cloud infrastructure from the same vendor used by the target agency, to both serve malicious web content to the agency's users, and to ex-filtration the agency's sensitive data. This may enable an adversary to circumvent the agency's use of security technologies such as whitelisting which domains and IP address ranges can be accessed, and which web sites can run active content such as JavaScript in the web browser.

(c) Dedicated Servers : Do I have some control over which physical computer runs my virtual machines? Can I pay extra to ensure that no other customer can use the same physical computer as me e.g. dedicated servers or virtual private cloud.

(d) Media Sanitization : When I delete portions of my data, what processes are used to sanitise the storage media before it is made available to another customer, and are the processes deemed appropriate by the ASD ISM? For example, a vendor advertises that when a customer deletes data, "the physical space on which the data was stored is zeroed over before the space is re-used by other data".

6.4.3 Protecting Data from Unauthorized Access by Rogue Vendor Employees

(a) Data Encryption Key Management : Does the vendor know the password or key used to decrypt my data, or do I encrypt and decrypt the data on my computer so the vendor only ever has encrypted data?

(b) Vetting of Vendor's Employees : What personnel employment checks and vetting processes does the vendor perform to ensure that employees are trustworthy? Examples include thorough police background checks, as well as citizenship checks, security clearances and psychological assessments especially for employees with administrative privileges or other access to customer data. For example, in September 2010 a major vendor acknowledged sacking an employee for allegedly deliberately violating the privacy of users by inappropriately reading their electronic communications during a timeframe of several months.

(c) Auditing Vendor's Employees : What robust identity and access management system do the vendor's employees use? What auditing process is used to log and review the actions performed by the vendor's employees?

(d) Visitors to Data Center : Are visitors to data centers escorted at all times, and are the name and other personal details of every visitor verified and recorded?

(e) Physical Tampering by Vendor's Employees : Is network cabling professionally installed to Australian standards or internationally acceptable standards, to help avoid the vendor's employees from accidentally connecting cables to the wrong computers, and to help readily highlight any deliberate attempts by the vendor's employees to tamper with the cabling?

(f) Vendor's Subcontractors : Do the answers to these questions apply equally to all of the vendor's subcontractors?

6.4.4 Handling Security Incidents

(a) Timely Vendor Support : Is the vendor readily contactable and responsive to requests for support, and is the maximum acceptable response time captured in the SLA or simply a marketing claim that the vendor will try their best? Is the support provided locally, or from a foreign country, or from several foreign countries using an approach that follows the sun? What mechanism does the vendor use to obtain a real-time understanding of the security posture of my use of the vendor's services so that the vendor can provide support?

(b) Vendor's Incident Response Plan : Does the vendor have a security incident response plan that specifies how to detect and respond to security incidents, in a way that is similar to incident handling procedures detailed in the ASD ISM? Can I thoroughly review a copy?

(c) Training of Vendor's Employees : What qualifications, certifications and regular information security awareness training do the vendor's employees require, to know how to use the vendor's systems in a secure manner and to identify potential security incidents?

(d) Notification of Security Incidents : Will the vendor notify me via secure communications of security incidents that are more serious than an agreed threshold, especially in cases where the vendor might be liable? Will the vendor automatically notify law enforcement or other authorities, who may confiscate computing equipment used to store or process my data?

(e) Extent of Vendor Support : How much assistance will the vendor provide me with investigations if there is a security breach such as an unauthorised disclosure of my data, or if there is a need to perform legal electronic discovery of evidence?

(f) My Access to Logs : How do I obtain access to time synchronised audit logs and other logs to perform a forensic investigation, and how are the logs created and stored to be suitable evidence for a court of law?

(g) Security Incident Compensation : How will the vendor adequately compensate me if the vendor's actions, faulty software or hardware contributed to a security breach?

(h) Data Spills : If data that I consider is too sensitive to be stored in the cloud is accidentally placed into the cloud, referred to as a data spill, how can the spilled data be deleted using forensic sanitisation techniques? Is the relevant portion of physical storage media zeroed whenever data is deleted? If not, how long does it take for deleted data to be overwritten by customers as part of normal operation, noting that clouds typically have significant spare unused storage capacity? Can the spilled data be forensically deleted from the vendor's backup media? Where else is the spilled data stored, and can it be forensically deleted?

6.5 CLOUD COMPUTING AND IDENTITY

- As per the pattern a cloud service provider is expected to provide security controls for DoS protection and protection of confidentiality and integrity for sessions originating from Mobile as well as PC.
- Typically these sessions initiated by browsers or client applications and are usually delivered using SSL/TLS terminated at the load balancers managed by the cloud service provider.
- Cloud service providers usually don't share the DoS protection mechanisms as hackers can easily abuse it.

Applications Security Services (In-House or Cloud Service Provider)

- Security services such as user identification, authentication, access enforcement, device identification, cryptographic services and key management can be located either with the cloud service provider, within the enterprise data center or some combination of the two.
- The second pattern illustrated below is the identity and access pattern derived from the CSA identity domain.
- This pattern illustrates a collection of common cloud access control use cases such as user registration, authentication, account provisioning, policy enforcement, logging, auditing and metering.
- It highlights the actors (end user, enterprise business user, third party auditor, cloud service owner) interacting with services that are hosted in the cloud, in-house (enterprise) and in third party locations.

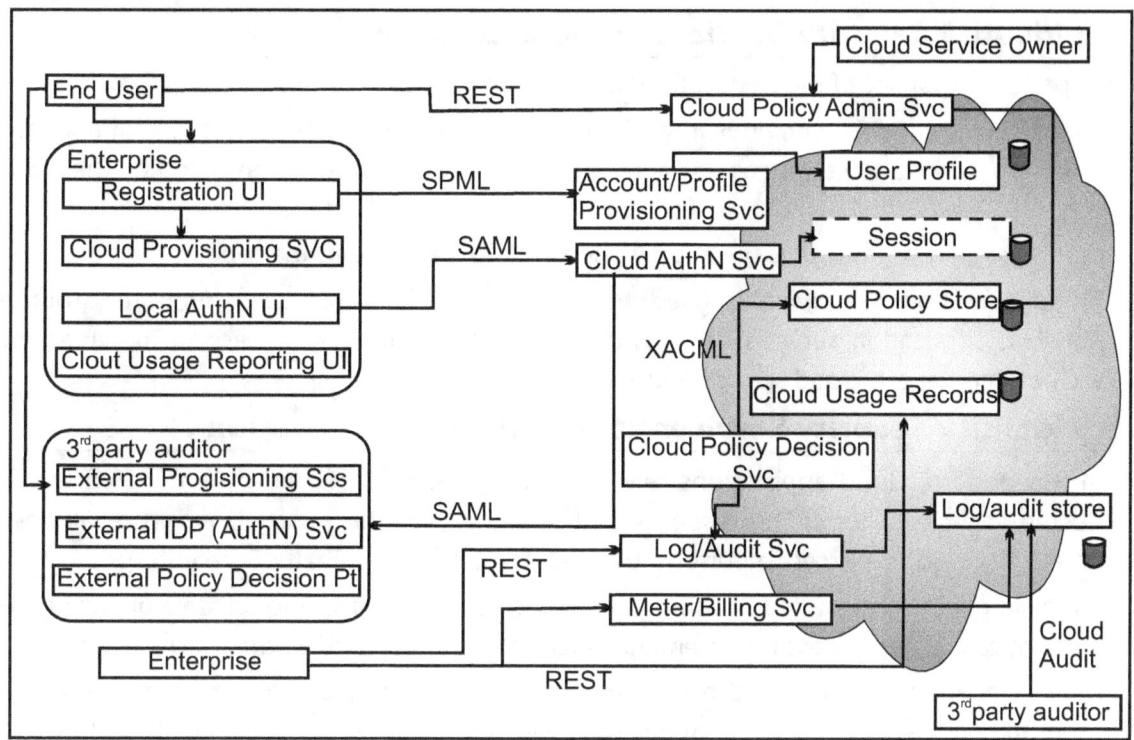

Fig. 6.5 : Cloud Identity/Access Architecture Pattern

6.5.1 Identity Security Services (Controls) at Cloud Service Providers

The cloud hosts the following services :

- Authentication service that supports user authentication originating from an enterprise portal (Local AuthN UI) and typically delivered using SAML protocol. The authenticated session state is maintained in a cloud session store.

- Account and profile provisioning service supports the provisioning of new accounts and user profiles, typically invoked via SPML (Service Provisioning Markup Language) or a cloud service provider specific API. Profiles are stored in the user profile store.

- Cloud policy admin service is used for managing policies that dictate which resources in the cloud can be accessed by end users. Using this service, cloud service owners (enterprise) can perform administrative functions and end users can request for access to cloud resources. Cloud policies are stored in the cloud policy store.

- Logging and auditing service supports dual functions. The first function is event logging, including security events, in the cloud and the second is for audit purposes. Cloud Audit protocols and APIs can be employed to access this service.

- Metering service keeps track of cloud resource usage. Finance departments can use this service for charge back as well as for billing reconciliation.

6.5.2 Identity Security Services in the Enterprise

In this pattern, a subset of the applications is hosted in the enterprise :

- Cloud registration UI provides the UI service for end users to register, manage and provision new cloud resources. Authentication and Authorization is enforced by the cloud services.
- Cloud usage reporting UI is utilized by end users to generate usage reports.
- Cloud provisioning service is used to provision cloud resources (compute, storage, network, application services). Access control (AuthN, AuthZ) and session management are enforced at the cloud service end.

6.5.3 Identity Security Services at the Third Party Location

- In this pattern, cloud applications rely on identity services offered by a third party and hosted at their location. These services offer support for third party users who will need access to cloud resources to perform business functions on behalf of the enterprise.
- For example backup and application monitoring services. In this model, user provisioning, authentication and access enforcement functions are delegated to the third party service.
- By understanding what you can leverage from your cloud platform or service provider, one can build security into your application without reinventing the capability within your application boundary thus avoiding costly "bolt-on" safeguards.
- A good practice is to create security principles and architectural patterns that can be leveraged in the design phase. Architectural patterns can help articulate where controls are enforced (Cloud versus third party versus enterprise) during the design phase so appropriate security controls are baked into the application design.
- Keep in mind the relevant threats and the principle of "risk appropriate" when creating cloud security patterns. Ultimately cloud security architecture should support the developer's needs to protect the confidentiality, integrity and availability of data processed and stored in the cloud.

6.5.4 Trusted Cloud Computing

- The trusted cloud initiative helps cloud providers to develop industry-recommended, secure and interoperable identity, access and compliance management configurations, and practices.
- The trusted cloud initiative will develop reference models and education in a vendor-neutral manner, inclusive of all CSA members and affiliates who wish to participate.
- The trusted cloud initiative reference architecture is both a methodology and a set of tools that enable security architects, enterprise architects and risk management professionals to leverage a common set of solutions that fulfil their common needs to be able to assess where their internal IT and their cloud providers are in terms of security capabilities and to plan a roadmap to meet the security needs of their business.

6.6 IDENTITY MANAGEMENT AND ACCESS CONTROL

Before we get into cloud specific Identity Management and Access control, let's understand some basics of it.

6.6.1 Identity Management

- Identity Management (IdM) describes the management of individual identities, their authentication, authorization, roles, and privileges/permissions within or across system and enterprise boundaries with the goal of increasing security and productivity while decreasing cost, downtime, and repetitive tasks.

- "Identity Management" and "Access and Identity Management" (or AIM) are terms that are used interchangeably under the title of Identity management while Identity management itself falls the umbrella of IT Security.

- Identity management systems, products, applications, and platforms are commercial Identity management solutions implemented for enterprises and organizations.

- Technologies, services, and terms related to Identity management include Active Directories, Service Providers, Identity Providers, Web Services, Access control, Digital Identities, Password Managers, Single Sign-on, Security Tokens, Security Token Services (STS), Workflows, OpenID, WS-Security, WS-Trust, SAML 2.0, OAuth, and RBAC.

- Identity Management (IdM) is a term related to how humans are authenticated (identified) and authorized across computer networks. It covers issues such as how users are given an identity, the protection of that identity, and the technologies supporting that protection (e.g., network protocols, digital certificates, passwords, etc.).

6.6.2 Digital Identity

- Personal Identifying Information (PII) selectively exposed over a network. Thus the term management is appended to "identity" to indicate that there is technological and best practice framework around a somewhat intractable philosophical concept.

- Digital identity can be interpreted as the codification of identity names and attributes of a physical instance in a way that facilitates processing.

- In each organization there is normally a role or department that is responsible for managing the schema of digital identities of their staff and their own objects, these represented by object identities or object identifiers (OID).

- The SAML protocol is a prominent means used to exchange identity information between two identity domains.

Perspectives on IdM

In the real-world context of engineering online systems, identity management can involve three perspectives :

- **The Pure Identity Paradigm :** Creation, management and deletion of identities without regard to access or entitlements.

- **The User Access (log-on) Paradigm :** For example : a smart card and its associated data used by a customer to log on to a service or services (a traditional view).
- **The Service Paradigm :** A system that delivers personalized role-based, online on-demand, multimedia (content), presence-based services to users and their devices.

6.6.3 Pure Identity Paradigm

- A general model of identity can be constructed from a small set of axiomatic principles, for example that all identities in a given abstract namespace are unique and distinctive, or that such identities bear a specific relationship to corresponding entities in the real world.
- An axiomatic model of this kind can be considered to express "pure identity" in the sense that the model is not constrained by the context in which it is applied. In general, an entity can have multiple identities, and each identity can consist of multiple attributes or identifiers, some of which are shared and some of which are unique within a given name space.
- The diagram below illustrates the conceptual relationship between identities and the entities they represent, as well as between identities and the attributes they consist of.

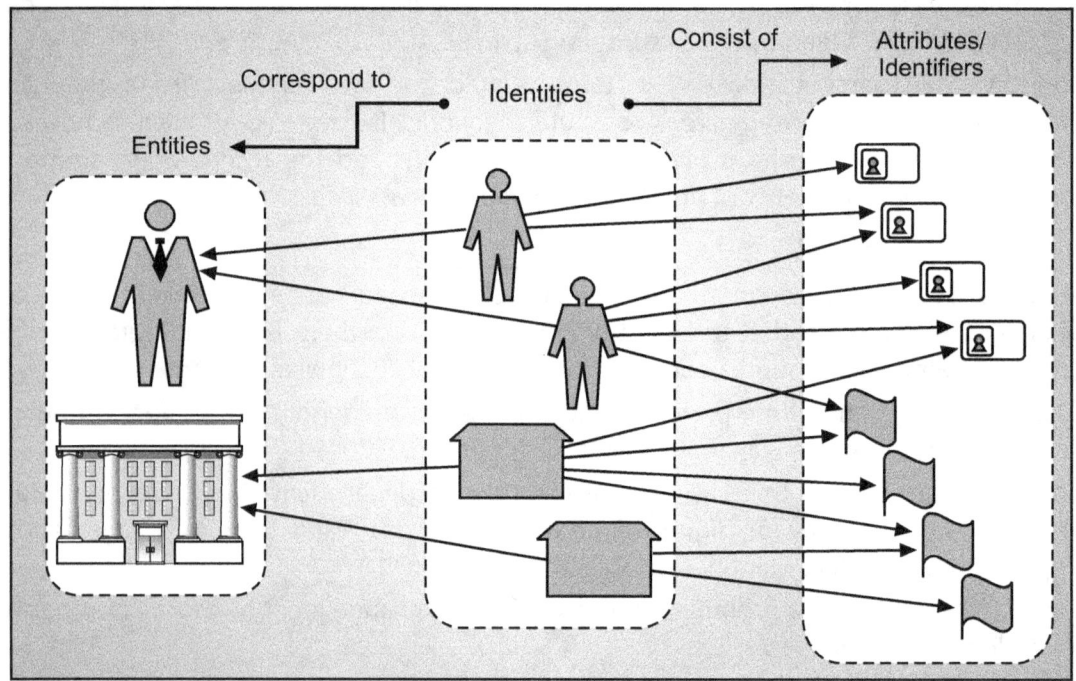

Fig. 6.6 : Identify Paradigms

- In most theoretical and all practical models of digital identity, a given identity object consists of a finite set of properties. These properties may be used to record information about the object, either for purposes external to the model itself or so as to assist the model operationally, for example in classification and retrieval.

- A "pure identity" model is strictly not concerned with the external semantics of these properties.
- The most common departure from "pure identity" in practice occurs with properties intended to assure some aspect of identity, for example a digital signature or software token which the model may use internally to verify some aspect of the identity in satisfaction of an external purpose.
- To the extent that the model attempts to express these semantics internally, it is not a pure model.
- Contrast this situation with properties which might be externally used for purposes of information security such as managing access or entitlement, but which are simply stored and retrieved, in other words not treated specially by the model. The absence of external semantics within the model qualifies it as a "pure identity" model.
- Identity management, then can be defined as a set of operations on a given identity model, or as a set of capabilities with reference to it.
- In practice, identity management is often used to express how identity information is to be provisioned and reconciled between multiple identity models.

6.6.4 User Access Paradigm

- User access requires each user to assume a unique "digital identity" across applications and networked infrastructures, which enables access controls to be assigned and evaluate against this identity.
- Technically, the use of a unique identity across all systems ease the monitoring and verification of potential unauthorized access, and allows the organization to keep tabs of excessive privileges granted to any individual within the company.
- From the user lifecycle perspective, user access can be tracked from new hire, suspension to termination of employee.

6.6.5 Service Paradigm

- In the service paradigm perspective, where organizations evolve their systems to the world of converged services, the scope of identity management becomes much larger, and its application more critical.
- The scope of identity management includes all the resources of the company deployed to deliver online services. These may include devices, network equipment, servers, portals, content, applications and/or products as well as a user's credentials, address books, preferences, entitlements and telephone numbers. See Service Delivery Platform and Directory service.
- Today, many organizations face a major clean-up in their systems if they are to bring identity coherence into their influence.
- Such coherence has become a prerequisite for delivering unified services to very large numbers of users on demand, cheaply, with security and single-customer viewing facilities.

6.6.6 Access Control

- Access control refers to exerting control over who can interact with a resource. Often but not always, this involves an authority, who does the controlling. The resource can be a given building, group of buildings, or computer-based information system.

- But it can also refer to a restroom stall where access is controlled by using a coin to open the door.

- Access control is, in reality, an everyday phenomenon. A lock on a car door is essentially a form of access control. A PIN on an ATM system at a bank is another means of access control.

- The possession of access control is of prime importance when persons seek to secure important, confidential, or sensitive information and equipment.

- Similarly, in cloud as we are accessing services hosted remotely by some other enterprise, and on a shared basis, we have to implement access control practices to make our data more secure.

6.7 DIGITAL IDENTITY AND ACCESS MANAGEMENT

Trust Boundaries and IAM

- In a typical organization where applications are deployed within the organization's perimeter the "trust boundary" is mostly static and is monitored and controlled by the IT department. In that traditional model, the trust boundary encompasses the network, systems, and applications hosted in a private data center managed by the IT department (sometimes third-party providers under IT supervision). And access to the network, systems, and applications is secured via network security controls including Virtual Private Networks (VPNs), Intrusion Detection Systems (IDSs), Intrusion Prevention Systems (IPSs), and multifactor authentication.

- With the adoption of cloud services, the organization's trust boundary will become dynamic and will move beyond the control of IT. With cloud computing, the network, system, and application boundary of an organization will extend into the service provider domain. (This may already be the case for most large enterprises engaged in e-commerce, supply chain management, outsourcing, and collaboration with partners and communities.) This loss of control continues to challenge the established trusted governance and control model (including the trusted source of information for employees and contractors), and, if not managed properly, will impede cloud service adoption within an organization.

- To compensate for the loss of network control and to strengthen risk assurance, organizations will be forced to rely on other higher-level software controls, such as application security and user access controls. These controls manifest as strong authentication, authorization based on role or claims, trusted sources with accurate attributes, identity federation, Single Sign-On (SSO), user activity monitoring, and auditing. In particular, organizations need to pay attention to the identity federation architecture and processes, as they can strengthen the controls and trust between organizations and Cloud Service Providers (CSPs).

- Identity federation is an emerging industry best practice for dealing with the heterogeneous, dynamic, loosely coupled trust relationships that characterize an organization's external and internal supply chains and collaboration model. Federation enables the interaction of systems and applications separated by an organization's trust boundary, e.g., a sales person interacting with Salesforce.com from a corporate network. Since federation coupled with good IAM practice can enable strong authentication by way of delegation, web single sign-on, and entitlement management via centralized access control services, it will play a central role in accelerating cloud computing adoption within organizations.

- In some cases, the practice of IAM within an organization may suffer due to a lack of central governance and identity information architecture. More often than not, identity storage is managed via manual entry by multiple administrators, and user provisioning processes are not well orchestrated. This process is not only inefficient, but it will also propagate existing bad practice to the cloud services. In such cases, the weak access model will extend excess privileges for unauthorized users to cloud   services.

- IAM is a two-way street. CSPs need to support IAM standards (e.g., SAML) and practices such as federation for customers to take advantage of and extend their practice to maintain compliance with internal policies and standards. Cloud services that support IAM features such as federation will accelerate the migration of traditional IT applications from trusted corporate networks into a trusted cloud service model. For customers, well-implemented user IAM practices and processes will help protect the confidentiality and integrity and manage compliance of the information stored in the cloud. Cloud services that support IAM standards such as SAML can accelerate the adoption of new cloud services and migration of IT applications from trusted corporate networks into a trusted cloud service model.

6.7.1 Why IAM?

Traditionally, organizations invest in IAM practices to improve operational efficiency and to comply with regulatory, privacy, and data protection requirements.

- Improve operational efficiency
- Properly architected IAM technology and processes can improve efficiency by automating user on boarding and other repetitive tasks (e.g., self-service for users requesting password resets that otherwise will require the intervention of system administrators using a help desk ticketing system).
- Regulatory compliance management.
- To protect systems, applications, and information from internal and external threats (e.g., disgruntled employees deleting sensitive files) and to comply with various regulatory, privacy, and data protection requirements (e.g., HIPAA, SOX), organizations implement an "IT general and application-level controls" framework derived from industry standard

frameworks such as ISO 27002 and Information Technology Infrastructure Library (ITIL). IAM processes and practices can help organizations meet objectives in the area of access control and operational security (e.g., enforcement of compliance requirements such as "segregation of duties" and assignment of limited privileges for staff members to perform their duties). Auditors routinely map internal controls to IT controls as they support management of regulatory compliance processes including Payment Card Industry (PCI), Data Security Standards (DSSs) and the Sarbanes-Oxley Act of 2003 (SOX).In addition to improving operational efficiencies and effective compliance management, IAM can enable new IT delivery and deployment models (i.e., cloud services). For example, federated identity, a key IAM component, enables the linking and portability of identity information across trust boundaries. As such, it enables enterprises and cloud service providers to bridge security domains through web single sign-on and federated user provisioning. Some of the cloud use cases that require IAM support from the CSP include :

- Employees and on-site contractors of an organization accessing a SaaS service using identity federation (e.g., sales and support staff members accessing Salesforce.com with corporate identities and credentials).

- IT administrators accessing the CSP management console to provision resources and access for users using a corporate identity (e.g., IT administrators of Newco.com provisioning virtual machines or VMs in Amazon's EC2 service, configured with identities, entitlements, and credentials for operating the VMs [i.e., start, stop, suspend, and delete VMs]).

- Developers creating accounts for partner users in a PaaS platform (e.g., developers from Newco.com provisioning accounts in Force.com for Partnerco.com employees contracted to perform business process tasks for Newco.com).

- End users accessing storage service in the cloud (e.g., Amazon S3) and sharing files and objects with users, within and outside a domain using access policy management features.

- An application residing in a cloud service provider (e.g., Amazon EC2) accessing storage from another cloud service (e.g., Mosso)

- Since IAM features such as SSO allow applications to externalize authentication features, businesses can rapidly adopt SaaS services (an example is Salesforce.com) by reducing the time required to integrate with service providers. IAM capabilities can also help a business outsource a process or service to partners with a reduced impact to the business's privacy and security, for example, employees of an order fulfillment partner of a merchant can use their federated identities to access real-time information stored in a merchant application to manage the product fulfillment process. In short, extending your IAM strategy, practice, and architecture allows your organization to extend your user access management practices and processes to the cloud. Hence, organizations with established IAM practices can rapidly adopt cloud services while maintaining the efficiency and efficacy of their security controls.

6.7.2 IAM Architecture and Practice

- IAM is not a monolithic solution that can be easily deployed to gain capabilities immediately. It is as much an aspect of architecture (see Fig. 6.7) as it is a collection of technology components, processes, and standard practices. Standard enterprise IAM architecture encompasses several layers of technology, services, and processes. At the core of the deployment architecture is a directory service (such as LDAP or Active Directory) that acts as a repository for the identity, credential, and user attributes of the organization's user pool. The directory interacts with IAM technology components such as authentication, user management, provisioning, and federation services that support the standard IAM practice and processes within the organization. It is not uncommon for organizations to use several directories that were deployed for environment-specific reasons (e.g., Windows systems using Active Directory, UNIX systems using LDAP) or that were integrated into the environment by way of business mergers and acquisitions.

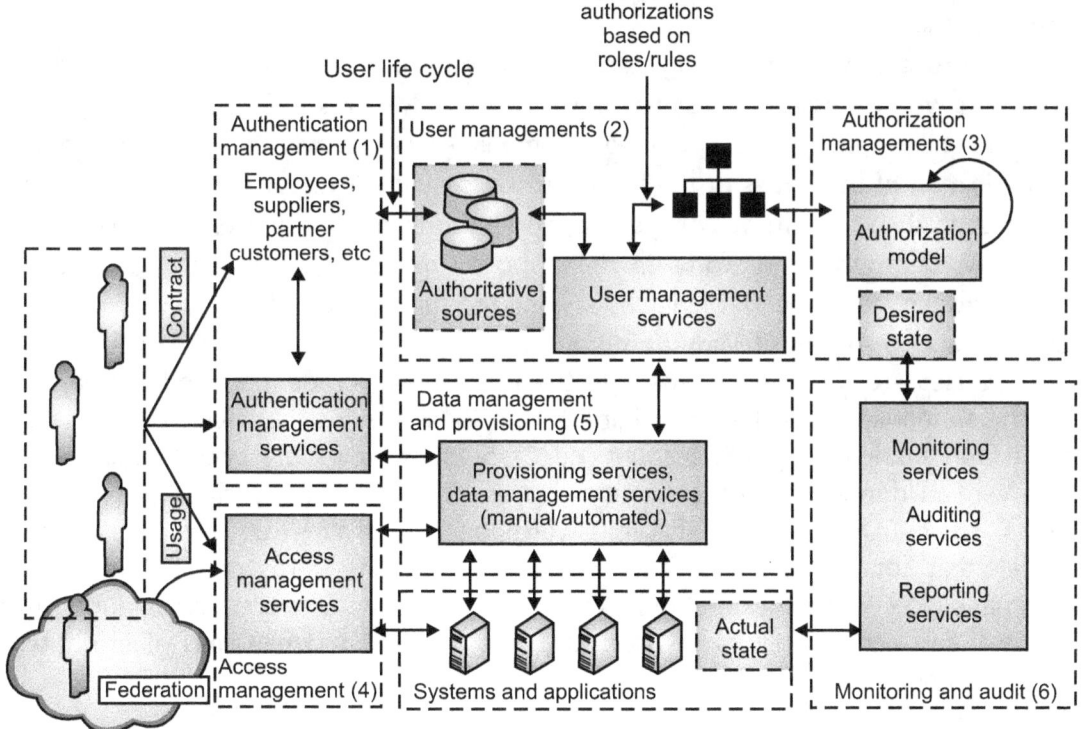

Fig. 6.7 : Enterprise IAM functional architecture

The IAM processes to support the business can be broadly categorized as follows :

- User management.
- Activities for the effective governance and management of identity life cycles.
- Authentication management.
- Activities for the effective governance and management of the process for determining that an entity is who or what it claims to be.

- Authorization management.
- Activities for the effective governance and management of the process for determining entitlement rights that decide what resources an entity is permitted to access in accordance with the organization's policies.
- Access management.
- Enforcement of policies for access control in response to a request from an entity (user, services) wanting to access an IT resource within the organization.
- Data management and provisioning.
- Propagation of identity and data for authorization to IT resources via automated or manual processes.
- Monitoring and auditing.
- Monitoring, auditing, and reporting compliance by users regarding access to resources within the organization based on the defined policies.

IAM processes support the following operational activities :

- **Provisioning**

This is the process of on-boarding users to systems and applications. These processes provide users with necessary access to data and technology resources. The term typically is used in reference to enterprise-level resource management. Provisioning can be thought of as a combination of the duties of the human resources and IT departments, where users are given access to data repositories or systems, applications, and databases based on a unique user identity. Deprovisioning works in the opposite manner, resulting in the deletion or deactivation of an identity or of privileges assigned to the user identity.

- **Credential and Attribute Management**

These processes are designed to manage the life cycle of credentials and user attributes create issue, manage, revoke to minimize the business risk associated with identity impersonation and inappropriate account use. Credentials are usually bound to an individual and are verified during the authentication process. The processes include provisioning of attributes, static (e.g., standard text password) and dynamic (e.g., one-time password) credentials that comply with a password standard (e.g., passwords resistant to dictionary attacks), handling password expiration, encryption management of credentials during transit and at rest, and access policies of user attributes (privacy and handling of attributes for various regulatory reasons).

- **Entitlement Management**

Entitlements are also referred to as authorization policies. The processes in this domain address the provisioning and deprovisioning of privileges needed for the user to access resources including systems, applications, and databases. Proper entitlement management ensures that users are assigned only the required privileges (least privileges) that match with their job functions. Entitlement management can be used to strengthen the security of web services, web applications, legacy applications, documents and files, and physical security systems.

- **Compliance Management**

This process implies that access rights and privileges are monitored and tracked to ensure the security of an enterprise's resources. The process also helps auditors verify compliance to various internal access control policies, and standards that include practices such as segregation of duties, access monitoring, periodic auditing, and reporting. An example is a user certification process that allows application owners to certify that only authorized users have the privileges necessary to access business-sensitive information.

- **Identity Federation Management**

Federation is the process of managing the trust relationships established beyond the internal network boundaries or administrative domain boundaries among distinct organizations. A federation is an association of organizations that come together to exchange information about their users and resources to enable collaborations and transactions (e.g., sharing user information with the organization's benefits systems managed by a third-party provider). Federation of identities to service providers will support SSO to cloud services.

- **Centralization of Authentication (authN) and Authorization (authZ)**

A central authentication and authorization infrastructure alleviates the need for application developers to build custom authentication and authorization features into their applications. Furthermore, it promotes a loose coupling architecture where applications become agnostic to the authentication methods and policies. This approach is also called an "externalization of authN and authZ" from applications.

6.7.3 Relevant IAM Standards and Protocols for Cloud Services

In the previous sections, we established the requirements and benefits of applying standard IAM principles and practices to cloud services. In this section, we will discuss the relevant IAM standards that act as catalysts for organizations adopting cloud services. Organizations that are currently evaluating cloud services based on business and operational criteria should also take into consideration the CSP's commitment to and support for IAM standards.

6.8 CONTENT LEVEL SECURITY

- Much of the substance of this chapter has described a new way of thinking about securing data, so that data within a cloud can remain fluid, accessible on multiple nodes and yet remain protected throughout its life cycle.
- The basis of this new security model has been described as "content or information-centric." What this means in reality is that the content that makes up any given data object (for example, a Word document) is protected, as opposed to the file that is, the carrier of that information being protected. This subtle difference in approach gives us a major advantage in terms of granularity and choice of protection level, as well as persistence of protection. We will take a Word document as our example here to outline the main pros and cons of this type of security approach.
- Imagine that I have just prepared a merger and acquisition (M and A) draft document using an on-line document authoring application, such as Google Apps. I need to share

this document with persons within my own company, across several departments, as well as with an external lawyer and with the third-party company to be acquired.

- In addition, I want to make sure that certain sections are only visible to certain of these parties and that they cannot change any item or copy the content (I don't want some of the sensitive clauses to be placed on an ex-employee's blog page, or leaked to the press to affect share prices). I also want to audit the access and use of the document and to limit the time that these people can read the draft of this document, because I want to close this acquisition within 2 weeks. Thereafter I need to publish the finished M and A document with new access rights and restrictions to reflect its new status. I am also acutely aware that the data center that is holding this sensitive document is being hosted by a cloud vendor, and I definitely do not want the administrator of that data center to see this transaction. How can I achieve this? I could create a shared on-line document portal that controls access to the document using a password login and set up user accounts for those persons I wish to share the document with.

- The main problem with this type of container-based security is that it relies on the user not sharing their password. In addition, once access is gained, the user can use the document without restriction, for example, copy the document content to their blog page, email the document to others, or download the document to a local computer and share it with anyone they wish to, across their network. In addition, the document is potentially accessible by the cloud vendor themselves.

- To prevent any of these unauthorized actions, I will need to control the document content itself and improve on the access control measures, because password access is far too insecure. This is where a content-centric approach delivers persistent and pervasive security. Content-centric security, which is also digital identity led (i.e., the identity used to access the content), also dictates the security policy applied to that content and will allow me to control who accesses my M and A draft, because at the time of protecting the draft I will decide who can access it and how access is controlled.

- This brings us back to the section on information cards. I could protect the draft document by assigning access to persons who hold a managed information card, which contains certain claims for example, specific email addresses, a security clearance level (set by a specified identity provider), or a specified company number, and so on. Only those persons could then access the document; and because the claims are managed by an identity provider (perhaps my own company), the claims can also be dynamically changed and, as such, if I need to revoke access to the document, I can arrange for the claims to change in line with this, revoke the information card of that user, or alternatively change the security applied to the document. Once access is gained, security policies that control what part of the document can be seen, by which person and what they can do with the content, will be applied, because the access is based on an individual identity, individual content controls can be applied and so some users can be given strong rights and restrictions than others. Importantly, even though the document is held on third party server, in the cloud it can't be accessed by even the system administrator of that server, because the access is controlled at the content level and is not dependent on the access to the database holding the data.

- You can easily see the advantages that are conferred on data protected at the content level : greater control, more focused access control, increased granular protection over content, and assurance within a cloud-hosted system. But what, if any, disadvantages come with this type of methodology?

- Container security is a much simpler way of securing data. Within a cloud computing environment you have the storage and transfer of data, both of which can be easily accommodated in terms of security by using encryption protocols already built for the purpose. It is fairly simple to apply database encryption, because it is applied natively to the data and decrypted, on-the-fly, when there is a query on that data. Similarly, transfer of the data between application and database, or human-to-human transfer, can protect the data as an encrypted package, decrypted when access is granted. Content-centric security measures need to be compatible with both database security and secure transfer of data within a cloud environment. Protecting the content of our word document needs to be done in such a manner that it does not impact the storage of that data.

- This may be problematic, especially across different storage types and in use with query engines, which is particularly pertinent with the use of dynamic data updating, as required by modern data storage operations. One of the other aspects of cloud computing data storage that can complicate the area of data security is the use of redundant storage in more than one location. However, at this juncture it is worth noting that this same issue causes more problems for a container approach than for a content-centric approach, in terms of synchronicity between databases.

- The current state of research, with respect to the protection of data within a cloud computing environment, is focused on the protection of data within the data centers hosting the cloud : The problems therein are compounded by the highly distributed nature of the cloud and the use of multi-center storage and replication of data. Content-centric security needs to overcome these same problems and also needs to retain protection of data within the structure of the database itself.

6.9 SECURITY AS A CLOUD SERVICE

So far, we have addressed the security provided by Cloud Service Providers (CSPS) as well as the security provided by customers using cloud services. In this chapter, the focus is on security provided as cloud services; that is security delivered through the cloud, also known as security-as-a-service.

Just like software-as-a-service (SaaS), the business model with security-as-a-service is subscription-based. In addition, security-as-a-service is also sometimes referred to as "SaaS," which is how we will address it specifically in this chapter.With SaaS, there are two emerging provider types. The first type comprises established information security vendors who are changing their delivery methods to include services delivered through the cloud. The second type comprises start-up information security companies that are also emerging in this field as pure, play CSPs that is, these companies provide security only as a cloud service, and do not provide traditional client/server security products for networks, hosts, and/or applications.

Among established information security companies that are changing their business models to also include SaaS, the most prominent are traditional anti-malware vendors. However, other established information security companies are also involved in the delivery of SaaS, especially with regard to email filtering.

6.9.1 Today's Offerings

Today's offerings in the SaaS segment involve several services to improve information security : email filtering (including backup, archival, and e-discovery), web content filtering, vulnerability management, and identity-as-a-service (spelled in this chapter as IDaaS).

Email Filtering

SaaS for email primarily involves cleansing spam, phishing emails, and malware included in email from an organization's incoming email stream, and then delivering that clean email securely to the organization so that it is effectively not repolluted. The touted benefits of this approach are not only more comprehensive security for clients due to the use of multiple engines, but also better performance of those client devices (because the anti-malware runs in the cloud and not on the endpoint directly), as well as far better anti-malware management. The anti-malware management is superior to endpoint solutions because that anti-malware is OS and processor agnostic, so it can be managed centrally through the cloud rather than working with multiple management systems, probably from multiple anti-malware vendors. This cleansing in the cloud service has corollary benefits : reduced bandwidth used by email, reduced loads on organizational email servers, and improved effectiveness of a (recipient) organization's own anti-malware efforts.

Although most attention on SaaS involving email tends to focus on inbound email, it is also often used with outgoing email. Many organizations want to ensure that they are not inadvertently sending malware-infected emails, and cleansing outbound email through SaaS is a good method for preventing such problems and embarrassments. Additionally, outside SaaS email can be used to enforce organizational policies around the encryption of email (e.g., between specified [email] domains, such as those belonging to business partners or customers). This email encryption is generally performed at the (email) server-to-server level so that individual user actions and key management are not required. This is accomplished by using either Secure Sockets Layer (SSL) or Transport Layer Security (TLS) on network communications at the transport layer.

A further benefit of SaaS anti-malware is the collective intelligence that is gained from the visibility of all malware threats to all endpoints across an enterprise, irrespective of type (e.g., server, desktop, laptop, or mobile device), location, OS, or processor architecture. Having this greater view in a timely manner is a significant help to organizational information security teams.

SaaS for email also includes email backup and archiving. This service usually involves storing and indexing an organization's email messages and attachments in a centralized repository. That centralized repository allows an organization to index and search by a number of parameters, including date range, recipient, sender, subject, and content. These capabilities are particularly useful for e-discovery purposes, which can be extremely expensive without such capabilities.

Web Content Filtering

As endpoints belonging to an organization whether they are within an organization's facilities, at home, or on the road try to retrieve web traffic, that traffic is diverted to a SaaS provider that scans for malware threats and ensures that only clean traffic is delivered to end users. Organizations can also enforce their web content policies by allowing, blocking, or throttling traffic (use of bandwidth for that traffic reduced). Because of the number of websites accessible today, earlier URL filtering solutions deployed on organizations' premises are increasingly inefficient. SaaS providers supplement that URL filtering with the examination of Hypertext Transfer Protocol (HTTP) header information, page content, and embedded links to better understand site content. Additionally, these services use a collective reputation scoring system to bolster the accuracy of this filtering.

SaaS for web content also involves scanning outbound web traffic for sensitive information (e.g., ID numbers, credit card information, intellectual property) that users could send externally without appropriate authorization (data leakage protection). Web traffic is also scanned for content analysis, file type, and pattern matching to prevent data exfiltration.

Fig. 6.8 illustrates SaaS web content filtering.

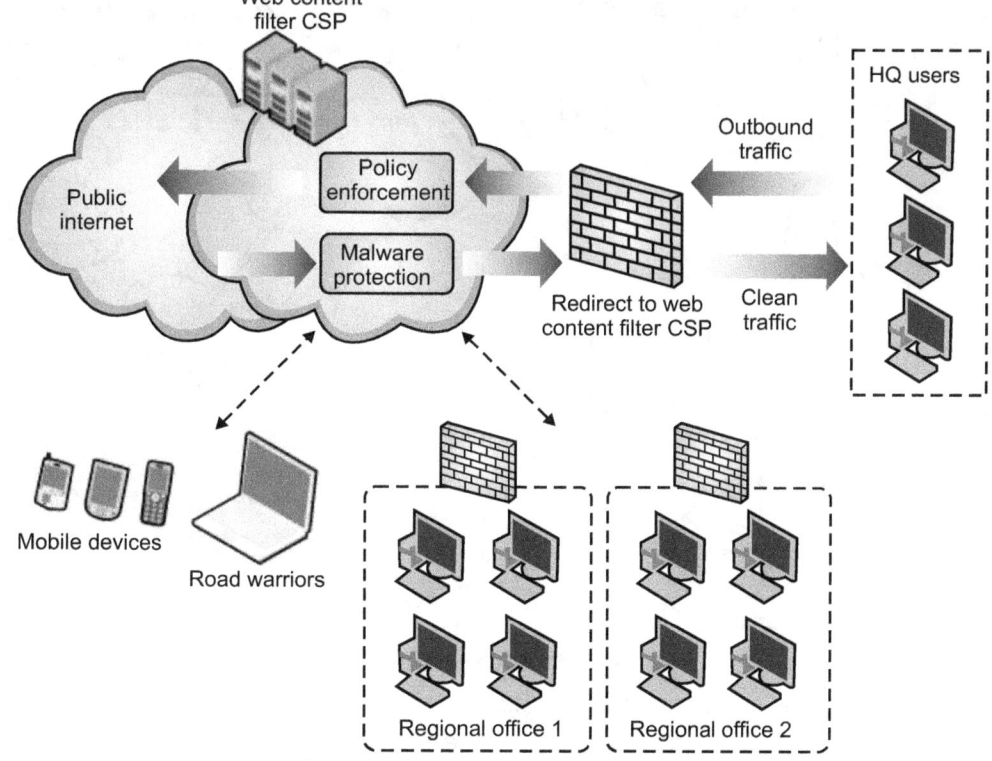

Fig. 6.8 : SaaS web content filtering

Identity Management-As-a-Service

Identity management-as-a-service (IDaaS) only recently emerged as an example of SaaS, in comparison to email filtering, web content filtering, and vulnerability management, which are more established as SaaS offerings. There are some significant deficiencies in today's Identity and Access Management (IAM) capabilities with regard to uses in cloud computing (e.g., scalability). IDaaS attempts to provide some IAM services in the cloud. Today's relatively early IDaaS offering tends to focus on authentication, because this is the most critical problem for customers, see Fig. 6.9. However, the most significant problem for CSPs concerns IDaaS providers, and developing some form of collaborative meta system. (Just as meta directories did not scale within organizations, virtual directories will not scale to a cloud level.) IDaaS providers will also need to provide other IAM services for cloud customers, including authorization (groups and roles at a minimum), provisioning, and auditing.

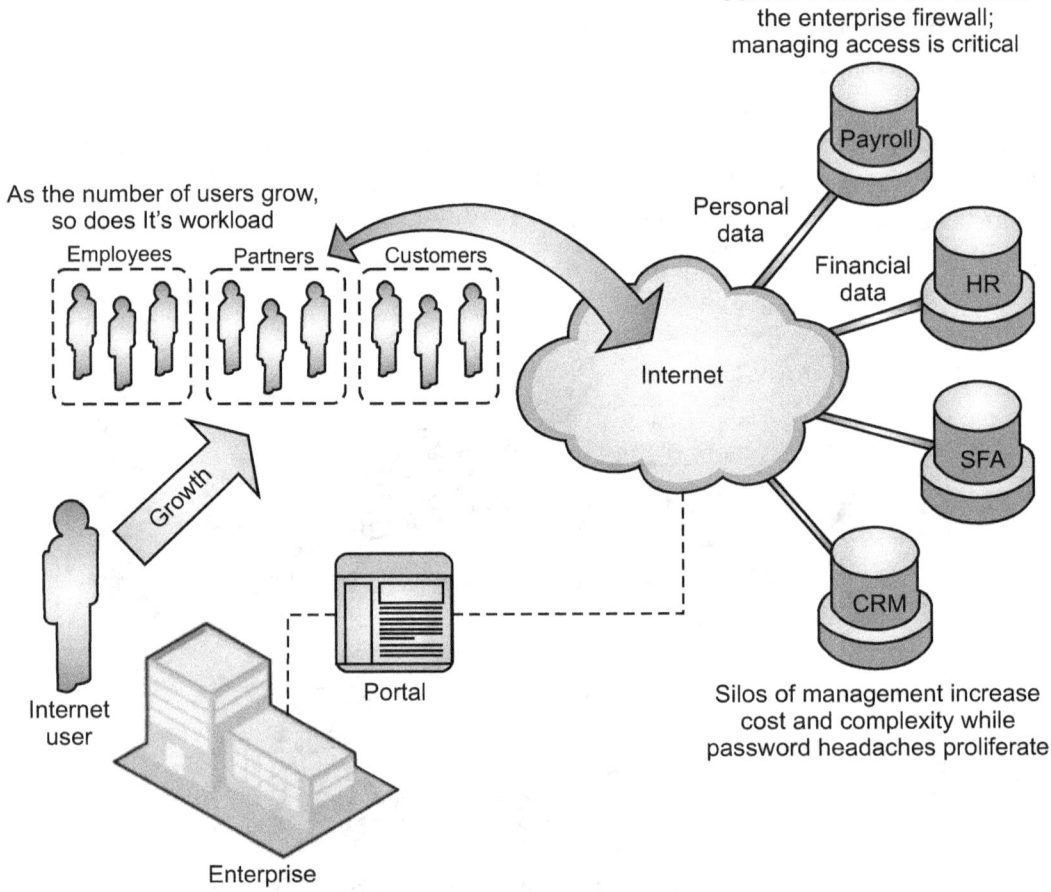

Fig. 6.9 : IDaaS model

- Security-as-a-service is already well established in the nascent cloud computing space. In fact, it is likely to continue to grow both in terms of market share against traditionally delivered security capabilities and in terms of depth of offerings. For example, not only is the relatively new Identity-as-a-Service (IDaaS) a needed alternative for individual organizations, but IDaaS will become even more desirable for growing organizational types, such as increasingly multistatus organizations (i.e., employees, contractors, interns, other companie's employees, and vendors, all working in the same shared workspace), co-petition (cooperative competition), and virtual organizations. Additionally, other important security services could be outsourced and provided in a cloud environment, such as logging, auditing, and Security Incident and Event Management (SIEM).

- Security-as-a-service is likely to see significant future growth for two reasons. First, it is likely that a continuing shift in information security work from in-house to outsource will continue. What started with email filtering and managed security services will continue and expand as organizations look to reduce Capital Expenditures (CapEx) further and increasingly concentrate on their core capabilities. Second, several other information security needs are present for organizations currently, but they will accelerate in need and complexity with the growing adoption of cloud computing. That growing complexity will further fuel the growth of SaaS. Specifically, we are referring to two preventive (proactive) controls and two detective (reactive) controls. The two proactive controls are also important to the growth of cloud computing : identity management that is intercloud and scalable to the cloud size, and (encryption) key management. Significant improvement in both is needed for cloud computing, and that will make potential solutions very valuable. The two reactive controls are needed for audit and compliance purposes as well: scalable and effective SIEM, and Data Leakage Prevention (DLP). Trying to provide solutions to each of these controls will be difficult and requires significant complexity that must be hugely scalable and yet easy to use. However, all of these needs also pose significant and growing opportunities for vendors as cloud computing continues to grow in adoption.

Impact of Cloud Computing on the Role of Corporate IT

- Almost certainly, many corporate IT departments will continue to be redefined by this latest model of outsourcing. As with earlier outsourcing (e.g., to large IT services firms such as CSC, EDS, and IBM Global Services, or application development to China or India), use of collocation facilities or Application Service Providers (ASPs) and IT functions previously done in-house are moving outside corporate IT departments. With growing IT needs at the cost of growing complexity, many organizations are deciding that IT is not a core competency for their organizations and much of the IT work required to run today's organizations is being turned over to specialist companies. Cloud computing is a further example of this.

- However, cloud computing is in some respects also a repudiation of traditional corporate IT departments. Business units are tired of hearing CIOs and IT departments telling them that the costs of their desired projects are excessively high and that there will be an excessive time delay until those projects can be implemented. Part of cloud computing's appeal is the speed with which business units can be up and running on their desired platform or application, along with the perceived lower costs of "pay as you go" and lack of upfront capital expenditures. As such, it really should be no surprise that the push for the use of cloud computing in most organizations is coming from business units and not from within IT. The long-standing tech mantra of better, faster, cheaper has come home to roost for corporate IT departments.

Security Leadership

Appropriate leadership needs to be involved with any strategy involving cloud computing. This applies to both CSPs and their customers. Customers are likely to have a decentralized approach as each business unit adopts its own plans for addressing the CSP. It is important to centralize this planning to ensure that consistent practices are adopted and that the maximum purchasing power is leveraged. Considerations of using the public, private, or hybrid clouds need to be standardized. Today, some customers of CSPs have IT departments whose staff members have little knowledge of how the CSPs are being used. It is important for management to have a deep understanding of the issues around cloud computing and it is vital that they are educated on the latest solutions and challenges with cloud computing. The traditional security paradigm is different for cloud computing, so it is essential for leadership to fully understand the complexities and capabilities of solutions in the cloud. Applying traditional security techniques is not sufficient .For CSPs, it is important to have adequate senior leadership involved in all security matters to ensure that they are appropriately addressed.

Security Governance

Another critical success factor is that appropriate governance needs to be in place. That is, is an appropriate organizational structure in place to manage the organization facing the cloud computing solution? A risk assessment framework should be adopted to ensure that consistent and reasonable practices are applied. Defining security metrics will be key to both the CSP and the customer. Each will have different perspectives and it is important to ensure that both understand their responsibilities well and none rely on each other.

Key security policies that would become critical would be the handling of data, storage of data, communication policy, vendor management (including external connections), trust reporting (i.e., how to give assurance to third parties and customers of the reliability and security of the solution), and awareness policy (both for customers and for internal users to the boundaries of responsibilities around security).

Security Assurance

Another key aspect to overcome is for the CSP to provide assurance to its customers that their operations are secure and reliable. SAS 70 is not an adequate reporting format and CSPs will need to develop a more transparent means of gaining the confidence of their customers.

Customers of CSPs need to perform their own audits and ensure that they have the right to audit for key operations. Clearly, this will become burdensome for CSPs, so they will need to develop more assurance by becoming compliant with standards such as ITIL, ISO 27001, and others to build up confidence from the market.

Security Management

Information governance, that is, the need to have controls over the life cycle of, is crucial for both the CSP and its customers. One of the biggest issues is the difficulty in tracking the exact location of data during processing times therefore, having control over its creation, storage, use, and destruction is important. Leveraging data mining tools and providing sound IT operational practices will be key to managing data.

Developing capabilities around information asset security will be challenging to CSPs. As we discussed earlier, although host-level security can be addressed, host-to-host communication and its integrity are much harder to secure due to the volume and dynamic nature of how data travels through the infrastructure. Although traditional security scanners can be deployed, it is critical to have real-time reporting around them therefore, an IT GRC solution would assist in providing management with a "dashboard" of key metrics to provide oversight of site security and reliability.

User Management

Identity access management can be leveraged to assist the CSP in providing access more seamlessly to its customers. However, IAM solutions today need to be enhanced to deal with having multiple CSPs providing access to the same customer. Also, these solutions need to provide the ability for self-provisioning in such a multitenancy environment. User awareness will be key, and more education is needed for the customers of CSPs to understand how the security posture will be changed with the CSP.

Technology Controls

A number of new and exciting technologies can be applied to both the CSP and its customers. A central question to ponder is who should manage the keys as they relate to the encryption of data? Can the CSP be trusted and does it have the expertise to hold the keys? Other factors to address would be browser security, image stabilization, and how access can be controlled.

Technology Protection and Continuity

CSPs provide for a resilient system, however, there will be times, perhaps due to a failure by the ISP or telecommunications carrier, when the customer may not be able to access the CSP's environment. Although most CSPs will build resiliency and redundancy into the design of their services, it is inevitable that there will be some outages. It is essential for both CSPs and their customers to have robust business and disaster recovery plans. The responsibilities for certain tasks will not be clear, so it is important for both parties to recognize who will be responsible for which part of the business continuity plan and/or the disaster recovery plan. The testing of each plan will be critical here to ensure that the right level of coordination between the CSP, ISP, and customer as well as others exists.

QUESTIONS

1. Explain Technologies for Data security.
2. Explain Data security risk.
3. Explain Content level security.
4. Write short note on:
   (a) Digital identity and access management
   (b) Security-As-A-Cloud Service

Sample Question Paper for
In-Semester Examination (30 Marks)

Time: 1 Hour   **Marks : 30**

---

1. (a) Explain the Roots of cloud computing.   **[6 M]**

   (b) Explain Characteristics of Virtualized environments   **[4 M]**

OR

2. (a) Explain benefits of Cloud Computing SOA.   **[6 M]**

   (b) Explain Cloud types and service models.   **[4 M]**

3. (a) Write short note on the following :

     (i) Eucalyptus

     (ii) Microsoft Hyper-V,

     (iii) KVM   **[6 M]**

   (b) State the types of virtualization and explain them in detail.   **[4 M]**

OR

4. (a) Write short note on the following :

     (i) Benefits of cloud computing

     (ii) Web 2.0,

     (iii) KVM   **[6 M]**

   (b) Explain Pros and Cons of Virtualization.   **[4 M]**

5. (a) Explain the Storage system architecture of cloud computing.   **[4 M]**

   (b) Explain Virtual Machine Components.   **[4 M]**

   (c) Explain Cloud file System   **[2 M]**

OR

6. (a) Explain in detail BigTable.   **[4 M]**

   (b) Explain Block and file level storage virtualization.   **[4 M]**

   (c) Explain Technology examples of cloud computing   **[2 M]**

Sample Question Paper for
End-Semester Examination (70 Marks)

Time: 2:30 Hours   **Marks: 70**

1. (a) Explain Roots of Cloud Computing. And benefits of cloud computing. [6 M]
    (b) List out web services of cloud computing? [4 M]

OR

2. (a) Explain Cloud types and service models. [6 M]
    (b) What are Benefits of Cloud Computing SOA? [4 M]

3. (a) Describe Taxonomy of Virtualization techniques ? [6 M]
    (b) Explain Virtualize Data Centre (VDC) architecture. [4 M]

OR

4. (a) Explain Characteristics of Virtualized environments? [6 M]
    (b) Explain KVM in detail.. [4 M]

5. (a) What are the security risks involved in cloud computing ? [6 M]
    (b) Draw and explain an architecture for federated cloud computing. [6 M]
    (c) Explain the monitoring tools in the context of cloud computing. [4 M]

OR

6. (a) What are Block and file level storage virtualization? [6 M]
    (b) Draw and explain Storage system architecture. [6 M]
    (c) Explain the monitoring tools in cloud computing. [4 M]

7. (a) Draw and Explain Life cycle of SLA? [6 M]
    (b) Short note on : (i) SOAP and REST (ii) Security-As-A-Cloud Service
        (iii) Cloud portal and its functions [6 M]
    (c) Explain scheduling techniques of Cloud computing. [6 M]

OR

8. (a) What are the security risks involved in cloud computing? [6 M]
    (b) Explain cloud infrastructure components [6 M]
    (c) Explain Digital identity and access management [6 M]

9. (a) Explain the Distributed management of virtual infrastructure. [6 M]
    (b) Write short note on Technologies for Data security [6 M]
    (c) What are the Types of SLA? [4 M]

OR

10. (a) Explain Global Risk and Compliance aspects in cloud environments. [6 M]
    (b) Short note on : (i) Work flow modelling (ii) SLA management. [6 M]
    (c) What are software defined approach and techniques for managing IT resources? [4 M]

Time : 1 Hour   **Max. Marks : 30**

Instructions to the candidates :

(1) Answer Q. 1 or Q.2, Q. 3 or Q. 4, Q. 5 or Q. 6.

(2) Neat diagrams must be drawn wherever necessary.

(3) Figures to the right side indicate full marks.

(4) Assume suitable data, if necessary.

---

1. **(a)** Define Cloud Computing. Explain essential characteristics of Cloud Computing.   **[5]**

   (b) Define the following: **[3]**

      (i)   Elastic Computing.

      (ii)   Utility Computing.

      (iii) Grid Computing.

   (c) Explain mashup.   **[2]**

OR

2. **(a)** Explain in brief enabling technologies for cloud computing.   **[5]**

   (b) Write a short note on Eucalyptus.   **[3]**

   (c) What do you mean by greenfield and brownfield deployment?   **[2]**

3. **(a)** Define virtualization. Explain its pros and cons.   **[3]**

   (b) Explain in detail Xen architecture.   **[5]**

   (c) Define the following: **[2]**

      (i)   Full virtualization.

      (ii)   Para virtualization.

4. **(a)** Explain taxonomy of virtualization techniques.   **[5]**

   (b) Explain in detail Hyper-V architecture.   **[5]**

5. **(a)** Explain virtual data centre architecture and its components.   **[5]**

   (b) Differentiate between GFS and HDFS.   **[5]**

OR

6. **(a)** What do you mean by storage tiering? How is it carried out in cloud storage?   **[5]**

   (b) Explain in detail google Big Table.   **[5]**

❀ ❀ ❀

END SEM. EXAM. MAY 2016

Time : $2\frac{1}{2}$ Hours   **Max. Marks : 70**

Instructions to the candidates :

(1) Answer Q.1 or Q.2, Q.3 or Q.4, Q.5 or Q.6, Q.7 or Q.8, Q.9 or Q.10.

(2) Figures to the right indicate full marks.

(3) Neat diagrams must be drawn wherever necessary.

(4) Assume suitable data, if necessary.

1. (a) Write a short note on open nimbus architecture.   **[4]**

    (b) Explain role of networking in cloud computing.   **[6]**

OR

2. (a) Explain service models of cloud computing in detail.   **[6]**

    (b) Write a short note on Vmware architecture.   **[4]**

3. (a) Write a short note on: **[6]**

      (i)   OS level virtualization.

      (ii) Application level virtualization.

    (b) Differentiate between SAN and NAS.   **[4]**

OR

4. (a) Elaborate HDFS architecture in detail.   **[6]**

    (b) Write a short note on HBase.   **[4]**

5. (a) Explain virtual machine life cycle in detail.   **[6]**

    (b) Explain virtual machine provisioning process in detail.   **[6]**

    (c) Elaborate benefits of converged infrastructure.   **[4]**

OR

6. (a) Explain anatomy of cloud infrastructure.   **[8]**

    (b) Explain virtual machine migration techniques in detail.   **[8]**

7. (a) Differentiate between "Classical" HPC and HPC in cloud environments.   **[6]**

    (b) Compare performance of HPC system and HPC on clouds.   **[6]**

    (c) Explain key components of SLA.   **[6]**

8. (a) Elaborate cloud service life cycle phases in detail.   **[6]**

    (b) Explain the phases of SLA management of application hosted on cloud platform. **[6]**

    (c) Write a short note on SOAP verses REST.   **[6]**

9. (a) Explain virtualization software security in detail.   [8]

   (b) Explain threads in cloud computing.   [8]

                                    OR

10. (a) Explain Iaas Host security in detail.   [8]

    (b) Explain identity life cycle management phases in detail.   [8]

END SEM. EXAM. NOVEMBER 2016

Time : $2\frac{1}{2}$ Hours   **Max. Marks : 70**

Instructions to the candidates :

(1) Solve Q.1 or Q.2, Q.3 or Q.4, Q.5 or Q.6, Q.7 or Q.8, Q.9 or Q.10.

(2) Figures to the right indicate full marks.

(3) Neat diagrams must be drawn wherever necessary.

(4) Assume suitable data, if necessary.

1. (a) Write a short note on openstack architecture.   [4]

   (b) Explain cloud deployment models in detail.   [6]

                                    OR

2. (a) Elaborate characteristics of cloud computing.   [6]

   (b) Explain cloud computing reference model.   [4]

3. (a) Explain characteristics of virtualized environments in detail.   [4]

   (b) Explain in detail KVM architecture.   [6]

                                    OR

4. (a) How does virtual provisioning simplifies cloud storage management?   [6]

   (b) Write a short note on Dynamo.   [4]

5. (a) Explain virtual machine migration techniques in detail.   [10]

   (b) Elaborate process of SLA commitment.   [6]

                                    OR

6. (a) How opennebula cloud models and manages VMS in virtualized infrastructure. [8]

   (b) Explain scheduling techniques in cloud computing.   [8]

7. (a) Explain the model for federated cloud computing.   [6]

   (b) Explain performance related issues for HPC in cloud computing.   [6]

   (c) What do you mean by SLA? Elaborate various types of SLA.   [6]

OR

8. **(a)** Write a short note on. [9]

    (i) SOAP versus REST.

    (ii) Work flow modelling

  (b) Explain traditional approaches of SLA. [9]

9. **(a)** Write a short note on following offering on saas segment to improve information security. [12]

    (i) Email filtering

    (ii) Web content filtering

    (iii) Vulnerability management

    (iv) Identity management – as – a – service (Ioaas)

  (b) What are data security risks? How will you mitigate these risks. [4]

OR

10. **(a)** Explain in detail IAM architecture. [8]

   (b) Explain information security concerns associated with data stored in cloud. [8]